D1084040

IMAGES OF A CONSTITUTION

In this remarkable conjunction of constitutional theory, jurisprudence, literary theory, constitutional law, and political theory, William Conklin first tells us what a constitution is not: it is not a text, nor a compendium of judicial and legislative decisions interpreting a text, nor a set of doctrines, nor moral/political values, nor customs, nor *a priori* conceptions. A constitution, he argues, is an image which exists through the legal consciousness of a community.

Using a wide range of Canadian judicial decisions as examples, Conklin shows that the classic cases have been those where the boundaries of two conflicting images clashed. In each instance, the subject-matter itself collapses into a search for a coherent image of what a constitution is all about.

The dominant image of a constitution in Canadian judicial discourse has been a rationalist one emanating from the Enlightenment understanding of knowledge. Turning to academic writings on Canadian federalism law, Conklin goes on to identify clearly the boundaries of three versions of rationalism, and to show that Canadian scholars have shared with judges the dominant image of rationalism.

In the third part of his essay, the author makes a prescriptive claim, namely that a text such as the Canadian Charter of Rights and Freedoms arguably raises issues which the rationalist image of a constitution precludes as legitimate inquiries. He identifies a further general image of a constitution in Canadian legal discourse, a teleological one which is rooted in the writings and judgments of Ivan Rand. Finally, he uses the contours of the Rand image to work out a further image of a constitution, an image that allows lawyers to entertain issues of both theory and social/cultural practice, thereby placing them in a position to alleviate the pain and suffering of those in need.

WILLIAM CONKLIN is Professor of Law, University of Windsor.

WILLIAM E. CONKLIN

Images
of a Constitution

UNIVERSITY OF TORONTO PRESS

Toronto Buffalo London

© University of Toronto Press 1989
Toronto Buffalo London
Printed in Canada

ISBN 0-8020-2669-9

Printed on acid-free paper

Canadian Cataloguing in Publication Data

Conklin, William E.
Images of a constitution

Includes bibliographical references and index.
ISBN 0-8020-2669-9

1. Canada – Constitutional law – Philosophy.
I. Title.

KE4219.C66 1989   342.71'001   c88-095102-8
KF4482.C66 1989

For Marjolijn

You also know how they make use of visible figures and discourse about them, though what they really have in mind is the originals of which these figures are images: they are not reasoning, for instance, about this particular square and diagonal which they have drawn, but about *the* Square and *the* Diagonal; and so in all cases. The diagrams they draw and the models they make are actual things, which may have their shadows or images in water; but now they serve in their turn as images, while the student is seeking to behold those realities which only thought can apprehend.

Plato, *Republic*
(Cornford transl.; Oxford: Oxford University Press 1941),
at 510

Reason is incapable of thinking this double infringement upon Nature: that there is *lack* in Nature and that *because of that very fact* something is added to it. Yet one should not say that Reason is *powerless to think this*; it is constituted by that lack of power. It is the principle of identity. It is the thought of the self-identity of the natural being. It cannot even determine the supplement as its other, as the irrational and the non-natural for the supplement comes *naturally* to put itself in Nature's place. The supplement is the image and the representation of Nature. The image is neither in or out of Nature. The supplement is therefore equally dangerous for Reason, the natural health of Reason.
Dangerous supplement.

Jacques Derrida, *Of Grammatology*
(Gayatri C. Spivak, transl.; Baltimore: John Hopkins
University Press 1976), at 149

A picture, however, is not destined to be cancelled out, for it is not a means to an end. Here the picture itself is what is meant ...

Hans-Georg Gadamer, *Truth and Method*
(New York: Crossroad 1985), at 123

Contents

Contents ix

x Contents

XIII. An Image of a Constitution 266

Preface

Many years ago, I began a book very different than this one. I wished to examine different theories of a constitution in Western thought. I particularly aimed to explain the role of social/cultural practice and of ethics within each theory. Slowly, I realized that most lawyers, judges, legal scholars, and law students would ignore such a study, claiming it to be impractical and irrelevant as a legitimate subject of legal knowledge. Further, such a focus upon social/cultural practice and ethics strangely destabilized some of my students and excited others. I had to ask 'why?' And this question took me to the rationalist horizons within which the Canadian legal fraternity had understood constitutional law at least since the 1920s.

During the process of writing, teaching, and understanding (not that they differ), I gradually lost faith in the very rationalist boundaries within which I had been raised and educated. I felt entrapped in an inherited rationalist technique which simply would not let me break from treating law as a self-contained end-in-itself. I felt imprisoned by the prospect that what was not objective simply had to be subjective, and that subjective values were invariably considered an illegitimate, irrelevant source of legal knowledge. This essay aspires to break from the trap.

While struggling to escape from the labyrinth, I gained an appreciation of the expression of judges and scholars, as the expression of who they are. I enter into a contemporaneous critical discourse with this expression. I claim that what Canadian judges/scholars have taken to be constitutional law really collapses into their deep search for a satisfactory image of 'what is a constitution?' (Part I); that one can clearly identify the specific boundaries of the dominant rationalist image in Canadian constitutional discourse (Part II), and that lawyers have it within their heritage to fall back upon a richer image of a constitution in order to gain a better understanding of legal texts, judicial decisions, legal scholarship, and themselves/the world (Part III).

I have been encouraged during the past several years by critics of formative drafts of sections of this essay which I presented to the Queen's (Kingston), Leiden, Tilburg, Detroit, Toledo, and Windsor law faculties, to the department of philosophy at Waterloo University, and to various conferences of the American Political Science Association, the Michigan Political Science Association, the Southwestern Ontario Political Theory Group, the Canadian Association of Law and Society, and the Canadian section of the International Association for Philosophy of Law and Social Philosophy. A condensed version of the last chapter was presented to a conference on the philosophy of law at Ottawa University during the fall of 1987. I have been particularly encouraged by new friends whom I discovered at the summer camps of the Critical Legal Studies Movement of 1986 and 1987, though many may object to my themes. The criticisms of the anonymous referees for the Social Science Federation and the University of Toronto Press encouraged me to rewrite much of the manuscript. Grants from the Ontario Law Foundation and the Canadian Social Science Research Council provided for the typing of the early drafts by Ann Spadafora and Fran Munroe, and for the typing and note checking by Celia Laframboise, Martha Mingay, Stephen Kirby, Rosemary Boscka, and Frank Handy, the latter four being law students. I appreciate Annette Pratt's help in typing the last draft. This book has been published with the help of a grant from the Social Science Federation of Canada, using funds provided by the Social Sciences and Humanities Research Council of Canada. Finally, I have been aided by Violet Bozanich through her tireless retrieval of library books, by Paul Murphy and his colleagues for making the Windsor Law Library an enviable research institution, by a continental philosophy study group at the University of Windsor for introducing me to a new world, and by Marjolijn Doedijns who alone believed in the sustenance of this essay during the long Darkness.

I alone take full responsibility for the claims, arguments, and research.

Kingsville, Ontario
26 November 1987

IMAGES OF A CONSTITUTION

I

Introduction:
Images of a Constitution

A constitution is not a text. Nor is it a compendium of judicial and legislative decisions interpreting a text. Nor is it a set of doctrines and arguments which lawyers and legal scholars usher forth in justification of opinions. A constitution is none of these things. Nor is it even the underlying moral/political values, the customs, or the conceptions which the political agent/lawyer/judge assumes or consciously chooses in her or his deliberations. A constitution cannot be these things because a constitution is not a thing separate from and autonomous of the legal community, whereas a text, textual interpretations, justificatory reasons, community values, customs, and conceptions are external to the legal community. One can neither perceive nor measure nor deduce a constitution because these events presuppose the existence of a thing called 'a constitution' external to the observer/scientist.

A constitution is an image; it is a product of the legal community's imagination. A constitution does not live except through the conscious-ness of a legal community. However separated from social/cultural practice, a shared consciousness makes persons feel as if they belong to a community. Lawyers experience this shared consciousness and sense of community. I call this shared consciousness an image. Its parameters make up what has hitherto been called a constitution. The more deeply an image is ingrained in the prejudgments of a lawyer, the more the lawyer thinks and feels as if the image actually exists as an objective fact. When that point in time arises, the lawyer begins to decide and act as if one can actually define, quantify, and justify the image's existence in the phenom-enal world. The constitution (that is, the image) takes on a life of its own. And the more one believes that the constitution actually exists 'out there' as an objective, scientifically verifiable fact, the more authoritatively and legitimately does one assert one's role as law professor, judge, lawyer, public official, or law student.

But a constitution is an image and, as such, it is subject to the scrutiny of critical self-reflection.

1. THE THESES

As a descriptivist thesis, I claim that the most critical issue in understanding the law of a constitution is neither a basic text such as the Constitution Acts, 1867–1987, nor ordinary texts such as a statute or 'reasons for judgment.' Rather, to understand the law of a constitution, one must identify and consider the presupposed image of a constitution which judges, scholars, lawyers, or political officials share in their discourse. The image rebounds off a text. Past lawyers, judges, and scholars have concentrated upon a text's surface issues. They have done so because of the dominant rule rationalist image of a constitution, as I shall show in Chapter VII. But surface issues merely serve as the intermediate juncture between a constitutional image and diverse social/cultural circumstances. A classic law suit is classic because it constitutes a forum for the clash of divergent images, each with a compelling heritage with coherent boundaries. Constitutional law is the expression of the shared images within a legal community's consciousness over time.

This descriptivist claim will be established in Part I of the essay. In Chapter II, I shall show that the representative judicial decisions which students study as an introduction to Canadian constitutional law – the 'rule of law,' the 'separation of powers,' and 'section 96' – exhibit a deep quest for 'what constitutes a constitution?' These 'subject-matters' merely offer an opportunity for any one scholar, judge, or lawyer to search within legal discourse for an image of 'what is a constitution?' Even technical, procedural subject-matters such as 'standing' or 'extrinsic evidence' – the traditional monopoly of rule rationalists – do not really concern the rules of standing or evidence. Rather, as Chapter III will demonstrate, procedural subject-matters serve as the outward expressions of inward responses to the first question of constitutional law: namely, 'what is a constitution?' A trilogy of constitutional amendment judgments during the early 1980s offers a pretext for the clash of responses to that question, as I shall demonstrate in Chapter IV. That the overpowering weight of a rule rationalist image of a constitution permeates one judgment after another in the demise of the Canadian Bill of Rights will be shown in Chapter V. Chapter VI will document how this rule rationalist image penetrates the initial trial court reactions to the Canadian Charter of Rights and Freedoms during the first five years of Charter experience. Lawyers, judges, and scholars find themselves entrapped in the scientistic image of the age. Dickson, Wilson, and some trial court judges, I shall demonstrate in Chapters vi and vii, are stridently aspiring to escape from the hold of rule rationalism during the Charter's first five years, only to find themselves caught within the interstices of another version of rationalism: policy rationalism. Chapters v, vi, and vii will show how human rights texts unnerve the otherwise staid catechism of rule rationalism. Part i, more generally, will make explicit what the Canadian legal community has hitherto left implicit in their search for an answer to the question, 'what is a constitution?'

What is the source of one's image of reality? On the one hand, the external world does not impose the image by *fiat*. Nor can one analytically and rationally cause the construction of an image in an *a priori* medium devoid of phenomenal experience. On the other hand, a constitutional image is not one particular judge's or scholar's set of subjective preferences. Rather, an image constitutes the shared signposts of communication. An image joins a lawyer to his/her past and projects him/her into the future. The image connects the lawyer with others in his/her apparent community, however reified the discourse of that community. I aim to demonstrate how this is so by working within the expression of representative judges and scholars in Canadian legal discourse since the 1920s. In a sense, I carry on a dialogue with them. Only slowly, imperceptibly, do the contours of identifiable images reveal themselves through the chapters. It is only well into Part i that we begin to identify the boundaries of the dominant images of a constitution.

The second general thesis, then, claims that one can clearly identify the boundaries of the shared images of a constitution in Canadian legal discourse. By the end of Part i, I shall have shown how the Canadian legal community has shared three such images of a constitution – three images which cross subject-matters, time, the common law/civil law systems, and the practitioner/scholar visions of law.

The first, an historicist image, focuses upon institutional history for the answer to the question, 'what is a constitution?' Historical evidence validates claims. But the evidence concerns institutional relationships between parliament, the courts, public officials, and the like, rather than economic or social history. Evidence of long-standing claims transforms norms with a social genesis into legal claims. Bracton assumes the importance of this image in the thirteenth century. Edward Coke refines its ramifications for legal validity as an author, reporter, chief justice of the Common Pleas (1606–13), and chief justice of the King's Bench (1613–16). Edmund Burke brings political rigour to the historicist image. And now, in Part I, we shall see how Canadian judges sometimes presuppose the historicist image in their expression. This image reaches its full fruition in the Martland/Ritchie dissent of the *Patriation Reference*.

The second image, rationalism, excludes history as a legitimate source of legal knowledge except to the extent that posited rules or posited values/policies incorporate an appeal to history. Similarly, the rationalist image shuts out a critical reflection of ideal-directed ends as legitimate legal knowledge unless the posited rules or values instruct the lawyer to consider such ends. The content of a constitution begins and terminates with posited rules and/or values. The lawyer who works within this image acts as if rational technique can actually cause legal answers. As a result, s/he pictures law as a cohesive, self-sufficient end-in-itself which historically, logically, morally, and politically needs no idea, argument, end, or social/cultural practice outside posited rules/values for its own legitimacy or justification.

Part II of this essay will work out the precise boundaries of different versions of the rationalist image by carrying on a dialogue with representative Canadian scholars who write about federalism law. Federalism scholars generally expound three versions of the rationalist image: rule rationalism, policy rationalism, and orthodox rationalism.

The first version pictures rules and doctrines along two axes. The one – a horizontal axis – compartmentalizes subject-matters which theoretically encompass a totality of social conduct. The image projects lines between each adjoining compartment. Beneath the horizontal spectrum, authorized institutions – courts, legislatures, or the like – vertically posit further rules. Parent posited rules, in turn, prescribe which institution can posit which rule. To the end of completing an encyclopaedic scheme of horizontal/vertical rules, the lawyer defines the inherent meaning of a text's words, discovers the original intent of the text's framers, or excruciatingly projects the framer's intent into unforeseen contemporary circumstances. S/he pre-understands constitutional law as objectively existing 'out there' in an external world. S/he imagines law as a complete, internally consistent, self-contained sum of legal propositions (sometimes called "tests" or "doctrines"). The lawyer imagines that the doctrines emanate from within the text itself or from the objective intent of the text's original framers. The lawyer accepts the posited rules, as well as the background horizontal/vertical spectrum, as 'givens,' as 'natural,' as 'fundamental.' Equipped with an arsenal of analytic techniques, s/he aims to predict with enviable precision how to apply the doctrines in complex future hypothetical cases. S/he seeks to do so abstractly, scientifically, and objectively. This image of a constitution takes root in the Canadian lawyers' consciousness during the 1920s and reaches its apex in the writings of Albert Abel, Louis-Phillippe Pigeon, and Jean Beetz. I call this image of a constitution "rule rationalism."

The second version of a rationalist image of a constitution, I name "policy rationalism." This picture begins with policies or values – rather than rules – as 'given' or 'fundamental.' To the cache of rationality techniques exploited within the rule rationalist image of a constitution, policy rationalism adds history, empirical research techniques, and moral/political theory. With this wealth of resource material, jurists seek to pierce the veil of formal rules to uncover the social policies/values lying behind, or presupposed in, the rules. The distinction between law and politics collapses with the recognition of the inevitable positing of policies/values in judicial decision-making. Having identified the values or policies, the jurist must define their meaning, delimit their scope, priorize them, and balance them off against each other. S/he must do all this scientifically, objectively, and impartially, sometimes hiding and sometimes acknowledging the positivistic character of constitutional law when s/he makes the ultimate choice of one value or policy over another in seemingly inevitable conflicts. This last stage is pictured as arbitrary, subjective, and irrational, because the jurist realizes that rational technique can carry her/him only so far. Ultimately, one must jump from the objective world of *a priori* concepts and rationality to the subjective world of one's own biases, prejudices, or feelings – or, for that matter, to the biases posited by the majority, an elite, a class, a gender, or whatever.

Bora Laskin, as a young scholar, gives policy rationalism a rigour and sophistication unmatched in Canadian constitutional history; he concentrates upon the indigenous social interests pressing for the enactment of Canadian statutes. Noel Lyon, meanwhile, aspires to scientize the resource base and the methodology of identifying community values. Finally, a group of Quebec and English-speaking scholars, led by Peter Russell, elaborate the political ramifications of the seemingly inevitable values posited in constitutional decision-making. Trial and appellate court judges in Canada share the two rationalist images of a constitution in their interpretation of the Canadian Charter of Rights and Freedoms. They differ only in terms of the rule or policy orientation of their rationalism.

Only Chief Justice Dickson and Madame Justice Wilson of the Canadian Supreme Court are seeking to break from the rationalist hold. They are doing so, though, only to fall back, in part, upon a third strain of the rationalist image of a constitution: namely, "orthodox" rationalism. This image supplements rules with policies. Pressing the exploitation of rational technique to the full, Dickson, Wilson, William Lederman, and others acknowledge the ultimate positing of policies or values in any rational elaboration of constitutional law. Rule rationalism, none the less, remains appealing.

Part III of this essay will identify a third image of a constitution in Canadian legal discourse. I call this image a teleological one. Here, the lawyer understands the content of a constitution in terms of two constituent elements: first, the end or *telos* toward which a society is evolving; and secondly, the social/cultural practices of the society. The lawyer's role is to grasp the *telos* from the evolution of the social/cultural practices of society. This image of a constitution reaches its full expression in the judgments, essays, and government studies of Ivan Rand, scholar and judge of the Canadian Supreme Court during the 1950s. In addition, we shall see in Chapters VI and VII that some lower and higher courts prejudge the Canadian Charter of Rights in terms of a teleological image of a constitution. And, I shall suggest in Chapters XII and XIII that the text of the Charter seems to trigger deep issues of Goodness on the one hand, and social/cultural practice on the other. I shall show that a lawyer can only face the former issues of Goodness, though, within the horizons of a teleological as opposed to a rationalist image of a constitution. Part III of this essay will not only explain why this is so, but will also show why it is so important for the legal community to bypass the rationalist hold which, in one strain or another, now entraps the consciousness of Canadian jurists. After elaborating Rand's image in Chapter XI and after returning to the text of the Charter in Chapter XII, I shall set out the contours of a further image of a constitution in Chapter XIII, an image which contemplates issues of both theory and practice.

2. WHAT IS AN "IMAGE"?

Issues of theory and practice are prejudged by an image of a constitution because an image demarcates what issues count as relevant, valid, and legitimate knowledge. A constitutional image sets out the parameters or boundaries of the lawyer's reality. Historicism assumes, for example, that a text is merely evidence of law and that the older and more revered the text, the weighter is the text as such evidence. Rationalism assumes that the text, the framer's intent, or the subject-matter posit relevance. Teleology assumes that the end(s) embedded within the evolution of social/ historical practice induce relevancy. One image excludes from consideration questions and factors which a second image deems relevant. The image identifies relevancy in terms of the scope of inquiry (the questions asked), the resource material (content), and standing (that is, 'who has a relevant claim?'). The image informs us how a constitution can be amended because it tells us what constitutes law, as opposed to non-law. And the image suggests the boundaries of the lawyer's and judge's role vis-à-vis other institutional actors. These questions infiltrate the lawyer's or judge's prejudgments in a manner which informs the surface issues posed by a basic text such as a charter of rights.

In addition to identifying the relevancy of expression, the image legitimates the judge/lawyer's questions, scope of inquiry, and resource material. This is the image's prime social function, whereas relevancy is an image's prime epistemological function. The text does not legitimate a lawyer's argument; nor do the values assumed or advocated by the lawyer; rather, the dominant image of a constitution performs that function. The lawyer/judge realizes the need to legitimate her/his argument or judgment by justifying her/his decision and by doing so in terms of an ultimate appeal to the prevailing constitutional image. Yes, the lawyer/ judge does use 'texts' such as statutes, the Constitution Acts, and prior judicial decisions. Lawyers usher forth these texts, however, against the legal community's prior expectations, its images of 'what counts.' The common reference points or boundaries of an image serve as the intellectual grounding for the 'rule of law,' 'separations of powers,' the institutional role of a judge, and other important questions.

Constitutional discourse occurs, then, on two levels. The surface level leaves the image largely unarticulated and works within the image's boundaries. The surface image goes unchallenged by judge or lawyer. Lawyers either incorporate the issues of a dispute within the assumed boundaries of their shared image of 'what is a constitution,' or, alternatively, subtly shift the image's boundaries in an effort to absorb the conflict before them. The second level of constitutional discourse, what I call the critical level, crystallizes when one of the participants – the judge, a scholar, a public figure, or the citizen – confronts the dominant prism through which lawyers have hitherto understood a constitution. This clash between two images makes for a classic constitutional case. I describe this clash as a critical discourse because the horizons of the dominant image are questioned. In a critical discourse, lawyers identify the competing images, reject one of them, synthesize them, or work out a new image. In the classic case the critical discourse no longer reflects a shared social outlook; instead, the discourse reflects social interaction and social conflict at least within the legal fraternity. When the lawyers and those affected share a common commitment to a similar image of what counts: only then can we say is there a real community.

An image of a constitution possesses a character of both artificiality and reality. An image is artificial because it is a cultural construct (as opposed to a product of Nature). But a constitutional image takes on an air of reality when the lawyer/judge lives it and when s/he decides or acts because of it. At that point, reality and legitimacy coincide. The image's artificial character is forgotten until critical discourse is reinvigorated and the legitimacy of the prevailing image is challenged.

The image serves to immunize or hide the lawyer from criticism of his/her self. By appealing to the boundaries of the image for social legitimacy, the image interjects between the self and the external world. So long as the image goes unchallenged, it reflects the ideology of a community – an ideology because the image shapes or pre-censors how one understands the self and the other. But once the image is challenged, the deliberator must defend his/her image vociferously. The image no longer protects one against intruders. His/her self is open to brutal and raw attack. One must dig in one's heels, abandon one's image for a new one, or modify one's image to incorporate or ameliorate the opponent. That is why, I think, critical constitutional discourse is political discourse. The image of 'what counts' is up for grabs. When social leaders consciously (or, for that matter, subconsciously) cling to a counter-image, the political intensity surrounding the discourse magnifies. Social conflict permeates all the more so when citizens do not share the dominant image of a legal discourse.

Because the image interfaces with the self, the self forms and evolves as one's image modifies, adjusts, or changes. The self is defined through the image. But the self changes from the inside by re-describing, remaking, and re-explaining the world through its own images. Thus, to understand the law we must understand the images of the law. And, to understand the images of law, we must understand the judge's or lawyer's expression of who she or he is.

3. WHY NOT RULES, CONCEPTIONS, OR FUNDAMENTAL VALUES?

Perhaps one can better appreciate constitutional imagery by distinguishing the image from certain concepts which have sometimes been said to ground the law of a constitution. First, why not entitle the essay "Rules of a Constitution"? A.V. Dicey, most certainly, understands the "true nature of constitutional law" as "all rules which directly or indirectly affect the distribution or the exercise of the sovereign power of the state."[1] H.L.A. Hart grounds the law in a "rule of recognition" which he defines as "the criteria by which the validity of other rules of the system is assessed ..."[2] But both lawyers assume that a rule is a measurable entity in an objective world, whereas I wish to suggest that an image is not. In addition, Dicey's scheme contemplates that one rule can be rationally derived from a prior rule, and Hart's that primary rules can be rationally grounded in the rule of recognition. I do not wish to suggest that an image can rationally cause the creation of rules. More importantly, rules contrast with the cluster of expectations, aspirations, dispositions, attitudes, commitments, and the like, all of which make up an image. Finally, Chapter VIII will show that rules are caught up in an objective world of fact, external to the observer. As Hart suggests, one can discover a rule of recognition by impartially studying whether the officials of a legal system adhere to it and whether they regularly criticize departures from the rule. The rule of recognition is observable much as the law of gravity is observable. But an image is not an observable part of the external world: it lies within expression, and expression, as a source of legal knowledge, bypasses the objective world of rules on the one hand and subjective feelings on the other.

If we are not talking about rules, would it be more appropriate to substitute 'conception' for 'image'? A conception, though, might suggest an *a priori* construct, whereas an image evolves subconsciously from the past. Furthermore, a conception has a definable meaning which can be substituted in place of the conception; an image, by contrast, is self-defining and grows in meaning. It varies, and evolves into different meanings over time. Indeed, one image may grow into an entirely different image, although the terms of the discourse remain the same. An image is as much a figment of the spirit as it is of the mind. But a conception is a creation of the mind.

Nor is an image a fundamental value. First, a value connotes a determinate entity which one can consciously choose, whereas an image is a network of prejudgments which we cannot consciously choose precisely because they are prejudgments. Secondly, a value is personal to the individual: one's values are subjective preferences beyond which rational argument cannot reach. Values are those given, indemonstrable first principles which, with the help of wisdom, we may identify yet not explain. In contrast, an image is a socially induced understanding which others share. We communicate with each other from within the contours of our image of the other and of our self. The sharing of an image makes for the culture of a community and the distinctiveness of that culture vis-à-vis other cultures. Finally, an image joins the past to the present and projects the present into the future. That temporal character contrasts with the limp, atemporal expression of a subjective value.

Interestingly, an image is created over time through a discourse, whereas a value can be posited in a once-and-for-all point of time in isolation from other human beings. Again, an image is created in the process of reaction to others. That is why a judicial decision is a judge's working out of his image of a constitution in response to counsel. The judge needs other participants in order to make the decision. The parties and institutions create the circumstance which envelops the judge. The judgment, with its often long reasons, is the judge's appeal to a legitimizing image. In contrast, one can posit a value, alone, without other human beings. One need not express one's value. Nor is one's value necessarily created in the process of reacting toward others. Images, then, are not values, and we would be misdirected to think otherwise.

By focusing upon images, I hope to redirect the attention of the legal community from a concern with legal doctrine and policy towards a focus upon the prejudgments embedded within critical constitutional discourse. I attempt, for the most part, to understand shared images on their own terms, by assimilating myself into the prisms through which Canadian jurists picture constitutional law. I converse with their expression. Finally, I aspire to show that the various forms of the rationalist image of a constitution protect the rationalist commitment from being questioned critically. The rationalist image immunizes the lawyer from an active role in her/his own self-discovery.

4. METHOD AS UNDERSTANDING EXPRESSION

If an image is neither a rule, nor a conception, nor a fundamental value (or set of values), what method do we use to find an image and where do we look? The questions of method and resource material are part of the very problem which this essay aims to overcome. Method, whatever its etymology, infers technique, observable behaviour, *a priori* concepts, and science. And, to ask 'where do we look?' assumes that we can find the image either in an objective world external to the observer/scientist or a subjective world of the individual's private self. But both technique and the objective/subjective alternatives of reality go to the core of the rationalist image of a constitution, just one of at least three competing images in Canadian legal discourse.

What constitutes reality has plagued the study of law for centuries. Two conceptions of reality have been offered.[3] The one, what Immanuel Kant calls the noumenal world, is composed of abstract *a priori* categories. The lawyer's role is to formulate and justify the categories. Lawyers understand law as a metaphysics. The tighter one's reasoning process and the more purged of empirical, emotional content, the purer is the metaphysics of law. The second reality, what Kant calls the phenomenal world, is the subject of social science or 'law and society' scrutiny. Concentrating upon the 'real' world of power, the lawyer/scholar in the phenomenal world aims to expose the empirical content lying behind the fictional abstractions of law. Whereas the noumenal lawyer enunciates duties which officials or citizens ought to fulfil in this imperfect phenomenal world, the phenomenal lawyer exposes the social/cultural reality hidden behind the appearances of legal categories. Objective rules and doctrines are the resource material of the noumenal lawyer. Subjective values are the resource material of the phenomenal 'law and society' lawyer. Rational technique is the methodology of both. And explanation is the aim of their enterprise.

Now, an image bypasses both horizons of reality. I, too, wish to expose reality, just as empiricism does.[4] Notwithstanding the absence of the social/empirical data of a 'law and society' student, the study of law as imagery gives a realistic account of Canadian constitutional law. I aim to show, as my first thesis, that constitutional reality lies embedded within the consciousness of the legal community. In the process, one may find that this essay goes beyond empiricism, for the latter assumes an objective reality 'out there,' separate from the student and explainable through social science methodology. Instead of seeking out the posited values and policies underlying the appearance of legal doctrine, I wish to understand law through the lived experience of written expansion. Expression is the lawyer's reality.

Conversely, my method is not *a priori*. The latter is grounded in Kant's noumenal world of categories and pure logic. Legal doctrines and the analytic technique dwell in the noumenal world. That the noumenal world is the intellectual and professional home of many Canadian scholars and judges, I shall demonstrate in Part II. I look to what is actually said without forming abstract conclusions or concepts until well into Part I, although I too undoubtedly have my own prejudgments. Instead of retroactively positing my concepts upon the judge or scholar, I try to make myself contemporary with the texts. That is why one will find so many explicit references to the actual words of the participants. That is also why I use the present tense when describing centuries-old texts. I look to *our* expression in an effort to understand the boundaries of *our* consciousness of what constitutes a constitution. I uncover my prejudgments as I seek out the prejudgments of judges and scholars because I too must share the same images for us to have a dialogue. Influenced, no doubt, by some of the writings of Hans Gadamer,[5] Jacques Derrida,[6] Michel Foucault,[7] and Paul Ricoeur,[8] I converse and interpret the texts through our shared understandings, the latter of which I call images. The image magnetically draws my Being into the past and into the future, notwithstanding my old subjective desire, as an independent and impartial spectator, to construct an ahistorical rational order which can rationally cause future events independent of the past and present. The image opens up as much as it forecloses communication. At last, law becomes a lived experience in contrast to the dead abstractions of the noumenal lawyer.

But what exactly is the relationship of the image to anything else which makes up reality?[9] Is the image a picture of a law whose reality may still lie beyond the image? Is the image merely a photocopy or reproduction of an objective law? If so, then the image would have to compete with the sophisticated war chest of social science techniques in the uncovering of phenomenal reality. An image, too, would serve as a mere surface issue, an appearance behind which there would rest a constitutional law as a 'thing-in-itself.' The image would merely intercede between the framer of the text and the 'real' world beyond the image.

Now, there is much to suggest that the law (imagery) is not all there is to reality, that law (imagery) constitutes only one set of expressions or discourses, that there does remain the possibility of *a priori* universals in a noumenal reality on the one hand and social/cultural practices in a phenomenal reality on the other, and that both the theory of the former and the practice of the latter remain untouched by the reified expression of legal discourse. Indeed, my final chapter offers an image of a constitution which entertains such a critical inquiry into theory and practice.

And yet, that other elements of reality beyond legal discourse might exist does not detract from my two theses identified above. Although a constitutional image says much about the self-image of a lawyer as an actor, I intend to leave the relationship between legal knowledge and the subjective/objective dichotomy to another study. To make my claims in this essay, I need only show that constitutional law is imagery and that one can identify competing images in Canadian legal discourse. I do not need to show that imagery is all there is to reality. Nor do I wish to do so at present. Indeed, the very possibility that legal knowledge constitutes only one constituent of social reality suggests the need for a piercing scrutiny of any image of a constitution which characterizes law (and, therefore, itself) as an end-in-itself.

PART I:

IMAGES AND THE LAW OF A CONSTITUTION

WHEN ONE STUDIES A SUBJECT, sooner or later one must reflect upon 'where one want to get to,' much as the Cheshire Cat counselled Alice. The image of a constitution responds to that question. The image sets out the boundary lines of the inquiry, the issues, the resource material, the evidence, and the assumptions which a discourse presupposes. This is so with respect to constitutional law as much as it is of any other subject. Canadian judges find the question of constitutional imagery unsettling. When confronted with the issue, they fall back defensively upon their own hitherto inarticulated images, images which years of reading cases, arguing cases, and judging cases have inculcated. With difficulty, they assert the parameters of an image in response to a lawyer's challenge.

This part of the essay does not identify the precise boundaries of alternative images of a constitution. Part II aims to do that. Rather, this part aspires to show that Canadian judges themselves have recognized that constitutional law really collapses into the judge's own image of a constitution. Obviously, space prevents me from examining every Canadian constitutional case since Confederation. However, one can choose representative cases in representative subjects. The subjects in this part represent the traditional subject-matter in contemporary constitutional discourse: the 'rule of law,' 'separation of powers,' the appointment of judges, standing, extrinsic evidence, constitutional amendment, the Canadian Bill of Rights, and the Charter of Rights. With respect to each of these subject-matters, this part intends to show, judges either assume or expressly acknowledge that the first issue is to identify the dominant image of 'what is a constitution?' Although we shall first concentrate upon judgments of the Canadian Supreme Court, Chapter VI will examine the different images of a constitution presupposed in lower court judgments concerning the Charter of Rights.

Traditionally, the Canadian constitutional lawyer has understood constitutional law in term of horizontal compartmentalized 'subject-matters' with posited rules flowing vertically from each subject-matter. In Part I, I accept the traditional compartments as a framework and aim to expose the consciousness of various judges in representative cases in the 'subject -matters.' In the process, we shall observe how the vision of law as a horizontal/vertical spectrum of compartmentalized 'subject-matters' invariably collapses into a search for a coherent image of a constitution. The 'subject-matters' merely pose surface issues which trigger an inquiry into the very nature of a constitution, the source of a constitution, its resource material (or content), the judiciary's institutional self-image, and other components of a constitutional image. By the end of Part I, the 'subject-matter' approach to constitutional law will have been under-mined as an appropriate descriptivist account of the law of a constitution. At that point we shall be justified in identifying and examining the contours of the dominant images more closely. Part II entertains the latter enterprise in the context of the evolution of Canadian thought about federalism law.

II

Images and Three Traditional Subjects of Canadian Constitutional Law

The first question in constitutional law is 'what is one's image of a constitution?' This is the first question because what has hitherto been taken as an objective law really breaks down into one's own image of a constitution. I shall show how this is so with respect to the 'subject-matters' of the 'rule of law,' 'separation of powers,' and the interpretation of section 96 of the Constitution Act, 1867 (formerly called the British North America Act). In this and in the following chapters in Part 1, I aim to demonstrate that the first question in the law of a constitution is 'what is one's image of a constitution?'

1. THE RULE OF LAW

The 'rule of law' serves as a core 'subject-matter' of ancient,[1] early modern,[2] and contemporary[3] commentaries on constitutional law. When one pries behind the words, one finds a diversity of content granted to the concept of the 'rule of law.' I shall identify three competing approaches to the content of the 'rule of law.' I shall join the three approaches to the deeper question of one's image of a constitution. Finally, I shall show how the Supreme Court of Canada in two representative judgments cannot ascertain the relevancy of the 'rule of law' to a given-fact situation without first appealing to a deeper, broader, and more cohesive image of a constitution. Nor can the Court interpret the concept without doing so. The two judgments are *Roncarelli* v. *Duplessis*[4] and *Re s. 23 of the Manitoba Act, 1870 and s. 133 of the Constitution Act, 1867.*[5]

(a) *The Approaches to the 'Rule of Law'*

In its most restricted meaning, the 'rule of law' connotes the equal and impartial *administration* of *rules* posited by a legislature or court. The Canadian Supreme Court, we shall see in Chapter v, took this to be the meaning of 'equality before the law' as enacted in section 1(b) of the Canadian Bill of Rights during the Bill's early history.[6] Similarly, in the more recent judgment of *Re Manitoba Language Rights*, the Supreme Court of Canada has held that Manitoban enactments and institutions were legally valid even though they had been "constitutionally invalid" since 1870. Why? Because "the rule of law requires the creation and maintenance of an actual order of *positive laws*";[7] and "[t]he rule of law simply cannot be fulfilled in a province that has *no positive law*."[8] Again, in interpreting the phrase "prescribed by law" in section 1 of the Charter, LeDain J., speaking for Dickson C.J.C. and McIntyre J., has asserted in *R. v. Therens* that "prescribed by law" "is chiefly concerned with the distinction between a limit imposed by law and one that is arbitrary."[9] A limit is "law" if it has been "expressly provided for by statute or regulation," or if the limit has resulted "by necessary implication from the terms of a statute or regulation or from its operating requirements ... [or] from the application of a common law rule." Police officers have contradicted the 'rule of law' when they have precluded a passenger's contact with counsel while administering a roadside breathalyser test, according to the *Therens* Court, because neither the legislature nor a court authorized this restriction of the right to counsel. Similarly, the Ontario High Court has applied this narrow sense of the 'rule of law' when the Court held that the tenure, directions, salary, political control, and status of a justice of the peace prevented the justice from acting as "an independent and impartial tribunal," as guaranteed by section 11(d) of the Charter.[10] The doctrines of natural justice in administrative law, fiduciary duties of directors in company law, trustee duties, and crimes proscribing bribery, obstruction of justice, breach of trust, and so on also reflect the key role for the equal and impartial *administration* of *rules* in a constitution.

Now, the common denominator in this first sense of the 'rule of law' is an image of a constitution. That image pictures law exclusively in terms of posited rules. First, the rules inform one as to what constitutes harm, and in what circumstances. Dicey shares this sense when he writes that the state cannot harm a person "except for a distinct breach of law established in the ordinary legal manner before the ordinary courts of the land."[11] If rules are absent, the state officials may not legitimately harm a citizen. Secondly, notwithstanding the social, economic, or political status of a citizen, posited rules govern relationships.[12] Finally, an official act of the legislature or a court posits the rules. The lawyer/judges's role is to apply the rules impartially. To question the wisdom of their content undermines the authoritative posit of the rules.

A second sense of the 'rule of law' involves a scrutiny of the policy content of the posited rules. According to this second sense, judges connect the content of the rules to the policy of procedural fairness. That policy emanates from outside the rules themselves. Lon Fuller, for example, identifies eight criteria for legality (clarity, consistency, publicity, prospectivity, and so on) as constituents of a procedurally fair constitution.[13] John Rawls understands the 'rule of law' in similar procedural terms:[14] "ought implies can,"[15] similar cases should be treated similarly (that is, consistently), "no offence without a law,"[16] and natural justice.

A constitution as policy underlies the European Court of Human Right's conclusion in *Sunday Times* v. *U.K.* that 'law' means much more than just 'the rule of posited rules.'[17] Posited rules must be clear, certain, and precise to enable the citizen to regulate his conduct. The European Court describes the contempt power in the common law as so inaccessible, imprecise, and uncertain as to fail to meet the minimum requirements for posited rules to be 'law.' Similarly, in *Ontario Film and Video Appreciation Society* v. *Ont. Bd. of Censors* the Ontario Divisional Court acknowledges that, although "prescribed by law" in section 1 of the Charter encompasses both judicially and legislatively established rules, the rules "must have legal force."[18] To have legal force, a posited rule must have been "established democratically through the legislative process or judicially through the operation of precedent over the years." Further, "law cannot be vague, undefined, and totally discretionary; it must be ascertainable and understandable."[19] Accordingly, a rule which grants wide discretion to a board to censor or prohibit the exhibition of a film simply "is not legal." Such a wide discretion undermines the policy of procedural fairness.

Along the same lines, the Federal Court of Appeal in *Luscher* v. *Dep. M.N.R. (Customs and Excise)* understands the requirement of 'prescribed by law' in section 1 of the Charter in terms of the policy of procedural fairness.[20] To be law, a rule "should be expressed in terms sufficiently clear to permit a determination of where and what the limit is."[21] The *Luscher* Court continues, "[a] limit which is vague, ambiguous, uncertain, or subject to discretionary determination is, by that fact alone, an unreasonable limit."[22] In *Luscher*, a customs tariff prohibited the importation of "books ... or representation of any kind of a treasonable or seditious, or of an immoral or indecent character,"[23] without defining "immoral" and "indecent." Consequently, the terms of the rule are "highly subjective and emotional in their content."[24] An overlay of such judicial doctrines as 'community standards' merely increases the uncertainty of the rule's content, according to the *Luscher* Court.[25]

Jurists understand the 'rule of law' in a third sense. This third conception, like the second, goes to a policy. In place of procedural fairness, the third sense appeals to the policy of a substantive justice external to the rule and external to the fairness of the procedure by which the rule is enacted and administered.[26] So, for example, the International Commission of Jurists believes that the 'rule of law' requires a policy of distributive justice.[27] Similarly, Third World scholars give great weight to social and economic policies in their discussions of the 'rule of law' concept.[28] And, one finds in *Roncarelli* v. *Duplessis* that Rand J. concerns himself with the economic consequence of administering a posited rule in circumstances unintended by the rule.[29] Let us now see how the Canadian Supreme Court's reliance upon the 'rule of law' in two judgments triggers a deeper self-examination of two very different images of a constitution.

(b) *Why Rand's Constitutional Image Matters*

The statute at issue in *Roncarelli* (the Alcoholic Liquor Act) provides that the "Commission may cancel any permit at its discretion." The Liquor Commission has denied Roncarelli's liquor licence "forever." Why? Not because of fraud or corruption but because Roncarelli has been using profits from his restaurant business in order to provide bail for Jehovah's Witnesses who, in turn, have been imprisoned pursuant to a local by-law. The Witnesses have sold two periodicals known as *The Watch Tower* and *Awake* at a low price without a licence for peddling wares as provided in the by-law. The periodicals have been highly critical of the Roman Catholic Church, Premier Duplessis, and the courts. The Supreme Court holds that the liquor commissioner has illegally severed Roncarelli's licence. The commissioner can only cancel a licence in "good faith," "with a rational appreciation" of the purpose of the statute. For if "an administration according to law is to be superseded by action dictated by and according to the arbitrary likes, dislikes and irrelevant purposes of public officers acting beyond their duty, [it] would signalize the beginning of disintegration of the rule of law as a fundamental postulate of our constitutional structure."[30]

But why has the liquor commissioner exercised his discretion in an improper manner or for an irrelevant purpose in the circumstances? The commissioner has revoked the permit precisely because, according to the Court, Roncarelli has been exercising an unchallengeable," "absolute" right. The core to Rand J.'s explanation lies in this paragraph:

To deny or revoke a permit because a citizen exercises an unchallengeable right totally irrelevant to the sale of liquor in a restaurant is equally beyond the scope of the discretion conferred. There was here not only revocation of the existing permit but a declaration of a future, definitive disqualification of the appellant to obtain one: it was to be "forever." This purports to divest his citizenship status of its incident of membership in the class of those of the public to whom such a privilege could be extended ... [W]hat could be more malicious than to punish this licensee for having done what he had an absolute right to do in a matter utterly irrelevant to the *Liquor Act*? Malice in the proper sense is simply acting for a reason and purpose knowingly foreign to the administration, to which was added here the element of intentional punishment by what was virtually vocation outlawry.[31]

But what is Roncarelli's "absolute" right? A right to grant bail? A right to freedom of speech? freedom of the press? freedom of assembly? A right to private property in the form of a liquor licence? Or a right to pursue the gaining of a livelihood of his choice (a right which was "destroyed")? And why is the right "unchallengeable" and "absolute"? If it is an unchallengeable and absolute right, how can it also be a privilege? What is the difference or is there one? In the above quotation, Rand J. talks about Roncarelli's "citizenship status." This concept, we shall see in Part III, is central to Rand J.'s image of a constitution. It begs the question, 'why is the denial of his unchallengeable right also a divesting of his "citizenship status"?' And 'what does the "citizenship status" mean?' Finally, why is "complete impartiality and integrity" in "a rational appreciation" of the purpose of an enactment so indispensable to the administration of posited rules? Why is law connected to reason rather than, say, fiat? Is "reason" understood as instrumental rationality or as a critical reflection of the ends of posited rules?[32]

Justice Rand does not consciously raise these questions. His assertions he accepts as 'givens.' They are his starting-points or prejudgments which form elements of a cohesive image of a constitution, as we shall see in Chapter XI. *Roncarelli* v. *Duplessis* represents for Rand an opportunity to work out his own image of a constitution in concrete circumstances. That is, the circumstances surrounding Duplessis's conduct challenge the very emotive and intellectual core of Rand J.'s image of 'what a constitution (and law) are supposed to be about.' The latter image is indispensable in understanding why Rand J. reacts the way he does to the facts. Indeed, Rand J. himself recognizes the role of constitutional imagery in his 'reasons for judgment' in *Roncarelli* v. *Duplessis*. The principle of "complete impartiality and integrity" in the administration of posited rules is "a matter of vital importance." Important in respect to what? To Rand J.'s image of 'what is a constitution.' That image plays a major role in the impartial administration of posited rules: without such an impartiality, the 'rule of law' would disintegrate. The 'rule of law,' in turn, constitutes "a fundamental postulate of our constitutional structure" or, more correctly, of Rand J.'s image of a constitutional structure. But Rand J.'s reaction would be neither inevitable nor predictable nor so forcefully worded if he shared one of the very different images of the constitution embedded in Canadian constitutional discourse. The latter images will demonstrate themselves in due course.

(c) *A 'Chaos and Anarchy' Image of a Constitution*

Let us now turn to a judgment where the surface discourse about the 'rule of law' triggers a very different image of a constitution: *Ref. re Certain Language Rights under s. 23 of the Manitoba Act, 1870 and s. 133 of the Constitution Act, 1867.*[33] There, the Supreme Court adopts the most restrictive sense of the 'rule of law' as 'the rule of posited rules.' The important question remains 'why?' Why does the *Manitoba Language Rights* Court adopt the restrictive 'posited rules' approach rather than a policy approach to the 'rule of law'? More important, why does the Court consider the 'rule of law' even relevant to the circumstances? After all, the Court finds invalid all post-1890 Manitoban statutes and regulations which have been printed and published only in English. They are of no force and effect. Having so decided, why does the Court find it necessary to create two new constitutional doctrines for Canada in the process (the *de facto* doctrine and the doctrine of state necessity), doctrines which Third World courts have used to constitutionalize illegal regimes in the past?[34] The answer cannot be found in any Canadian text, although the Court certainly does its best to find textual *indicia* to support its reaction.[35] Rather, the Court recognizes that the answer can be found only within the minds of individual judges. It is to those images of a constitution that they collectively appeal.

The *Manitoba Language Rights* Court begins the 'rule of law' portion of its judgment by *asserting* that the rule of law constitutes "a fundamental principle of our Constitution."[36] The Court also cites single line assertions from Rand J. in *Roncarelli* and Dicey in *The Law of the Constitution* to the effect that the rule of law is "a fundamental postulate of our constitutional structure," "the very basis of the English Constitution" since the Norman Conquest. But the Court realizes that assertions do not constitute arguments and so it goes on to ground the 'rule of law' "in the very nature of a Constitution."[37] Once the Court elaborates a constitution's nature ("a purposive ordering of social relations providing a basis upon which an actual order of positive laws can be brought into existence"),[38] the Court projects into the state of mind of the framers of the Constitution Act, 1867 an intent to ground the text in posited rules: "the founders of this nation," the Court reasons, "*must have intended*, as one of the basic principles of nation building, that Canada be a society of legal order and normative structure: one governed by rule of law."[39] Admitting that the 'rule of posited rules' is not explicitly set out "in a specific provision," the principle still remains "clearly a principle of our Constitution." Or, as it insists toward the end of the judgment, "the unwritten but inherent principle of rule of law ... must provide the foundation of any constitution."[40]

The Supreme Court assures us that its derivation of a principle from "the very nature of a Constitution" is nothing new. Indeed, the Canadian courts have "inferred" and "found" the federal principle itself, along with other principles, from preambles "and the general object and purpose of the Constitution."[41] The Court quotes approvingly from the *Patriation Reference*, a case which will be discussed at length below, where the Supreme Court acknowledged that "*none* [of a whole series of judically developed legal principles and doctrines] *is to be found in the express provisions of the 'British North America Act' or other constitutional enactments.*"[42] The *Manitoba Language Rights* Court admits that these doctrines have been derived from the federal principle which, in turn, the courts have created from "the Constitution." Summarizing its position, the Court affirms that the "unwritten postulates ... form the very foundation of the Constitution of Canada."[43] Federalism and the rule of law represent such unwritten postulates.

Having recognized the source of a constitution as being within each judge's own image of 'what is a constitution' rather than in some external text or some objectivist interpretation of a text, the judges then proceed to work out the content of their image. One theme shapes that content: namely, a very deep and pervasive fear that if the judges do not support the 'rule of posited rules,' "chaos and anarchy" will result. The *Manitoba Language Rights* judges *create* and *add* the *de facto* doctrine to the corpus of Canadian constitutional law because, without such doctrines, there would result "chaos and anarchy,"[44] "legal chaos,"[45] "chaos and disorder,"[46] a "vacuum and chaos,"[47] and "uncertainty and confusion."[48] In short, the absence of the *de facto* doctrine would lead to the break up of "the order and quiet of all civil administration."[49] The judges are willing to allow the government a "temporary reprieve" from compliance with the Constitution "in order to preserve society."[50] The *de facto* doctrine does not extend to all of the rights, duties, and other legal consequences arising pursuant to the 1890 Manitoba Act, according to the Supreme Court. "The only appropriate solution" to preserve those posited rules not saved by the *de facto* and other doctrines is to extend the latter in order to protect all unconstitutional posited rules. For, "[t]he Province of Manitoba would be faced with *chaos and anarchy* if the [posited rules] ... were suddenly open to challenge."[51] The Court's image of a constitution simply cannot tolerate such chaos and anarchy. In the Court's words, "t[he] constitutional guarantee of rule of law *will not tolerate such chaos and anarchy*." And, again "n[or] will the constitutional guarantee of rule of law *tolerate* the Province of Manitoba being without a valid and effectual legal system for the present and future."[52]

Realizing the lack of an explicit precedent for the 'chaos and anarchy' element of their image of a constitution, the *Manitoba Language Rights* judges gather "analagous support" from the doctrine of 'state necessity' elaborated in Third World courts during the past quarter-century.[53] The Court distinguishes that doctrine from the Manitoba facts because the doctrine has concerned the legal situation under insurrectionary governments, whereas Manitoba's government is not insurrectionary. In addition, the doctrine has left constitutional guarantees protected whereas, in the Manitoba facts, the Court wishes to save posited rules which *do* in fact impair constitutional rights. Thus, the Court *extends* the doctrine, originally created for insurrectionary and revolutionary governments, so as to give effect to invalid laws where "necessary" to preserve 'the Rule of Law' (that is, 'the rule of posited rules'). And that necessity arises "in order to preserve society and maintain, as nearly as possible, normal conditions."[54] More particularly, the three circumstances of state necessity share a common theme: namely, that judges "will recognise unconstitutional enactments as valid where a failure to do so would lead to *legal chaos* and thus violate the constitutional requirement of the rule of law."[55] Applying the 'chaos and anarchy' image to the Manitoba facts "*[t]he Constitution* will not suffer a province without laws." "Thus *the Constitution requires*" the temporary validity of invalid rules. "It is only in this way," the Court concludes, "that *legal chaos* can be avoided and the rule of law preserved."[56]

2. THE SEPARATION OF POWERS

Let us now journey to a second pivotal 'subject-matter' of contemporary constitutional commentaries: the 'separation of powers.' Aristotle tells us in the *Politics* that there are three elements or 'powers' in each constitution.[57] The first, called the 'deliberative' element, is sovereign on issues of war, the enactment of rules, cases involving the sanction of death, exile, and confiscation, and the appointment of magistrates.[58] The second, named the 'magistracy,' is charged "with the duty, in some given field, of deliberating, deciding, and giving instructions – and more especially with the duty of giving instructions, which is the special mark of the magistrate."[59] The third is the judicial power.[60] Modern constitutionalists restate the importance of Aristotle's threefold division of constitutional powers. Montesquieu stresses, for example, that "there is no liberty, if the power of judging be not separated from the legislative and executive powers."[61] Thomas Jefferson takes up the same point by emphasizing that the concentration of legislative, executive, and judicial powers "in the same hands is precisely the definition of despotic government."[62] And, the Founding Fathers designed the American constitution with the separation of powers in mind, modified by checks and balances.

In contrast, commentators of the Canadian constitution do not take a consistent position as to the acceptance or legitimacy of a separation of powers. Noel Lyon and William Lederman claim that the Canadian constitution possesses a separation of the judicial from the legislative and executive powers.[63] Other commentators deny a 'separation of powers' in the Canadian constitution.[64] The important question is 'why?' Why can learned commentators render such conflicting opinions about a principle which Aristotle, Montesquieu, and Jefferson assume to be an inherent part of any constitution?

The answer, once again, lies in the conflicting images of a constitution which jurists presuppose in their opinions concerning the surface issue. I intend to demonstrate this by reference to the two conflicting sets of Canadian opinions noted above. Each scholar or judge faces a surface issue by working out an image of a constitution. When a counsel appeals to the doctrine of 'separation of powers' in argument, I wish to show that the counsel tries to justify the doctrine in terms of the counsel's or judges' boundaries of 'what constitutes a constitution?' The more forceful and rigorous counsel's argument, the clearer will be the boundaries and the more searching will be the scholar's or judge's reaction to the argument.

(a) *An Historicist Image of a Constitution*

The first set of Canadian opinions claims that there *does* exist a 'separation of powers' in the Canadian constitution. In particular, jurists hold that there exists a constitutional limit beyond which the legislative and executive branches of government may not infringe upon the functions of the judiciary. One can find this claim, for example, in the appellate decision of *R. v. Hess (No. 2)*[65] and the trial court decision of *Beauregard v. R.*[66] Chief Justice Dickson affirms the principle in the Supreme Court judgment of *Beauregard* by emphasizing the critical connection of the financial security of a judge to "complete freedom from arbitrary interference by both the executive and the legislature."[67] And LeDain J. identifies three conditions for judicial independence in the context of section 11(d) of the Canadian Charter of Rights and Freedoms in *Valente v. The Queen*: security of tenure, financial security, and independent control of the court's internal administration.[68] I intend to show that the 'separation of powers' claim is an intellectual construct, a creation of the mind, an idea. Behind it, there lies a deep image of 'what is a constitution.' The individual judge or scholar works out that image through his or her 'separation of powers' construct. The image explains the construct; the image is expressed through the construct.

In *R. v. Hess (No. 2)* (1949), as an example, O'Halloran J.A. denies to Parliament the constitutional authority to authorize the detention of a person pending an appeal to the Supreme Court of Canada, after one has already been acquitted in an appellate court.[69] The Criminal Code of the time provided that the acquitted person could be detained within the time allowed for appeal or until its determination, if the Crown appealed, unless the Crown gave written notice that it did not intend to appeal or unless the trial judge had granted bail. O'Halloran J.A. holds that this legislative provision infringes the judiciary's independent function of reviewing detention. That function is separate from the legislative and executive functions. In the *Hess* circumstances, Parliament has invaded the judicial function, according to O'Halloran J.A. The Constitution protects the latter.

But what is this thing called a 'Constitution'? Where does O'Halloran find it? O'Halloran J.A. cannot discover his constitution in some specific text. It does not live 'out there' in some objective world, only to be applied at the asking. The 'Constitution' rests in Judge O'Halloran's consciousness. He *imagines* the contours of a constitution. Once he has consciously identified his image of a constitution, O'Halloran J.A. can ascertain the legitimate scope of the judicial power.

What, then, is the character of O'Halloran J.A.'s image? His image of a constitution is an historicist one. Early in his judgment he declares that *"[l]ong-established principles* are unconcernedly infringed to [such] a degree that I find it judicially impossible to attach to the assembled words any rational meaning ..."[70] That is, history makes the posited legislative rule irrational. If Parliament can set aside a judicial decision or interfere with the enforcement of a court's judgment, Parliament "would break down the independence of the judiciary and destroy the judicial system Canada and its common law Provinces have inherited."[71] O'Halloran J.A.'s "reading of constitutional history" leads him to his conclusion. He quotes extensively from Coke's early seventeenth-century opinions concerning the independence of the courts. And Coke, in turn, grounded his opinions in centuries-old statutes and *"the ancient law of the land."*[72] According to O'Halloran J.A., Canada has adopted "the same constitutional principles" as the United Kingdom, in that the preamble of the British North America Act, 1867 has provided for a constitution "similar in Principle to that of the United Kingdom." And the written constitution of the latter is *"reflected in"* such documents as Magna Carta (1215), the Petition of Right (1628), the Bill of Rights (1688), and the Act of Settlement (1700–1).[73]

Let us now take a more recent judgment: that of Addy J. in the Federal Court, Trial Division decision of *Beauregard* v. *R.* in 1981.[74] After Beauregard J. has been appointed a judge, Parliament amends the Judges Act so as to require previously non-contributory pension payments to be contributory, retroactive to a date prior to Beauregard J.'s appointment. Beauregard J.'s salary is thereby reduced to the extent of the contributory payments. Addy J. of the Federal Court, Trial Division holds that Parliament is "constitutionally prevented" from reducing any judge's salary directly or indirectly. The majority of the Appeal Division of the Federal Court later affirms his decision, although the three appellate judges presuppose a textualist as opposed to Addy J.'s historicist image of a constitution.[75] Chief Justice Dickson, speaking for the majority of the Supreme Court of Canada, confirms Addy J.'s trial court opinion.[76] Although the federal character of "the Constitution," the text of the Constitution Act, 1867, "the fundamental values" underlying "the Constitution," and international documents combine to concretize Dickson C.J.'s picture of the place of judicial independence in a constitution, tradition certainly makes its mark upon him, as much as it does upon LeDain in *Valente.*[77] The question persists: 'why is a parliament "constitutionally prevented" from reducing a judge's salary?' Why are judges constitutionally guaranteed security of tenure, financial security, and administrative independence? Once again, I wish to suggest, our judges collapse these questions into a wider search for a coherent image of a constitution. The common boundary of the shared images in the Addy J., Dickson C.J., and LeDain line of judgments is the heavy weight of history.[78] Let us look closely at the trial court judgment in *Beauregard* to experience this factor.

Addy does not work out some construct of "citizenship status" as we have seen Rand J. do in a series of cases beginning with *Roncarelli* v. *Duplessis*.[79] Nor does Addy J. preoccupy himself with the actual wording of the Constitution Act, 1867. No. He shares with O'Halloran J.A. a historicist image of a constitution where the content, the character, and the source of constitutional obligation emanate from institutional history. As to the content of the constitution in this case, Addy J. discovers an "intrinsic and fundamental principle of constitutional law" embedded within the seventeenth-century constitutional battles. These battles culminate in the doctrine of the 'independence of the courts' in the Act of Settlement, 1700–1. Sections 99 and 100 of the Constitution Act, 1867 offer institutional support for the existence of the constitutional principle,[80] according to Addy J. That is, the Constitution Act, 1867 does not posit the principle in 1867; rather, the principle grows out of institutional history of which the Act is mere evidence.

As to the character of a constitution, Addy J. has this to say: a constitutional rule is "much more fundamental and essential" than a "rule which is regarded as obligatory by the officials to whom it applies."[81] The security of judicial salaries is "constitutionally guaranteed," "a legal constitutional requirement."[82] Addy J. concludes that "there exists *a legal constitutional requirement* derived from the federal nature of our Constitution to the effect that the rights of federally appointed judiciary, as they existed at the time of Confederation, cannot be abrogated, curtailed, or changed without an amendment to the Constitution."[83] That is, the functions of the judges are constitutionally (and legally, if that adds anything) separate from the legislative and executive functions. Indeed, only a formal amendment to the Constitution Act could alter the constitutional requirement of 'separation of powers.' And yet, even express provincial consent to such alteration would not suffice to modify the 'separation of powers' principle, Addy continues, "because a constitutional power or obligation cannot be legally changed or abandoned in a federal state by mere consent."[84] The principle of 'separation of powers,' he restates, "arises out of an intrinsic and fundamental principle of constitutional law."[85] The character of Addy J.'s image of a constitution is clear: something called "the Constitution" is supreme over posited law. The 'separation of powers' doctrine represents the intellectual construct through which Addy J. transposes his image of a constitution into legal discourse.

Finally, Addy J. tells us something about the source of constitutional obligation within his image. A constitutional rule is *not* obligatory because officials consider it obligatory, as H.L.A. Hart has claimed in his discussion of secondary rules.[86] Rather, institutional history provides the source of constitutional obligation, whatever the officials – or the populace, for that matter – think or feel about the 'separation of powers' doctrine in general or the circumstance of this case.

(b) *Deference to Posited Legislative Rules*

In contrast to an historicist constitutional image and the supporting 'separation of powers' doctrine of O'Halloran and Addy J.J., a counter-strain of contemporary Canadian discourse suggests that no such doctrine exists in Canada.[87] Again, the crucial question is 'why?'[88] Is there a rational grounding? If so, what is the grounding of these latter esteemed opinions? Must they also be understood in terms of an historicist perspective? No, for one can trace the counter-strain to the writings and teaching materials of an earlier generation of legal scholars. In one of the earliest comprehensive statements concerning judicial independence, John Willis concludes, citing cases as authority, that "[t]here is *no constitutional rule* against taking away the jurisdiction of the higher courts or against conferring judicial powers on administrative officers[.]"[89] Laskin repeatedly affirms Willis's claim in the various editions of his text, *Canadian Constitutional Law*.[90] Laskin insists in each edition that "[t]his proposition is surely not open to challenge in relation to substantive original and appellate jurisdiction where curtailment is by the competent legislature."[91]

Why do Willis and Laskin believe that their counter-proposition is not open to challenge? O'Halloran, Addy, Lyon, and Lederman certainly believe it is. The explanation for Laskin's presumed unchallengeability to the counter-claim lies in the starting premise of his teaching materials: the posited text, the British North America Act, 1867.[92] Laskin believes that that document establishes a totality of legislative power from which no institution or human conduct can theoretically escape. Accordingly, Laskin subtitles his text, for example, *Cases, Text and Notes on Distribution of Legislative Power*. That is, he equates Canadian constitutional law with the division of the totality of legislative power. Further, he begins each edition of his text with *dicta* affirming the totality of legislative power.[93] And he follows this up on the same page with Lord Watson's statement that the British North America Act, 1867 has aimed to distribute *"all* powers executive and legislative, and all public property and revenues which had previously belonged to the provinces," so that what powers the dominion government does not retain the provincial governments do.[94] Some pages later Laskin approvingly begins a "Note on Limitation of Legislative Power" with judicial *dicta* that "whatever belongs to self-government in Canada belongs either to the Dominion or to the provinces, within the limits of the British North America Act."[95] He traces this proposition to *Bank of Toronto* v. *Lambe* where the Judicial Committee has asserted that "the Federation Act exhausts the whole range of legislative power, and ... whatever is not thereby given to the provincial legislatures rests with the parliament."[96] The remainder of Laskin's text delimits the respective spheres of power for the two levels of government.

Given Laskin's prejudgment that no human behaviour is theoretically immune from potential restriction by the two sets of legislatures, a legislature can legislate a court out of existence. In Laskin's words, although "a superior court is (apart from appeal) not accountable to any other judicial tribunal, and hence may properly determine its own jurisdiction," the legislature ultimately controls a court: "the *competent* legislature may confer or curtail, may shape or condition jurisdiction of a court."[97] The British North America Act, 1867 does impliedly guarantee that the courts can rule upon the validity of a legislative enactment. And the Act does assume "but without explicitly so declaring, that provincial superior Courts have a constitutional existence."[98] But a court cannot hold an alleged legislative infringement of judicial power invalid. Rather, a court can determine validity only in terms of the distribution of legislative authority between the two levels of government. A text, the British North America Act, 1867, posits that distribution and the corresponding subordinate position of a court. There is nothing to prevent the appropriate institution (that is, the United Kingdom Parliament with the advice and consent of the provincial and federal legislatures)[99] from amending the rules in the text. Nor is there any logical barrier to prevent federal and provincial governments from restricting or denying judicial independence at the same time. In his words, "[t]here is nothing in the *British North America Act* which expressly protects the courts in any claim to particular jurisdiction against both Parliament and provincial Legislatures."[100] Laskin does contemplate some minor limitations to the exhaustive totality of legislative power.[101] But Laskin's image of a constitution does not contemplate that the existence and functions of a court could exist independently of the legislature. Parliament and provincial legislatures share a totality of rule-making authority subject to the few minor exceptions where another legislature – the United Kingdom Parliament – can legislate upon a subject-matter.

In sum, Canadian jurists express contradictory opinions as to whether the Canadian constitution possesses a principle of 'separation of powers.' The one view, represented in the scholarship of Professors Lyon and Lederman and in the judgments of *Hess, Beauregard,* and *Valente,* suggests an affirmative response. The second, expressed in the writings of Willis and Laskin, opines in the negative. Both responses search for the legitimate boundaries of a constitution. 'Separation of powers' merely poses as a surface issue for a deeper dialogue about constitutional imagery.

3. THE JUDICIAL FUNCTION, THE CHARACTER OF A CONSTITUTION, AND SECTION 96

We have seen how two 'subject-matters' of constitutional law –the 'rule of law' and the 'separation of powers' – collapse, upon close scrutiny, into a search for a coherent image of a constitution. Admittedly, it is difficult to decipher the full boundaries of identifiable images. The contours vary from Rand's unlimited citizenship rights in *Roncarelli,* to a fear of 'chaos and anarchy' on the part of the *Manitoba Language Rights* Court, to an historicism, and, finally, to a deference to legislated rules. With respect to each 'subject-matter,' the surface issue, whether the 'rule of law' or the 'separation of powers,' triggers a need on a jurist's part to express his image of 'what is a constitution?' A judgment offers an opportunity for a judge to work out his/her constitutional image.

Section 96 of the Constitution Act, 1867 differs little from this phenomenon, nothwithstanding that the surface issues surround a code, as opposed to judicially created doctrine. Section 96 provides as follows:

96. The Governor General shall appoint the Judges of the Superior, District, and County Courts in each Province, except those of the Courts of Probate in Nova Scotia and New Brunswick.

As with the 'rule of law' and the 'separation of powers,' counsel frame their arguments in terms of a surface issue: the meaning of section 96. But

Supreme Court judgments do not really seek out some inherent meaning of the words in section 96. Rather, judges use the opportunity of a section 96 challenge to elaborate their own expectations of the judicial function. And they hint that the judicial function plays only one element in one's broader image of a constitution.

(a) *Dickson's Search for an Image of a Constitution*

The judgment of Dickson J. in *Re Residential Tenancies Act* serves as the take-off point for recent opinions concerning section 96.[102] The Supreme Court is asked whether the Ontario legislature could empower a tribunal to evict a tenant or to compel landlords and tenants to fulfil certain duties posited by a provincial statute. Dickson J. sets his frame of reference in traditional 'separation of powers' terms. First, "there is no general 'separation of powers' in the *British North America Act, 1867*."[103] Secondly, although section 92(14) of the BNA Act 1867 authorizes "a wide power" to the provincial legislatures in relation to the administration of justice, section 96 grants to the Federal Cabinet the sole authority to appoint judges of the superior, district, and county courts. Dickson J. understands the role of section 96 against the *historical* background of Confederation. Section 96, along with sections 92(14) and 97–100, represents "one of the important compromises of the Father of Confederation." Section 96 provides "a strong constitutional base for national unity, through a unitary judicial system" in a federal system of government.[104]

Having placed section 96 upon "a strong constitutional base," Dickson J. then proceeds to elaborate a three-pronged test for resolving whether a provincial tribunal is really a superior, district, or county court.[105] First, is the tribunal's power within "the power or jurisdiction" of a superior, district, or county court at confederation? Secondly, does the tribunal exercise a judicial function? And thirdly, is that judicial function "a sole or central function" of the tribunal; or, alternatively, is it "necessarily incidental" to a broader social goal? When Dickson J. applies this threefold test to the residential tenancy commission he concludes, first, that the power of the tribunal is "broadly conformable" to the pre-1867 jurisdiction of the superior, district, and county courts; secondly, that the tribunal's functions are in fact "judicial powers"; and thirdly that, when viewed in its contemporary institutional setting, the tribunal performs an adjudicative function. As a consequence, "[t]he provincial Legislature has sought to withdraw historically entrenched and important judicial functions from the superior court and vest them in one of its tribunals."[106]

Now, many a law student has memorized Dickson J.'s three-pronged test in the expectation that constitutional law equals legal rules and their rational application. And Dickson J., it will be thought, deduces his three rules from the parent rule in section 96 of the Constitution Act, 1867. But a leading doctrinal lawyer in English-speaking Canada describes the application of the parent rule as "vague and disputable in many situations," casting doubt upon the constitutionality of many provincial administrative tribunals and encouraging "a spate of litigation."[107] Given a textualist image of a constitution, a formal amendment to the parent text would offer "the only solution" to overcome the vague rules. But *Re Residential Tenancies* does not hang upon an inherent meaning of section 96 or even in Dickson J.'s three rules. Rather, one can understand Dickson J.'s judgment only in terms of his own image of a constitution and his effort to express that image in response to a text which triggers a surface issue. Dickson J. himself realizes that his deeper image of a constitution is all important; more than that, he realizes that he is working out his constitutional image in the form of 'reasons for judgment.'

Dickson J. begins that process when he initially denies the existence of a 'separation of powers' doctrine. More affirmatively, he concentrates upon two important constituents of his image: first, 'what is the function of a judge?'; and secondly, 'what is the character or nature of a constitution?' He responds to the first question in the context of his threefold rule. He reacts to the second in terms of the relationship between a posited legislative rule, on the one hand, and 'the constitution,' on the other. Let us now consider these two constituents of his image.

First, what is the function of a judge? Dickson J. poses three models of a court. First, a court is any institution called a court in 1867. Secondly, a court is any institution whose formal trappings, apparatus, and, presumably, name resemble a court. Thirdly, a court is any institution which performs the functions of a court. Dickson's threefold test adopts an amalgam of the first and third models of a court. The first stage of his test instructs the lawyer to go to Canadian institutional history, especially the history surrounding judicial institutions in 1867. The second and third stages of his test advise the lawyer to reject the second formal institutionalist model of a court in favour of a functional theory of 'what courts in fact do.' In Dickson J.'s view – and that of many others in the legal community – a judicial function, first, involves "a private dispute between parties"; secondly, the officer must adjudicate the dispute through "the application of a recognised body of rules"; and thirdly, he must do so "in a manner consistent with fairness and impartiality."[108] Dickson superimposes this latter functionalist theory of a court upon his historicist test. He informs us that that is really what section 96 involves. And he then applies his functionalist/historicist theory of a court to the history and functions of the residential tenancies tribunal.

The second element of Dickson J.'s image of a constitution as expressed in *Re Residential Tenancies* involves his understanding of the character of a constitution. Is a constitution posited by the legislature, is it embedded in institutional history, or is it some overbearing text, principle, or abstract 'thing' to which the legislature and court are subject? By rendering the proposed provincial legislation invalid in *Residential Tenancies*, Judge Dickson opens himself to the charge that his interpretation of section 96 "thwart[s] or unduly restrict[s]" a legislative policy for which there is a genuine "social need": namely the need to restrict the inflation of tenancy rates. But Dickson J. has a deeper sense of obligation to "the Constitution" as opposed to posited law. In his words, "Yet, however worthy the policy objectives, it must be recognized that we, as a Court, *are not given the freedom to choose* whether the problem is such that provincial, rather than federal, authority should deal with it. We must seek to give effect to *the Constitution as we understand it* and with due regard for the manner in which it has been judicially interpreted in the past."[109] Dickson J. does not believe himself as having "the freedom to choose" because his image of a constitution possesses a sense of compulsion or obligatoriness about it. Within that image he assigns a special adjudicative function to a court. He also assigns a secondary function to both the legislature and the court vis-à-vis this almost mythical thing which he calls "the Constitution." That is, both the legislature and the court are subject to "the Constitution." And "the Constitution" is really Dickson J.'s image of a constitution. In that sense, the proposed provincial legislation does not violate section 96 of the British North America Act, 1867. Rather, it violates Dickson J.'s image of a constitution, an image which he expresses when interpreting section 96 and when applying that interpretation to the proposed legislation.

(b) *The Early Theme of the Judicial Function*

The claim that section 96 really triggers the general question 'what is a constitution?' applies to the old precedents as much as it does to the new ones. Judges infrequently inform us what actually is a 'court' or what precisely is the role of a court. But they insist that whatever a court and its role are, these are the key issues arising out of section 96.

In one of the earlier cases, *Toronto* v. *York Township*, it is claimed that the Ontario Municipal Board has been invalidly constituted as a superior court in violation of sections 96, 99, and 100 of the British North America Act, that the board's authority can only be exercised by a court, and that the Ontario Municipal Board Act has purported to vest the jurisdiction of a superior court in the Municipal Board.[110] Lord Atkin severs as invalid such sections of the Act which purport to vest the functions of a court in the provincial board. Although Lord Atkin is uncertain what constitutes the judicial function, he is certain that the Municipal Board does in fact exercise judicial functions.[111] In the same year Duff C.J. also relies upon "the judicial function" as the key determinant to a section 96 problem in *Reference re Adoption Act*.[112] After a detailed examination of the precedents before his time, Duff C.J. assesses his general approach in terms of his own institutional self-image:

Then, it should be observed that, if you have a provincial Court outside the scope of section 96 and the province enlarges its jurisdiction or its powers, but not in such a manner as to constitute a [c]ourt of a class within the intendment of section 96, *I, as a Judge, charged solely with the application of the law*, have no further concern with what the Legislature has done. *It is no part of my function as a Judge* to consider whether, if the Province should go on enlarging the jurisdiction and powers of the [C]ourt, it might arrive at a point when the tribunal ceases to be one outside the ambit of section 96. I have nothing to do with that. It may be a very excellent ground for disallowance of the legislation by the Governor-General. Even if I am satisfied that there is something in the nature of an abuse of power, that in itself is no concern of mine ...[113]

After so declaring, Duff examines a series of Ontario statutes which authorize the adjudication of disputes by provincially appointed magistrates. He concludes that such magistrates do not exercise a function historically belonging to the superior courts.

And again, in *Labour Relations Board of Sask.* v. *John East Iron Works Ltd.*, the Judicial Committee faces the claim that the Saskatchewan labour relations board resembles a court of King's Bench and that the board is thereby invalidly constituted as contrary to section 96 of the British North America Act, 1867.[114] The Judicial Committee frames the issue solely in terms of whether the board exercises "judicial power." If the board does not exercise a judicial function, it is not a court. That is, the board cannot possibly be a "Superior, District or County Court" as contemplated in section 96. The Privy Council then defines the function of a court as follows: "It is a truism that the conception of the judicial function is inseparably bound up with the idea of *a suit between parties*, whether between Crown and subject or between subject and subject, and that it is *the duty of the court* to decide the issue between those parties, with whom alone it rests to initiate or defend or compromise the proceedings."[115] The Privy Council continues that the labour board is "a striking departure from the traditional conception of a [c]ourt."[116] Although an industrial conflict may be described as a *lis* or suit between parties, such a dispute is remote from the judicial function in 1867. As an "analogous" point, members of a labour board other than an independent president "bring an experience and knowledge acquired extra-judicially," in contrast to judges. Board members represent the litigants and the general public equally.[117] Although this bias or interest would not lead them to act injudiciously, it does distinguish a labour board's function from a court's. Accordingly, the labour board cannot possibly resemble a court. Thus, labour board orders do not offend section 96 of the British North America Act, 1867.

(c) Laskin's Early Textualism

(i) *The role of a court* Dickson J.'s amalgam of historicist and functionalist elements in his *Re Residential Tenancies Act* judgment certainly contrasts with Professor Laskin's deference to legislative rules in his 'separation of powers' commentary. We saw above that Laskin, through his teaching materials, expresses a constitutional image in terms of a set of legislated rules posited in the British North America Act, 1867. He grants little independent weight to history, in contrast to O'Halloran and Addy J.J. Consistent with his 'separation of powers' commentary, the early Laskin (Laskin, the scholar) reacts strongly against the judicial "rewriting" of section 96 in the "functional" terms which eventually come to fruition in Dickson J.'s *Residential Tenancies Act* judgment.[118] He explains his reaction in terms of his own picture of the proper role of a judge.

In an essay which he published in 1955, Professor Laskin describes the judiciary's functionalist "rewriting" of section 96 as "one of the paradoxes of Canadian constitutional interpretation."[119] The fact that the courts would subordinate sections 97–100 to section 96 he finds "baffling" and "unreasonable." Interestingly, Professor Laskin appeals to the Quebec Resolutions of 1864 and the Confederation Debates as providing no evidence that the Fathers of Confederation had actually intended section 96 to be pivotal. Nor, in his view, did the participants contemplate that the appointing power in section 96 should encompass any inquiry into 'what is the function of a court?' According to Laskin, historical evidence establishes that the federal appointing power has not "meant anything more than what it formally involved."[120]

(ii) *A posited text* For Laskin, the teacher, the British North America Act, 1867 posits rules and those rules constitute the exclusive resource material for constitutional law.[121] Whatever the subject-matter of law, Laskin believes, law does not concern a self-examination of the judiciary's function. To read "judicial power" or "question of law" into the duties of a provincially appointed tribunal and then to elevate that "judicial power" or "question of law" to "a constitutional prohibition" by reading "judicial power" into section 96 is "stranger still," he remarks. By talking about the role of a court in the context of section 96, Laskin believes, the judges create "a needless artificiality."[122] Laskin finds all this talk about the judicial function as "stranger still" because Laskin's image of a constitution focuses upon written posited rules rather than some unwritten intangible notion of a court's role or, more generally, a judge's institutional self-image. The latter inquiry goes beyond the explicit rule laid down in section 96. It also goes beyond Laskin's own image of what a court is supposed to do and what a constitution is supposed to be about.

(d) *Laskin's Revised Functionalism*
As chief justice, Laskin modifies his early hostility to the above "needless artificiality" of imputing the judicial function into section 96. Indeed, as his judgment in *Crevier* v. *A.G. Canada* demonstrates, he reads a functionalist conception of a court into section 96.[123] But he does so in a manner which retains earlier elements of his image of a constitution. The *Crevier* case involved Quebec's professions tribunal, which heard appeals from thirty-eight discipline committees of thirty-eight respective professions. The tribunal consisted of six provincial court judges with authority to confirm, alter, or quash any decision of a discipline committee. Their decisions were final and the Professional Code, section 193, guaranteed them immunity from prosecution for acts done in good faith.

As with Dickson J.'s judgment in *Re Residential Tenancies Act* and the early precedents discussed above, Laskin C.J.'s *Crevier* judgment does not represent a scientific application of section 96 of the BNA Act, 1867 to the *Crevier* statute. Rather, the judgment expresses Laskin's own self-image as a judge. Laskin C.J. posits two models of a court. The one assumes a court "in non-functional formal terms," to use his terms. The other adopts a behaviourist concern for the *de facto* function of a court, presumably in contemporary society. If Laskin adopted the formalist model, he believes, he "would make a mockery of [the BNA Act, 1867]."[124] The behaviourist model, in contrast, allows Laskin to focus upon the final review function of a superior court in matters of law, jurisdiction, and constitutionality. By being immunized from further review of its own decisions on issues of jurisdiction, the professions tribunal thereby functions with the same "hallmark" traits as a superior court.

At the same time Laskin C.J. assumes that the most important element in "the constitution" is the posited text, the British North America Act, 1867. "[G]iven that s. 96 is in the *British North America Act, 1867*," "in the face of s. 96," "it cannot be left to a provincial statutory tribunal, in the face of s. 96, to determine the limits of its own jurisdiction without appeal or review."[125] And again, the interests of a legislature contrast with those of the courts which, in turn, are the "ultimate interpreters of the *British North America Act, 1867* and s. 96 thereof."[126] The posited rules in the British North America Act, 1867 provide the source of constitutional obligation for Laskin. The courts are bound to apply those rules, come what may.

(e) *The Refinement of the Dickson Court's Self-Image*

Recent Supreme Court judgments refine the judiciary's self-image in response to section 96 challenges. In *Massey-Ferguson Indust. Ltd.* v. *Sask.*, for example, a provincially appointed board could grant fair compensation against loss or damage arising from the purchase or use of agricultural implements.[127] If one proceeded before the board, s/he was precluded from seeking recovery in a court. Does the board perform the functions of a court? To ask that question the *Massey-Ferguson* Court inquires into the nature of a court. A court is bound by "legal considerations" (such as blameworthiness in a legal sense) in assessing the validity of a claim.[128] A court resolves a dispute between two parties (a *lis inter partes*).[129] Finally, a court plays a "neutral," adjudicative function as opposed to an investigative or an administrative function. The Supreme Court then concludes that the provincial board has not met these *indicia* of a court.

Justice Estey has recently added to these *indicia* of a court's function in a challenge to a provincially appointed court in *Re B.C. Family Relations Act*. A statute had granted jurisdiction to the court over guardianship, custody, access to a child, occupancy of family residence, use of the residence's contents, and non-entry to the premises.[130] Estey J. begins with "the generally accepted theory" that the purpose of section 96 is "to ensure a quality of independence and impartiality in the courtroom ... and an aura of detachment said to be analogous to that of the royal justices on circuit from Westminster."[131] In addition to the independent and impartial aura of detachment surrounding a court, Estey J. notes the formal, demanding, "highly refined" techniques and procedures of a court.[132] Further, issues before a court involve, "the more serious claims and issues in the community" and the "serious and frequently profound difficulties arising in the community ..."[133] These *indicia*, Estey J. observes, distinguish a superior from the provincially appointed court at issue.

4. SUMMARY

I have tried to dislodge the old notion expressed in the teaching materials of the early Laskin that constitutional law equals the strict application of a posited text. As Peter Hogg suggests with respect to the interpretation of section 96, "[i]f ss. 96 to 100 of the Constitution Act, 1867 were read literally, they could easily be evaded by a province which wanted to assume control of its judicial appointments."[134] I have also tried to show that Canadian Supreme Court judges do not even treat this seemingly technical subject-matter of constitutional law as if it were an objective subject-matter 'out there,' separate from the judge's self and open to neutral interpretation. When a lawyer raises section 96 in his or her argument, appellate judges feel compelled to examine their institutional self-image as judges. That is, 'what function should a judge perform in Canadian society?' has been the real issue in section 96 litigation. In the words of the most recent Supreme Court judgment "concerning" section 96, it is "the key constitutional issue in the present case[.]"[135] If an institution performs the adjudicative function of a court, then it is a 'superior, district or county court' and the federal government alone may appoint its officers. The deep issue is the judge's self-image as a judge. That issue permeates 'rule of law' and 'separation of power' judgments as much as it does the judiciary's interpretation of section 96.

The resolution of that issue ultimately connects with other boundaries of a judge's overall image of a constitution. We have experienced in our study of 'rule of law' and 'separation of powers' judgments that a further such constituent is the resource material of a constitution. For O'Halloran J.A. and Addy J. the content of a constitution is uncovered in institutional history. For Laskin, a posited text, the British North America Act, 1867, gives content to a constitution. Laskin expresses his opinions as if the posited text actually causes his opinions: "given that s. 96 is in the British North America Act, 1867" and "in the face of s. 96." To read a court's proper function into section 96 imposes a "needless artificiality" upon the textual rules and, therefore, is "stranger still," Laskin writes in his early essays. In contrast, Dickson J. explicitly rejects a posited legislative text as the core to a constitution in *Re Residential Tenancies*. The Dickson Court does not consider itself bound to legislated posited rules "however worthy the policy objectives." An objective Constitution simply overrides the judiciary's "freedom to choose." The Constitution binds or compels judges to decide one way over another. But the Constitution is "the Constitution as we understand it." That is, the Constitution is really Dickson J.'s image of a constitution. Section 96 analysis, not unlike 'rule of law' and 'separation of powers' judgments, collapses into a discourse about which boundaries should dominate that discourse.

The judicial and scholarly analysis of the 'separation of powers' doctrine and the Supreme Court's interpretation of section 96 of the Constitution Act, 1867 concentrate upon two such boundaries of an image of a constitution: first, the judiciary's institutional self-image or proper role; and secondly, the resource material of a constitution. 'Leading' contemporary Supreme Court judgments which discuss the 'rule of law,' however, add a third arena of conflicting boundaries. The latter context focuses upon the character of constitutional law. That is, is constitutional law made up of rules previously posited by a legislature or a court, as the early *Canadian Bill of Rights* judgments, the *Manitoba Language Rights* Court, LeDain in *Therens*, and Dicey in his classic, *The Law of the Constitution*, presuppose? Or, does constitutional law, to be law, mean that not all rules are law? Rather, to be law, must the rules comply with procedural conditions of fairness such as clarity, consistency, publicity, prospectivity, and the like as the *Sunday Times*, *Ontario Film and Video Appreciation Society*, and *Luscher* Courts assume? Or, thirdly, must constitutional law, to be law, satisfy certain standards of distributive justice which each and every citizen deserves, as Rand suggests in *Roncarelli* v. *Duplessis*? Each approach to the 'rule of law' presupposes a different boundary to the question 'what is the character of law?'

From all this we can reasonably conclude that the formality of titles such as 'C.J.' and the objectification of humans as 'the Court' really masks an inquiry into law as imagery. Whereas the former begins with an Enlightenment picture of knowledge as objective, external, rationally causal, and posited, 'law as imagery' begins with a psychosocial prism through which a person pictures the external world. Dickson, Laskin, Addy, and the others write their judgments as human beings who are seriously and consciously trying to express their innermost images in an effort to understand themselves and the world. An objective, rational world underlies only one such image. The abstract, formal words 'the Court' and the title "J." following a judge's name merely prolong the domination of an objectivist image. Such objectifying words make one think that the authors of past decisions do not really possess deeply felt thoughts or feelings about a constitution. They induce a rationalistic picture of the decision-making process. In that respect, the formal titles themselves symbolize one image of a constitution: the rationalist one. The latter serves as the subject of Chapters VIII, IX, and X. As that image itself is the subject of this essay's scrutiny, one is justified in disbanding the formal titles of legal discourse in an effort to understand a judgment as it really is: the expression of a judge's image of a constitution.

III

Images and Constitutional Procedure

The descriptivist power of the 'subject-matter approach' to constitutional law has collapsed into a search for a coherent and dominant image of a constitution – at least, for the three subjects of the 'rule of law,' 'separation of powers,' and section 96 of the British North America Act, 1867. We have discovered that any one judgment has represented a particular judge's expression of his or her image of 'what a constitution is about.' One's child rearing, formal education, peer influences, and interpersonal experiences no doubt contribute to the eventual crystallization of one's image. 'Reasons for judgment' have served as the judge's only available means for expressing his or her innermost images of the outside world. The fact that any one judge – such as a Laskin – could more or less consistently appeal to the same boundaries of an image from one doctrine to the next reinforces our suspicion in Chapter 1 that the law of a constitution is synonymous with constitutional imagery. The fact that several jurists can express the same coherent image over different 'subject-matters' (as did Laskin, Peter Hogg, and Barry Strayer, for example) demonstrates the domination of one particular image over time within legal discourse. That several jurists can share the same image may well point more to the nexus between that image and legal culture than it does to any objectivist law discovered in some text.

Now, one might respond to the above by suggesting that vague, indeterminate, and judicially created subjects such as the 'rule of law' or 'separation of powers' lend themselves to a search for the legitimizing boundaries of a constitutional image. Admittedly, a subject grounded in a code, such as section 96, might be less open to a search for a constitutional image. And yet, here too the subject-matter collapses into constitutional imagery. But, it might be thought, imagery might not be forthcoming with technical rules. With that in mind, let us venture into the procedure of constitutional litigation. For if there is one area of legal practice which has been conceived as synonymous with legal technicality and objective legal rules, it has been civil, criminal, and administrative procedure. This chapter intends to demonstrate that, indeed, two of the more important issues of constitutional procedure – standing and extrinsic evidence – also collapse into a search for constitutional images.

1. WHO MAY INITIATE CONSTITUTIONAL PROCEEDINGS?

Over the decades our courts and legislatures have elaborated two general methods by which a court may review the constitutionality of statutes, regulation, administrative proceedings, and executive orders. First, the courts must resolve any constitutional issues flowing from litigation between two parties. This method occurs in any lawsuit, civil or criminal, before any level of the judicial or administrative hierarchy. The central "procedural" issue involves the question '*who* may initiate a constitutional issue as a ground for litigation?' That is, 'who has standing?' Secondly, a government may initiate a proceeding by referring constitutional issues to a court for an advisory opinion. Let us consider several representative higher court decisions involving both methods, in an effort to show why an image of a constitution is so important in judicial decision-making.

The first modern decision on the subject-matter of 'standing' is the 1975 Supreme Court judgment of *Nova Scotia Board of Censors* v. *McNeil*.[1] McNeil, a concerned citizen, had challenged Nova Scotia's Theatres and Amusements Act. The Act had granted wide discretionary authority to the Board of Censors for the purpose of censoring films and video tapes before they were sold to theatres. McNeil requested the Cabinet to overrule the board's decision to censor *Last Tango in Paris*. But the Cabinet did not recognize him as having any standing. McNeil claimed that the Attorney-General would not respond affirmatively or negatively to his request, although the Attorney-General took the position that McNeil had no right to attack the validity of the statute. The Supreme Court of Canada, per Laskin, held that McNeil *did* have standing to challenge the constitutionality of the enactment. Why?

(a) *Laskin's Rule Rationalism*
Now, in the introduction to this essay, I suggested that an image of a constitution expresses 'what counts' or 'what is relevant' in a judge's reaction to a lawyer's challenge before him/her. We saw in Chapter II that

an image demarcates what is relevant doctrine from what is irrelevant, what counts in interpreting a section of the Constitution Act from what does not. Laskin's judgment in *McNeil* demonstrates that an image of a constitution also explains why a judge perceives one set of facts as relevant. The very notion of relevancy requires that one ask 'relevant with respect to what?' This essay claims that facts are relevant in terms of one's presupposed image of a constitution.

Laskin identifies three facts which he considers important to his decision in *McNeil*. First, he identifies "a serious, a substantial constitutional issue" in McNeil's declaratory proceeding: namely, 'was the legislation an infringement of the criminal law power of section 91 of the British North America Act, 1867 and an infringement of freedom of expression as allegedly guaranteed in Canada's implied Bill of Rights?'[2] Secondly, although the Act applied to "a manageable group of entrepreneurs in the theatre and film distribution businesses," it also "directly affected" and "strikes at" the "members of the Nova Scotia public": namely, in the public's restraint from viewing censored films.[3] Thirdly, since McNeil had already taken "all the steps that he could reasonably be required to take in order to make the question of his standing ripe for consideration," Laskin reasons, "there appears to be no other way, practically speaking, to subject the challenged Act to judicial review" than to grant him standing.[4] Why does Laskin choose these three sets of facts as the relevant ones?

The answer, I suggest, lies embedded in the way in which he envisions a constitution. The relevancy of facts particularly hangs upon Laskin's picture of the source of a constitution in a posited text. The judge's role is simply to apply the text's rules, analogously if necessary, to fact situations presented by a lawyer, and to do so neutrally, impartially, and scientifically. The posited source of a constitution bears upon the relevancy of the *McNeil* facts in two ways. First, the rule – that is, section 92(27) – in the posited text (the British North America Act, 1867) has not authorized the creation of the rules in the Theatres and Amusements Act. The parent rule has only authorized the federal parliament – not a provincial legislature – to create such a rule. Because the parent rule has not authorized the creation of the theatre rules, the theatre rules prevent McNeil from certain conduct (viewing the film) when the theatre rules themselves are not authorized in the parent rules. Secondly, McNeil claims that a court can imply a freedom of expression from the 'criminal law' rule in section 91(27) of the British North America Act, 1867. Indeed, he argues that previous Supreme Court judges in *Reference Re Alberta*

Statutes,[5] *Saumur* v. *Que.,*[6] *Switzman* v. *Ebling,*[7] and other judgments have accomplished just that. Precisely because McNeil has grounded his argument in the parent posited text, Laskin realizes that he has to take cognizance of McNeil's claim. But Laskin's presupposed image of a constitution, not the text itself, induces Laskin to recognize McNeil's claim for standing.

Appreciating the connection between Laskin's image of a constitution and why he chooses the three facts as "relevant," one must ask whether Laskin consistently expresses his image in his other 'standing' judgments. Let us turn to his dissent in *Min. of Justice of Can.* v. *Borowski*[8] where, on the surface, Laskin seems to take a more conservative result by denying standing to an interested citizen. And yet, Laskin's judgments are reconcilable in the two cases. Borowski sought a declaration that Criminal Code provisions authorizing an abortion contravened the right to life of the foetus as allegedly protected in section 1 of the Canadian Bill of Rights.[9] Laskin, dissenting, holds that Borowski did not have standing to challenge the Code. Why not? Because Laskin's image of a constitution does not allow Borowski to have standing. What elements of his image of a constitution, then, does Laskin articulate in *Borowski?*

First, Laskin emphasizes the apolitical character of constitutional law. This is not the first time we have seen Laskin insisting that the court is and ought to be apolitical.[10] Politics, for Laskin, is a matter for the legislature. This protrudes at the start and finish of his *Borowski* judgment. At the start he emphasizes that "however passionately a person may believe" that a law is wrong, "the courts are not open to such a believer ..."[11] That is, a citizen's mere distaste of the content of a statute does not serve as a justifiable ground for the courts to entertain a citizen's claim. Such distaste, Laskin insists at the end of his judgment, rests with the legislature's function. If Borowski had been granted standing, Laskin hypothesizes, "other persons with an opposite point of view might seek to intervene and would be allowed to do so, [and] the result would be to set up a battle between parties who do not have a direct interest, to wage it in a judicial arena."[12] Borowski should have challenged the legislation in the "political" arena.

This raises a second element of Laskin's image of a constitution; namely, 'what is the role of a court?' In reacting to the *Borowski* challenge, Laskin falls back upon his innermost self-image of passive deference to the "legislature." If Laskin had granted Borowski standing, Borowski (and the courts) would have pre-empted the legislature from considering the abortion claim. McNeil, in contrast, had initially gone to the legislative arena. By expressly emphasizing that point in *McNeil*, Laskin consistently upholds his belief in the judiciary's deference to the legislature.

Laskin's *Borowski* dissent expresses a third boundary of his image of a constitution. As we saw in Laskin's early writings about section 96 of the British North America Act, 1867 in Chapter II, a constitution's character derives from a text's posited rules. Given this rule character of a constitution, it is only a short step for Laskin to conclude in *Borowski* that a citizen should have standing to challenge a statute only if he/she comes within the scope of a posited statutory rule. The British North America Acts as well as Canadian statutes posited the rules. Admittedly, McNeil and other citizens are "directly affected" by freedom of expression (or its infringement). But no text posits freedom of expression. Indeed, Borowski does not come within the scope of any legislated rule, according to Laskin. Borowski is neither a pregnant woman nor a foetus. Nor does he have any "special interest" in the abortion rule "beyond the general interest that is common to all members of the relevant society."[13]

From this, one can appreciate why Laskin's positions in *McNeil* and *Borowski* are reconcilable, even though the results seem to conflict on the surface. They are reconcilable because they emanate from a person who shares a fairly coherent rule-positivist image of a constitution. In *McNeil* the Court focuses upon an alleged *constitutional* rule (freedom of expression and the criminal law power) whereas in *Borowski*, by contrast, the citizen challenges a legislative rule in the Criminal Code. The only issue, for Laskin, is whether the claimant falls within the scope of a posited legislative rule. One can find the rule in the British North America Act, 1867 as in *McNeil*, or in a Canadian statute as in *Borowski*. Laskin places the 'basic' posited constitutional document (the British North America Act, 1867) on the same level of legitimate authority and with the same weight as a statute (the Criminal Code). "Constitutionality and legality must be synonymous," he insists in his *Patriation Reference* dissent.[14] And do it is in the standing cases, in Laskin's view. In *McNeil* the challenged posited rule encompasses the scope of the citizen's conduct (the freedom to see the film). In contrast, in *Borowski* the posited rule in the Criminal Code does not and cannot extend to Borowski's conduct (because he could be neither a pregnant woman nor a foetus nor the legal representative of either).

(b) *Martland's Constitutional Supremacy*

Laskin's appeal to posited rules contrasts sharply with Martland's appeal to a higher ordered 'Constitution' in *Borowski*. Martland affirms Laskin's *dicta* in *Thorson* v. *A.G. Can.*[15] to the effect that "It is not the alleged waste of public funds alone that will support standing but rather *the right of the citizenry to constitutional behaviour* by Parliament where the issue in such behaviour is justiciable as a legal question."[16] That is, 'the Constitution' overrides posited rules. Martland explains, further, that "the constitution" encompasses more than the British North America Act, 1867 because British North America Act issues are "no different" than an action regarding the operative effect of the Canadian Bill of Rights. Both the British North America Act and the Canadian Bill of Rights are of equal weight in terms of the harm caused to a plaintiff, according to Martland and his colleagues. That is, even though the Canadian Bill of Rights merely embodies the form of a statute, the *Borowski* majority has extended the resource material constitutive of the character of a constitution. The *Borowski* majority has elevated a statute to the status of a constitutional text.

Just as important, the *Borowski* majority does not equate constitutionality with legality, as does Laskin. The majority focuses upon "the *constitutional*" right infringed (the foetus's right to liberty under the Bill) rather than the legislative rule authorizing the right's infringement (s. 251 (4)–(6) of the Criminal Code). Martland thereby appreciates that neither of the parties subject to the legislative rule (the pregnant woman and the hospital committee) had an interest in enforcing the constitutional rule. Accordingly, unless standing were granted to an "interested citizen," there would be "no reasonable way" in which the constitutional right could be brought into court. The citizen's right is a constitutional, as opposed to a legislative, right. But what gives it status and legitimacy as a constitutional right is Martland's inward image of 'what is a constitution?'

(c) *LeDain's Policy Interests*

A more recent 'standing' judgment expresses a further departure from Laskin's rule rationalist image of law. In *Finlay* v. *Canada (Min. of Finance)*, Finlay claims standing to seek a declaration that a provincial assistance scheme has not complied with the conditions established in the Canada assistance plan pursuant to which the federal government shares in the assistance costs.[17] Although Finlay does not possess a sufficiently direct personal interest in the legality of the federal shared-cost payments to warrant standing without the consent of the attorney-general, LeDain explains that Finlay could be granted "public interest standing." That is, LeDain grants Finlay standing to bring a non-constitutional challenge to administrative action. In the process of so holding, LeDain unmasks the content of Laskin's apparent rules in *Thorson*, *McNeil*, and *Borowski* in an effort to expose "the policy considerations underlying judicial attitudes to public interest standing."[18] Behind the Laskin rule requiring "a serious, a substantial constitutional issue,"[19] for example, there lies "the judicial concern about the allocation of scarce resources and the need to screen out the mere busybody."[20] According to LeDain, the latter "policy" matters also underlie Laskin's second rule that a citizen have a genuine interest in the issue.[21] In addition, this rule requiring justiciability responds to the judicial concern about "the proper role of the courts" vis-à-vis other branches of government.[22] LeDain explains how that is so. And behind Laskin's third rule requiring that there be no other reasonable and effective manner in which to seek a remedy,[23] LeDain explains, there lies the judicial concern of receiving full information from those most directly affected.[24] Once LeDain has identified the social policies lying behind the posited standing rules, he finds that he could consistently extend "public interest" standing to a non-constitutional challenge to administrative action. What bears notice in LeDain's excursus is how his picture of what constitutes 'law' differs from Laskin's in the subject-matter of 'standing.' Whereas both judges express deep concern about the proper role of a judge vis-à-vis political actors, Laskin's boundary of 'law' begins and ends with posited rules, whereas LeDain's boundary goes to the social interests underlying the rules. This contrast marks the beginning of what I shall identify in Chapters VIII and IX as two versions of a rationalist image of a constitution.

(d) References

Now, the *McNeil* and *Borowski* courts granted standing to the litigants in particular disputes. But federal and provincial governments may intervene in such ordinary litigation whenever a constitutional issues is raised. Governments may also raise constitutional issues by another procedure, however: they may direct a court to advise them as to the constitutionality of a proposed or existing enactment. At first sight, one might react that such a procedure involves a gross interference with the 'separation of powers.' But we have already seen that whether one is of the opinion that a 'separation of powers' doctrine even exists in Canada hangs upon one's deeper image of a constitution. So too, the boundaries of one's image of a constitution presuppose the judiciary's response to the issue concerning whether the executive arm of government may constitutionally direct the courts to address constitutional issues. In the 1912 *Validity of References Case* the Judicial Committee hold that the executive can legitimately refer matters without violating the Constitution.[25] Once again, however, both counsel and court frame the issue and their respective responses in terms of their own respective images of a constitution. The issue of 'the validity' of a constitutional reference triggers within their consciousness the deeper question already noted with respect to a section 96 claim: namely, 'what is the proper role of a judge?' More accurately, 'what is one's own self-image as a judge?'

In 1875 the Canadian Parliament had authorized the executive to request a Supreme Court opinion directly upon any matter. Parliament had passed more detailed, yet narrower, enactments in 1891 and 1906. The Supreme Court had repeatedly rendered opinions at the government's request in accordance with these statutes. In six instances the Judicial Committee had entertained appeals from the reference opinions of the Supreme Court. Similarly, nearly all the provincial legislatures had passed similar legislation authorizing references to their own courts. In the *Validity of Reference Case* the lawyer for the provinces argues that Parliament could not validly authorize the federal government to require the Supreme Court of answer it.

The lawyer for the provinces frames his arguments in a manner which expresses an image of a constitution very similar to Laskin's. The lawyer, in particular, identifies his expectations of the role which a judge should play in society. He argues that reference legislation seriously violates that role. The federal reference legislation is so wide "as to admit of a gross interference with the judicial character of that [c]ourt."[26] Why? Because within his image, impartiality characterizes the judiciary. Once a judge has pronounced upon an issue in a reference case, "it is not in human nature to expect that, if the same matter is again raised upon a concrete case by an individual litigant before the same [c]ourt, its members can divest themselves of their pre-conceived opinions." The court "will in fact, however unintentionally, be biased."[27] This would result in "actual injustice" as well as "a distrust of their freedom from prepossession." To require the courts to answer questions is "incompatible with the maintenance of such judicial character [as impartiality] ..."[28] From whence does counsel find this important doctrine of impartiality? Does he appeal to the posited text, the British North America Act? Does he go to the framers' intent and imply 'impartiality' from their expressed intent? No. Counsel derives the impartiality requirement from the very existence of a court. Once Parliament has established a Supreme Court of Appeal pursuant to section 101 of the British North America Act, 1867, "that carries with it an implied condition that the Court of Appeal shall be in truth a judicial body *according to the conception of judicial character* obtaining *in civilized countries* and especially obtaining in Great Britain, to whose Constitution the Constitution of Canada is intended to be similar, as recited in the British North America Act, 1867 ."[29]

The Privy Council responds to the lawyer's argument in terms of the Privy Council's own institutional self-image vis-à-vis the legislative arm of government. First, counsel's fear of bias serves as "a commentary upon the wisdom" of the reference process.[30] But, "[w]ith that this Board is in no sense concerned. A court of law has nothing to do with a Canadian Act of Parliament, lawfully passed, except to give it effect according to its tenor," the Privy Council continues. The executive arm of government – not the judiciary – can entertain issues which go to the efficacy or abuse of the reference process. Indeed, judges *must* assume that Parliament would duly weigh the risk of judicial bias before Parliament had enacted the reference legislation. Whereas British and other courts have held transactions of individuals void as contrary to public policy, "no such doctrine can apply to an Act of Parliament." A court can only legitimately question whether reference legislation has been enacted "outside the authority of the Canadian Parliament." And this is "purely a question of the constitutional law of Canada." In other words, constitutional law does not involve "the wisdom or expediency or policy of an Act."[31]

The Privy Council suggests a second reason why its self-image prevents it from rendering all reference legislation invalid. Although counsel had argued that *no* Legislature or Parliament had the constitutional authority to request any opinion outside of litigation,[32] the Privy Council surmises that this question would "never" have been raised except for the nature of the particular questions which the federal government had put to the court.[33] Further, the Privy Council equates the claim that all references are *ultra vires* with the claim that the executive has "rightly or wrongly" used the reference power. They "must be the same," the Privy Council asserts. But the Privy Council then restates counsel's argument: "it is *intra vires* to put some kinds of question, but *ultra vires* to put other kinds of question." But that requires that a court draw lines as to what is "judicious or wise" to ask and what is not. And that line-drawing, in turn, "can in no sense rest upon considerations of law."[34] The point in noting these passages is not to underline how the Privy Council restates counsel's argument in a manner very different from counsel's explicit claim (the Privy Council believed that it had restated the "substance" of counsel's argument), but to emphasize how the Privy Council uses that restatement to show how the restated claim would contradict the Privy Council's image of the function of a court vis-à-vis the legislature. For, having speculated about the necessity for "line-drawing" between good and bad reference questions, the Privy Council goes on to conclude that this line-drawing would invite courts to depart "from their legitimate province." "They would really be pronouncing upon the policy of the Canadian Parliament," the Privy Council concludes, "which is exclusively the business of the Canadian people, and is no concern of this Board."[35]

If the Privy Council recognizes what constitutional law is not (that it is not a matter of wisdom, expediency, policy, or line-drawing), does the Privy Council inform us as to what constitutes constitutional law? Providing the strains for Laskin's partially expressed image described above, the Privy Council claims that the Constitution is grounded in "a written organic instrument"; namely, the British North America Act.[36] The rules posited in this instrument constitute the whole of the Constitution. When the text posits "explicit" rules, the text is "conclusive." With ambiguous rules, the lawyer resorts to "the context and scheme" of the instrument. And when the organic instrument is silent, then the legislature must enact its own rules. The latter possesses constitutional authority. Why? Because the Privy Council assumes that posited rules encompassed the whole of the Constitution. Rules are encyclopaedic, all-encompassing, total in the sense that no human conduct is immune from their potential grasp. One may complete a constitution merely by adding more rules. In the words of the Privy Council, "whatever belongs to self-government in Canada belongs either to the Dominion or to the provinces within the limits of *The British North America Act*."[37] One simply cannot escape from the tentacles of rules. Posited rules constitute the starting-point of all legal analysis. The context of the rules, whatever their content, constitutes the ends of the Constitution. As the Privy Council remarks in the *Validity of Reference Case*, "[i]t certainly would not be sufficient to say that the exercise of a power might be oppressive."[38] The Privy Council continues, "[i]ndeed it [oppressiveness] might ensue from the breach of almost any power [rule]." Thus, a court could not evaluate the ethical content of a rule or the oppressive application of a rule. Indeed, the very fact that oppressiveness might result from "almost any power" (that is, rule) does not distract from the rightness of the rules themselves. An image of a constitution as posited rules lies at the heart of the *Validity of Reference Case*.

2. EVIDENCE IN CONSTITUTIONAL PROCEEDINGS

There remains a second important issue in the subject-matter of 'constitutional procedure.' What sorts of evidence may a judge admit to aid in the resolution of a constitutional issue? And what weight should s/he give to such evidence? For example, may a judge admit evidence documenting the expressed intent of the minister, a parliamentary committee, a draftsperson, royal commission, or task force, when the latter first recommends and/or drafts a text? May the judge admit evidence to demonstrate whether the original framers specifically intend a section to cover the circumstances before the judge? May the judge admit evidence to show the political values of the framers with a view to speculating and analogizing whether the values would support one interpretation over another in unforeseen contemporary circumstances? Finally, may the court admit social or economic evidence showing the empirical consequences of interpreting a section one way over another, or of rendering a statute invalid in contemporary circumstances? Even if any or all of these questions can be answered affirmatively, what weight should a court give to the evidence?

Once again, the surface issues of the admissibility and weight of evidence have served merely as an opportunity for judges to express their inward images of a constitution. Rather than representing objective *ratios*, 'reasons for judgment' have really expressed a judge's image of a constitution. And legal controversy has really centred upon which competing image of a constitution should prevail in legal discourse. From out study of various 'subject-matters' so far, we can now observe the bare outlines of three such images: the first looks to posited legislatively created rules which judges are supposed to apply impartially; the second possesses a more realistic or functionalist picture of the role of judges; and the third appeals to institutional history. Evidentiary issues have afforded an opportunity for the judiciary to work out some of the details of these three images of a constitution.

(a) *Laskin's Rule Rationalism*

We have already detected fairly consistent themes in Laskin's commentaries about the 'separation of powers,' section 96, and standing. He claims that there is no 'separation of powers' in the Canadian Constitution. His early writings concerning section 96 explain that the rules in the British North America Act, 1867 constitute the character of a constitution. From that claim, he explains that jurists should not journey into their innermost beliefs about a judge's proper function. Posited rules alone inform the judge as to who may challenge the validity of a statute.

One cannot help but note, at this point, how rationalistic is Laskin's image of a constitution. The content of a constitution can be found in a text which the judge can touch and see. The document lives 'out there' in an objective observable world, separate and independent of the judge, a world into itself. Given the wall between the text and the judge as a person, the judge's duty is to apply the rules in the text. He should do so passively, always subservient to the author of the rules: the legislature. Only when the text is silent or ambiguous can the judge be 'creative' and then only in a manner which, through analogical reasoning, has accepted the prior posited rules as a 'given.' Through this rational process, the judge can make the rules more consistent, cohesive, ordered, and legitimate.

Higher court judges articulate the above image of a constitution in response to claims to admit extrinsic evidence – extrinsic to the words of the given posited text itself. Indeed, one is incorrect to suggest that judges deliberately choose to express their presupposed image. Rather, they feel *compelled* to join evidentiary issues to their deeper image of a constitution because they realize that the image – not some pre-existing rule – determines the 'validity' of any decision to exclude extrinsic evidence.[39] The image legitimizes any ultimate outcome. To demonstrate the importance of a constitutional image in resolving evidentiary issues, let us examine one of Laskin's judgments and his teaching materials with a view to understanding why he believes that extrinsic evidence, if admitted, should be given little weight.

In *Re Anti-Inflation Act*[40] Laskin acknowledges the real difficulty of finding or even establishing a precise rule which could govern future cases. First, Laskin stresses that "no general principle of admissibility or inadmissibility can or ought to be propounded by this Court" because its admissibility and, if relevant, its weight depend upon "the ambit of the legislative power" of any particular statute.[41] That is, the scope of the term of a legislative rule determines the admissibility of evidence. Because a rule may have different purposes, so too admissibility varies. Sometimes, as with tax regulations, the issue is the *purpose* or *meaning* of the legislation, he explains. Sometimes, evidence as to the *effect* of the legislation shines light upon its purpose or meaning. At other times it does not do so. On still other occasions, as here, a court considers whether social and economic circumstances external to the enactment justify the federal use of the emergency power. Accordingly, "the questions of resort to extrinsic evidence and what kind of extrinsic evidence may be admitted must depend on the constitutional issues on which it is sought to adduce such evidence."[42]

But how does a lawyer know what is a "constitutional issue" and what is not? Surely the rule at issue cannot state that there is a constitutional issue emanating from the rule itself. A constitutional issue must be triggered from something external to the rule. Earlier sections of this essay have suggested that what consitutes a "constitutional issue" in traditional subject-matters of constitutional law emanates from within one's image of a constitution. What is considered an issue within one image is excluded in another. This has been so for doctrinal issues such as the 'rule of law,' the 'separation of powers,' and the section 96 problem, as it has been for issues of procedure. We have also seen that Laskin articulated a particular image of a constitution as a compendium of posited rules. His image infiltrates all elements of his judgments and scholarship concerning these subjects. The admissibility and weight of extrinsic evidence is no exception.

Laskin, as author, admits the crucial role of his image of a constitution when he elaborates the doctrine of extrinsic evidence in his *Canadian Constitutional Law*. In a note entitled "Extrinsic Aids in Determining Meaning of B.N.A. Act" Laskin assures us that "[c]onstitutional cases are unique illustrations of the need for some rationalisation of the use and admissibility of extrinsic aids in interpretation."[43] In his note and accompanying precedents, Laskin offers the reader an explanation for this need. Laskin explains that evidence in constitutional cases goes to the interpretation of textual rules, unlike civil or criminal cases where evidence goes to disputed issues of fact. There are only two types of textual rules: statutory rules (involving "the object or purpose, the 'constitutional value,' or the pith and substance of the impugned statute") and the parent rules posited in the British North America Act. The latter, he suggests, collapse into or, in his words, "inevitably involve" the first. Only by incorporating "contemporary references on a Canadian level" in the form of indigenous statutory rules: only then can the Constitution adapt to changing Canadian social conditions. Laskin then reprints *dicta* from three "illustrative cases." In the first, James asserts that "[w]e shall not be influenced by anything then said" when counsel refers, during argument, to the speech of the Earl of Carnarvon, who had introduced the British North America Bill into the British Parliament.[44] In the second, the Privy Council determines that the London Resolutions which had preceded the British North America Act, 1867, were inadmissible, let alone of little evidentiary weight.[45] But, in the third, a dissenting judge in the Supreme Court holds the converse: the courts are "not only entitled but bound to apply that well established rule which requires us ... to have recourse to external aids derived from the surrounding circumstances and the history of the subject-matter dealt with, and to construe the enactment by the light derived from such sources, and so to put ourselves as far as possible in the position of the legislature whose language we have to expound."[46] On the surface, the first two *dicta* obviously contradict the third in terms of admitting extrinsic aids.

But there are two common premises. First, as with other subjects, Laskin begins his analysis with a posited rule in a text. For each judgment, as for Laskin generally, posited rules constitute the starting-point of all constitutional analysis. They differ only as to whether the starting-point should be a Canadian rule or a British rule and, if the latter, whether their meaning should be gleaned from the rules themselves or from the historical context surrounding their origins. Secondly, Laskin, in addition to the scholars and judges he cites, assumes that the process of interpreting a rule places the rule external to the interpreter. That is, one finds the meaning of a rule in an external world, external to the interpreter's expectations, values, and premises. Laskin and his cited commentators project an objectivist character to law. The scope or reach of any particular posited rule itself determines the admissibility and weight of evidence, not the interpreter's image of a constitution, or the interpreter's more general image of the external world. If a rule's scope reaches certain human or institutional conduct, then Laskin advises admission of the evidence. If the rule does not reach that conduct to which the evidence relates, then the court should exclude the evidence.

Laskin explicitly expresses both common themes in "A Note on Constitutional Facts" a few pages later when he writes that "[t]he scope of a legislative power, its breadth or narrowness as the case may be, has a decided bearing on the kind of material (whether called facts or extrinsic evidence or simply extrinsic aids) that may be relevant to support a statute addressed to that power."[47] That is, a legislated rule serves as his starting-point of analysis. Meaning inheres from the rule, not extrinsic context. Furthermore, there remains a problem of "constitutional construction" which "although realted to, stands above the use of extrinsic materials in connection with impugned statutes." That problem concerns whether the courts should rely upon "anything more than precedent and logic" in constitutional construction. According to Laskin, the scope and content of the British North America Act rules themselves determine the outcome of that question.[48] Because the scope of the POGG, 91(2) and 92(13) rules is so "apparently wide," so "broad or ample," the lawyer had better steer cautiously within "precedent and logic."

(b) *Dickson's Values and Evidence*

Now, we have already seen in other contexts that although many jurists share Laskin's rule rationalism, this is not always so. Dockson's majority judgment in *Re Residential Tenancies Act, 1979*,[49] which we have already discussed in the context of 'separation of powers' and section 96, counters with a more realistic assessment of the judicial function.[50] Dickson openly challenges the sole use of precedent and logic in constitutional construction. More than that, Dickson's challenge to rule rationalism speaks to a very different image of a constitution which guides him in identifying the sorts of evidence a court should consider. Dickson approves of Lederman's opinion that constitutional analysis "joins logic with social fact, value decisions and the authority of precedents."[51] A court needs relevant facts from which to "draw logical inferences, determine *social impact*, make *value decisions* and select governing precedents." Quoting again from the Lederman teaching materials, Dickson emphasizes that a constitutional challenge "raises a need for evidence of facts of *social context* and legislative *effect.*"

This wider resource material, in turn, triggers a series of questions which go to the heart of Dickson's image of a constitution. Where does a judge obtain evidence of 'social impact' and 'value decisions'? And what criterion makes one 'value decision' more legitimate than another? Where does one find these values? Why are they a part of constitutional law? Dickson asserts several paragraphs after his Lederman quotation that "[m]aterial relevant to the issues before the court, and not inherently unreliable or offending against public policy should be admissible ..."[52] But what is 'public policy' or 'a value decision'? Where are judges and lawyers to find them? And what standard or justificatory argument will differentiate the legitimacy of one 'public policy' over another? One cannot respond to these questions within a world of posited, objective rules. Rather, one must seek out a wider frame of reference. Dickson finally begins to elaborate such a framework in his Charter judgments.[53]

(c) *McIntyre's Rationalism and Evidence*

Indeed, a response to the above questions in terms of fixed posited rules takes on an aura of irrationality once one realizes that the competent lawyer must identify competing images of a constitution to serve as reference points. In *Churchill Falls (Labrador Corp.)* v. *A.G. Nfld.*,[54] for example, the Supreme Court shares Laskin's rule rationalist image of a constitution, on the one hand, and yet faces issues which that image simply cannot entertain, on the other. McIntyre begins his judgment by repeating Laskin's rule that "no inflexible rule governing the admission of extrinsic evidence in constitutional references should be formulated."[55] After interspacing his "rule" with one-sentence quotations from Dickson and Laskin, the Supreme Court assures us that a court may receive and consider extrinsic evidence "in a proper case." But if no rule exists, one must ask, what is "a proper case"? When faced with this quandary, McIntyre himself presents us with four rules:

first, "extrinsic evidence is admissible to show the background against which the legislation was enacted";
second, it "is not receivable as an aid to construction";
third, it may be considered to ascertain the "operation and effect of the impugned legislation";
and fourth, it may be considered to ascertain its "true object and purpose."[56]

It is a mystery how the assessment of the operation, effect, true object, and purpose of an enactment could differ from the construction of a statute. And yet, McIntyre insists in his second rule that evidence is inadmissible to construe a statute. Conversely, his third and fourth rules authorize the admissibility of evidence for the construction of a statute. Perhaps to assure us that his rules (derived from the non-rule or non-existence of a rule) are rational, McIntyre on behalf of the Court appeals to a pre-existing rule posited by Dickson in *Re Residential Tenancies*. Ironically, contrary to McIntyre's first rule, Dickson asserts in this further rule that "speeches made in the Legislature at the time of enactment of the measure are inadmissible as having little evidential weight."[57]

And this is not the end of the matter. If one views the world rationalistically, much as does Laskin, one must appeal to a rule (or, we shall see in Chapter IX, a policy) as a 'given' in order to validate one's analysis. This is so even when one wishes to incorporate ideal-directed matters from a noumenal world. Whether or not this indirect assimilation of 'ought' claims in the form of a rule undermines the apolitical character of one's analysis, McIntyre clearly incorporates rule oriented 'ought' claims. And yet, he considers the rules as constituting the phenomenal 'is' world. Specifically, McIntyre initially asserts a rule which incorporates political morality: "only evidence which is not inherently unreliable *or offending against public policy* should be admissible."[58] But that rule he derives from Dickson's pre-existing "living tree" rule in *Re Residential Tenancies*. And Dickson, in turn, derives that rule from Lord Sankey's prior, given rule in *Edwards and Others* v. *Attorney General for Canada and Others* (1930).[59] And on it goes.

Having now six clear rules before him, McIntyre proceeds to apply the rules impartially and neutrally to the *Churchill Falls* facts. He believes speeches and public declarations of prominent figures inadmissible because they violate the fifth rule (that is, such speeches "cannot be said to be expressions of the intent of the Legislative Assembly").[60] Although such persons are probably closer to the final product, McIntyre feels compelled to fall back upon the first rule which, in contrast, admits "the background of the negotiations." In addition, he holds a government pamphlet admissible because it comes within the sixth rule: that is, "the categorization of materials which are 'not inherently unreliable or offending against public policy'."[61]

All in all, McIntyre expresses his inward image of a constitution very rationalistically. But does his rationalism produce internal consistency? Does his rationalism even allow lawyers (or citizens for that matter) to predict with any accuracy how McIntyre himself, let alone any other judge, would react to extrinsic evidence in a future case? Although no rule is said to exist, a rationalistically inclined lawyer/judge feels compelled to find a rule. Having done so, s/he then feels "bound." In his or her self-image, a judge/lawyer should apply the rule impartially. But a rationalist self-image deceives the judge/lawyer. On the one hand, the rationalist image excludes the issue 'what is a constitution?' as an irrelevant and illegitimate issue. It is a political, not a legal, question. On the other hand, we now understand that one's image of a constitution informs one as to what evidence to admit. McIntyre's image of a constitution induces him to equate law with posited rules, to understand the rules to be external to his self, and to imagine his institutional self in terms of the neutral administration of given rules – 'public policy' or political values being outside the world of law. *Churchill Falls* concerns the admissibility of extrinsic evidence only on the surface. The evidentiary claim triggers within McIntyre's self the desire to express his innermost image of a constitution, this being a rule rationalist one. His image, not some posited rules, provides him with his answer as to whether extrinsic evidence is admissible. But his image shapes his response to the surface issue in a manner which renders his responses incoherent.

3. SUMMARY

Two critical questions rise to the fore when a citizen wishes to challenge the constitutional conduct of a government: first, may s/he initiate a constitutional challenge; and secondly, what evidence may s/he introduce into court in order to shed light onto the meaning of a text described as 'the Constitution'? Texts in most jurisdictions in the common law world usually offer a compendium of intricate rules to aid the citizen. The texts usually admit that the rules are slowly widening and that, upon close inspection, the rules oscillate. The explanation for this oscillation, we have seen, lies neither in the content of the rules nor in their application. Rather, the explanation lies embedded within the inward images of a constitution and the crucial role of those images in day-to-day decision-making. We have seen, for example, that Laskin has pictured a constitution through the prism of a rule rationalist. We shall see in Chapter ix that this image departs from the policy rationalism of Laskin's early scholarship. Suffice it to note at this point that Laskin, as a judge, grounds his constitution in posited rules. This rule rationalist image explains his apparent divergent attitudes toward standing in *McNeil* and *Borowski*. And it contrasts with LeDain's exposition of the social policies underlying the posited rules in *Finlay*. The reference cases demonstrate how judges of an earlier era from another society shared Laskin's rationalism. His textual writings about evidence show how one's image of a constitution can be formed many, many years before one ever ventures onto the bench. And McIntyre's judgment in *Churchill Falls* reflects the hold which rationalism has had upon the consciousness of the legal community to the present day.

We have also seen counter images of a constitution in judgments about constitutional procedure. In *Borowski*, Martland does not find himself entrapped in some hierarchy of posited texts. Rather, the legislated rules are subject to a higher "Constitution," although legislated rules can sometimes be elevated to constitutional status as occurred with the Canadian Bill of Rights. Predicting his later *Constitutional Amendment Reference* judgment, Martland distinguishes between constitutionality and legality in an effort to resolve whether Borowski has standing.[62] Whether Dickson shares Martland's image of a constitution as expressed in *Borowski*, one cannot say on the basis of his one judgment in *Re Residential Tenancies Act, 1979*. But we can state with assurance that Dickson begins *Re Residential Tenancies Act, 1979* with an image of a constitution very different from Laskin's. Dickson understands constitutional judgments to be "value decisions" whereas for Laskin, the judge, values constitute an illegitimate source of law. Dickson incorporates values and public policy as constituent elements of his image whereas Laskin, as a judge, relies entirely upon posited rules for his image of a constitution. The constitutional amendment judgments, we shall now see, provide the classic opportunity for our judges to articulate the boundaries of the full competing images of a constitution embedded within the consciousness of the Canadian legal community.

IV

Constitutional Amendment

Chapters II and III of this essay reinterpreted representative doctrines and judgments usually discussed in Canadian constitutional discourse. The second chapter showed that the 'rule of law,' 'separation of powers,' and 'section 96' judgments were not really determinate subject-matters *per se*. Rather, what judges have hitherto taken as carefully delineated subject-matters collapses into a deeper exposition of 'what is a constitution?' The third chapter reread representative Supreme Court judgments concerning the subject-matter of constitutional procedure. Notwithstanding the apparently straightforward, ostensibly rules oriented character of procedure issues, I have demonstrated how the macro-issue of 'what is a constitution?' permeates each judgment. Whether the surface issue be a matter of substantive law or procedural law, it triggers a deep search on the part of each judge as to how s/he envisions the boundaries of a constitution. The boundaries of that image delimit a judge's response to the surface issue. Indeed, what constitutes a relevant issue or a relevant fact hangs upon the image. The law of a constitution, on close inspection, collapses into a judge's image of a constitution.

The images of a constitution embedded in both substantive and procedural constitutional law come to a head during the early 1980s in a series of judgments concerning constitutional amendment. Lawyers frame the surface issues in each judgment in terms of the "legitimate," "proper," "legal," or "constitutional" manner and form requirements for an amendment to "the Constitution." Once again, though, we see that the surface issues quickly disintegrate into the deeper macro-issue of 'what is a constitution?' The first judgment, characterized as the *Upper House Reference*, examines the extent to which parliament could amend the senate.[1] The remaining two sets of judgments, cited as the *Patriation*

Reference[2] and the *Quebec Veto Reference*,[3] consider first, the "appropriate" amending procedure required for the repatriation of the Canadian Constitution from the United Kingdom; and, secondly, the inclusion of a charter of rights in a written constitution. This chapter aims to show that the three sets of judgments are preoccupied with the issue 'what is a constitution?' In facing that first question, Supreme Court judges draw out from within their legal consciousness their responses to four elements of a constitutional image: the resource material of a constitution, the role of courts, the source of constitutional obligation, and the (a)political character of constitutional law. Their responses to the latter four issues complete our intent, begun in Chapter II, of demonstrating that the law of a constitution really collapses into the expression of a jurist's deep-felt image of 'what a constitution is all about.'

1. BACKGROUND

In the *Upper House Reference* the Supreme Court asks itself, first, whether a parliament may amend the British North America Act, 1867 by omitting any reference to the senate; and, secondly, whether a parliament may alter or replace the senate in order to change, among other things, the numbers and proportions of senators representing a province or territory, to provide for the direct election of senators, and to bypass approval of laws by the senate. The Court in a *per curiam* judgment holds in the negative.

The Supreme Court has unanimously expressed its opinion in the *Upper House Reference*. There, the Court expresses a historicist image of a constitution which Martland and Ritchie share, with some inconsistency, with their position in the *Patriation Reference* one year later. But Laskin departs from the historicist image in the latter case. That he does so is quite understandable in the light of the rationalist underpinnings of his 'separation of powers' and 'section 96' writings, teaching materials, and judgments discussed above in Chapter II. The clash between an historicist and rationalist image of a constitution presents an opportunity to look closely at the boundaries of the conflicting images.

The *Patriation Reference* poses three surface issues. First, does the proposed patriation of the Constitution from the United Kingdom affect federal-provincial relationships or the powers, rights, or privileges granted to the provinces? Secondly, is it a constitutional convention that, in such a situation, a federal parliament should first obtain "the agreement of the provinces" before it lays the proposed amendment before the United Kingdom Parliament? Thirdly, is the agreement of the provinces of Canada "constitutionally required" for such a constitutional amendment? The Court unanimously responds affirmatively to the first issue. As to the third question, a majority of seven (Laskin, Estey, McIntyre, Dickson, Beetz, Chouinard, and Lamer) holds that the agreement of the provinces is not constitutionally required "as a matter of law." Martland and Ritchie, dissenting,[4] hold that such agreement is constitutionally required. As to the second question, a majority of six (Martland, Ritchie, Dickson, Beetz, Chouinard, and Lamer) finds that a constitutional convention requiring provincial consent for the proposed amendment does exist and is required "as a matter of constitutional convention." Laskin, Estey, and McIntyre dissent on the latter point.[5] Since the principal author of each opinion is not identified, the judgments will be described as the Majority of Seven and the Minority of Two, the Majority of Six and the Minority of Three respectively.[6]

Following the *Patriation Reference* the Federal Government held a constitutional conference with the ten provinces. Nine of the ten provinces agreed to the patriation of the Constitution together with a charter of rights and an amending formula. Quebec, dissenting, referred the matter to the courts, questioning whether the consent of the Province of Quebec is constitutionally required, by convention. In particular, Quebec argues that convention requires unanimous consent, or alternatively, convention allows Quebec to have a veto power. The Supreme Court responds negatively and unanimously to both questions.[7] In so doing, however, the Court refines the historicist Martland/Ritchie position as to the nature of constitutional obligation.

This chapter intends to show that the various judgments in the three cases are important attempts, on the part of distinguished spokespersons for the legal community, to express their respective images of a constitution. These images have rarely been confronted so openly in the evolution of Canadian constitutional law. This is not a novel claim. William Lederman, probably the foremost living constitutional law scholar in Canada, argues that the judges in each of the four *Patriation Reference Judgments* are responding to "three primary constitutional questions." These questions go to the boundaries of what I have called an image of a constitution, although Lederman would refrain from any suggestion that constitutional law concerns inward images rather than rules and values.[8] He identified the key questions as 'what is the nature of law, convention, their relationship, and their sources?'; and 'what is the proper function of the traditional courts, especially of the Supreme Court

of Canada, as the final guardians of compliance with the Constitution?'
His colleague, Noel Lyon, suggests that it is in the construction "from first
principles [of] a sound theoretical model within which to locate difficult
legal questions for analysis and decision" that one can best understand the
divergent opinions in the *Patriation Reference*.[9] And the late Robert Samek
suggests that "[u]nfortunately, the real significance of the Supreme Court
decision has been misunderstood by interpreting and debating it in
precisely those legalistic terms which had been rejected by the majority.
To understand it correctly, we must go one step further than the majority
was able to do as a court of law."[10] That "one step further," this essay
suggests, is to identify the competing images of a constitution which the
judges presuppose. Unlike Lederman and Lyon, however, the images are
not metaphysical constructs, models or theories. Nor are the images
'values,' to use their term —whether the values be personal to the judge (as
in Lederman's image) or embedded in the community (as in Lyon's
image).[11] Rather, the images emanate from within the conscious and
subconscious self of the individual judges. Formed over a lifetime of
formal and informal education, experience, and childhood rearing, these
images serve as a prism through which the lawyer/judge understands the
world. The images or prisms are called into question in the constitutional
amendment references. The judiciary feel compelled to react to immi-
nent challenges to their lifelong images of a constitution (and of the
world) and to react in a manner which would express and defend those
images.[12]

We shall see that Laskin, Estey, and McIntyre identify constitutional law
with rules in both the Majority of Seven and in their dissenting judgment
of the *Patriation Reference*. The unanimous *Upper House* Court as well as
the Martland/Ritchie dissent in the *Patriation Reference* concentrate upon
institutional history. Unfortunately, Martland and Ritchie share a contradictory image of a constitution in the Majority of Six. Or so this essay aims
to show. Whereas one of Canada's most eminent scholars is convinced that
"the absence of a complete theoretical model of the Canadian Constitution" explains the difference between majority and dissenters in the
Patriation Reference,[13] I wish to show that both the Laskin group (Laskin,
Estey, and McIntyre) on the one hand and the Martland group (Martland
and Ritchie) on the other actually do possess respective "theoretical
models" of a constitution. Further, they express the "models" through
their images in their respective judgments. The Laskin group shares what
we can describe as an "imperative," rule rationalistic image whereas the
Martland group shares an historicist image. The *Quebec Veto* Court refines

the latter image. The two images oppose each other in every fundamental: the resource material of constitutional law, the institutional self-image of a court, the source of constitutional obligation, and the (a)political character of constitutional law. The clash of the two images, rather than their absence, explains the various judgments.

2. AN INTRODUCTION TO HISTORICISM:
THE UPPER HOUSE COURT

The first reference in the trilogy of constitutional amendment cases examines whether the Federal Parliament can alter, replace, or omit any reference to the Senate pursuant to an amendment to the British North America Act, 1867. The Court initially looks to section 91(1.1) of the British North America Act, 1949 which allowed for Parliament's exclusive jurisdiction to amend "the Constitution of Canada, except [amongst other things] as regards matters coming within the classes of subjects by this Act assigned exclusively to the Legislatures of the provinces." The proposed federal legislation does not directly affect federal-provincial relationships "in the sense of changing federal and provincial legislative powers," according to the Court. But the Act does "envision the elimination" of the Senate and this "would alter the structure of the federal Parliament."[14] But why is this offensive to the constitution in the Supreme Court's eyes? Because the judges, in this case, share an historicist image of a constitution. That is, must as did O'Halloran and Addy in the 'separation of powers' judgments discussed above, the Supreme Court assumes that history advises lawyers as to which arguments are "valid" and which are "invalid."

How does the Court apply its historicist image of a constitution in the case before it? First, it holds that in the light of the framers' parliamentary statements in 1867, "[a] primary purpose of the creation of the Senate" is "to afford protection to the various sectional interests in Canada in relation to the enactment of federal legislation."[15] Interestingly, the Court does not proceed to ask whether that purpose survives today. Nor can it do so without violating the coherency of its own historicist image of a constitution. For it is the past − not the present − which validates any proposed legislative action.

Secondly, the Court presupposes an historicist image of a constitution in response to whether Parliament can provide for the direct election of senators. The Court grounds its negative answer in this way: "[t]he substitution of a system of election for a system of appointment would involve *a radical change* in the nature of one of the component parts of Parliament."[16] The framers intend "to make the Senate a thoroughly independent body which could canvass dispassionately the measures of the House of Commons."[17] Tenure for life, according to the Court, accomplishes this. But why would a system of election involve a "radical change"? One can appreciate why the election of senators would constitute a 'radical change' once one assumes an historicist image of a constitution. Given the originally understood purpose of the senate, the proposed change is radical. Given its existing purpose (as a forum for patronage), the change might not be. But these judges could not consider existing circumstances. Their shared historicist image of a constitution would react strongly against any attempt to analyse the contemporary – as opposed to the past – role of the Senate.

3. LASKIN'S RULE RATIONALIST IMAGE OF A CONSTITUTION

The *Upper House Reference* constitutes a unanimous judgment of the Supreme Court. An historicist image of a constitution is openly shared, with some inconsistency, by the Minority of Two and Majority of Six in the *Patriation Reference* one year later.[18] But we have seen from representative cases in such 'subject-matters' as the 'separation of powers,' 'section 96,' 'standing,' 'references,' and 'extrinsic evidence' that Laskin does not share such an historicist image. Laskin understands the British North America Act, 1867 as encompassing clearly defined rules. He pictures his own function and that of all judges in terms of discovering the meaning of the words in the rules from an analysis of the words themselves. The judge's proper function is to do so objectively without speculative excursions into one's own preferences, as had happened with respect to section 96. Finally, Laskin defers to the scope of the rule in identifying who should have standing and what evidence to admit. Martland and Ritchie finally and openly confront Laskin's image of a constitution in the *Patriation Reference*. Accordingly, Laskin finds it necessary to defend and to refine his image with a rigour which even he had not yet experienced as a scholar or judge.

(a) *The Resource Material of a Constitution*
Laskin explicitly rejects any historicist image of a constitution such as the Court unanimously expressed only a year earlier in the *Upper House Reference*. The surface issues, as noted above, concern the questions, first, whether the convention of provincial consent to an amendment is

"constitutionally required" as a matter of law and, secondly, whether there exists any such convention in the first place. Laskin's Majority of Seven responds in the negative with respect to the 'question of law' issue and his Minority of Three responds in the negative concerning the 'existence of a convention' issue.[19] In both of his judgments Laskin emphasizes several points which go to his own image of a constitution. First, being political in inception and historical in nature, conventions are not law.[20] Secondly, Laskin disclaims the historicist underpinnings of the *Upper House Case* discussed above. In his words: "Although the Court referred to certain historical background for perspective on the position of the Senate as it was dealt with under the *British North America Act*, its fundamental duty was to examine the validity of a proposed federal measure sought to be justified under a grant of federal power under that Act."[21] And, thirdly, in response to the historicist claim of the provinces concerning the binding quality of the principle of provincial consent, Laskin responds the "[t]he arguments from history do not lead to any consistent view or any single view of the nature of the *British North America Act*." He continues, "... [h]istory cannot alter the fact that in law there is a British statute to construe and apply ..."[22] Indeed, in response to the very question of whether a convention exists, Laskin asserts that "no legal question is raised ... and, ordinarily, the Court would not undertake to answer them for it is not the function of the Court to go beyond legal determinations."[23] In short, history is not and ought not to be considered the resource material of law.

Then, what should? Laskin exclusively confines his constitution to an "imperative constitutional text of statute."[24] For Canada, that imperative text is the British North America Act, 1867. Political practice, no matter how long it has been followed, "counted for nothing" unless statute law posits the practice as law.[25] The court's sole duty is to examine the validity of a statute in the light of the British North America Act.[26] Any other role would be "judicial legislation."[27]

If Laskin intended to express an historicist image of a constitution, then his "law" would have included principles other than those posited by a legislature or parliament. But he rejects an historicist image and, in place thereof, he insists that the constitution and law can only be found in posited enactments. Thus, his image of an imperative constitution requires that he restate the surface issue in his own terms: namely, 'how does one reconcile the supremacy of provincial legislatures *vis-à-vis* the federal Parliament in the amending process?'[28] After dealing at length with the nature of a convention, Laskin ineluctably returns to his concern for the supremacy of the sovereign state: "[t]he convention sought to be advanced here," according to Laskin, "would truncate the functioning of the executive and legislative branches at the federal level. This would impose a limitation on the sovereign body itself within the Constitution."[29] Once he has posed the issue in terms of the boundary of an imperative state, Laskin could note that the "supremacy position, taken alone, needs no further justification than that found in the respective formulations of the powers of Parliament and the provincial legislatures in ss. 91 and 92 of the *British North America Act.*"[30]

Of course the legislative supremacy doctrine needs no further justification, given the imperative character of posited rules. A constitution equals an "imperative, constitutional text or statute." Therefore, the legislative or executive source of a text is unchallengeable. It follows, further, that the norms of other sources cannot logically constitute part of a constitution. All this logically flows from Laskin's premise of posited rules being a constitution's resource material. But his premise serves as the very target of the opposed Martland/Ritchie historicist image in the *Patriation Reference.*

In his Minority of Three dissent, Laskin explains the imperative character of his picture of law in response to the question 'what are conventions and, particularly, what are constitutional conventions?' A convention is not law, according to Laskin: "These rules have an historical origin and bind, and have bound, the actors in constitutional matters in Canada for generations. No one can doubt their operative force or the reality of their existence as an effective part of the Canadian constitution. They are, nonetheless, conventional and, therefore, *distinct from purely legal rules*"[31] Although it may be "a matter of some surprise to many Canadians," he continues, "these conventions have no legal force." "*Constitutionality and legality must be synonymous,*" he holds.[32] Why? Because "[s]uch law cannot be ascribed to informal or customary origins, but *must be found in a formal document* which is the source of authority, legal authority, through which the central and regional units function and exercise their powers."[33]

This formal text constitutes Laskin's 'given,' his starting-point and the grounding for his image of a constitution as he expresses that image in the *Patriation Reference.* His 'given' explains why he has rejected conventions in favour of tangible rules. It explains why courts cannot and do not enforce conventions. And it supports why courts cannot provide sanctions for the non-observance of conventions.[34]

What, then, is the nature of a constitutional convention? Quoting approvingly from Dicey, himself a student of John Austin, Laskin affirms that conventions are "constitutional morality"[35] or "politics." Conventions "need trouble no lawyer or the class of any professor of law."[36] And why does Dicey not consider conventions law? Conventions "are not in reality laws at all since they are not enforced by the courts."[37] But we have seen above that, for Laskin, conventions are unenforceable because they are not law. How, then, can the student escape from the circularity of Laskin's claims? One can do so only when one realizes that both Dicey and Laskin share a similar image of a constitution.[38] Their shared image grounds the constitutional law in an imperative written text posited by a legislature, albeit a far more refined, sophisticated, and rigorous image in Laskin's case. Given that imperative character of law, all principles emanating from some source, other than a legislated text, cannot be law. Nor is it for the courts to enforce non-textual sources: "it is our view that it is not for the Courts to raise a convention to the status of a legal principle."[39]

(b) *The Judiciary's Institutional Self-Image*

In the *Patriation Reference* Laskin represents that judges should play a passive role in the elaboration of the content of a constitution. A determinant text constitutes the content of the constitution, we have seen. The courts ought not to add to it by recognizing the existence of some constitutional convention outside and independent of the text. In his words: "The attempted assimilation of the growth of a convention to the growth of the common law is *misconceived*. The latter is the product of judicial effort, ... *in obedience to statutes or constitutional directives*. No such parental role is played by the courts with respect to conventions."[40] Laskin reinterprets the *Upper House Reference* in a manner which rejects any backward-looking role for a court: "its fundamental duty was to examine the validity of a proposed federal measure sought to be justified under a grant of federal power under that Act."[41] To hold that a convention of unanimous consent of the provinces exists would constitute "judicial legislation."[42] To entertain such a convention would involve the court in the world of political values; the court's duty is to avoid the latter incursion. As he notes in the first paragraph of his dissenting Minority of Three judgment, a court does not ordinarily undertake to deal with the question of whether a convention in fact exists because "it is not the function of the Court to go beyond legal determinations."[43] And again, "it is not for the Courts to raise a convention to the status of a legal principle."[44] Nor is it "for the Court to express views on the wisdom or lack of wisdom of these proposals [before the Court]."[45]

Laskin does not inform us why the latter is excluded from a judge's role.

Or does he? We can ascertain his answer only by appreciating that his 'reasons for judgment' express Laskin's picture of 'what is a constitution.' One can understand why Laskin projects a passive role for judges only by seeing that issue as one element of several, all of which go to inform his deep image of a constitution.

(c) *The Source of Constitutional Obligation*

Laskin admits that the crucial issue concerning a constitutional convention is whether the parties act and speak *as if they are bound by the convention.* Conventions "bind, and have bound, the actors ... for generations."[46] "They are observed without demur," he continues, 'because all parties concerned recognize their existence and accept the obligation of observance, considering themselves to be bound.' This binding quality constitutes an "operative force," a "reality." Laskin proceeds to study the institutional evidence to ascertain whether all parties have considered themselves bound to a practice requiring provincial consent to constitutional amendments which affect federal/provincial relations.

Notwithstanding the sense of obligation surrounding an established convention Laskin, as judge, does not consider himself bound by it. Nor can he. He is bound only to posited rules delineated in an imperative text. And posited rules constitute the only kind of law there can be, for him. Accordingly, constitutional obligation for Laskin is not grounded in some immanent sense of obligation internal to the parties. No. It is grounded in a determinant positive enactment. The latter possesses an imperative character. And that imperative character binds the judge. The imperative character renders the rules enforceable.

(d) *The Apolitical Character of Constitutional Law*

It need hardly be mentioned, then, that constitutional law for Laskin possesses an apolitical character. First, given his sole focus upon the posited legal rules and upon a determinative imperative text, any historical argument is a theory, not reality. And "[t]heories, whether of a full compact theory ... or of a modified compact theory ... operate in the political realm, in political science studies. They do not engage the law ..."[47] Even federalism, as a "theory," can only be used "as an aid" to interpreting "the *imperative character* of the distribution of legislative power" in the British North America Act.[48] Laskin expresses this apolitical character of constitutional law, secondly, by feeling compelled to conclude his Majority judgment with the disclaimer that his 'reasons for judgment' have no political content: "Nothing said in these reasons is to be construed as either favouring or disapproving the proposed amending formula or the *Charter of Rights and Freedoms* or any of the other provisions of which enactment is sought. The questions put to this Court do not ask for its approval or disapproval of the contents of the so-called 'package.'"[49] Thirdly, he believes, any inquiry into the existence or non-existence of a constitutional convention (such as the second question itself) is political and thus non-legal. The enforcement of a convention is political. Accordingly, its enforcement "will not engage the attention of the courts which are limited to matters of law alone."[50] Finally, Laskin expresses his concern about the apolitical character of a constitution in a fourth manner: he concludes his dissenting judgment with the same disclaimer as his Majority of Seven judgment. More particularly, he insists that: "[i]t is not for the Court to express views on the wisdom or lack of wisdom of these proposals. We are concerned solely with their constitutionality."[51]

Having emphasized that other judges ought to exclude theory, history, activism, and considerations about the wisdom of an enactment from their decision-making, Laskin assures himself that the patriation resolution "does not, save for the enactment of the *Charter of Rights*, ... truly amend the Canadian Constitution. Its effect is to complete the formation of an incomplete constitution by supplying its present deficiency *i.e.* an amending formula ..."[52] Not only does he play an apolitical role in this reference, but the actual content of the reference, Laskin imagines, has little political consequence. Canada now has a complete constitution – but only given Laskin's premises as to the resource material of the constitution, the institutional self-image of a judge, constitutional obligation, and the apolitical character of constitutional law. Because a constitution is posited in an imperative text and because the imperative text has not allowed for the amendment of the rules governing the source of the text (the Canadian parliament and United Kingdom parliament), the constitution is necessarily incomplete. The patriation resolution fills the gap in rule-making. Canada's constitution, as Laskin imagines it, is now complete.

4. THE MARTLAND/RITCHIE HISTORICIST IMAGE

Now, we have already seen that not all Canadian judges and scholars share Laskin's rule rationalist image of a constitution. One would have difficulty in associating Laskin's image, for example, with Rand's beliefs in "an unchallengeable right," "citizenship status," and irreparable economic harm as he expresses them in *Roncarelli* v. *Duplessis*. Whereas Laskin equates posited rights with "the Constitution," Dickson elevates "the Constitution" to a higher status in his discussion of the 'separation of powers' doctrine in *Ref. re Residential Tenancies Act*. And several judgments arising out of both the 'separation of powers' and the *Upper House Reference* understand a constitution through an historicist prism. As they did in Laskin's case, counsel in the *Patriation Reference* challenge the deepest inward feelings of Martland and Ritchie. Martland and Ritchie believe that the Federal Government's attempt to seek a United Kingdom amendment to the British North America Act, 1867 without substantial provincial consent violates what they have assumed to be the fundamental constitutional norms of society. More than that, those norms have the legal effect of rendering the proposed amendment invalid.

(a) *The Resource Material of a Constitution*

In Martland and Ritchie's view, one does not discover a constitution in some *a priori* imperative text, such as the British North America Act, 1867. Rather, one uncovers the content of a constitution by looking backward into a society's institutional history. History offers evidence of a binding norm. A posited text is not imperative. A text does not impose or declare duties and rights. And it is only one source of evidence to which one can appeal in identifying the content of a constitution. Rather than declaring the content of a constitution, a posited text such as the British North America Act, 1867 merely offers evidence of a constitutional standard. Other *indicia*, documented in writing, can provide weighty resource material. The duty of the court is to sort out that evidence and to ascertain its accuracy, its weight, and its coherency with other evidence. If one can find a consistent acknowledgment of a particular norm embedded in past institutional materials, then the norm constitutes a part of a constitution.

In their response to the third question (whether agreement of the provinces is "constitutionally required"), the Martland/Ritchie dissent utilizes historical evidence to invalidate the federal resolution. "Never before" has the federal Parliament proceeded this way, according to the dissent.[53] After reviewing the evidence, the dissent concludes that the early evidence acknowledged the existence of a norm: "[t]he practice has developed, since 1895, to have the formal approach to the Imperial Parliament made by means of a joint address of both Houses of Parliament. This form of procedure had been followed earlier in respect of amendments to the *Act of Union, 1840*."[54] This practice had also been followed in the events leading up to the enactment of section 146 of the

British North America Act, 1867. Section 146 admitted existing colonies, or territories, into Canada. Martland then describes the practice followed in fourteen amendments to the Constitution beginning in 1871. But "[i]n no instance has an amendment to the *B.N.A. Act* been enacted which directly affected federal-provincial relationships in the sense of changing provincial legislative powers, in the absence of federal consultation with and the consent of all the provinces."[55] And this process occurs, he explains, because "the *normal constitutional principles* recognizing the inviolability of separate and exclusive legislative powers were carried into and *considered* an integral part of the operation of the resolution procedure."[56] But what Martland considers as "the normal constitutional principles" is grounded in pre-existing historical evidence.

In addition to reviewing past practices of governments, the Martland/Ritchie dissent examines a series of judgments which go to show that "the basic principles of the Constitution" are not necessarily posited in "the express terms of the *B.N.A. Act*."[57] The "legal principles and doctrines" of the Constitution have been "judicially created." They share these four characteristics:

First, none is to be found in express provisions of the *British North America Acts* or other constitutional enactments;
Second, all have been perceived to represent constitutional requirements that are derived from the federal character of Canada's Constitution;
Third, they have been accorded full legal force in the sense of being employed to strike down legislative enactments;
Fourth, each was judicially developed ...[58]

That is, Martland and Ritchie claim that the courts have created an enforceable part of constitutional law outside and independent of any determinative imperative document. The unwritten conventions of the federal character of the body politic generate much law. Historicist principles can even strike down legislated enactments.

But, if express provisions of the British North America Acts or other constitutional enactments do not create legally binding doctrines, as the Martland/Ritchie dissent disclaims in its first summary point, where are judges to look for evidence of the law of a constitution? Martland and Ritchie respond to that question in their Majority of Six judgment. That judgment claims that there has been a constitutional convention requiring provincial consent in the patriation circumstances before the court. Ironically, the Martland/Ritchie Majority of Six characterizes as non-law the very judicially created principles which the Martland/Ritchie dissent considers as law. Notwithstanding the apparent contradiction, the re-source material of the law of a constitution remains the same. As the Majority of Six explains, courts can find constitutional principles embed-ded within "the prevailing constitutional values or principles of the period."[59] For that reason, the Majority of Six describes constitutional principles as largely "unwritten."[60]

Again, the Majority of Six contradicts the Martland/Ritchie dissent with respect to the issue 'what qualifies as law?' As with opposed positions with respect to other surface issues which we have already examined in earlier chapters, the explanation of the contradiction lies within the opposed images of a constitution expressed in the 'reasons for judgment.' Whereas the dissent assumes an historicist image which pictures constitutional law in terms of historical evidence of decades past, the Majority of Six adopts a rule rationalist image of a constitution not unlike that described by Laskin. For example, the Majority of Six begins its 'reasons of judgment' this way: the "Constitution of Canada ... embraces the global system of rules and principles ... in the whole and in every part of the Canadian state."[61] Falling back upon Dicey's classification, Martland then identifies two elements of the Constitution: first, the "law of the Constitution" which he describes as statutes, order in council, and common law rules; secondly, "essential rules" and "requirement[s]," which Dicey calls con-ventions.

In an even more ironic ambiguity, the Majority of Six still insists that conventions are "important parts" of a constitution. Indeed, conventions really provide the foundation of the legal system (and the society), according to the Majority of Six, because their "main purpose" is "to ensure that the legal framework of the constitution will be operated in accordance with the prevailing constitutional values and principles of the period."[62] So, for example, majority rule is actually a "requirement of the Constitution." There also exists "a constitutional requirement" that the prime minister enjoy the support of the elected branch of the legisla-ture.[63] Indeed, "some conventions may be more important than some laws."[64] And yet, the Majority of Six remains adamant that conventions are not law. Conventions are unenforceable. And, when in conflict with the legal rules "which they postulate," the courts are bound to enforce only the legal rules.[65] The sanctions of conventions lie in the political world. A convention crystallizes into law only when the legislature posits a rule expressly adopting it.

(b) The Judiciary's Institutional Self-Image
What is the role of judges in the Martland/Ritchie historicist image of a

constitution? In contrast to Laskin's apolitical role, Martland and Ritchie believe that judges will inevitably involve themselves in the identification and application of a community's social values.

In their dissenting judgment Martland and Ritchie note that although the British North America Act "confided the whole area of self-government within Canada" to the two levels of government, it "did not make any specific provision as to the means of determining the constitutionality of any federal or provincial legislation." Accordingly, "[t]hat task has been assumed and performed by the courts."[66] And, "[i]n performing this function, the courts ... have had occasion to develop legal principles based on the necessity of preserving the integrity of the federal structure."[67] In this process Martland and Ritchie project their own self-image onto others: a judge's duty is to examine issues "from the point of view of substance rather than of form."[68] If the United Kingdom Parliament were to amend the constitution upon a Joint Resolution of the Senate and House of Commons without provincial consent, this "could disturb and even destroy the federal system of constitutional government in Canada."[69] Against this possibility, Martland insists, "[i]t is the duty of this Court to consider this assertion of rights with a view to the preservation of the Constitution [that is, the judicially created principle of federalism]."[70] The court has been "active" in fulfilling this role "since its inception," sometimes by interpreting the express terms of the British North America Act and sometimes by using "the basic principles of the Constitution" to strike down legislation.[71] This active role is "the proper function of this court."[72]

In contrast to this activist judicial role in their dissent, the Martland Majority of Six contemplates a passive role for the courts. Since constitutional law embraces a "global system of rules and principles," law is tangible and determinative. It can be found only for the asking. Accordingly, the function of a judge is simply to find the relevant rule and then to apply it. As the Majority of Six imagines the situation, "it is the function of the courts *to declare what the law is* and since the law is sometimes breached, it is generally the function of the courts to ascertain whether it has in fact been breached in specific instances and, if so, *to apply such sanctions* as are contemplated *by the law* [that is, posited rules]."[73] Thus, the Majority of Six judges see their institutional duty in terms of adhering to express rules rather than wandering into the world of political values. That duty explains why the sanctions of a convention rest with institutions of the state other than courts. And that duty underlies why courts cannot enforce conventions.

(c) *The Source of Constitutional Obligation*

The Martland/Ritchie dissent goes one step deeper than many of the judgments which we have examined in earlier chapters. Martland and Ritchie do so by identifying the source of constitutional obligation as one of the indispensable questions for a full image of a constitution. Judges are not obligated to follow a constitution because some formal document calling itself 'the constitution' says so. No. Constitutional obligation emanates from within the social fabric rather than from without. It emanates from a judge's sense of obligation. The source of that obligation, then, is neither the state nor to its formal institutions (such as the legislature). Rather, the obligation emanates from the values presupposed by a judge or a community as projected by a judge.

Martland and Ritchie emphasize in their four-point summary, quoted above,[74] that judicially created principles "have been *perceived* to represent constitutional requirements."[75] If standards are not so perceived, then they are not constitutional requirements. Perception goes to the empirical world. It goes to evidence. Accordingly, if officials cannot support a claim with sufficient empirical evidence that it exists then, in the eyes of a judge, the claim has no legal force. The Martland/Ritchie dissent informs us, in its first summary point, that the "express provisions of the B.N.A. Acts or other constitutional *enactments*" do not qualify as such empirical evidence. Were they to do so, the judicial role would be an easy one. We could then rightfully agree with the Laskin group that imperative rules posited from an exterior institution constitute the sole source of constitutional obligation. But the Martland/Ritchie dissent expresses that constitutional requirements are perceived from *within* the minds of officials and/or citizens rather than from without. The only remaining question is, then, 'where do judges find the resource material with which to perceive the world?'

The answer to that question, we have already seen, lies within the Martland/Ritchie Majority of Six. There, the Majority finds conventions in "the prevailing constitutional values or principles of the time." The values are largely unwritten. The Martland/Ritchie dissent would find the source of constitutional obligation in those unwritten values and principles at any particular period of society's history. Martland and Ritchie imagine that those unwritten social values, not externally posited rules, serve as the source of constitutional obligation.

What weight do Martland and Ritchie attribute to an unwritten social value? Although the Majority of Six responds that no legal weight should be given to a social value, they do explain that the importance of conventions "depends on that of the value or principle which they are meant to safeguard."[76] Thus, the crucial question in ascertaining the existence of a convention is 'did the actors believe themselves bound by the alleged convention?' That is, as an empirical question, do officials possess an internal sense of obligation toward the principle? In an effort to ascertain whether there is such a sense of obligation in the *Patriation Reference* Martland plods tirelessly through a Federal Government White Paper of 1965, and statements by Prime Minister King in 1938 and 1940, Justice Minister Lapointe in 1940, Prime Minister Bennett in 1931, Justice Minister St Laurent in 1943, and Prime Minister Diefenbaker in 1960. He concludes that federal officials have believed themselves bound to a requirement of provincial consent for at least fifty years. Such an exercise in historical research would be unnecessary for a judge whose boundaries begin and end with externally posited rules.

(d) *The Apolitical Character of Constitutional Law*

The Martland and Ritchie image of a constitution in the *Patriation Reference* is not without a contradiction. On the one hand we have seen that, for Martland and Ritchie, social values are more important than legal (that is, posited or legislative) rules; a judge is obligated to resist offensive incursions into social values; and the values themselves emanate from within society rather than externally from a legislature or previous court. Social-constitutional values are more "legitimate" than legal rules.[77] On the other hand, Martland's Majority of Six believes that constitutional values are judicially unenforceable. They do not form part of "the laws of the Constitution." The Majority of Six claims that "the courts would be bound to enforce the law, not the convention."[78] In a mystifying explanation, the Majority of Six asserts that "[p]erhaps the main reason why conventional rules cannot be enforced by the courts is that they are generally in conflict with the legal rules which they postulate and the courts are bound to enforce the legal rules."[79] But why would a court be more bound to the latter if, as the Martland/Ritchie dissent pictures the law, a court could be bound by a convention (once established)?

The explanation, but not justification, of this contradiction would seem to be that the Majority of Six cannot sever its image of a constitution from the rationalist roots in Dicey. The historicist image of a constitution in the Martland/Ritchie dissent consistently requires that a judge invalidate contemporary legislation which contradicts historically derived social values. But the hold of Dicey's heritage induces the Majority of Six to distinguish arbitrarily a convention from a legal rule, a constitution from a constitutional law. In the words of the Majority of Six, "to violate a convention is to do something which is unconstitutional although it entails no direct legal consequence."[80] Assuming the logical validity of the arbitrary distinction, the Majority can describe the distinction as "perfectly appropriate." Given Martland and Ritchie's otherwise coherent image of a constitution in their dissent, the distinction between a constitution and constitutional law is entirely inappropriate. If the Majority of Six applied the first three boundaries of the Martland/Ritchie constitutional image (the historicist resource material, an active judicial role, and an immanent source of constitutional obligation), then the judge's duty would be to enforce the more important, fundamental, legitimate social values upon which the legal rules and legal institutions allegedly rest. But the Majority of Six would then have to admit that constitutional law possesses a political character. And *that*, the Majority is unwilling to do.

5. AN IMMANENT CONSTITUTIONAL OBLIGATION: THE QUEBEC VETO REFERENCE

The Supreme Court takes the occasion of a further constitutional amendment reference, the *Quebec Veto Reference*,[81] to express more refined views about constitutional obligation. Quebec argued that, by convention, Quebec could veto any amendment to the Constitution if an amendment affects federal/provincial relations. The Court responds to Quebec's claim by delving deeply into the very core of its image: 'what is the source of constitutional obligation?' The Court raises this issue in three contexts.

First, the Court connects its conception of constitutional obligation to the nature of a convention. The Court affirms Freedman's definition of a convention in the *Patriation Reference*. That definition, in turn, approvingly quotes Peter Hogg as stating that 'a convention is a rule which is *regarded as obligatory by the officials to whom it applies.*'[82] The *Quebec Veto Reference* Court also approves of Jennings's assertion, affirmed by the Majority of Seven in the *Patriation Reference*, that one of the three crucial issues surrounding a convention is "did the actors in the precedents believe that they were *bound* by a rule?"[83] An alleged convention might possess a compulsive character even if there were no reason for it; but this compulsion would only lie if "it is perfectly certain that the persons concerned *regarded them[selves] as bound by it.*"[84] The Supreme Court approvingly quotes Jennings in two different parts of its judgment. In the second set of references to it, the Court affirms Jennings's position that "[c]onvention implies some form of agreement, whether expressed or implied ..." Again, "conventions are like most fundamental rules of any constitution in that they rest essentially upon general acquiescence."[85] Officials must believe they *ought* to follow an alleged convention before the latter can be recognized as a convention. In that sense one can characterize a convention as normative or ideal-directed. To this end, Quebec's counsel ushers forth an abundance of evidence demonstrating that Quebec officials have hitherto believed themselves bound by a Quebec veto power convention. This evidence includes parliamentary speeches, royal commission reports, and the opinions of historians, political scientists, and constitutional experts. But the Supreme Court believes that Quebec's counsel has failed to adduce sufficient evidence showing that federal officials and officials from the provinces other than Quebec have recognized a conventional power of veto either explicitly or by necessary implication.

Secondly, the *Quebec Veto Reference* Court characterizes conventions in the same vein as Martland and Ritchie do in their *Patriation Reference* dissent. More particularly, on the one hand, the Court acknowledges that conventional rules are "quite distinct from legal ones." On the other hand, the Court distinguishes conventions from "rules of morality, rules of expediency and subjective rules."[86] The Court explains toward the end of the *Veto Reference* that a *sense of obligation* shared by the actors toward any standard "unmistakably" distinguishes that standard as a *constitutional* rule from a rule of convenience or political expediency.[87] The Court incorrectly describes conventions as "positive rules." The Court seems to mean by a positive rule that there must be institutional evidence (court documents, legislative enactments, orders-in-council, and other *written* evidence) supporting the positive acquiescence in the principle or the negative absence thereof. Consistent with this interpretation, the Court adds that conventions must be ascertained by reference to "objective standards." Objectivity inheres in the institutional evidence of the past. Tradition exists independently of a judge's subjective values. And the source of obligation emanates from a sense of obligation toward the standard shared by all the interested institutional parties.

Finally, because proof of a convention requires proof of a sense of obligation, a convention appears to be more "fundamental" than a posited rule. "The main purpose of constitutional conventions," the unanimous Court emphasizes, "is to ensure that the legal framework of the constitution will be operated in accordance with generally accepted principles."[88] That is, the day-to-day posited rules provide "the legal framework." And yet, that "legal framework" does not exist in a vacuum. Generally accepted principles embedded in institutional history legitimize the posited legal framework. One must characterize the former, then, as more fundamental or of a higher priority of legitimacy than the latter.

V

The Canadian Bill of Rights

Let us now consider a further 'subject-matter' of Canadian constitutional law, the Canadian Bill of Rights.[1] Although the Supreme Court's judgment in *R. v. Drybones*[2] elevated the expectations which liberal constitutionalists had for the Canadian Bill of Rights, subsequent judgments slowly have whittled away the meaning, scope, and legal effect of the Bill.[3] Explanations for the demise of the Bill have varied from its statutory – as opposed to constitutional – character,[4] to its draftmanship,[5] to the influence of Dicey,[6] and to faulty legal analysis.[7] I wish to connect the demise of the Canadian Bill of Rights to a constitutional image, one whose boundaries we have just experienced in Laskin's constitutional amendment judgments. In other words, I aim to show, once again, that Canadian Bill of Rights judgments speak to constitutional imagery. Early in the Bill's life, Canadian higher and lower court judges realized that in examining the meaning of the text, judges are inevitably called upon to ask a prior question: namely, 'how can the judiciary account for, explain, differentiate, assimilate, or respond to the Bill, given a constitutional image which begins and ends with externally posited rules?' Is the Bill really a part of 'the Constitution'? If so, why? If not, why not?

Let us first reread the text of the Canadian Bill of Rights itself. The long title, section one, and the preamble of the Canadian Bill of Rights all describe the enacted rights as *human* rights and freedoms as *fundamental* ones. The preamble provides that in enacting the Bill, the Canadian Parliament affirms that Canada is founded upon human rights and fundamental freedoms. Parliament's directive seems emphatic: the rights and freedoms "have existed" and "shall continue to exist"; and *every* law in Canada "*shall* ... be so construed and applied as not to abrogate, abridge or infringe ... the rights and freedoms herein."[8] The text provides that

Parliament believes the rights and freedoms to be fundamental, and so the Bill's rights are to prevail over any conflict with "every law of Canada." Section 5(2) defines the expression "law of Canada" to mean an act, "any order, rule or regulation thereunder," "and any law in force in Canada or in any part of Canada ... that is subject to be repealed, abolished or altered by the Parliament of Canada."[9] The latter definition incorporates judicially created principles, prerogative, custom, and practice as subject to the purview of the Canadian Bill of Rights since Parliament can repeal, abolish, or alter rules emanating from each of these sources of law. Furthermore, the Bill explicitly applies to acts and orders thereunder enacted "*before* or *after* the coming into force of this Act."[10] The terms of the Bill are to be subservient to ordinary statutes or orders on only one occasion: namely, when Parliament has "expressly declared" that the latter conflicting statute or order is to operate "notwithstanding the Canadian Bill of Rights." *No court* and *no parliament* have authority to restrict a right or freedom unless Parliament has prefaced such a restriction with a "notwithstanding" clause.

In spite of the wording of the Canadian Bill of Rights, Canadian judges have gradually rendered the Bill ineffective. Judges admittedly used the Bill to render legislation inoperative in *R. v. Drybones*.[11] On occasion, they gave an old common law right more weight and scope in the light of the Canadian Bill of Rights.[12] In *Curr* v. *The Queen*, Fauteaux acknowledges "the all embracing scope of the *Canadian Bill of Rights*" and Laskin affirms that the Bill does not freeze the federal statute book as of 10 August 1960, nor is a court restricted to sterilizing federal law enacted prior to the enactment of the Bill.[13] And in *Brownridge* v. *The Queen* the Supreme Court widens the scope of the right to retain and instruct counsel, as protected in section 2(c)(ii) of the Bill, in order to afford a citizen a "reasonable excuse" to refuse to comply with a breathalyser demand.[14] Justice Beetz has recently resurrected the force and effect of the Canadian Bill of Rights to broaden the previous understanding of "the right to a fair hearing in accordance with the principles of fundamental justice" as protected in section 2(e) of the Bill.[15] Notwithstanding these cases, however, lower and higher court judges rendered the Bill a "paper tiger" by the late 1970s, the last resort in any lawyer's fledging argument. The Supreme Court finally recognizes the demise of the Bill by reading an "implied notwithstanding clause" into the text of the Bill itself: unless Parliament has expressly declared that the Canadian Bill of Rights could operate against a specifically named statute, the courts are to presume that Parliament has not intended the Bill to operate.[16]

The question remains. Why? Why did Canadian judges render the Canadian Bill of Rights ineffective by the late 1970s despite the seemingly clear, emphatic text? One can understand why judges interpreted the text in this manner only by addressing the first question of constitutional law: namely, what image of a constitution did Canadian judges share amongst themselves when confronted with a challenge under the Canadian Bill of Rights? I intend to argue that in their Canadian Bill of Rights judgments, judges (and the lawyers arguing before them) express their inward image of a constitution. I aim to do so by looking closely at a series of Supreme Court justices who played the dominant role in the demise of the Canadian Bill of Rights. We shall scrutinize the judgments in terms of three of the four boundaries which crystallize in the constitutional amendment cases. First, and most important for the Canadian Bill of Rights judgments, 'what is a court's institutional self-image vis-à-vis other institutions?' Secondly, 'is constitutional law apolitical?' And thirdly, 'what is the resource material of a constitution?' In the process of identifying these horizons of a judge's image of a constitution, I aim to show how these judges tried so fervently to protect their shared image from the potentially destabilizing and threatening impact of the Canadian Bill of Rights.

1. THE JUDICIARY'S INSTITUTIONAL SELF-IMAGE

The most important element in the judiciary's image of a constitution as expressed in the Canadian Bill of Rights cases is a judge's institutional self-image. Although I shall restrict myself to the Supreme Court of Canada decisions, the judiciary's institutional self-image plays an even weightier role with respect to lower court decisions, much as Chapter VI shows concerning the Canadian Charter of Rights and Freedoms. Those judges instrumental to the Bill's demise picture that they ought merely to apply posited rules: judges ought not to create rules. Conversely, the judiciary projects onto parliament the sole responsibility for changing the rules. Let us look more closely at how several judges express their self-image.

In his Canadian Bill of Rights judgments Pigeon consistently projects a passive self-image not unlike Laskin's. In his dissenting judgment in *R. v. Drybones* Pigeon holds that judges simply cannot use the Canadian Bill of Rights to render another legislative enactment inoperative.[17] The judiciary's passive self-image constitutes a "compelling reason" for his judgment, he explains:

Parliament must not be presumed to have intended to depart from the existing law any further than expressly stated (Maxwell ...). In the present case, the judgments below hold in effect that Parliament in enacting the *Bill* has implicitly repealed not only a large part of the *Indian Act* but also the fundamental principle that *the duty of the courts* is to apply the law as written and they are in no case authorized to fail to give effect to the clearly expressed will of Parliament. It would be a *radical departure from this basic British constitutional rule* to enact that henceforth the courts are to declare inoperative all enactments that are considered as not in conformity with some legal principles stated in very general language ...[18]

According to Pigeon, the meaning of such expressions as 'freedom of religion' and 'freedom of speech' is "in truth largely unlimited and undefined."[19] Meaning expands and varies over time. But, he continues, "in the traditional British system that is our own by virtue of the *British North America Act, 1867*, the responsibility for updating the statutes in this changing world rests exclusively upon Parliament."[20] He describes this as a "traditional principle." And he believes it synonymous with the principle of legislative supremacy.[21] The Canadian Bill of Rights embodies this "traditional principle," according to Pigeon. Because the role for updating statutes rests with parliaments rather than the courts, Pigeon claims that the Bill's import is merely to declare that "human rights and fundamental freedoms" have existed in the past and shall continue to exist in the future. The human rights have existed in the past because and only to the extent that Parliament has posited their existence. Pigeon adopts this reasoning in *Lavell* v. *A.-G. Canada*,[22] *The Queen* v. *Burnshine*,[23] and *A.-G. Canada* v. *Canard*.[24]

Pigeon is not alone in restricting his interpretation of the Canadian Bill of Rights to the boundary of a passive institutional self-image. Abbott accompanies Pigeon's dissenting opinion in *Drybones*.[25] Indeed, Abbott relies upon the judiciary's passive role as the core explanation for restrictively interpreting the Canadian Bill of Rights:

[t]he interpretation of the *Bill of Rights*, adopted by the courts below, necessarily implies a wide delegation of the legislative authority of Parliament to the courts. The power to make such a delegation cannot be questioned but, in my view, *it would require the plainest words* to impute to Parliament an intention *to extend to the courts, such an invitation to engage in judicial legislation*. I cannot find that intention expressed in s.2 of the *Bill*.[26]

Even the judiciary's oft-repeated "frozen meaning" doctrine presupposes a passive institutional self-image vis-à-vis the legislature. The frozen meaning doctrine states that the common law has protected all Canadian Bill of Rights guarantees prior to the Bill's enactment. The Bill does not purport to create new rights or to enlarge the scope of some alleged inherent meaning of the old rights. The Bill merely reaffirms their "frozen" existence in the form of a statute. What underlies this doctrine of the 'frozen meaning' is not the actual wording of the Bill (section one reads that the rights and freedoms "have existed," not that they have always existed),[27] but rather the passive, apolitical self-image of the judiciary. In *Lavell* v. *A.-G. Can.*[28] and *R.* v. *Miller and Cockreill*,[29] for example, Ritchie insists that judges possess a heavy negative duty to defer to all legislative enactments so long as the legislature has posited the challenged enactment within its jurisdiction as posited in sections 91 and 92 of the British North America Act, 1867. Further, in *Lavell*, Ritchie exclaims that if the Canadian Bill of Rights overrode other federal enactments Parliament would be rendered powerless.[30] Given this passive institutional self-image, Ritchie finds little difficulty in supporting the 'frozen meaning' doctrine.[31] When counsel confront Ritchie in *Miller and Cockreill* with the claim that the mandatory death penalty constitutes cruel and unusual punishment contrary to section 2(d) of the Bill,[32] he reacts that 'cruel and unusual punishment' means whatever meaning it bore in 1960. In that year, "there did not exist and had never existed in Canada the right not to be deprived of life."[33] It follows that Parliament could not possibly have intended to abolish the death penalty "by such an oblique method" as proscribing 'cruel and unusual punishment' in the Canadian Bill of Rights.[34]

Ritchie gives a great deal of weight in *Miller and Cockreill* to the fact that Parliament has seen fit to retain the death penalty pursuant to certain Criminal Code amendments *after* the passage of the Canadian Bill of Rights. Accordingly, the Criminal Code amendments constitute "strong evidence" of the nature and scope of the individual's right not to be subjected to 'cruel and unusual punishment.' Although Ritchie believes that he does not possess explicit duty to assess current community standards of morality, he speculates that he can implicitly do so by relying heavily upon Parliament's latest criminal code enactments. Politicians deal with policy; judges with rules. In Ritchie's words, current community standards of morality involve "essentially questions of policy and as such they are of necessity considerations effecting the decision of Parliament as to whether or not the death penalty should be retained."[35] The boundaries of Ritchie's frame of reference clearly contemplate that Parliament quite properly functions as the source of policy because, in contrast to judges, politicians more accurately reflect the contemporary values of the Canadian society. The judiciary's resource material – rules of law – possesses an apolitical, non-normative character. That character would be undermined if judges could read the Bill in a manner which overrides later policy statements of Parliament.

Finally, let us look at the last occasion when the Supreme Court discusses the Canadian Bill of Rights prior to the enactment of the Charter. In *MacKay* v. *The Queen*, the appellant has been tried by a Standing Court Martial pursuant to charges under the National Defence Act and the Narcotic Control Act.[36] The single surface issue is whether the manner of prosecution, trial, and exposure to conviction offends ss. 2(f) and 1(b) of the Canadian Bill of Rights. Concerning section 2(f), MacKay has been charged with a criminal offence (as contrasted with a disciplinary offence under military law). And yet, a Court Martial has tried him. Counsel alleges that a Court Martial is not an independent and impartial tribunal as required by section 2(f) of the Bill. Concerning section 1(b) of the Bill, MacKay has allegedly been denied 'equality before the law' because he has been subjected to a procedure and tribunal to which other Canadians are not subjected for the same offence. Also, he has been exposed to a civil proceeding after having been tried for the same offence by a military service tribunal. Ritchie, who delivers the majority judgment, is quick to quote Laskin from *Curr* v. *The Queen* as noted below.[37] For Ritchie, the crucial point is that Parliament has enacted the National Defence Act within Parliament's section 91 jurisdiction as posited in the parent British North America Act. "There can be no doubt that the National Defence Act," he asserts, "was enacted by Parliament 'constitutionally competent to do so and exercising its powers in accordance with the tenets of responsible government.'"[38] Given its constitutional validity, Ritchie places the onus upon any claimant "to demonstrate that Parliament was not seeking to achieve a valid federal objective."[39]

Martland, Laskin, and others share the same deferential attitude to the policy-making role of politicians in their Canadian Bill of Rights judgments. Martland explains his majority judgment in *Burnshine*, for example, in that when the Canadian Bill of Rights was enacted, the concept of 'equality before the law' could not possibly have been wider in scope than at the time of the *Burnshine* case because such a meaning "would have involved *a substantial impairment of the sovereignty of Parliament* in the exercise of its legislative powers under s. 91 of the *British North America Act* and could only have been created by constitutional amendment, or by statute."[40] Martland insists that "*it is not the function of this Court, under the Bill of Rights*, to prevent the operation of a federal enactment, designed for this purpose, on the ground that it applies only to one class of persons, or to a particular area."[41]

Laskin often dissents from the conclusions of Pigeon, Abbott, Ritchie, and Martland in Canadian Bill of Rights cases. And yet, he too shares the same apolitical, passive institutional self-image. Indeed, one would be more correct to suggest that Ritchie and Martland share Laskin's image of a court's role (in contrast to their opposed position in the constitutional amendment cases). In *dicta* which Laskin lays down in *Curr* v. *The Queen*[42] and which the majority of the Supreme Court subsequently adopts in *Burnshine*,[43] Laskin announces that whether section 1(a) of the Canadian Bill of Rights or, indeed, any other provision of the *Bill* controls substantive federal legislation "did not directly arise in *R.* v. *Drybones*." Laskin continues that when the substantive or policy content – as opposed to the procedural application – of the law is at stake, "compelling reasons ought to be advances to justify the Court in this case to employ a statutory (as contrasted with a constitutional) jurisdiction to deny operative effect to a *substantive measure duly enacted by a Parliament constitutionally competent to do so,* and exercising its powers in accordance with the *tenets of responsible government,* which underlie the discharge of legislative authority under the *British North America Act.*"[44] Laskin demonstrates his deference to the legislature as the sole source of policy once again, when he goes on to assert in *Curr* that the American experience with the "due process" clause has little application to Canada because, in Canada, "*the major role is played by elected representatives of the people.*"[45] And Laskin connects his passive institutional self-image to policy matters by emphasizing in *Burnshine* that "the primary injunction of the Bill" is "to determine whether a challenged measure is open to a compatible construction that would enable it to remain an effective enactment. If the process of construction in the light of the Bill yields this result, it is unnecessary and, indeed, it would be *an abuse of judicial power to sterilize the federal measure.*"[46]

In virtually every one of his Canadian Bill of Rights judgments, Laskin imagines that the Canadian Constitution requires a judge to play a passive secondary role. To the suggestion that the Criminal Code abortion provisions deny Morgentaler 'equality before the law' and 'the protection of the law,' in that the Code grants advantages to some Canadians on grounds of economic status and geographic location, for example, Laskin reacts that this argument would require a court to consider the distribution of abortion facilities.[47] And this, in turn, triggers policy issues: the equal distribution of abortion facilities is a reach for equality by *judicially unmanageable standards*, and *is posited on the theory* that the Court should either give directions for the achievement of relative equality of access to therapeutic abortion committees and approved hospitals ...

I do not regard s. 1(b) of the *Canadian Bill of Rights as charging the courts with supervising* the administrative efficiency of legislation *or with evaluating* the regional or national organization of its administration ...[48]

Evaluative matters of distributive justice are for the politicians: "Parliament has made a judgment which does not admit of any interference by the courts."[49] An issue of policy (such as the composition of an abortion committee and the restriction of abortions to accredited hospitals) cannot raise "a judicially reviewable question." And why not, one might ask? Because Laskin's institutional self-image precludes him from entertaining arguments which question the policy content of legislation. This self-image – not the text of the Canadian Bill of Rights – prevents Morgentaler's claims from being considered "a judicially reviewable question."

One is tempted to appreciate Laskin as a friend of the Canadian Bill of Rights because he frequently dissents during the Bill's demise. But even when he holds out the Bill as having some weight, he does so in terms of his own picture of a judge's passive institutional role. So, for example, his dissent in *A.-G. Can. v. Canard*[50] rebuts Pigeon's claim in *Lavell* that Indians have been designated as a special class under section 91(24) of the British North America Act and that, therefore, Parliament has not contravened 'equality before the law' by treating natives differently from other Canadians. Laskin explains that "it is open to Parliament" to interpret section 91(24) of the British North America Act, 1867 widely, although he himself had not regarded section 91(24) as authorizing Parliament to offend the Bill's protections. Whatever the scope of the Act, it was "not, in my opinion, an invitation to the [c]ourts to do what Parliament has not chosen to do ..."[51]

2. THE APOLITICAL LAW

Joined with institutional passivity, there is a pre-understanding that law is apolitical. Once the legislature posits a rule, the rule somehow becomes immunized from the power struggles of society and autonomous of external ethical claims thrust upon it. Judges especially express this second boundary of their image of a constitution in 'equality before the law' cases where counsel urge a departure from the judiciary's passive, apolitical self-image. When their apolitical image of a constitution is challenged in Canadian Bill of Rights cases, judges retrench. They do so through their creation of two doctrines consonant with the prior boundaries of their passive, apolitical law.

(a) The 'Formal Equality' Doctrine

The first doctrinal boundary takes the content of a posited legislative rule as a 'given.' The courts project a meaning into 'equality before the law' which goes to the *application* of the 'given' rule. Politics enters into the content of a rule, not its application. By confining the judiciary's role to a scrutiny of a rule's application, judges imagine that they can remain apolitical. The doctrine immunizes judges from a charge that they are questioning the political wisdom or public preferences of the elected legislators. Further, the doctrine states that judges should administer rules *impartially*, ensuring that rules reach all intended persons whatever their political or economic class. The content of the rule alone – not the judiciary's subjective values – serves to inform a judge as to the scope or reach of a rule.[52] Formal equality ensues.

Ironically, the Supreme Court falls back upon this judicially created doctrine in two important judgments solidifying the Canadian Bill of Rights's demise prior to the Charter's enactment in 1982. In the first, *Lavell* v. *A.-G. Can.*,[53] section 12(1)(b) of the Indian Act has provided that a woman married to a non-Indian is not entitled to be registered as an Indian. The registrar has struck Mrs Lavell's name from the Indian register on the grounds that, having married a non-Indian, she is not entitled to be registered as an Indian. The Federal Court of Appeal has held that section 12(1)(b) contravenes the 'equality before the law' provision of the Canadian Bill of Rights. The Supreme Court responds by interpreting 'equality before the law' in the narrow 'formal equality' sense expressed above. Relying upon Dicey as a source of legitimacy for the doctrine, the Supreme Court reaffirms that "the same law applies to the highest official of government as to any other ordinary citizen."[54] Ritchie understands 'equality before the law' as "equality in the *administration* or *application* of the law by the law enforcement authorities and the ordinary courts of the land."[55] Any alleged inequality in the administration or application of the law must flow "as a *necessary* result" from the statute.

The formal equality doctrine, as has been mentioned, speaks to an apolitical autonomous law. In its *Burnshine* judgment the Supreme Court refines the connection between the doctrine and the judiciary's boundary of an apolitical law.[56] Martland, speaking for the majority, simply does not allow counsel to use 'equality before the law' to undermine the givenness of a legislative rule. If 'equality before the law' incorporated universal rights theory (that is, that rights be universally shared by each and all), then the judiciary would be challenging the very content of posited legislated rules. In Martland's words, "the concept of 'equality before the law' did not [in 1960] and could not include the right of each individual to insist that no statute could be enacted which did not have application to everyone and in all areas of Canada."[57] Why not? Because, he continues, "[s]uch a right would have involved a substantial impairment of the sovereignty of Parliament in the exercise of its legislative powers under s. 91 of the *British North America Act*, and could only have been created by constitutional amendment, or by statute." Notwithstanding Parliament's direction to the courts in the text of the Bill that the posited rules are to be "so construed and applied ... as not to abrogate, abridge, or infringe ... the rights and freedoms herein," Martland insists that the Bill cannot require statute law to apply "to everyone and in all areas of Canada" "because ... by its express wording it declared and continued *existing* rights and freedoms."[58] That is, Martland deceptively adds the adjective "existing" to the text.[59]

Martland assumes that the 'sovereignty of Parliament' would be so impaired if he gave any wider interpretation to 'equality before the law.' He assumes that section 91 of the British North America Act, 1867 has posited the 'sovereignty of Parliament.' He assumes that the constitution can be modified only by constitutional amendment or statute. He assumes that rights and freedoms mean existing rights and freedoms. But why does Martland make these assumptions? Why? Because his image of a constitution, which the Canadian Bill of Rights cases trigger, cannot allow him coherently to make contrary assumptions. The image is a network of boundaries. The boundaries delimit what questions Martland considers legitimate and what questions he thinks illegitimate. Martland's particular boundaries allow judges merely to apply existing posited rules: politicians alone can posit those rules, not judges. And the boundaries project that laws, once enacted, are an apolitical, autonomous thing. The judiciary uses the 'formal equality' doctrine to transpose these boundaries into legal discourse.

(b) *The 'Reasonable Relationship' Doctrine*

Now, Canadian judges elaborate a second doctrine – called the 'reasonable relationship' doctrine – in their interpretation of 'equality before the law.' As with formal equality, this doctrine speaks to the boundary of an apolitical character to law. Being autonomous of the judge, the law dwells in an objective noumenal world of concepts. The judge's sole duty is to formulate and explain the concepts. S/he must purge herself/himself of all desire to question the wisdom of the rules or to incorporate her/his subjective feelings in interpretative analysis. Briefly, the doctrine states that a judge should only assess whether a challenged legislative enactment possesses a reasonable connection between the statute's classification and the statute's overall purpose. With some exceptions (notably, Laskin in *Lavell*),[60] Canadian judges read this doctrine into 'equality before the law' in the Canadian Bill of Rights.[61] In the process, they equate law with the posited legislative rules and they accept the purpose of a legislated rule as a 'given.' Indeed, both American and Canadian courts have made extraordinary efforts, from time to time, to hypothesize, speculate upon, or construct the purpose against which the allegedly discriminatory classification is measured.[62] Upon constructing a purpose, they self-impose the minimal duty of ensuring that one can make an *ex post facto* rationalization for the classification vis-à-vis the constructed purpose.[63] It is unnecessary to scrutinize either the purpose of the legislated rule or the availability of less onerous means to accomplish the purpose. In this manner, judges assure themselves that their analytic process remains purified of any subjective or political content. That is, they can assure themselves that law is composed of legislated rules, that the rules possess an apolitical character, and that their application remains true to an autonomous *a priori* world of abstract concepts.

A close look at two important judgments in the Bill's demise reflects the above. For example, at the beginning and end of his reasons for judgment in *Burnshine*,[64] Martland appears to hold that the alleged discriminatory classification of persons under twenty-two years in British Columbia is reasonably related to the purpose of section 150. The statutory purpose, according to Martland, is "the reform and training of young offenders."[65] The classification is reasonably related to that purpose because British Columbia is "equipped with the necessary institutions and staff for that purpose."[66]

Martland does not even require that the classification have "some reasonable basis." He places the onus upon Burnshine to establish "compelling reasons" why the classification is unrelated to the purpose.[67] Additionally, Martland ascertains the legislative purpose of section 150 simply by quoting from earlier judgments. If he were to employ the various techniques of statutory interpretation and if he were to consider section 150 in its complete internal and external context, he might very well come to a different conclusion as to the enactment's purpose. Indeed, by defining the statutory purpose as the reform of young offenders, Martland in effect disposes of the question of whether or not the classification is reasonably related to the statutory purpose, for the classification collapses into the purpose. Finally, because his construct of the legislative purpose conditions the reasonableness of the classification, the 'reasonable classification' doctrine becomes simply tautological. The moral/political content of a statutory rule remains untouched. The challenged legislative rule creates and conditions the very possibility of 'equality before the law.' It could not have been otherwise. The boundaries of a judiciary's passive self-image and of an apolitical, autonomous law remain entrenched.

Similarly, in *Bliss* v. *A.-G. Can.* sections 46 and 30 of the Unemployment Insurance Act entitle a woman to benefits if she has had ten weeks of insurable employment in the twenty weeks that immediately precede confinement due to pregnancy.[68] Bliss interrupts her employment four days before the birth of her child. Although she has not fulfilled the ten-week employment requirement, she would have been entitled to the regular benefits enjoyed by all non-pregnant persons had she not been pregnant. Ritchie holds that this does not constitute discrimination by reason of sex resulting in the denial of 'equality before the law.' Why not? Because Ritchie accepts the legislative scheme as a 'given.' The treatment of Mrs Bliss constitutes "a relevant distinction" – relevant, that is, to the purpose of the posited rule.[69] "Whatever may be thought of the wisdom" of the content of the rule, Ritchie asserts, he places the onus upon Mrs Bliss to advance "compelling reasons" why the distinction of pregnancy is "clearly irrelevant."[70] In the process, Ritchie remains true to his passive self-image and an apolitical, autonomous law.

3. A VERTICAL HIERARCHY OF POSITED RULES

The 'reasons for judgment' in the demise of the Canadian Bill of Rights express a third prejudgment: namely, that one finds the law of 'the Constitution' in the rules of the British North America Act, 1867. One can "perceive" the rules in the text. One can even "touch" the rules – or, at least, touch the text where one discovers the rules. In the case of the British North America Act, judges find themselves looking mainly at two sets of rules in sections 91 and 92. These rules, the judges believe, entrench what they take to be the super-rule of the 'supremacy of Parliament.' The latter super-rule, in turn, reinforces a subservient, passive, apolitical judge who applies apolitical rules of law. Rules constitute the sole resource material of a constitution. And the rules lie in a vertical hierarchy of legitimacy with the British North America Acts, at the top.

Judges express this rule-oriented picture of a constitution's content, in the first place, in the very peculiar manner in which they apply the 'reasonable relationship' doctrine. Instead of inquiring into the relationship between the means and purpose of a statutory rule, they merely ask whether the statutory rule is posited ("is authorized") by the appropriate section of the British North America Act, 1867.[71] For example, Pigeon believes that the alleged discrimination in *Drybones* is coloured by the fact that section 91(24) of the British North America Act, 1867 enables Parliament to make legislation applicable only to Indians.[72] In addition, although Parliament used terms which are "in truth largely unlimited and undefined," the British North America Act, 1867 grants Canada "the traditional British system that is our own." And with that system, "the responsibility for updating the statutes in this changing world rests exclusively upon Parliament."[73]

Similarly, Ritchie's majority judgment in *Lavell* begins with the claim that the Bill "is not effective to amend or in any way alter the terms of the *British North America Act.*"[74] He explains this point in the very terms of a vertical hierarchy of rules.[75] The British North America Act, 1867, we are told, is "the Constitution." The British North America Act, 1867 posits "Parliament's constitutional function." So long as Parliament posits a rule within the scope of section 91, Parliament's constitutional function remains unlimited —notwithstanding the Canadian Bill of Rights to the contrary. Martland, too, accepts his hierarchical image of rules in *Burnshine* when he insists that in enacting section 150 of the Prisons and Reformatories Act Parliament has been "seeking to achieve *a valid federal objective.*"[76] What makes a statutory objective "valid"? The higher ordered rules in section 91 of the British North America Act, 1867.

Whereas Beetz positions the Canadian Bill of Rights in an intermediate status between statutory rules and the rules in the British North America Act in *A.-G. Can.* v. *Canard,*[77] Ritchie, Martland, and others locate the Bill at the bottom rung of the hierarchy of rules. Beetz describes the British North America Act as "the fundamental law of the land" in contrast to the "quasi-constitutional" character of the Canadian Bill of Rights.[78] Ritchie, in contrast, narrows the hierarchy of posited rules in *Canard* to the point of making the Canadian Bill of Rights redundant.[79] Ritchie reinforces this vertical hierarchy of rules in *Bliss* v. *A.-G. Can.* by adding that the British North America Acts posit along a horizontal spectrum a set of 'subject-matters' under which all social conduct —including inequality between the sexes – is subsumed.[80] In *MacKay* v. *The Queen*, Ritchie again reorders the vertical hierarchy of posited rules so as to place the Canadian Bill of Rights rules below posited statutory rules.[81] He informs us that "[t]here can be no doubt that the *National Defence Act* is enacted by Parliament 'constitutionally competent to do so and exercising its powers in accordance with the tenets of responsible government'."[82] From this premise Ritchie concludes that "no effort was made *or indeed could have been made* to demonstrate that Parliament was not seeking to achieve a valid federal objective."[83] Ritchie's reasoning is sound. No effort could be made to use the Bill so as to challenge the "validity" of a federal objective. His picture of a horizontal/vertical spectrum of posited rules prevents that. By granting a low status to the Canadian Bill of Rights on the vertical hierarchy of rules, Ritchie reinforces the boundary of a judiciary's passive self-image with an apolitical law. Being so low on the vertical hierarchy, it is difficult to contemplate any circumstances when a judge could use the Bill's rights to supersede statutory rules. Ritchie's horizons of a constitution render the Canadian Bill of Rights redundant.

4. CONCLUSION

Canadian jurists have for too long focused their diagnosis of the Canadian Bill of Rights experience upon the shortcomings of the text's actual wording or upon the statutory – as opposed to the constitutional – status of the text. I have aimed to demonstrate that an explanation for the demise of the Canadian Bill of Rights during the 1960s and 1970s must go to the shared rationalistic image of a constitution which Supreme Court judges presupposed in their judgments. In the past, lawyers have understood judgments in terms of the ratiocination process. In contrast, I have shown that the Canadian Bill of Rights claims presented mere surface issues which, in turn, triggered a searching examination of the boundaries of 'what constitutes a constitution?' This chapter has made explicit the hitherto implicit boundaries of a constitution. The boundaries lay embedded within the judiciary's consciousness – not a text. The judiciary responded to the text in a manner which rendered coherent their rationalistic image of a constitution.

Supreme Court justices identified three boundaries to their shared image of a constitution in their Canadian Bill of Rights judgments. First, they shared an institutional self-image which projected the judiciary as passive appliers of posited statutory rules. The judges superimposed that self-image upon the Canadian Bill of Rights. Parliament being the sole source of policy, judges could naturally presume that Parliament should consciously and explicitly alter policy only through "special legislation" rather than through some vaguely worded statute such as the Canadian Bill of Rights. Secondly, by virtue of their passive self-image, judges characterized their enterprise as apolitical. That projected apolitical character permeated their 'formal equality' and 'reasonable relationship' doctrines. Thirdly, the apolitical and passive self-image of judges joined with a vertical hierarchy of all-encompassing, encyclopaedic rules to form a fairly coherent image of a constitution.

As Ritchie demonstrated in *MacKay*, these three constituents of an image of a constitution combined to render the text of the Canadian Bill of Rights redundant. Judges denied to themselves any role of placing policy content into the terms of the Bill. They created doctrines which reaffirmed the court's apolitical role. And their constitution, they believed, was exclusively composed of rules posited in a higher ordered text. In the process of expounding their image of a constitution, Canadian judges delegitimized the role and effectiveness of the Canadian Bill of Rights. Their image of a constitution could not absorb or incorporate the Bill. Much like an old body with a newly transplanted heart, their image rejected the Bill as a foreign, unassimilable object.

VI

Lower Court Images of a
Charter of Rights

In our reading of traditional 'subject-matters' of Canadian constitutional discourse, we have experienced that what some judges take to be an objective law collapses into an expression of deeply ingrained images or prisms through which the lawyer projects that objectivity. The law of the Canadian constitution is not 'discovered' in texts such as the Constitution Acts, 1867–present, the Canadian Bill of Rights, or 'Reasons for judgment.' Nor is law found in the traditional discrete 'subject-matters' which encyclopaedic digests, treatises, learned articles, and teaching materials identify as 'the law.' Texts and 'subject-matters' are presumed to exist 'out there,' independently of the lawyer in an objective world. This essay did begin with these supposed 'objective' sources. But we soon experienced that much hangs upon the lawyer/judge's legal conscious- ness: that is, what does the lawyer/judge prejudge as socially legitimate and epistemologically valid knowledge? We uncovered that the lawyer/ judge shares different pre-understandings of 'what constitutes a constitu- tion?' Those pre-understandings, in turn, filter out how the lawyer/judge interprets a text, what role s/he gives to the text, history, or theory, who has standing to press a constitutional claim, what constitutes relevant evidence, what role a lawyer or judge should play vis-à-vis other institutions, and other issues. The responses to these questions constitute boundaries or signposts beyond which the lawyer/judge should not delve. An image of a constitution pre-censors the manner in which one interprets a text, reads a judicial decision, writes an article, teaches a course, or even identifies a relevant issue. A lawyer's challenge on behalf of his or her client merely ignites the felt need for an opposing counsel, judge, or pedagogue to articulate the boundaries of his or her own image of a constitution. We find judges defending the boundaries, incorporating a challenge within them, modifying their boundaries, or, very rarely, rejecting existing boundaries entirely for another set. 'Reasons for judgment' express a particular judge's image of a constitution. Objective law collapses into the expression of competing images of 'what constitutes law.'

Now, the legal community does not always share the same image of a constitution. Indeed, one describes certain constitutional cases in British and Canadian history as classic precisely because at least two sets of boundaries clash in every fundamental way. Such occurs in *Patriation Reference*.[1] More often, judges and scholars leave their images of a constitution unarticulated and presupposed in their written expression because all or most members of the legal community to whom they write share the image.

This chapter aims to show that Charter of Rights judgments similarly express identifiable boundaries of identifiable images of a constitution. At the provincial, county, divisional, high court, and first appellate court levels, the images are generally left unsaid. Judges identify a Charter section being used by counsel, summarize counsels' arguments, then quote one or two passages from a colleague, and, finally, conclude with an "I think that the sections means," "I feel that," "I am of the opinion that," or "I believe that," without argument or analysis. The general thesis of this essay would appear fallacious in this context, for one is hard-pressed to find any articulated image of a constitution, let alone place the Charter within that image, when a judge merely asserts his or her conclusions. One has even greater difficulty to explain the judgments in terms of some inarticulated deeply felt image of a Charter.

And yet, that is precisely what I intend to demonstrate. I shall argue that the above seemingly vacuous response to Charter claims expresses and presupposes a particular image of a constitution which I identify as rule rationalism. A judge finds it unnecessary to articulate a defence of the image because s/he and her/his interpretative community accepts the boundaries without question. But, with the Charter of Rights as a new textual resource, lawyers and judges begin to reconsider their role, a constitution's resource material, a constitution's character, the objectivity of meaning, and other critical themes which one finds earlier in this essay. I wish to show that, in the process, clearly identifiable boundaries of rationalist images of the Charter of Rights emerge during the first five years of the Charter's history. In Chapter VII I shall demonstrate how two Supreme Court judges strain to break from the rationalist hold.

1. RULE RATIONALISM

When one slowly digests the volumes of judgments interpreting the Charter of Rights during its first five years, one is struck by the extraordinary desire on the part of lower court judges to understand the Charter rationally as an entity which can rationally cause or move social behaviour. These judges believe that all law does and ought to have a rational basis. Posited rules constitute the whole of the law. The posited rules flow vertically from given horizontal clusters of subject-matters. Rational technique discovers and deduces the rules. A judge's role is to apply the rules to any given circumstance, bearing in mind the complete horizontal/vertical picture. Rigid adherence to rational rechnique cleanses the judicial process from any political or evaluative taint. The latter's absence ensures that the judge conduct himself or herself as an impartial scientist. Legal knowledge in the form of posited rules exists in an objective world, independent of the actors in the legal process. What we find is that the lower court judges intriguingly project this rationalist enterprise out of a deep fear of rational disorder.

(a) *The Fear of Rational Disorder*

The fear of rational disorder is reflected in an often quoted passage of Ontario High Court judge Eberle shortly after the Charter's enactment. Eberle comments in *Re R. and Potma* that it might take years before higher court judges have elucidated the complete and correct meaning of the Charter. "As is all too common," he complains, "Parliament had said virtually nothing" as to whether the Charter is retrospective or retroactive. Nevertheless, the law always exists to fill the void: "I think it is fair to say that the Charter of Rights was not passed in a vacuum,' he exclaims. He continues, "We have in this country a long established legal system, both as to the principles of law and the physical framework of courts to deal with them, and it must be taken that Parliament was aware of the basic principles of law existing and applied in this country."[2] According to a "basic" principle of statutory interpretation, the legal community presumes that "substantive" (as opposed to "procedural" or "adjectival") legislative changes simply cannot be retroactive, according to Eberle. Eberle then proceeds to the text of sections 7 and 11(d). "Looking at them, as I have many times ... I am unable *to find* any *express* words" directing a judge to consider the Charter retrospective. The Charter's text, he insists, "appear[s] *to me* to adopt and restate what has been the law of Canada for generations."[3] That is, Eberle admits that it is *his* image of the text's words and of the past law that counts. After further discussion of the past law and the *Charter's* words he reminds himself and the reader of his background concern of rational disorder:

I have said earlier that the Charter was not passed in *a vacuum*. This country has a well developed and long established system of laws, including many presumptions in favour of an accused person. We have a whole body of legal principles and concepts, substantive and adjectival, together with a system of tribunals to apply that whole complex of laws to the cases that arise from day to day. *It cannot be thought that the intent of the provisions of the Charter that are in issue in this case, is to undermine and bring to the ground the whole framework of laws and the legal system of the country at the stroke of a pen, even if it be a royal pen. I can see nothing* in the provisions of the Charter relied on in this case to suggest that they are intended to alter the principles on which courts have acted traditionally in relation to the *subject-matter* of this case ...[4]

This belief that "it cannot be thought" that the intent of the Charter's text is "to undermine and to bring to the ground the whole framework of laws and the legal system" motivates an Ontario provincial court judge, Lewis, to admit proof of a prior criminal record in an accused's trial.[5] Other judges, too, share Eberle's fear of a rational vacuum of posited rules.[6] If there were a hiatus in the legal order, from what determinate source could judges rationally deduce new sub-rules? There just *must* be prior posited rules to being rational analysis. As the Ontario Court of Appeal unanimously expresses in *Re Federal Republic of Germany and Rauca*, "the Charter was not enacted in a *vacuum* and the rights set out therein *must* be interpreted *rationally* having regard to *the then existing laws* ...[7] Without pre-existing background rules, a judge who presupposes a rationalist image of the Charter (and law) simply cannot cope. Therein lies the source of a judiciary's anxiety.

Aside from relying upon the fear of disorder where the Charter's words have not expressly posited a rule or where the text uses a word with a vague, open-ended meaning, many judges simply project their fear into the overall intent of the Charter's framers. They do so by approvingly supporting well-known *dicta* of Zuber in multiple circumstances. In *R. v. Altseimer*, Zuber can "find nothing in the Charter of Rights and Freedoms which affects this case," where the accused has argued that breathalyser tests violate one's right against self-incrimination as guaranteed in sections 11(c) and 13 of the Charter.[8] The key to Zuber's failure "to find" anything in the Charter's text is his concluding paragraph:

In view of the number of cases in Ontario trial courts in which Charter provisions are being argued, and especially in view of some of the bizarre and colourful arguments being advanced, it may be appropriate to observe that *the Charter does not intend a transformation of our legal system or the paralysis of law enforcement.* Extravagant interpretations can only trivialize and diminish respect for the Charter which is a part of the supreme law of this country.[9]

In judgment after judgment Canadian judges expressly adopt Zuber's *dicta* as expressing their own feelings about the Charter's "intent."[10]

At times, judges equate rational disorder with civil disorder. In *R. v. Newall et al.* a B.C. Supreme Court judge considers a legislated fixed minimum sentence, for example.[11] Because the sentence attaches to the crime of importing any mind-altering drug and "*[n]o country can survive* if there is widespread use of mind-altering drugs," the fixed sentence constitutes a "reasonable limit demonstrably justifiable in a free and democratic society."[12] Similarly, where the legislature has imposed compulsory arbitration for labour disputes involving public servants, the Alberta Court of Appeal excludes the freedom to *act* from the freedom of association, for to add the freedom to act to the freedom to form an association would cause a "remarkable effect in our present society." "The argument leads to the conclusion, for example," the Court speculates, "that a lynch mob has a prima facie right to act!" The Court then extends the civil disorder ramification so as to undermine all laws: "Indeed, all laws regulating group activity – from those dealing with family life to those dealing with local government – would be required to pass muster under s. 1. One is hard put to think of a piece of major legislation in this century which would not be suspect, including of course the very laws which give the opposing intervenants legal vitality."[13]

The nexus between rational disorder and civil disorder underlies the judgments in *R. v. Hayden* of three Manitoba Court of Appeal judges who were faced with the question as to whether section 7 of the Charter encompasses substantive as well as procedural justice.[14] "*My* reading leads *me* to the conclusion," Hall states, that section 7 does not go beyond fair procedure. *His* reading leads him to fear the rational disorder brought on by a substantive justice interpretation: "To hold otherwise *would require all legislative enactments* creating offences to be submitted to the test of whether they offend the principles of fundamental justice."[15] Hall admits in the next two sentences that this constitutes "judicial policy," "an *acceptable* area for judicial reviews," and, at the same time, "in my view."

One final example of the judiciary's extension of rational disorder to civil disorder occurs in *Reynolds* v. *A.G.B.C.* where the Canada Elections Act proscribed Reynolds, as a parolee, from being a candidate in an election. Craig of the British Columbia Court of Appeal, dissenting, holds that society is "entitled to suspend the voting right of a person who has breached certain laws of society." The Charter, he explains, deals with rights without specifically mentioning a citizen's obligations. "*Obviously*, however, its *premise*" is that if one has a right he also has an obligation. "A citizen *must* obey the law," he insists.[16] Why must one always obey the law? Because. Nemetz just does not answer this question because he does not ask it. It is just "obviously."

(b) *Law as Posited Rules*

Posited rules fill the vacuum which a text, such as the Charter, otherwise creates. Judges usher forth posited rules from the pre-Charter era. Absent the previously posited rules, there would be a hiatus and the Charter, by filling the vacuum, would constitute a genuinely revolutionary document. Posited rules do more than provide a background to the Charter. They give meaning to the Charter's text and they answer the question 'what is law?'

The lower court judges openly face the question 'what is law?' during the first five years of the Charter experience when they interpret the phrase 'by law' in section 1 of the Charter. LeDain speaks for many of the Supreme Court judges, no doubt, when he states that "by law" means that a limit to a right must be "expressly provided for *by statute* or *regulation*, or results *by necessary implication* from the terms of a statute or regulation or from its operating requirements. The limit may also result from the application of a *common law rule*."[17] The Ontario Divisional Court affirms this positivistic conception of law in *Re Ont. Film and Video Appreciation Society and Ont. Bd. of Censors* when it unanimously holds that "law cannot be vague, undefined, and totally discretionary; it must be ascertainable and understandable." Statutory law, regulations, and common law rules constitute law. "But the limit, to be acceptable, must have legal force." To have "legal force," the rule must be "established" by the legislature or the courts. The latter must occur "through the operation of precedent over the years."[18] The federal court draws upon the same conception when it insists that in order to constitute a law, one must be able to see it in written form. Written rules define their own content. In *Luscher* v. *Dep. M.N.R. (Customs and Excise)* Hugesson of the Federal Court of Appeal observes that the words "immoral" and "indecent" are "nowhere defined in the legislation." The words in the written form are insufficiently certain and particular to be seen, to be identified.[19] And unless one can rationally identify the content of a rule, one cannot vertically ratiocinate further sub-rules from the parent rule at issue.

Many judges picture law through this rationalistic lens during our time period under study. Law is a written law. After citing counsel's arguments, the judge reads a section of the Charter as if the Charter imposed a set of rules and as if meaning emanated inherently from those rules. The text of the Charter lives 'out there,' independent of judge and politician.[20] After "restating" the rule in his own words, the judge invariably cites *dicta* from a colleague who has expressed a fear of rational disorder. Thereupon, the judges render their conclusions prefaced with 'in my opinion,' 'obviously,' or 'of course.' Against the fear of rational disorder, meaning inheres in the text.

The judgment of Essen of the British Columbia Court of Appeal in *Dolphin Delivery Ltd.* v. *R.W.D.S.U., Loc. 580* exemplifies this format.[21] After identifying the issue (the right to picket guaranteed in the Charter?), the facts and the arguments of the plaintiff and defendant, Essen quickly responds to the issue after restating it: "[i]n my view, it is not, for the simple reason that the activity described as picketing is not within any known meaning of the word 'association'."[22] The Charter guarantees the freedom of the individual to unite, combine, or enter into a union or association with a common purpose. But "it does not follow," Essen reasons, that the Charter guarantees the purposes of the union or the means by which the union can achieve its purposes. The Charter only removes the power of Parliament or a legislature to limit or abolish the freedom of association (except via section 1). "But it [freedom of association] does not affect laws which limit or control picketing."[23] Why not? Essen does not tell the reader. For Essen, as for so many other judges, the meaning exists inherently in the rule. When confronted with cases suggesting that the right of association includes the right to organize trade unions, to bargain collectively, and to strike, the latter do not "touch upon the right to picket," according to Essen. Further, neither the right to bargain collectively nor the right to strike can be brought "*within the ordinary meaning* of association." The precedents do not consider "*the ordinary meaning* of 'association'." To extend the word 'association' to its purposes and the means of obtaining its purposes simply "*cannot be right*" because some associations have purposes or means of achieving them which the Charter's framers "cannot have intended to protect." "The basic fallacy in the approach" is that judges believe themselves empowered "to construct edifices of policy without regard for the plain meaning of the words of the Charter."[24] Indeed, Essen acknowledges that "that cardinal principle" is "equally applicable to a written constitution" as to a statutory rule. This is so even when international law contradicts the "plain meaning" of the posited rule. Essen assures himself that the "plain meaning" of freedom of association in combination with the individual right to vote in section 3 and the section 4 requirement of elections within five years constitute "a potent combination" with which "any government" must reckon.[25]

Further, posited rules sometimes determine the meaning of the Charter's text. One of the text's great question-begging terms is "a free and democratic society" in section 1. Canadian judges often look to other societies to discover the meaning of the term without asking what makes these societies free and democratic. But even when the Ontario Court of Appeal cites the norms in other jurisdictions for the first time in *Re Southam Inc. and the Queen (No. 1)*, Chief Justice MacKinnon claims that, ultimately, the meaning of freedom and democracy is discoverable within existing posited rules in Canada.[26] As he explains, "In any event I believe the court must come back, ultimately, having derived whatever assistance can be secured from the experience of other free and democratic societies, *to the facts of our own free and democratic* society to answer the question ..."[27] Indeed, it is not unknown for a lower court judge during the period under study to understand "free and democratic society" "by definition."[28] In case after case lower court judges presume that the meaning of freedom and democracy objectively inheres within previously posited rules.

Finally, it is a short jump for some judges to declare posited law as effectively supreme over the Charter, much as they held posited law to operate notwithstanding the Canadian Bill of Rights.[29] Ontario High Court judge Evans explains in *Federal Republic of Germany* v. *Rauca*, for example, that "a procedure which has been accepted in our country for over a century and in most other democratic societies" *must* be considered reasonable under section 1. If a posited criminal rule has as its objective "the protection and preservation of society from serious criminal activity," the latter rule should prevail over a Charter claim.[30] An Alberta Queen's Bench judge similarly presupposes the paramountcy of posited rules over Charter claims when he understands "just" in section 24(1) in this manner: "while furthering the object of the right guaranteed by the Charter that has been infringed, nevertheless [a just remedy] does that, as far as possible, in a way that does not offend the reasonable expectations of the community for *the enforcement of the criminal law*, an interest which is evoked by one meaning of '*the rule of the law*' that the preamble to the Charter asserts is one of the founding principles of Canada."[31] In *Broadway Manor Nursing Home* Smith goes so far as to extend the Charter's subservience to the rules of the economy: "the Charter must surely yield in a general way to the management of the economy by the body politic, as it must yield to national security and to the control of criminal activity."[32] And Zuber appeals to the rational stability of pre-Charter rules when he cautions that "[g]ranted that the Charter has changed the law but it has not, overnight, transformed the healthy repute of the administration of justice into a fragile flower ready to wilt because of the admission of evidence obtained as a result of a violation of the Charter rights of an accused."[33]

(c) *Objective Meaning*

These judges express more than that posited rules can support a sense of rational order. In addition, meaning inheres objectively within the words of a rule itself. Words which lend themselves to "subjective" interpretation are vague, ambiguous, and, therefore, unconstitutional.[34] Essen assumes in *Dolphin Delivery*, for example, that the meaning of the word 'association' inheres in that word.[35] In like vein, Collings shudders in *R*. v. *G.* that to impute an ideal-directed character to the words "free and democratic society" would be "unworkably subjective."[36] In contrast, "the general practice of civilised nations" can be discovered "by objective inquiry." Such a practice is "rationally appealing" and offers "an objective standard."[37] Similarly, a rational objectivity permeates the construction of "reasonable limits" in section 1 of the Charter. In *Shewchuk* v. *Ricard*, for example, Auxier insists that the phrase "reasonable limits" "imports an objective test of validity."[38] A personal censure of a legislative limitation of a right is, of course, illegitimate. Rather, the key is the "rational basis" of the limitation. Evidence of the latter lies "within the bounds of reason by fair-minded [*sic*] people accustomed to the norms of a free and democratic society."

By way of a more considered example, one might look to Seaton's dissenting judgment in *P.P.G. Industs. Can. Ltd.* v. *A.-G. Can.*[39] At issue is whether a corporation is guaranteed a trial by jury pursuant to section 11(f) of the Charter. Section 11(f) applies to "any person." The majority of the British Columbia Court of Appeal expresses that the context requires that 'person' mean natural person. Seaton, dissenting, believes that the word 'person' cannot have "a shifting meaning." The "plain meaning" of section 11 gives a corporation a trial by jury. He then explains: "Where the language of the Charter is straightforward, there is no need for presumptions or for aids to interpretation. Such aids might lead the courts to interpret the Charter so as to give only those rights that the court thinks ought to be given. The Charter is entitled to greater respect than that. In this new field we are followers, the Charter is the leader, and we must give effect to its plain meaning. There is no need for judicial tampering. If the plain meaning of a provision gives a wholly unacceptable result, then s. 1 of the Charter provides the remedy."[40] Consistent with this textualist perspective, Seaton rejects as "unhelpful" extrinsic evidence of parliamentary debates on the Charter as well as an historical review of the right guaranteed. He concludes this portion of his judgment by approving Zuber's *dicta* that "the Charter does not intend a transformation of our legal system, or the paralysis of law enforcement."[41]

Although Seaton conditions his textualism to Charter sections "where the language of the *Charter* is straightforward," judges who share the rule rationalist image of the Charter believe that the Charter's words are invariably quite simple. In *R. v. Nelson*, Scollin of the Manitoba Queen's Bench explains, for example, that an accused "whose mental condition should at least have raised a query" should be offered a "real opportunity" to retain counsel.[42] "Real opportunity is what is meant by the provision of the Charter ... *the form of words* in the Charter *is not complicated* and should be followed unless the exigencies of the situation render that course impractical ..."[43] Ruttan of the Yukon Territory Supreme Court understands the word "punishment" in section 11(h) of the Charter in equally simple equivalents: "the plain and ordinary meaning of the word 'punishment' should not be enlarged in s. 11(h) of the Charter, because *that would transform and change our legal system* and remove the ability to use the suspended sentence as a sentencing option entirely. It would really destroy the whole probation pattern."[44]

The objectivist prism through which rationalist judges understand meaning does not stop them, strangely, from ignoring words in the text. For example, the chief justice of the British Columbia Supreme Court finds it unnecessary to consider the word "fundamental" in section 7 because "in my view, 'fundamental' in this context is an unnecessary adjective because fundamental justice is justice and fairness, nothing more and nothing less."[45] However, on the other hand, objectivism prevents the *Dolphon Delivery* judges from adding or imputing meaning to the text's words.[46] In that case counsel wanted the judges to impute a right to picket into the meaning of "freedom of association." Similarly, at least one judge believes himself compelled not to read a 'right of access' into 'freedom of expression.'[47] Judge Dea of the Alberta Queen's Bench expresses his objectivist compulsion in this manner: "*In view of the wording* of the Charter a finding of a right of access incorporated into the guaranteed freedom of expression by necessary implication, *would be tantamount to writing into the Charter* what parliament chose to leave out."[48]

The objectivity of meaning induces judges to be cautious in altering the inherent meaning intended by the legislature. This caution emulates from Judge Dea's *dicta* above. One can also find this caution in the Ontario Divisional Court judgment of *Service Employees' International Union, Local 204* v. *Broadway Manor Nursing Home et al.*[49] Counsel argued there that 'freedom of association' included the right to organize, to bargain, and to strike. Galligan reacts that "[t]he Charter is *very precise* ... It enumerates the guaranteed freedoms in s. 2, and specifically confers guaranteed rights in other sections."[50] Galligan believes that one cannot equate the meaning of the word 'freedom' with that of the word 'right.' Galligan continues, "It is my opinion that while still in the early days of interpreting as important a document as the Constitution of our country, the courts should be *cautious* indeed before interpreting the document any way but in accordance with the *ordinary meaning* of the words chosen. And they should be *cautious* before using words which may have *fundamentally different meanings* interchangeably."[51] Galligan confidently proceeds to define the words 'right' and 'freedom' (the words "*fundamentally seem[ed]* to mean").[52] The Charter has not "explicitly or implicitly" set out a right to choose one's union, to bargain, or to strike. "The *Charter* only guarantees those rights and freedoms set out in it," Galligan reminds himself.[53]

(d) *Objectivist Tests to Discover Meaning*

The inherent objective meaning of a right does not always spring from the words of the text. Judges do not invariably "see" the meaning posited in the text. Consequently, they design objectivist tests to discover the inherent meaning.

One such test is for the judge to cite the meaning granted by some previous Canadian judge.[54] Absent some Canadian declaration, our lower court judges deferentially adopt the meaning which American (and sometimes U.K., Australian, and New Zealand) judges posit. As the Ontario Court of Appeal describes the test in *Re Southam Inc. and the Queen*

(No. 1): "[t]he wording [in section 1] imposes a positive obligation on those seeking to uphold the limit or limits to establish to the satisfaction of the court by evidence, by the terms and purpose of the limiting law, its economic, social and political background, and, *if felt helpful, by references to comparable legislation of other acknowledged free and democratic societies*, that such limit or limits are reasonable and demonstrably justified in a free and democratic society."[55] No Canadian judge, during the five-year period under study, identified the factors, let alone political theory, which should ground a "free and democratic" society.[56] Nor does any judge explain why one may legitimately borrow themes from some free and democratic societies (usually the United Kingdom, Australia, New Zealand, and the United States) and not others (such as France, Germany, Sweden, Switzerland, or some Third World societies such as India). Perhaps, the rationalist prism through which these judges prejudge 'what is a constitution' forecloses these questions. Because the meaning of a "free and democratic society" – or any word – exists in an objective world independently of the interpreter, the discovery of posited meanings in other societies reinforces the pre-understood objectivity of law. The more often cited, the more certain is the judge that a declared meaning coincides with the objective meaning.

Citing the declarations of one's Canadian and American peers consti-tutes two objectivist tests to discover the text's meaning. A third test is for lower court judges to project that meaning which a "reasonable" or "fair-minded" member of the public would give to the text. In *P.P.G. Industs. Can. Ltd.* v. *A.G. Can.*, for example, the British Columbia Court of Appeal rejects a "technical" or literalist approach to discover the Charter's meaning. In its place the judges offer this test: "[i]n my view, wherever possible, we should, instead, take the approach which would be taken *by a reasonable member of the public* when discussing the rights afforded to him by the Charter."[57] The key is the assumption that a "reasonable member of the public" would give a rational objective to the meaning. As an Ontario High Court judge put it in *Federal Republic of Germany* v. *Rauca*, the meaning of "reasonable limits" in section 1 is "not whether the judge agrees with the limitation [personally] but whether he considers that there is *a rational basis for it* – a basis that would be regarded as being *within the bounds of reason by fair-minded people accustomed to the norms of a free and democratic society*. That is *the crucible* in which the concept of reasonableness must be tested."[58] Scollin distinguishes "the practical and fair-minded member of the community at large" from "idealists or jurists at large" in *R. v. Nelson*.[59] Rationality and objectivism permeate the test.[60]

On occasion, judges adopt an even more general test in order to discover the inherent objective meaning of a word. In *R. v. Collins*, for example, the judges had to decide whether the admission of evidence resulting from a Charter violation would "bring the administration of justice into disrepute."[61] Seaton responds in this way: "Disrepute in whose eyes? That which would bring the administration of justice into disrepute in the eyes of a *policeman* might be the precise action that would be highly regarded in the eyes of a law teacher. I do not think that we are to look at this matter through the eyes of a policeman *or a law teacher, or a judge for that matter*. I think that it is *the community at large, including the policeman and the law teacher and the judge*, through whose eyes we are to see this question."[62] Seaton emphasizes that this does not invite judges to appeal to "public clamour or opinion polls." Rather, "the views of the *community at large*, developed by *concerned and thinking citizens* ought to guide the courts ..." Some judges find this exceedingly non-empirical, abstract test very easy to apply.[63]

(e) *The Court's Institutional Self-Image*

The fear of rational disorder, the totality of posited rules, the objectivity of meaning, and the construction of objectivist tests to discover meaning all share a common theme: judges must passively, impartially, and neutrally apply the rules posited by the legislature. Chief Justice Deschênes of the Quebec superior court expresses the theme when he writes that "[t]he courts must not yield to the temptation of too readily substituting their opinion for that of the Legislature."[64] In the judgment from which this *dicta* is quoted, Deschênes considers the empirical justification for the Quebec legislature's objective to francize education. He believes that Quebec's Bill 101 is disproportionate to the objective pursued and exceeds "unnecessarily the limits of what is reasonable." Deschênes and his colleagues have "difficulty understanding" why Quebec has refused to accept a political position giving rise to the litigation even though Quebec recently took that very position a few months earlier. Having said all this, Deschênes insists that he is not evaluating the political content of Quebec's legislation: "The court's decision is made quite independently of the results which might ensue: the latter belong to the realm of politics. The court's task is to interpret and apply the law while respecting the provisions of the Constitution."[65] We have already noted how most lower court judges project as a boundary of legal knowledge a totality of rules, whether the rules be posited in the Charter or in statutory form.[66] Accordingly, when Parliament or a legislature posits a specific rule dealing with an issue before a judge, arguments designed to override the rule are "not supported by the Charter."[67]

Judges sometimes explain this deferential self-image, on the one hand, in terms of the openness of the political process and the contrasting 'closed' life appointments of the judiciary. In *Broadway Manor Nursing Home*, for example, after equating democracy with majority rule, Galligan understands his self-image in terms of a democratic political process: "*I remind myself* that in a democracy ultimate responsibility rests with the elected representatives. It does not rest with the judiciary ..."[68] He denies to himself any role in scrutinizing the good motives or the rational motives of politicians who have voted for a statute.[69]

On the other hand, this student's study of lower court judgments during the Charter's first five years suggests that judges also express their deferential self-image in terms of their rationalist pre-understanding of reality. Objective meaning and objective tests contrast with subjective values, preferences, opinions, or policies. Their boundary of reality excludes policy matters as a legitimate source of law for judges. Practically speaking, judges can "interpret and apply" the Charter by appealing to the objective meaning inherent in posited rules. In contrast, elected officials alone ought to consider policy matters.[70] Conversely, the equation of objective reality with rules renders it more appropriate for a judge to authorize a search and seizure than a minister who, precisely because of his or her "public interest" considerations, is "not capable in law of constitution a neutral and impartial arbiter in weighing the interests of the individual's right to privacy against the conflicting interests of the state."[71]

Because the substantive content of legislation is thought to attain the subjective values and preferences of the legislators (that is, the policy of the legislation), it follows that judges should interpret Charter provisions in a manner which deters them from evaluating the substantive content of legislation. This underlies a series of judgments which restrict the term "fundamental justice" in section 7 to an evaluation of the fairness of the procedures by which government officials apply the rules. Strayer of the Federal Court, Trial Division, explains his proceduralist interpretation of section 7 in this way: "[i]ndeed, to give them a substantive content would be to assume that those legislative bodies and governments which adopted the Charter were prepared to commit to initial determination by the courts issues such as the propriety of abortion or capital punishment or the proper length of prison sentences. This flies in the face of history."[72]

The historically dominant image of reality excludes values and policies as a legitimate resource material for judges.

(f) *The Rationalist Technique*

The crucible of the above five themes is their rationalistic technique and intent. First, the anxiety which the Charter triggers is not a fear of civil violence and unrest, although we have noted how some judges project such a possibility. It is a fear of *rational* disorder. Without rules, there would be "a vacuum." And *that* would leave the legal community with no given starting-points with which to work. Should the Charter trigger a new meaning for old words, again there would ensue rational disorder, uncertainty, indeterminacy, and insecurity.

Secondly, a totality of posited rules constitutes the subject-matter of constitutional law. The Charter is understood to have posited rules, not open-ended principles, existing societal values, or vague ideal-directed aspirations. Judges analyse Charter claims through a rules prism. Existing posited rules give meaning to the Charter's words. And posited rules are sometimes held to prevail even over the Charter's rules themselves. The rules are the starting-point for legal analysis and, without them, the judge simply cannot understand the law to be rational.

Thirdly, the content of the rules exists independently of the judge. Meaning inheres in a word. One can work with words as if they are cubes or mathematical formulae. One can 'reason' with them objectively as if the reasoning process were a scientific enterprise.

Fourth, when faced with a word without an obvious meaning, the judges find it necessary to design objectivist tests to discover the meaning. Sometimes they cite the meaning declared by other Canadian judges, sometimes they look to other jurisdictions, sometimes they project what meaning the "reasonable" or "fair-minded" member of the community would give, and sometimes they discover what "the community at large" understands to be the meaning of a word. At all times, the respective tests are abstract or non-empirical. This abstractness informs the rational process of discovering meaning. It seems as if one can even add and substract words because a word is equated with something, a word represents an abstract thing, a word can actually be seen on a page, unlike policy, values, or feelings.

All this requires, and is supported by, a passive judiciary. So long as judges discover meaning without imputing their subjective values, they can remain rational. So long as they can elaborate and apply objectivist tests to discover the inherent meaning of words, they can remain rational.

So long as they can begin their analyses with a written rule which is certain, clear, ascertainable, understandable, and precise, they can remain rational. All these themes support a passive judiciary vis-à-vis the institution which imposes policy. These themes also require that the judiciary remain passive. Once a judge interprets the Charter as if the text does not posit self-contained, inherently objective rules, the judge needs an alternative set of boundaries within which to understand law.

2. VALUES AS SUPPLEMENTS

Other lower court judgments during the five-year period under study offer such an alternative: they supplement rules with policies or values. These judges begin with posited rules as the major component of law. They presuppose that meaning objectively inheres from within a word. They even elaborate objectivist tests for the meaning of such terms as 'free and democratic.' And they imagine themselves as passively and apolitically applying rules. But a realism tempers their subservience to posited rules in that they come to realize that the inevitably vague, open-ended, and ideal-directed character of rules invites subjectivist values and policy matters. Accordingly, they supplement rules with values in Charter interpretation. Values underlie particular sections. The rights to life, liberty, and security of the person in section 7 are said to be grounded in the value of privacy. So too, the legal rights in sections 8 to 14. The freedoms of thought, conscience, and expression are sometimes held to presuppose the values of an open political process or human dignity. Freedom and democracy are thought to be grounded in majority rule, privacy in 'man as a social being.' And sometimes judges uncover the values embedded within the legislative or common law rule being tested. The role of the court, within this picture of Charter law, is to identify the values and impartially to balance them as if they were fruits being weighed at the market. The weightier the value, the more legitimate is the Charter right in the circumstances.

(a) *The Balancing of Values in Discovering Meaning*

One can best appreciate how lower court judges supplement rules with values by considering how they go about discovering the objective meaning of the guaranteed rights. In *M.N.R.* v. *Kruger*, for example, the federal court of appeal finds that section 8's "right to be secure against unreasonable search and seizue" "obviously" constitutes "a solemn confirmation" of the deeper right to privacy.[73] To understand the "unreasonableness" of a search or seizure, one must balance privacy against "the need that the laws of the land be properly enforced." The Charter's standard "requires that a proper choice be made" between "the safeguard of privacy" and the community's interest "in uncovering a possible breach of the law." In balancing the two interests there is "not much room there for broad and easily applicable propositions." Rather, "practical aspects" are determinant: the circumstances, the manner of seizure, the nature of the objects seized, the extent of the privacy infringed, and the importance of the posited rule. This balancing of the two competing interests "verified" "the validity" of a Charter claim.[74] The Ontario Court of Appeal ascertains the reasonableness of a search or seizure in much the same way.[75]

Judges take a similar "balancing of interests" approach in uncovering the meaning of other Charter sections during our five-year period. In *Re R. and Speid*, for example, the Ontario Court of Appeal holds that although an accused's right to retain a counsel of his choice "is a fundamental right and one to be zealously protected by the court, it is not an absolute right and is subject to reasonable limitations."[76] In deciding whether a judge can remove a lawyer as counsel, the Court believes that it "must balance the individual's right to select counsel of his own choice, public policy and the public interest in the administration of justice and basic principles of fundamental fairness."[77]

Similarly, in *R. v. Reed*, a British Columbia County Court holds that freedom of expression does not extend to a Jehovah's Witnesses' dissenter who has driven his car onto church property within ten feet of the front door and, with a loud hailer, has derided the beliefs of those entering the church. The Court believes there that "[t]he right of the individual to freedom of expression must be balanced by the right of society to peaceful enjoyment of public places, the latter being a substantial interest in furtherance of which the State should be able to legislate."[78] Along the same line, the right of a person charged with an offence "to be informed without unreasonable delay of the specific offence" as guaranteed in section 11(a) is balanced against "the rights" of the state.[79] So was the right to be tried within a reasonable time as guaranteed in section 11(b).[80] Indeed, the Ontario Court of Appeal describes "the general approach" under section 11(b) as an "*ad hoc* balancing basis."[81] And again, section 7's guarantee of "in accordance with the principles of fundamental justice" requires a balancing between efficiency and justice when the Extradition Act is at issue.[82] On the one hand, "the common good requires that extradition proceedings be efficient and practical." On the other, "if in any situation justice is not compatible with expediency it is mandatory that the choice be justice." What section 7 requires, according to more than one court, is "a proper, practical, workable balance" of the embedded values.

(b) *The Balancing of Values in Section 1*

Having identified the meaning of a right and having concluded its *prima facie* infringement, judges sometimes imagine section 1 as triggering a balancing of values. The Ontario Court of Appeal puts it this way: "Section 1 of the Charter requires that the courts engage in a balancing process. The permissible limits of government action, on the one hand, must be measured against the rights of the individual on the other. Courts must be flexible in their approach to Charter cases ..."[83] This acknowledgment of the section 1 balancing process is often preceded by the claim that the Charter's rights are not absolute. Ewaschuk, one of the more ardent exponents of the scientific role of a judge, expresses the connection in *R. v. Rowbotham* in a typical manner: "Rights and freedoms as guaranteed in the Charter are not absolute. The constitutional rights and freedoms require a balancing between the rights of society as a collectivity of individuals and the rights of individual members of society. To strike the proper balance is a difficult task."[84]

Notwithstanding their adoption of a balancing role, Canadian lower court judges do not surprisingly have difficulty in identifying which interests are important. Nor is it difficult for them to assign an appropriate weight to each interest. The Quebec Superior Court identified "le droit à la dignité de la personne, la liberté des autres ..., le droit à un procès impartial, la sécurité nationale, etc." as "[c]ertaines valeurs concurrentielles" which "peuvent avoir priorité" within section 1.[85] In *National Citizens' Coalition* v. *A.G. Can.*, and Alberta Queen's Bench judge suggests that one must balance the value which a freedom is intended to serve on the one hand, and the "real value to society" of restricting the freedom on the other. The latter must be measured in terms of the "harm" "caused to other values in society" should the freedom not be restricted.[86] Other judges offer that a judge should turn the scales in favour of "values of superordinate importance," although they do not identify what makes the values superordinate or important.[87] The courts have presupposed the interests to be identifiable and quantifiable, although we have yet to know how and why.

The *Oakes* proportionally test does not help the lower court judges in quantifying the Charter's values.[88] That test asks, first, whether the legislated means is "carefully designed" to achieve the legislative objective. Secondly, do the means impair the right "as little as possible"? Thirdly, is there a proportionality between the effects upon the right and the given legislative objective? This three-pronged test allows lower court judges to hide the posit of the legislative objective behind rationalistic technique. In *Re Rebic and Collver*, for example, MacFarlane asserts his "conclusion" that the "objective" for detaining a person found not guilty by reason of insanity is "rational, relevant, necessary and desirable in a legal as well as in a social sense, and is of sufficient importance to warrant overriding a constitutionally protected right or freedom."[89] But he accepts the objective of the criminal procedure as a 'given' and, 'for argument,' he quotes paragraphs from an American judgment which, in turn, posits the objectives on the basis of previously posited rules.[90] Only once does a Canadian lower court judge expand upon his understanding of freedom and democracy in an effort to weigh the importance of a posited legislative objective.[91]

(c) *Values as Supplementary to Posited Rules*

Values do not replace the posited rules during the first five years of the Charter's history. Rather, values merely supplement the posited rules. A group of judges incorporate values into their analyses by asking 'what value underlies a Charter freedom?' or 'what value underlies a posited rule or practice which restricts the freedom?' Values (or policy) lie embedded behind the formal rules.[92] Those members of the judiciary who contemplate a role for values still share the 'givenness' of rules, whether the rules be enacted in a statute or in the Charter. But, this group of judges understands the Charter with a hint of realism, in that they recognize that rules can possess an indeterminate character. 'Balancing' judges see it as their role to articulate the presupposed purposes of a rule and, without going beyond the 'givenness' of the rule, to balance the purposes (or interests or values) as if they are mathematically quantifiable.[93]

(d) *The Judge's Self-Image*

Notwithstanding their incorporation of the newly discovered, seemingly subjectivist values into 'the law,' judges still see themselves as impartial adjudicators. For, they insist that they are not actually positing the values. Rather, the values emanate from within the text of the Charter and of a challenged statute. As to Charter values, Tarnopolsky differentiates in *R. v. Videoflicks* between the policy of a Charter right and its definition.[94] The enterprise of definition-seeking insulates the judge from imposing her or his values upon the law. Similarly, lower court judges during the early years particularly disclaim any role in evaluating the content of legislated or common law rules. Notwithstanding the fact that the Ontario Court of Appeal in *Morgentaler* believes that it can "review the substance of legislation," for example, it insists that "the policy and wisdom of legislation should remain first and foremost a matter for Parliament and the Legislatures."[95] Though values/policy inevitably supplement rules, the judiciary's self-image at this point in time restrains judges from questioning the justifiability of the values/policy. This impartial self-image also extends to their refusal to fill gaps in a statutory rule to save it from the threat of an unconstitutional decree.[96] And the judiciary's institutional self-image excludes the executive from exercising decisions which need a 'natural' neutrality.[97]

The question which suggests itself is 'how can judges insist upon their apolitical role and, at the same time, admit to balancing values?' Part of the answer lies in their retained belief in the objectivity of meaning and in the objectivity of the analytic process. As the Ontario Court of Appeal expresses it in the *Southam* judgment, "[w]e are left, at present, to a certain extent wandering in *unexplored terrain* in which we have to set up our own *guide-posts* in interpreting the meaning and effect of the words of s. 1 of the Charter. In determining the reasonableness of the limit in each particular case, the court must examine *objectively* its argued *rational basis* ..."[98] Part of the answer to the judiciary's retained apolitical self-image is also connected to its image of the actual balancing process as an apolitical one. Much as a cashier weighs apples in a market and calculates a price based upon the weight, so too judges assume that the same mathematical process inheres in the balancing of values.[99]

(e) *The Rationality of the Analytic Process*
The key, then, to the judge's realistic reassessment of 'what constitutes Charter law?' is his or her supplementation of posited rules, rational technique, and an impartial, apolitical self-image with values. Law goes to the *technique* of reasoning on the part of the judge or on the part of the original legislature which posits a challenged rule. We have seen that lower court judges generally accept the rule itself as a 'given.' Values merely supplement the law because values are embedded within the posited rules, the rules being the starting-point. To be 'law,' judges assure themselves that the posited rules, or the interests presupposed in them, are justifiable. But the justification possesses an instrumental character, in that judges examine whether the legislative or doctrinal means fulfil the

objective of the legislated posited rule. Issues of Goodness and Justice are an aside. The instrumental connection between the legislated means and the posited legislative objective is what judges mean by the "rational basis" of a challenged rule.

That the 'balancing of values' focus of Charter judgments precludes a questioning of the ethical ends sought in the values, interests, or rules, there can be little doubt. Dubé insists in a federal trial court judgment, for example, that "It is *not for the court* to agree or disagree with *the merits* of a programme limiting the liberty of the individual. It must consider whether such a programme as legislated by Parliament has *a rational basis*, whether it is within *the bounds of reason* acceptable in a democratic state. That is the crucible in which the concept of reasonableness must be tested."[100] By "the merits," Dubé means the Goodness or Justice of the limitation rule. That is a matter for the legislature. Reflecting what later judges are to reaffirm, Deschênes's *Quebec Protestant School Bds* judgment reflects this acceptance of the posited end when he expresses the proposition that "[t]he courts must not yield to the temptation of too readily substituting their opinion for that of the Legislature."[101] And virtually all Canadian courts accept the given ethical goodness of posited rules when, in elaborating "the meaning" of "free and democratic society" in section 1, they appeal to the *existing* posited rules in Canada and three or four English-speaking societies as evidence of what constituted a free and democratic society.[102] "[U]ltimately," Mackinnon says on behalf of Ontario Court of Appeal judges, "having derived whatever assistance can be secured from the experience of other free and democratic societies, [we should look] to *the facts of our own free and democratic society ...*"[103] And, as Deschênes assures himself, "one only needs to have travelled a little ... The court need go no further to demonstrate that Canadian society is a free society, among the freest in the world.[104]

If judges do not allow themselves to question the 'givenness' of the values embedded within a rule, what are "the bounds of reason" which judges share among themselves? How does one test "the rationality" of a posited rule? The key is the means which a legislature uses to fulfil the "interest," "value," or "objective" embedded within the rule. Judicial scrutiny goes to technique, not to ends. Judges question whether a rule is "a sensible necessary rule," given the posited ends.[105] Judges sometimes ask whether a legislated minimum sentence is "so obviously excessive as going beyond all rational bounds of punishment in the eyes of reasonable and right thinking Canadians ..."[106] Sometimes, judges question the "disproportionality" of a posited rule as in the case of cruel and unusual punishment where judges ask whether the treatment or punishment is disproportionate to a given posited offence.[107] Or, in the context of section 1, proportionality is understood more generally as "[t]he extent of the limitation which is to be balanced against its rationality."[108] That is, does the posited limit overshoot the purpose (interest) which it is designed to serve? Sometimes, one questions whether the interest or value underlying a limit is irrelevant and unconnected with a Charter right.[109] Sometimes one asks whether the legislature can fulfil the same interest underlying the posited limit without harming the interests or values embedded within a Charter rule. And sometimes, we have already seen, one compares a rule with other posited *indicia* in Canada or other countries.[110] All this is done without questioning the content of the posited rules themselves; without asking, for example, 'what is the nature of freedom or democracy?' or 'what makes one society (that is, the United States, the United Kingdom, Australia, New Zealand, and Canada) free and others not?'

This concentration upon the technique, rather than the ends, of analysis can be appreciated by closely noting the often cited Deschênes judgment in *Quebec Protestant School Bds*, a judgment which serves as a prelude to the later *Oakes'* proportionality test.[111] After an extensive survey of tests which European, American, British, and other judges apply in balancing the reasonableness of a posited limit, he enunciates three propositions:

1 A limit is reasonable if it is a *proportionate* means to attain the purpose of the law;
2 Proof of the contrary involves proof not only of *a wrong*, but of a wrong which runs against common sense; and
3 The courts must not yield to the temptation of too readily substituting their opinion for that of the Legislature.[112]

The first proposition affirms the key to Deschênes's image of rationality: one must test the appropriateness of the means, given the posited end. In the second proposition Deschênes acknowledges the wrongness of a rule in terms of the efficacy of the means chosen by the legislature to *implement* the objective of the rule. He does not understand the wrongness of a posited rule in terms of the content of the posited rule itself. The latter inquiry he leaves to the legislature, as suggested in his third proposition. A scrutiny of the means to accomplish a given posited interest is what Deschênes and others understand by "rationality"[113] or "validity."[114]

When judges share a 'balancing of values' image of Charter law, they imagine their decision-making rational because of the apparently objective, apolitical, almost scientific process involved. In that way, judges can apply their rationality without acknowledging to themselves or to others that they are actually incorporating their own values or effectively evaluating the content of the rules themselves. A rule is rational if it uses "a proportionate means" to achieve a given purpose. The rule's purpose, as posited, serves as a 'given.' It is not for a judge to question that 'given.' Thus, the judge acknowledges the supplementary character of values without openly questioning the Goodness of their content. To do so would return him or her from the objective to the subjective world. And the latter world constitutes non-knowledge for most lower court judges under study.

3. A CAUTIOUS RECONSIDERATION OF RATIONALISM

A rationalistic image of the Charter has been presupposed in the majority of Canadian judgments at the trial and first appellate court level. One finds in another strain of judgments, however, a cautious reconsideration of rationalism. This reconsideration is reflected in three ways: first, a conscious attempt to differentiate the legal community's image of the Charter from its image of the Canadian Bill of Rights; secondly, a desire to distinguish constitutional law from posited rules, granting a higher status or legitimacy to the former over the latter; and thirdly, a concern for the effectiveness of constitutional rights in the real world. These three themes lead judges to express two counter-images to rationalism. I shall discuss the latter in sections 4 and 5. In the meantime, let us look closely at the judiciary's cautious reconsideration of the rationalist image.

(a) *The Image of the Charter vs. the Image of the Canadian Bill of Rights*
The first indicator of a reassessment of the rationalist image of the Charter comes with the judiciary's distinction of the Charter as a constitutional document with constitutional status as opposed to the statutory status of the Canadian Bill of Rights. Generally, judges do not explain why the one has constitutional status whereas the other has not. The British Columbia Court of Appeal believes the key factor to be section 52 of the Constitution Act, 1982 "which can be viewed as effecting a fundamental change in the role of the courts."[115] An Alberta provincial court attributes the difference in status to the fact that the Canadian Bill of Rights is not an "*entrenched* Bill of Rights" whereas the Charter is entrenched.[116] A Quebec Superior Court judge distinguishes the two on

the grounds that the Charter is more difficult to amend: the Charter is "not merely an Act of Parliament" but "part of a fundamental law enshrined in the Constitution which can only be amended in accordance with the complicated process ..."[117] An Ontario County court judge claims that "the Supreme Court of Canada has in the past *specifically* pointed out that the *Canadian Bill of Rights* ... is not constitutional, but merely statutory."[118] Finally, a New Brunswick queen's bench judge distinguishes the two instruments simply by virtue of the fact that one can find the Charter in an underlined document self-described as a Constitution Act.[119]

What weight do these judges grant to their different respective images of the Charter and the Canadian Bill of Rights? First, previous higher court interpretations of Canadian Bill of Rights rights are not given weight in the judiciary's new self-image as interpreter of identical rights in the Charter. The former supreme court judgments cannot be taken as "final and definitive."[120] More assertively, "it is basically of little use to consider those cases decided under the Bill of Rights."[121] Secondly, "the constitutional status" of the Charter as opposed to the Bill induces judges to believe that they can legitimately grant a wider scope to the identical terms in both documents.[122] Thirdly, the attribution of a different status to the Charter as opposed to the Bill usually serves as a trigger for a judge to try to work out an alternative image of the Charter, an alternative to rationalism, that is. Sometimes, this is phrased in terms of reading the words with "a large and liberal interpretation rather than a narrow and technical construction."[123] A liberal construction is taken as "a necessary step in the progressive development of the Constitution of this country."[124] Often quoting from Lord Sankey in *Edwards et al.* v. *A.G. Can.*,[125] judges infer an elevated status to the Charter by picturing the text as "a living tree capable of growth and expansion within its natural limits."[126] More generally, upon picturing the elevated status of the Charter, judges see themselves compelled to "approach the task with an informed concern for the social, political and economic consequences of each decision."[127]

(b) *The Higher Law of a Constitution*

We experienced in the *Patriation Reference* in Chapter IV that Laskin and others equate constitutionality with legality whereas Martland and Ritchie hypothesize the two as sometimes contradictory. Martland and Ritchie elevate a constitution above and apart from posited rules. By granting a higher status to the Charter than to the Canadian Bill of Rights, our judges under study grant the Charter more legitimacy. In addition to legitimacy, a condition for effectiveness within a legal community, these judges share the Martland/Ritchie picture that a constitution exists separately and above posited legislative rules.

Judges express this higher law character of the Charter in different ways. In the words of one Ontario High Court judge, "[w]hile the Constitution is not technically a statute, it is *a higher law* and a broad interpretation of it must be taken to give it meaning in relation to the rules of this Court."[128] And a Supreme Court judge of the Northwest Territories places the constitution above and apart from posited rules in this way: "[t]he Charter is the supreme law of our country. The Constitution represents the public's limitation on the powers of the legislatures – in this case to truncate or curtail the right of the individual to a fair trial. The courts are the guardians of those rights: see s. 24(1), *Canadian Charter of Rights and Freedoms*"[129] Whereas a posited rule applies only to those persons intended within the scope of the rule, the charter, having acquired "adult status," is pictured as belonging universally to each and all.[130] Utilitarian considerations, such as the seriousness of an offence or an accused's apparent guilt, cannot outweigh the universal character of the Charter's rights.[131] Further, the Charter imposes a "mild blow" upon the supremacy of the legislature.[132]

(c) *Effective Constitutional Rights*

Lower court judges share a third boundary in their reconsideration of rationalist images of the Charter: namely, the Charter's rights must be effective rights. Since the Charter is thought to differ from an ordinary legislative enactment such as the Canadian Bill of Rights and since the Charter possesses an independent and elevated status over posited rules, judges begin to realize their "awesome role" in making the Charter's claims a reality.[133] This, in turn, contemplates a positive duty for the state's official's, through legislatures and courts, to create conditions for the effective exercise of rights. So, for example, the Ontario Court of Appeal interprets the right to retain and instruct counsel without delay as "a mere ritual without significance or meaning" and "wholly illusory and chimerical" if the arrested person or detainee has not been given a realistic opportunity to consult with his lawyer.[134] The right to counsel raises a correlative obligation upon the state's officials to facilitate contact with counsel. Similarly, the British Columbia Court of Appeal interprets the right to vote against "the exigencies of pursuing a course of education out of the province" and against the need to travel out of province to gain a livelihood.[135] The Court understands the Charter as imposing a new duty upon the state to provide a voting mechanism for persons out of province on election day. One Ontario county court judge contrasts effective procedural safeguards against the clearly drafted, "abstract rights" "in most of the show-piece constitutions of totalitarian States."[136] The latter exist "in a vacuum and on paper only." This same concern underlies one judge's realization of the nexus between the freedom of association and the right to strike. The latter renders the former "*effective economic clout* in dealing with ... employers."[137] If the right to strike were removed, "the workers' freedom of association is more than merely infringed, it is *emasculated*." The freedom would become "meaningless, empty and devoid of substance." Similarly, Ontario court of appeal judges speculate that a journalist's free access to the courts is "an integral and implicit part" of the freedoms of expression and of the press as well as a "necessary" element in the administration of justice.[138] This theme of the nexus between Charter rights and their social/cultural effectiveness sets the course for a more expansive reconsideration of the judiciary's traditionally passive self-image during the five-year period under study. And that reconsideration crystallizes into two relatively coherent images of the Charter.

4. AN HISTORICIST IMAGE

We saw in Chapters III and IV that the boundaries of Laskin's image of a constitution clash with the historicist image elaborated in the Martland/Ritchie dissent in the *Patriation Reference* and in Addy's judgment in *Beauregard*. Posited rules and institutional history constitute the resource material of the two images respectively. The historicist image does not include the history of social classes, economic practices, or even political theory as legitimate resource material. Rather, the historicist boundaries restrict the lawyer to institutional materials: precedents, statutes, legal practices, official proclamations, government reports, and the like.[139] Further, whereas Laskin's rationalist image equates a constitution with posited rules, the historicist boundaries place the constitution separate and apart from posited rules. Whereas with the former, one has standing only if the scope of a posited rule encompasses the conduct of the litigant, the lawyer with historicist boundaries seeks out institutional historical support for a claimant's standing before the courts. Whereas the rationalist understands the 'rule of law' as the rule of posited law, the historicist prejudges law in terms of historically embedded general principles which might well contradict a posited rule. Whereas the rationalist image confines the lawyer to a posited text, the Constitution Act, 1867 to present, to discover whether judges are institutionally independent of the legislative/executive arms of government, the historicist image shifts the lawyer's inquiry to the issue of whether institutional historical evidence supports judicial independence. The Constitution Act, 1867 serves as only one *indicia*, albeit an important one, going to the inquiry.

Given that the Canadian legal community shared such a coherent historicist image prior to the Charter, it is not surprising that one can identify similar boundaries in lower court Charter litigation. One can find the historicist image protruding in a variety of circumstances and of subject-matters.

In *R. v. Valente (No. 2)*, for example, counsel challenges the independence of provincial courts because of the attorney-general's effective control over them.[140] This independence has been guaranteed, according to counsel, in section 11(d) of the Charter. Section 11(d) provides that one charged with an offence is "to be presumed innocent until proven guilty according to law in a fair and public hearing by an independent and impartial tribunal." But what is "an independent and impartial tribunal"? The Ontario Court of Appeal believes that it can understand the meaning of an "independent and impartial tribunal," as guaranteed, only by tracing the evolution of common law and Chancery courts from thirteenth-century England to Parliament's protection of judicial independence in the Act of Settlement, 1701 and to contemporary manifestations of "independent" tribunals in the appointment process, salaries, pensions, and removal proceedings. Sections 96, 99, and 100 of the Constitution Act, 1867 offer further institutional evidence of the principle of judicial independence: the Act does not posit the principle, it merely offers evidence of pre-existing principles. Having so decided, the Court of Appeal then evaluates the independent and impartial character of provincial courts by reviewing their origins and evolution. From British and Canadian institutional history the Court concludes that judicial "independence" means independent *adjudication* as opposed to independent administration.[141] The key test for the meaning of "independence" in section 11(d) is "whether a reasonable person, who was informed of the relevant statutory provisions, their *historical background* and *the traditions surrounding them*, after viewing the matter realistically and practically would conclude that a provincial court judge ... was a tribunal which could make an independent and impartial adjudication."[142] Their presupposed historicist image of the Charter leads the judges to conclude that counsel's concerns "neither singly nor collectively would result in a reasonable apprehension that they would impair the ability of Judge Sharpe to make an independent and impartial adjudication."[143]

Similarly, in *R. v. Morgentaler, Smoling and Scott*, counsel confront the Ontario High Court with the claim that Criminal Code abortion provisions contradict "the right to life, liberty and security of the person, and the right not to be deprived thereof except in accordance with ... fundamental justice" as guaranteed in section 7 of the Charter.[144] Responding, Parker appeal to history: "In my opinion, a determination of the rights encompassed by s. 7 should begin by an inquiry into the legal rights Canadians have at common law or by statute. If the claimed right is not protected by our system of positive law, the inquiry should then consider if it is *so deeply 'rooted in the traditions and conscience of our people as to be ranked as fundamental,' per* Cardozo J. in *Palko* v. *Connecticut* (1937), 302 U.S. 319 at p. 325 [quoting himself in *Snyder* v. *Mass.* (1934), 291 U.S. at p. 105]."[145] Parker continues that Canadian judges invariably "looked to *our history* to determine the extent of the freedom under discussion." After providing the reader with three judgments sharing his historicist image,[146] he reviews the history of the posited laws since the early nineteenth century. Posited laws in Canada prohibit abortion at any stage of pregnancy for over one hundred years. "The fact" exists, in Parker's eyes, that "no unfettered legal right to an abortion *can be found* in our law, nor can it be said that a right to an abortion is *deeply rooted in the traditions or conscience* of this country. For these reasons, I cannot find a right an an abortion in s. 7 of the *Charter*."[147] Interestingly, the Ontario Court of Appeal overrules Parker's judgments and does so in a manner which openly rejects the historicist image of the Charter in favour of a rationalist one.[148]

The Ontario Court of Appeal presupposes the acceptability and legitimacy of its historicist boundaries, as a further example, when counsel challenges summary contempt proceedings as in violation of section 7, 11(c), 11(d), and 11(f) of the Charter in *R. v. Cohn*.[149] There, the judiciary identify the following *indicia* of institutional history as shedding insight on the challenge: that for over a century judges have held it a contempt for one to refuse to be a witness at a criminal trial; and that the historical practice has been a maximum sentence of two years for a contempt, notwithstanding that a superior court exercises inherent authority to set an unlimited term of imprisonment.[150] The latter historical evidence goes to exclude contempt proceedings from the purview of section 11(f) of the Charter since section 11(f) only guarantees a jury trial "where the maximum punishment for the offence is imprisonment *for five years* or a more severe punishment." More generally, the *Cohn* judges do not understand the common law in terms of some self-contained encyclopaedic set of posited rules. Rather, it is "*an evolving body of law* which constantly develops to take into account the social, economic and political conditions and circumstances which prevail from time to time in the territorial area in which the court applying the common law has jurisdiction."[151] And again, when summarizing their judgment in their last paragraph, the Court of Appeal judges make their *image* of the constitution the "bottom-line" of their judgment: "[s]imply put, it is a matter of the common law *continuing to evolve as it has done for centuries* but henceforth, in Canada, it must evolve within the framework provided by the Charter to safeguard individual rights."[152]

On at least one occasion Ontario court of appeal judges intermix historicism with their overreaching rationalist boundaries.[153] In *R. v. Bryant*, Bryant elected trial by judge and jury, absconded, and is tried by a judge sitting without a jury pursuant to a Criminal Code provision. Bryant's counsel claims that this Code provision contravenes the right to trial by jury as guaranteed in section 11(f) of the Charter. After holding that the posited rule *prima facie* infringes section 11(f), the judges go to section 1 and balance the purpose of the posited rule against "the significance of the right to trial by jury." In order to identify the significance of that latter, Blair surveys the detailed history of the jury system in England, the United States, and Canada. Blair concludes that "*[t]his history demonstrates* that the right of trial by jury is not only an essential part of our criminal justice system but also is an important constitutional guarantee of the rights of the individual in our democratic society. In all common law countries it has, for this reason, been treated as almost sacrosanct and has been interfered with only to a minimal extent."[154]

We saw with respect to the rationalist image of the Charter, particularly rule rationalism, that judges often assume the legitimacy and utility of the image without much ado. Why that is so is an open question. Perhaps the answer lies in the fact that both opposing counsel express the same image (but disagree as to how one should work it out, given the posited rule and circumstances). Perhaps a judge finds it unnecessary to articulate the image's contours because the professional milieu within which s/he has lived has never questioned it. Or, perhaps, the judge has not been faced with an opposing image in his legal education and professional experiences. *Valente (No. 2)* similarly serves as an exception to historicist judgments in that counsel and judges in *Valente* methodically trace the institutional history bearing upon the conception of the Charter right at issue and they do so by reminding themselves of the historicist underpinnings of their enterprise. More often, judges simply presuppose the acceptability and legitimacy of the historicist image and assert the conclusion they assume one would gather if one seriously studies the historical evidence.

So, for example, Judge Holland of the Ontario High Court assumes the legitimacy and acceptability of his historicist image of the Charter when he asserts that section 11(b) (the right to be tried within a reasonable time) is "a constitutional guarantee of a right which existed before the Charter, and while that right has been strengthened by entrenchment, the jurisdiction of the provincial court judge acting under Part xv is no different with respect to this relief than it was pre-Charter with respect to 'abuse of process'."[155] Since a provincial court judge does not possess authority to invoke an 'abuse of process' in the past, he does not possess it now. Similarly, Bayda, chief justice of the Saskatchewan court of appeal, at one point asserts, without more ado: "I do not subscribe to the view that the Parliament of Canada in drafting the Charter intended to depart completely from the law as it existed the day before the Charter became effective."[156] Given his historicist image, he interprets the word 'detained' in the Charter in the same manner which judges had interpreted the 'detained' in the Canadian Bill of Rights litigation. The fact that these judges do not feel compelled to elaborate the content of their historicist image of the Charter does not mean that they do not possess such an image. Rather, they presuppose the image. The focus upon historical continuity emerges in the brief occasions when lower court judges find it necessary to identify their core starting-points or 'bottom lines.'

5. A TELEOLOGICAL IMAGE

Some Canadian lower court judges express still different boundaries of 'what constitutes Charter law?' than that experienced so far. Instead of looking to contemporary posited rules and institutional history, they cling to the future. The boundary of this third judicial prism of Charter law entertains an inquiry into social goals as a legitimate project for a competent lawyer. In this strain of judgments, judges feel compelled to identify the purpose (or *telos*) of the Charter section at issue, the purpose of the Charter as a whole, and the purpose of the social/political arrangements under scrutiny. Judges then try to connect the goal(s) in the three contexts to the posited rule being challenged. We shall see in Chapter VII that Dickson and Wilson of the Canadian Supreme Court aspire to elaborate and to refine the boundaries of this image. Suffice it to say at this point, we shall acknowledge its presence within the thoughts and affections of some lower and first-level appellate justices.

First, this group of lower court judges believes that the content of the Charter evolves and grows over time. The Charter rights are simply not a 'given,' imposed in some text, in the values presupposed in the text, or in the institutional history of society. Rather, the meaning and scope – indeed, even the very existence – of the Charter rights grow like "a living tree," as Viscount Sankey describes the British North America Act in *Edwards* v. *A.-G. for Can.*: "The British North America Act planted in Canada *a living tree capable of growth and expansion* within its *natural* limits ... Their Lordships do not conceive it to be the duty of this Board – it is certainly not their desire – to cut down the provision of the Act by a narrow and technical construction, but rather to give it a large and liberal construction."[157] Referring to the 'living tree' metaphor, for example, the Ontario Court of Appeal judges in *Southam (No. 1)* express that "[t]he Charter as part of a constitutional document should be given a large and liberal construction. The spirit of this new 'living tree' planted in friendly Canadian soil should not be stultified by narrow technical, literal interpretations without regard to its background and purpose; capability for growth must be recognized ... Although said in a very different connection, it is apposite here: '*For the letter killeth but the spirit giveth life*'."[158] The Charter embodies a forward-looking image of a constitution, it is thought, rather than a backward-looking or contemporaneous focus as the historicist and rationalist images express.[159]

Secondly, the purpose of a Charter section as well as the Charter as a whole is thought to evolve with the social fabric of society. The Ontario Court of Appeal expresses the connection between the purpose and the social fabric in *Re Potma and the Queen*: "[t]he principles or standards of fairness essential to the attainment of fundamental justice are in no sense static, and will continue as they have in the past to evolve and develop *in response to society's changing perception* of what is arbitrary, unfair or unjust."[160] Veit of the Alberta Queen's Bench emphasizes that one must identify the *telos* of the Charter by examining the *Canadian* social fabric, not the American: "It seems to me in assessing the value of the American precedents ... that the *Constitution Act, 1982*, is very much the fruit of Canadian political maturity, *that this is a tree which has been grown in our own backyard, not a plastic tree, in my view, that we bought in a store and put in our yard.* It seems to me that we have to consider *the roots* from which this tree has grown up and that involves the Canadian and the Anglo-Canadian jurisprudence surrounding the words that eventually were chosen to be used in the Charter."[161] That is, one can only appreciate the purpose of the Charter by connecting the abstract words to the social fabric. And one can only make that connection by appreciating the genesis from which society has evolved.

Thirdly, within the boundaries of a socially evolving purposive Charter, judges share a belief in the ideal-directed character of the Charter's rights. The rule rationalist image of the Charter delimits a lawyer's understanding of a constitution to posited rules. The 'balancing of values' image has a lawyer beginning with the values or interests presupposed in the posited rules. And the historicist image starts with the principles embedded within institutional history. In contrast, the teleological image contemplates that the text triggers 'ought' claims about how the state, the state's officials, non-state organizations, and citizens ought to relate to each other. That is, the character of Charter rights lies in ideal-directed questions of a noumenal world rather than descriptive claims about the present in a phenomenal world. Kerans remarks in *Black* v. *Law Society of Alberta*, for example, that the words "free and democratic society" in section 1 "describe an ideal, not a place. And ... the ideal is at once broad and changing."[162] Kerans thereupon proceeds to survey the leading conceptions of "freedom" and "democracy" in the philosophical works on liberal-democracy.[163] Kerans urges that we weigh the social "interest" or "objective" of a posited rule, not in terms of the means posited to accomplish that objective, but against "the ideal society." The legal community is called upon to evaluate the content of a posited rule vis-à-vis the goal of fostering that ideal society.[164]

The most important example of the set of issues entertained within the ideal-directed boundaries is 'what is the nature of a person and how ought s/he to be?' Traditionally, liberal legal and political theory portrays the person as self-sufficient, atomistic, and the source of all values and decisions. The person is a subjectivist or empirical being. One *chooses* one value over another. Others are pictured as a threat to our inner, subjectivist self. Freedom, then, is a negative protective shield about the individual's choice of values. In contrast, judges who share a teleological image of the Charter during the five-year period under study understand the human person as a social being. Rather than presenting an obstacle to one's freedom, other persons are understood as potential contributors to one's own growth. Whereas rights demarcate the boundary between the self and others in the former context, rights demonstrate one's respect for others as a social being in the teleological image. Several Canadian lower court judges take the noumenal boundaries of the teleological image as an opportunity to express who we are as social beings.

In *Broadway Manor Nursing Home*, for example, Smith of the Ontario Divisional Court imagines the Charter as a "living tree."[165] Given this metaphor, he re-examines and then rejects the traditional role which judges leave for themselves vis-à-vis the legislature: the "[s]overeignty of Parliament as we have known it is a thing of history."[166] Having set the stage, Smith supports Alexis de Tocqueville's opinion that "in order that men remain civilized or become such, it is essential *that the art of associating be developed* and perfected among them." To act as a social being is the "most natural privilege" subject only to the right to act for oneself, he suggests. To be a social being means to *combine* one's exertions *with one's fellows* and *to act in common* with others.[167] Smith explains that the Canadian legal community has not previously discussed the "conceptual and philosophical terms" of de Tocqueville because, he thinks, Canada has only recently enacted a Charter. Statute law does not confer the freedom to associate, to bargain, and to strike. What, then, is the source of these freedoms? The *nature of man as a social being*, he responds. In his words, the freedoms "were developed under *a dynamic of their own*. The various statutes dealing with labour relations merely served to recognize and regulate them in the interest of order and industrial peace. It is perhaps therefore more accurate to speak of 'freedom' which *inheres the very nature of man as a social being*, rather than of 'right' which may be thought of as something conferred."[168] Because Charter rights inhere in the very nature of a person in contrast to being posited by civil authority, they are permanent. Accordingly, judges should reject doctrines and tests which effectively qualify the freedoms "lest the Charter become emasculated by some indefinable process that would proceed from one case to the next on the basis of ad hockery."[169]

In the same vein, Anderson at the British Columbia Court of Appeal responds to a Charter challenge to obscenity rules by evaluating the content of obscene videotapes in terms of the goal or end of the person as a social being.[170] Although he accepts that the Criminal Code rules offend freedom of expression as protected in section 2(b) of the Charter, the videotapes cannot be "demonstrably justified in a free and democratic society" simply because they cause harm to society. How do the videotapes harm a free and democratic society? The videos cause such harm by directly clashing with the nature or *telos* of a person as one should aspire to be. In his words, "[t]hey tend to *dehumanize* and *degrade* both men and women in an excessive and revolting way. They exalt the concept that in some perverted way *domination* of women by men is accepted in our society."[171] Accordingly, he claims, section 1 should be resolved, not in a vacuum, but in terms of the goal of equality between male and female persons as sought in section 28 of the Charter. The video material at issue tends "to make men more tolerant of violence to women and creates *a social climate* encouraging men to act in a callous and discriminatory way towards women."[172]

The teleological image of 'what is Charter law?' does more than entertain ideal-directed enquiries as to 'what is the telos of a person?' The image begs questions as to 'who we actually are.' With respect to both sets of inquiry, the person is understood as a social being. Bayda insists upon this point in the Saskatchewan Court of Appeal judgment in *Re Retail, Wholesale & Dept. Store Union, Locals 544, 496, 635 & 955 et al. and Gov't of Sask. et al.*[173] He claims that "the freedom *to be* in association" includes more than the freedom of an association to exist and the freedom of an individual to join and to choose one's associates: "*To be* in association means *to act* in association, for, it is metaphysically impossible for a human being to exist in a state of inanimateness, or in a state of no movement, or as it were, in a state of mere beingness. For a human being, to be is to act."[174] Bayda proceeds to wade through the thoughts of Aquinas (*Summa Contra Gentiles*), Etienne Gilson (*Being and Some Philosophers*), and Alexis de Tocqueville (*Democracy in America*) in order to glean insights into the nature of persons. Their common theme is that *to be* a person one must *relate with others*. That is, the nature of a person is to *act with others*, to be social. Bayda believes that this "fact" grounds his understanding of the meaning of 'association' in section 2(d) of the Charter. 'Association' just *must* mean something more than being a member of a union since Bayda says he grounds the nature of a person in something very different from the negative freedom of choosing subjectivist values, a freedom which separates the chooser from others.

6. SUMMARY

It is oftentimes said that the Canadian Charter of Rights and Freedoms introduces a major change in Canadian constitutional law. We have now seen that the document does stimulate judges to re-examine their inbred boundaries of what constitutes 'law.' Lower court judges share the same quest for an understanding of 'what is a constitution?' which, as we saw, Supreme Court judges sought with respect to the 'rule of law,' 'separation of powers,' and the like. The text of the Charter triggers within each lawyer and judge a searching examination of his or her image of a constitution. The image rebounds off the text.

The early years of the Charter's history bear witness to the overpowering weight of a rule rationalist prism in Canadian legal discourse. The deep fear of rational disorder invites an encyclopaedic totality of posited rules. Judges picture an objectivist meaning to the words of the Charter text. Accordingly, they set about to elaborate objectivist tests to discover meaning. Against all this, judges generally project themselves as passively, impartially, and neutrally applying the rules posited by the Charter and the legislature.

But the early years of the Charter do not demonstrate a uniform adherence to the boundaries of a rule rationalism. More realistically inclined, some judges shared an image of the Charter which envisages the text's meaning in terms of values lying behind the text. Section 1 of the Charter especially offers an opportunity to identify and scientifically to balance one value against another. Values supplement the legislatively posited rules: values do not replace the latter as the prime source of law. Once again, the analytic process begins with the external text, for the text seems to dwell 'out there' in an objective world. The text posits rules with supplementary values and policies. A rationalist technique permeates each step of the analytic discovery of that resource material.

Not unlike the traditional 'subject-matters' of Canadian constitutional discourse, there emerges in Charter litigation a cautious reconsideration of the rationalist boundaries of a constitution. Our study of the first five years of lower and first appellate level Charter judgments note this reassessment in three contexts: a conscious desire to differentiate the Charter from the Canadian Bill of Rights, the granting of a higher status or legitimacy to constitutional law over posited rules, and a concern for effective constitutional rights in the socio-economic world. Two full images of a constitution begin to emerge: an historicist and teleological image. We have experienced the teleological image as especially intriguing because it entertains questions about the nature of the person. Further, it encourages the lawyer to undertake speculative inquiry of an ideal-directed nature.

VII

Supreme Court Images of a Charter of Rights

In Chapters v and vi we have seen how one can understand the Canadian Bill of Rights and lower court Canadian Charter of Rights and Freedoms judgments only by understanding a judge's prejudgment of what constitutes a constitution. What initially appears to be an exegesis of the meaning of a text opens up into a judge's searching analysis of his institutional self-image vis-à-vis the legislature. This self-image joins with other themes: the objectivity of legal texts, the objectivity of judicial decision-making, the character of the Charter's rights, and the resource material to which one may appeal in interpreting the text. Even when judges do little more than briefly identify a surface issue, summarize counsel's arguments, give a quotation, and conclude with 'I feel that ...' or 'I think that ...,' one can still identify a judge's prejudgments. In particular, judicial expression takes us into four very different sets of boundaries delimiting the world: a rule rationalism, policy rationalism, historicism, and teleological image. I now wish to demonstrate how, for the initial five years following the Charter's enactment, higher court judges similarly collapsed Charter 'law' into a search for a coherent image of a constitution. Only in this chapter I wish to delve deeper into constitutional imagery. I aim to test whether one can pick a judge and identify the boundaries of her/his image of a constitution. I shall look closely at the judgments of Dickson and Wilson.

1. IN SEARCH OF AN IMAGE

In Charter judgment after Charter judgment, Supreme Court justices have felt compelled to identify their image of the Charter as the first task in justifying their decisions. Let us first describe this process in the one *coram* judgment during the first five years under study, *Quebec Protestant Separate School Bds.*[1] There, the surface issue is whether the provisions regarding English instruction in Chapter vii of Quebec's Charter of the French Language (Bill 101) are inconsistent with section 23 of the Charter of Rights.[2] What does section 23 of the Charter of Rights mean? And does section 23 encompass the sorts of requirements posited in Quebec's Charter? After summarizing the arguments of counsel and the reasoning processes of the lower courts, the unanimous Supreme Court justices attempt to come to terms with the place of the Charter of Rights within a coherent image of "the Constitution." The Court refuses to characterize the Charter, in its words, as "a codification of essential, pre-existing and more or less universal rights that are being confirmed and perhaps clarified, extended or amended."[3] Nor does the Court even picture the Charter rights as being granted "a new primacy and inviolability by their entrenchment in the supreme law of the land." Rather, section 23 of the Charter makes the whole text "a unique set of constitutional provisions, quite peculiar to Canada." Section 23 distinguishes the Charter from "the kind [of provisions] generally found in such charters and declarations of fundamental rights."

One can appreciate this "unique" character of Canada's Charter only by understanding it in its *historical* context, the Supreme Court judges insist: "This set of constitutional provisions was *not* enacted by the framers *in a vacuum*. When it was adopted, the framers *knew*, and *clearly had in mind* the regimes governing the Anglophone and Francophone linguistic minorities in various provinces in Canada so far as the language of instruction was concerned. They also had in mind *the history* of these regimes, both earlier ones ... as well as more recent ones ..."[4] Unlike the historicist focus of the lower courts,[5] the Supreme Court pictures section 23 as a departure from history: "the framers of the Constitution *manifestly* regarded as inadequate some – and perhaps all –of the regimes in force at the time the *Charter* was enacted."[6] But history, for the Supreme Court, is an objective thing, separate from the judge's own values, from his/her own reading of history, and from the impact of contemporary affairs upon his/her interpretation of history.

Much as we have seen in the previous chapter how lower courts objectify the meaning of words and create objective tests to identity that meaning, the *Quebec Protestant Separate School Board* Court objectifies the framers' intent. The Court projects into the Charter the framers' intention "to remedy the perceived defects of these regimes by uniform corrective measures" and to give the text "the status of a constitutional guarantee."[7] Two sentences later the Court asserts that the Charter's framers have "unquestionably intended" to establish a general uniform regime for the language of instruction in the whole of Canada.[8] The Court gathers this "unquestionable intent" by reviewing pre-1969 Quebec laws pertaining to the language of instruction, the federal Official Languages Act, 1974, the posited laws in other provinces prior to the Charter, and the actual wording of comparative texts. This institutional evidence leads the Court to conclude that past Quebec legislation has tended to give preferred treatment to French as the language of instruction and correspondingly lesser benefits to English "in fact if not in law."[9] Not surprisingly, then, Bill 101 very much occupies the minds of the Charter's framers when they have enacted section 23 of the Charter.[10] Indeed, "it may be wondered whether the framers of the Constitution would have drafted s. 23 of the *Charter* as they did if they had not had in view the model which s. 23 was indeed in large measure meant to override."[11] Two paragraphs later, the Court goes further, suggesting that "as is apparent, Chapter VIII of *Bill 101* is the prototype of regime which the framers of the Constitution wished to remedy by adopting s. 23 of the *Charter* ..."[12] The framers' intent exists 'out there' in the documents, to be discovered only for the asking: their "objective appears simple, and may readily be inferred from the concrete method [of drafting] used by them."[13] The simple intent of the text is separate and independent of the Court's own reading of historical or contemporary affairs: "[r]ightly or wrongly, – and it is not for the courts to decide, – the framers of the Constitution manifestly regarded ..."[14]

Since the Charter's text departs from objective history, one is hard pressed to describe the Court's image of a constitution as historicist. Yes, the Courts appeals to history. But that does not end the matter. What, then, constitutes "the Constitution"? A text called the Constitution Acts, 1867–1982? The Supreme Court suggests a clue towards the end of its historical study: "The reasons of Beauregard J.A., *like those developed above*, are based on *a teleological interpretation* of s. 23 of the *Charter*, that is to say, on a method of interpretation which looks to *the purpose* sought by the framers in drafting this section."[15] Although Greek thought offers very different versions of the meaning of "teleological," *telos* does connote "completion, end, purpose."[16] For the Supreme Court, then, history sheds light upon the purpose or end toward which the constitution is evolving. That is, the Charter does not describe or codify "pre-existing" rights, as the Court notes at the start.[17] Rather, the Charter assumes than an end exists. A constitution embodies the aims or ends of a society. One can identify those ends by reading the text called "the Constitution" against the institutional history of a society.

2. THE BOUNDARIES OF DICKSON'S IMAGE

Let us look a little closer at the key boundaries of Dickson's image of a constitution. Does Dickson share the dominating rule rationalist image of a constitution? Alternatively, does he try to depart from, or even to escape from it? If the latter, what is the relationship of posited law to a constitution, what role does history play, what is the character of a constitution, what is its relationship with the social/cultural world, and what is Dickson's institutional self-image as a judge? If Dickson succeeds in expressing an original or, perhaps, untraditional image of a constitution, does he entirely succeed in escaping from the rationalist influences about him? Much like the lower court and provincial appellate justices before him, Dickson uses the Charter of Rights to break from rule rationalism's hold upon the legal community. One can appreciate Dickson's painful reassessment of rule rationalism through three of his early themes.

First, Dickson maintains that one cannot treat the Charter as if it is a statutory set of self-contained rules. "The task of expounding a constitution is crucially different from that of construing a statute," he urgently exclaims in *Hunter* v. *Southam*.[18] "A statute *defines* [or posits] present rights and obligations" whereas a constitution, he insists, looks to the future. Dickson affirms Viscount Sankey's *dicta* that judges should give a constitution "a large and liberal interpretation," unlike textual rationalism where a court can "cut down the provisions of the Act by a narrow and technical construction."[19] Or, in the words of Lord Wilberforce in *Minister of Home Affairs* v. *Fisher*, a constitution with a bill of rights calls for "a generous interpretation avoiding what has been called 'that austerity of tabulated legalism'."[20] Dickson describes his own approach as "a broad, purposive analysis, which interprets specific provisions of a constitutional document *in the light of its larger objects*."[21] Again in *Big M Drug Mart*, Dickson describes his approach very differently from the textual rationalism which begins with horizontally posited given rules and which vertically deduces secondary rules from the 'givens': a court's interpretation, he writes, should be "*a generous rather than a legalistic one,* aimed at fulfilling the purpose of the guarantee and securing for individuals the full benefit of the *Charter*'s protection."[22] Again and again, Dickson differentiates his "liberal construction" with "a narrow reading" of the Charter.

Secondly, Dickson consistently differentiates the "enhanced status" of the Charter from "the distinctive nature and status" of the Canadian Bill of Rights.[23] Judicial reasoning under the Bill simply cannot "easily be transferred to a *constitutional* document like the *Charter*."[24] Further, whereas the Charter's text possesses an "imperative" character, the Court has previously viewed the Bill's language as merely declaratory of existing freedoms.[25] That is, the Canadian Bill of Rights declares a posited set of statutory rules whereas the Charter, because of its higher or elevated legitimacy, deserves a more generous weight.

Thirdly, Dickson wishes to depart from the abstractness of rationalistic reasoning. He aims to make the Charter's rights meaningful. This he can achieve only by joining the rights to their social context. This nexus would contrast with the abstract ratiocination process of Canadian Bill of Rights reasoning. A constitution, he notes in *Hunter* v. *Southam*, "must, therefore, be capable of growth and development over time to *meet new social, political and historical realities often unimagined by its framers.*"[26] In *Big M Drug Mart* Dickson insists that one should interpret the Charter in an effort to secure for each and every individual "the full benefit of the Charter's protection."[27] To the end of making the Charter effective, Dickson searches for new boundaries of constitutional analysis.

(a) *The Separation and Subordination of Posited Rules from a Constitution*
For the rule rationalist prism, posited rules constitute the whole of a constitution. According to the policy rationalist image of a constitution, social policies or values presupposed within "the community," the judge, or the posited rules themselves compose a constitution. Both images begin and end with posited rules or posited values. In contrast, Dickson pictures a constitution as separate from posited rules or the policies embedded within the rules. Whether the constitution hovers above the posited rules/policies or whether the constitution intellectually grounds or provides the rational foundation for the posited rules/policies, the constitution is supreme vis-à-vis the rules/policies in terms of legitimate authority.[28] From that characteristic, Dickson deduces "the undoubted corollary" that "no one can be convicted of an offence under an unconstitutional law."[29] Of course, if Dickson began with a rationalist image of a constitution, either the posited rules or the interests (or values) presupposed in the rules would be the supreme source of law. According to the rationalist image, one cannot have been convicted for an unconstitutional offence because, the legislature's posited rules/policies being supreme, a posited offence constitutes a part of the constitution so long as

the proper manner and form requirements have been followed in the positing enactment. In a manner not unlike that followed in his *Residential Tenancies* judgment,[30] Dickson consistently separates "the Constitution" from posited law in his Charter judgments.

Dickson elevates "the Constitution" to a higher plane of legitimacy. He does so in his conscious rejection of rule rationalism. And he does so in his explicit differentiation of the "status" of the Canadian Bill of Rights, a posited set of rules, from the "status" of the Charter, a constitutional document. Having placed the constitution upon a separate and elevated plane of legitimacy, it follows that judges should function as "the guardians of the constitution,"[31] legislatures being the guardians of posited rules.[32] As guardians of the constitution, judges possess the authority and "the duty" to review the posited practices and rules of the executive arm of government.[33] Further, it follows that Dickson would consider it "irrelevant" that a corporation, being an artificial construct (in contradistinction with a human being), might not be able to enjoy or exercise a Charter right in fact.[34] Such a suggestion simply "confuses the nature of this appeal." The key for Dickson grows out of the elevated status which he projects onto the Charter. If a posited set of rules contradicts the higher supreme law, then the former is void against whoever claims the supreme law's protection. Finally, as "interpreter of the law and defender of the constitution," the new legitimate role of courts "requires" that courts "be completely separate in authority and function from *all* other participants in the justice system."[35]

(b) *The Teleological Character of a Constitution*

A constitution, then, is separate from and elevated over posited rules. But if posited rules do not constitute a constitution, how does a constitution derive its character? Dickson responds clearly and emphatically: a constitution derives its character from its *telos* or end. Dickson describes a constitution as "purposive" or "teleological."[36] In contrast, a rationalist image of a constitution is characterized by *a priori* rules/policies and an historicist image projected backward into the norms of earlier generations. "A constitution, by contrast, is drafted with *an eye to the future*," he insists in *Hunter* v. *Southam*.[37] "Its function is to provide a *continuing* framework for the legitimate exercise of govermental power ...," he continues. Similarly, in *Big M Drug Mart*, Dickson notes in italics that "the *Charter* is intended to set a standard upon which *present as well as future legislation* is to be tested."[38] He repeatedly affirms Sankey's "classic formulation"[39] of a constitution as "a *living* tree capable of *growth* and *expansion* within its natural limits."[40] A constitution grows from within itself toward an end or *telos* shaped by its own natural limits.

Now, what exactly does Dickson mean by the term "teleological"? The concept is a Greek one. Yet, to cite a Greek notion does not necessarily mean that Dickson understands the term in the same sense as the Greeks. Indeed, Greek thought shares several different senses of the term, and so it is to Dickson's own understanding that we should turn. Dickson uses the term "teleological" in three different senses during the first five years of the Charter's history.

Sometimes, Dickson adopts the Aristotelian sense of the *telos*. For Aristotle, nature is composed of two elements: first, matter, being "the absolutely primary and formless substrate"; and secondly, the *telos* or end of matter's perpetual movement.[41] Matter's end constitutes the consummation of its growth in its healthy state.[42] When an object reaches its end (or purpose toward which it grows), it moves into a new and different entity which, in turn, possesses a different *telos*.[43] Constitutions are not immune from nature's movement.[44] Sankey's organic metaphor of "a living tree capable of growth and expansion within its *natural* limits" certainly reflects this Aristotelian image of a constitution, for the metaphor suggests that a constitution grows from within a society over time. In *The Queen* v. *Beauregard* Dickson similarly likens a constitution to a natural organism whose limits grow from within its own natural constituents: "[i]t lives and breathes and is capable of growing to keep pace with the growth of the country and its people."[45] Any particular Charter guarantee serves "the *larger* objects of the *Charter* itself," Dickson repeats in *Big M* and later cases.[46] One can appreciate the latter larger objects only if one identifies the genesis and evolving principle (or purpose) of a particular guarantee and of the Charter as a whole, Dickson advises. Dickson remains vague as to what the "larger objects" are.

One reason for this vagueness, no doubt, lies with Dickson's infrequent use of a Platonic sense of *telos*. For Plato, the *telos* of an object lies in the ideal standards of excellence in an invisible world.[47] Our visible or empirical world merely imitates the abstract forms, the latter alone constituting reality. Dickson sometimes describes a Charter guarantee in like terms as an abstract standard humanly designed or constructed to measure evolving posited law.[48] That is, a Charter provision is understood as an ideal standard or goal in a noumenal world, although Plato himself understands the latter alone to be reality in contrast to the mere imitations of the ideal standards in this visible world. In like vein, in *Société des Acadiens* v. *Association of Parents*, Dickson identifies the purpose of the

French/English equality guarantee in section 16 as a "goal."[49] The goal calls upon legislatures "to advance" the equality of status of the two official languages. The lawyer should not so much seek out the common genetic and evolving principle of section 19 as appreciate the mischief which section 19 aims to correct. Section 19's purpose, in other words, is a reaction to its genesis rather than a continuing, consistent flow from it. In this goal-oriented Platonic sense, the Charter's language provisions are described as having "broad remedial purposes."[50]

Now, Dickson expresses a third, less dominant sense of a *telos* during his early Charter judgments. This sense understands a *telos* in instrumental terms.[51] The competent lawyer aims to identify the utility of a Charter provision in fulfilling values which s/he, the lawyer, accepts as a 'given.' His/her role is not to question the ethical, political, or philosophic content of the 'given' values. Rather, justice lies in the efficacy of the Charter guarantees in serving the 'given' ends or ideals. That requires the judge to define, qualify, and balance the Charter "guarantees" so as to render overall benefits vis-à-vis the 'given' ends. This utilitarian or instrumentalist sense of a *telos* or purpose brings with it a very different package of issues than the organic Aristotelian or the ideal Platonic senses of a *telos*.

(c) *History as a Resource Material*

During the first five years following the enactment of the Charter, Dickson's picture of a constitution takes the Aristotelian sense of a *telos* as a pivotal horizon. Not surprisingly, history figures well in these early judgments. The Sankey *dicta*, noted above, describes a constitution's organic *telos* in terms of temporality. The "historic underpinnings" of a Charter guarantee or a challenged statute enlighten their purposes. In *Hunter* v. *Southam*, for example, Dickson describes a constitution as "a continuing framework" which, once enacted, must be "capable of growth and development over time to meet new social, political, and historical realities often unimagined by its framers."[52] Sections 10(1) and 10(3) of the Combines Investigation Act serve as the surface issue. Section 10(1) authorizes the director of the combines investigation branch to enter "any premises" in order to inquire into, examine, copy, or seize any document or evidence which the director considers relevant for his investigation. Prior to exercising this power, a member of the restrictive trade practices commission must sign a certificate authorizing the exercise of the investigatory power. Counsel claims that sections 10(1) and (3) contravene the guarantee against "unreasonable searches and seizures" in section 8 of the Charter. The "crux" of the case, according to Dickson, is the meaning to be given to the "vague and open" word "unreasonable" in section 8 of the Charter. To respond to that question Dickson distinguishes a constitution from posited law,[53] openly rejects a rule rationalist image of a constitution,[54] and expounds upon the teleological character of a constitution.[55] In order to identify the end of section 8 and of the Charter generally, Dickson seeks out the common law origins of the section 8 guarantee.[56] He traces the evolution of the common law doctrine in an effort to detect a common end.[57] And he concludes that "[a]nglo-Canadian legal and political traditions point to a higher standard" for the reasonableness of a search and seizure than the standard suggested by counsel.[58]

Similarly, in an effort to identify the purpose of the "freedom of conscience and religion" in *R.* v. *Big M Drug Mart*, Dickson demonstrates a breadth of historical research unappreciated since Rand's judgments.[59] Counsel challenged the very constitutionality of the Lord's Day Act, arguing that the compulsion of religious observance offends "freedom of conscience and religion" as guaranteed in section 2 of the Charter. After elaborating the facts, the posited rules, and the holdings of the trial and appellate courts, Dickson resolves the 'standing' and 'freedom of religion' issues by feeling compelled to outline his inward image of a constitution. After distinguishing a constitution from posited rules[60] and the Charter from the Canadian Bill of Rights,[61] Dickson elaborates the purposive character of a constitution.[62] Once again, Dickson seeks out the *telos* of posited legislation and the *telos* of the text's guarantee by returning to the "historic underpinnings" of the Lord's Day Act in the Fourth Commandment (Exodus 20:8–11) and by tracing its repeated re-enactments over the centuries.[63] He reviews the evolution of American and Canadian judicial decisions during this century.[64] And he joins the historical context to what he understands to be the underlying concepts or *telos* of the text's "guarantees."[65] After all, he cautions, "the *Charter* was not enacted in a vacuum and must therefore ... be placed in its proper linguistic, philosophic and historical contexts."[66] Indeed, later in his judgment he goes so far as to suggest that "[t]he values that underlie our political and philosophic *traditions demand*" a particular purpose or end for the freedom of conscience and religion.[67]

Again, in *Société des Acadiens* v. *Association of Parents*, Dickson tries to identify the purpose of the text's language guarantees by reviewing their genesis and evolution.[68] Appellants argue that their right to choose to use French in court includes the right to be fully understood by their judges. Dickson so holds, although in the absence of any clear evidentiary basis to the contrary, the judge under scrutiny is presumed capable of understanding French. When confronted with the request to extend section 19 to include the right to be fully understood, Dickson "firmly endorsed a purposive approach."[69] And that, in turn, opens the door for an examination of "the constitutional antecedents of the *Charter* language protections." This draws him to the *telos* of linguistic duality: "[l]inguistic duality has been a longstanding concern in our nation. Canada is a country with both French and English solidly embedded in its history."[70] Section 19 of the Charter, then, has as its purpose or end the "continued and renewed efforts *in the direction of bilingualism.*" That direction constitutes "the spirit and purpose of the guarantee."[71] Having identified this *telos* by studying Canada's past, Dickson now appreciates the need for "a liberal construction" which would render the *telos* "meaningful," "effective," and "coherent."

Finally, in *The Queen* v. *Beauregard*, Dickson goes to British and Canadian constitutional history in order to find a common principle – the independence of the courts – which can be used to strike down parliamentary enactments.[72] Parliament has retroactively required that judges contribute to a pension scheme even though section 100 of the Constitution Act, 1867 has simply provided that pensions "shall be fixed and provided" by Parliament. Again and again, Dickson appeals to history – not the Constitution Act – in order to identify "the foundations" of the principle and its constituent requirements: "historically, the generally accepted core of the principle ...," "it is trite history ...," "[t]he fundamental traditions of those courts ...," "the deep roots ...," and "at least since the *Act of Settlement, 1700 ...*"[73] Indeed, Dickson acknowledges that two other principles – parliamentary supremacy and the rule of law – have also been "the cornerstone of the constitutional system for centuries." It is not just their ancient roots, though, that help Dickson detect the ends of the constitution. He traces the expanding *telos* of the 'judicial independence' principle: "of recent years the general understanding of the principle has grown and been transformed," "the history of the Constitution of the United Kingdom reveals continuous growth towards independent judicial authority," and its evolution demonstrates its "vitality and vibrancy."

(d) *The Social Nexus*

Dickson clearly aspires to break from the abstract *ratiocination* process which has characterized the rule rationalist image of a constitution. The notions of a *telos* and historical context offer two boundaries of his alternative image of a constitution. But, having identified a guarantee's purpose against history, Dickson methodically works out the social impact of that purpose: "[p]urpose and effect respectively, in the sense of the legislation's object and its ultimate impact, are clearly linked, if not indivisible."[74] In *Hunter* v. *Southam*, for example, he assesses the actual impact of a search and seizure upon an actual subject in contrast to past inquiries of the simple "rationality in furthering some valid government objective."[75] An effects analysis, he considers, would offer a "more ready and more vigorous protection of constitutional rights."[76] Similarly, in *R.* v. *Oakes* he reads section 11(d)'s guarantee of a 'presumption of innocence' against the personal, social, psychological, and economic harm caused to a citizen who has been charged with a criminal offence.[77] And in *Société des Acadiens* v. *Association of Parents*, Dickson argues that the right to speak and make written submissions in French before a New Brunswick court, to be meaningful, extends to the right to be understood by a judge in French.[78] This extended right flows from the "fundamental [need] ... to any effective and coherent guarantee of language rights in the courtroom ..."[79]

The best example of Dickson's linkage of the *telos* of a guarantee to the social context is his arduous *Retail Business Holidays* case. There, he construes the 'freedom of religion' guarantee to include protection against indirect and unintentional burdens upon religious practices.[80] Dickson describes how, in the absence of legislative intervention, Saturday and Sunday observers compete upon an equal footing. But the Retail Business Holidays Act has the effect of driving the Saturday observer to a "natural disadvantage" relative to a non-believer: the Act requires that the Saturday observer remain closed an extra day relative to the Sunday observer. In addition, Dickson notes how the Act exempts some Saturday-observing retailers who meet employee and square-footage restrictions. The Act also impacts upon Saturday-observing consumers. By working out the social/cultural ramifications of the Act, Dickson aims to join the purpose of the 'religious freedom' guarantee to social reality.

(e) The Judiciary's Institutional Self-Image

Dickson's rejection of rule rationalism, his elevation of the status of the Charter over the Canadian Bill of Rights, and his concern that Charter rights be meaningful and effective in the real world: these three factors reflect how Dickson wishes to break out of the rationalist hold in which he has found himself. Although the source of a constitution appears unclear, the character of a constitution emanates from its *telos*. He believes that one can best identify a constitution's *telos* by studying the historical origins and evolution of any particular Charter guarantee.

Against these components of his image of a constitution, Dickson continually interjects his own self-image as a judge. Most important, he sees himself and he sees the judiciary as "the guardian of the constitution."[81] This is the same self-image which has induced Dickson to overrule the Residential Tenancies Act.[82] As a guardian of the constitution, a judge not only possesses "the power, but *the duty*, to regard the inconsistent statute, to the extent of the inconsistency, as being no longer 'of force or effect'."[83] Indeed, the court's dury extends beyond a scrutiny of legislation. In *Operation Dismantle* Dickson claims that decisions of a federal cabinet are in fact reviewable by the courts under the Charter.[84] From his own self-image as a judge, Dickson projects a corresponding institutional role for a legislature and executive. On the one hand, the government bears "a general duty to act in accordance with the Charter's dictates."[85] Although the courts serve as the "guardians of the Constitution ...," it is the legislature's responsibility to enact legislation that embodies appropriate safeguards to comply with the Constitution's requirements."[86] On the other hand, Dickson's institutional self-image necessitates that legislatures and the executive arm of government leave judges "totally free to render decisions," as his judgment in *Beauregard* underlines.[87]

3. DICKSON'S RATIONALIST HANGOVER

Dickson desperately wishes to depart, if not entirely escape, from the rationalist hold which, we have seen in earlier chapters, permeates the images of the contemporary legal community. To a large extent he succeeds in doing so by picturing the Charter of Rights historically, socially, and teleologically. And yet, it is not easy for him to do so, for Dickson arguably shares two key elements of a rationalist image of a constitution.

First, we have noted above that Dickson sometimes adopts an instrumentalist conception of the *telos* of a constitution. Instrumental rationality permeates a 'balancing of interests' role for judges. In *Hunter* v. *Southam*, for example, Dickson represents the "proper" approach as "in other words, to delineate the nature of the interests it [that is, a Charter guarantee] is meant to protect."[88] And when he applies his teleological approach in *Hunter*, one is hard-pressed to distinguish his approach from the expression of policy rationalism which we studied in Chapter VI.[89] 'When is the balance of interests to be assessed?' 'On what basis must the balance of interests be assessed?' and 'what further balancing of interests, if any, may be contemplated by section 1, beyond that evisaged by section 8?': these constitute the very issues which Dickson faces when he unpacks his image of a constitution expressed in the earlier portion of his *Hunter* judgment.[90]

Dickson's instrumentalist "interest balancing" role reaches its zenith in the Charter's early years in *Re Fraser*, where a public servant has publicly criticized the government's policy on metric conversion in several forums: first, a letter to a local newspaper; second, his attendance at a municipal meeting where a motion opposing the government's policy has been presented; and, third, a journalist's article which quotes Fraser's original letter with a photograph of him carrying a placard bearing the slogan "Your freedom to measure is a measure of your freedom."[91] Fraser is discharged from his job as an income tax auditor, a decision which Dickson affirms. Dickson does not seek out the *telos* of 'freedom of expression' in our history as he aims to do in other judgments. Rather, he accepts the competing values of "an impartial and effective public service" as a 'given.' Impartiality and effectiveness, in turn, require knowledge, fairness, integrity, neutrality, and loyalty.[92] 'Freedom of expression' must be defined, qualified, and balanced against each of these posited competing values, according to Dickson. And, in the circumstances, loyalty to the government outweighs "the value" of 'freedom of expression.'

Dickson departs most frequently from his Aristotelian sense of a *telos* when faced with the "limitations" clause of the Charter. In *Big M Drug Mart*, *Oakes*, and the *Retail Business Holidays* cases he understands section 1 of the Charter entirely through a prism which balances social policies. Government objectives which are "of sufficient importance" can override a constitutionally protected right.[93] Once a judge "recognises" "a sufficiently significant government interest," then the judge's proper role is to examine the legislative means used to achieve the posited objective. In particular, does the legislature adopt a means to achieve the end "by impairing as little as possible the right or freedom in question"? Dickson's self-described 'proportionality' doctrine accepts the posited statutory objectives, if "significant," as a 'given.' And his "balancing of social interests' assumes that the Charter's rights are mathematically quantifiable, as if they were apples in a fruit market. Instrumental rationality permeates the application of his teleological image of a constitution to such a degree as to render his judgments (and image) incoherent.

Nowhere does Dickson, in any of his section 1 judgments, try to explain why one social objective is more important than another. In *Oakes* Dickson can only suggest that an objective should be "pressing and substantial in a free and democratic society."[94] Dickson's *Oakes* and *Public Service Alliance* judgments ignore the critical concepts of "freedom" and "democracy" in section 1 of the Charter: no genealogy of the concepts "freedom" and "democracy"; no examination of the evolution of the concepts since the seventeenth century; no contemplation of the possibility that there inheres in our history two very different traditions of freedom (negative and positive freedom) and two very different traditions of democracy (procedural majoritarianism and the flourishing of the self).[95] Dickson accepts the posited objectives of challenged legislation as a 'given.' Further, that is the very point of his 'proportionality' test. The test concentrates upon the efficacy of the legislated means in achieving the legislated objective. As he expresses it in the *Retail Business Holidays* case, "[t]he requirement of rational connection calls for an assessment of how well the legislative garment has been tailored to suit its purpose."[96] His inspired search for new boundaries of a constitution collapses into the very rationalist enterprise from which, in early reflective moments, he seems so determined to escape.

Dickson reflects this rationalist hangover in a second way. Although he obviously acknowledges the importance of an image of a constitution, Dickson still treats constitutional law as if it were objective, 'out there,' separate from the very prism through which he pictures constitutional law. "Some objective standard must be established," he insists, in order to locate "the constitutional balance between a justifiable expectation of privacy and the legitimate needs of the state."[97] Such an objective standard contrasts with "the subjective appreciation of individual adjudicators." His belief in an objective law independent of the adjudicator/interpreter underlies his contemporaneous judgment in *Towne Cinema Theatres Ltd.* v. *R.*[98] There, he insists that it is possible "to determine *in an objective way* what is tolerable in accordance with the contemporary standards of the Canadian community and not merely to project one's *own personal ideas* of what is tolerable."[99] In like manner, Dickson leaves the reasonableness of a limit in section 1 of the Charter to the legislature: for the judge to draw lines of reasonableness would take him/her beyond the objective role which Dickson sees for himself and his peers.

It is difficult not to describe Dickson in these passages as one would a scientist. The "interests," the balancing role, the objectivity of constitutional law: these all exist 'out there' as natural determinate facts to be discovered, investigated, quantified, and balanced. Dickson as a scientist sees himself as a neutral, impartial, and apolitical observer whose job it is to investigate and weigh the natural elements.

Indeed, he more or less writes such in his *Operation Dismantle* judgment.[100] Dickson rejects the section 7 claim that the testing of cruise missiles harms the 'right to life' and 'security of the person' because he cannot scientifically treat the allegations as fact. The speculated harm is mere "opinion and belief" in his words. As such, the harm is not entitled to the character of rational knowledge. More particularly, one cannot establish a link between the cabinet decision to allow the testing of cruise missiles on the one hand and the increased risk of nuclear war on the other.[101] The nature of foreign policy decisions is "a matter of speculation,"[102] "not possible" to predict,[103] and mere "hypothesis."[104] To claim that the development of the cruise would escalate the nuclear arms race is mere "speculation."[105] Generally, the claim that 'life,' 'liberty,' or 'security of the person' would be risked is "premised on assumptions and hypotheses about how independent and soveriegn nations, operating in an international arena of radical uncertainty, and continually changing circumstances, will react to the Canadian government's decision to permit the testing of the cruise missile."[106] After surveying the unclear, speculative, uncertain character of the plaintiff's allegations, Dickson concludes: "I wish to highlight that they are raising matters that, in my opinion, lie *in the realm of conjecture, rather than fact.* In brief, it is simply not possible for a court, even with the best available evidence, to do more than speculate ..."[107] He continues in the next paragraph that "[t]he very nature of such an allegation is that it cannot be proven to be true by the adduction of evidence."[108] In the same way that a judge must concern himself with facts in an 'is' world as wholly constitutive of legal knowledge, so too "[a] duty of the federal cabinet cannot arise on the basis of speculation and hypothesis about possible effects of government action. Such a duty *only* arises, *in my view,* where it can be said that a deprivation of life and security of the person *could be proven to result* from the impugned government act."[109] Presumably, Dickson's delimitation of law to scientific fact logically compels him to wait for a nuclear "accident"/holocaust before speculation, hypothesis, or values transform into "fact" and thereby become a ripe subject of constitutional investigation.

4. WILSON'S REVISION OF DICKSON'S IMAGE

Madame Justice Wilson's early judgments share Dickson's desire to break from the dominant rationalist image of a constitution. She gives more legitimacy to the Charter than the Canadian Bill of Rights because "the recent adoption of the Charter by Parliament and nine of the ten provinces as part of the Canadian constitutional framework has sent a clear message to the courts that the restrictive attitude which at times characterized their approach to the *Canadian Bill of Rights* ought to be re-examined."[110] She consciously rejects a textual rationalism which accepts the Charter's rights as if they posited abstract determinant rules.[111] She expresses a need to breathe life into the Charter's rights by making them effective and meaningful in social circumstances.[112] And she pictures a constitution as independent and separate from posited rules.[113] Thus, she shares some of the essentials of Dickson's image of a constitution. Her affinity to his image is reflected in her adoption of the *coram* judgment in *Quebec Protestant Separate School Bds*, her affirmation of Dickson's *Hunter* v. *Southam* judgment, and Dickson's adoption of her reasons in *Singh et al* v. *M.E.I.*

But Wilson expresses concern that Dickson's analytic framework does not accomplish what he wishes for it in concrete circumstances. She feels compelled to write separate judgments in several cases.[114] She openly rejects Dickson's teleological or purposive approach. She calls her image of a constitution an "effects" image because it incorporates, she thinks, the empirical reality lying beyond the theoretical and formal rights. As with Dickson, however, her image of a constitution retains rationalist strains within it.

We have seen that Dickson finds himself entrapped within the overpowering hold of rationalism. First, he contemplates a utilitarian balancing of interests which accepts posited ends as 'givens' and which quantifies their weights as if they are elements of nature. Secondly, he pictures law as an objective entity, separate from the interpreter and a subject-matter of scientific investigation. Wilson addresses both issues in her early judgments. She seems to acknowledge that both balancing and objectivity serve as serious stumbling-blocks to the effectiveness of the Charter. And she recognizes the desperate need to elaborate different boundaries from Dickson if she is to escape from the rationalist legal culture in which she finds herself.

(a) *Wilson's Rejection of Utilitarian Balancing*

First, Wilson sometimes claims that prudential or efficacious factors should not outweigh a constitutional right. In the *Saskatchewan Dairy Workers Case*, for example, Wilson Differentiates the Charter from "past discussion" in this way: in the past, lawyers have "always focused on the question of when it is *best* for government to intervene [to prohibit strikes] not on the question of when it is *constitutional* for government to do so."[115] Similarly, in *Singh et al.* v. *M.E.I.*, Singh has claimed "convention refugee status" as defined in a posited rule (section 2(1) of the Immigration Act, 1976).[116] The minister, upon the advice of a legislatively created committee, has denied the applicants "convention refugee status." Both the Immigration Appeal Board and the Federal Court of Appeal deny Singh's application for a redetermination of his refugee status. Singh's counsel claims that the posited procedures for the adjudication of refugee status violate the right to life, liberty, and security of the person, and the right not to be deprived thereof except in accordance with fundamental justice as guaranteed in section 7 of the Charter.[117] Wilson's image of a constitution clashes with the denial of Singh's refugee status.

Wilson asks whether the rules authorizing the denial can be saved by section 1 of the Charter. She answers that section 1 cannot save the rules, notwithstanding the government's attractiveness to Dickson's utilitarian balancing. First, she consciously refuses to allow utilitarian factors to outweigh the Charter's rights in her consideration of section 1. Secondly, she wishes to reject a ultilitarian conception of a right.[118] For a utilitarian, a right is a social interest or privilege which the legislature or executive may grant or take away as a testator bestows benefits.[119] Since a portion of her *Operation Dismantle* judgment reflects a very weak sense of rights,[120] let us look more closely at a situation where she explicitly rejects a utilitarian balancing role in *Singh*.

In *Singh*, Wilson begins her section 1 discussion by emphasizing how a court's response to section 1 is "without a doubt, a question of enormous significance for the operation of the *Charter*."[121] The government lawyer has argued that the immigration appeal board "was already subjected to a considerable strain in terms of the volumes of cases which it was required to hear."[122] Further, if the supreme court should require an oral hearing in every case where an application for redetermination of a refugee claim has been made, this decision "would constitute an unreasonable burden on the Board's resources." Wilson reacts to these utilitarian arguments by elevating the status to the Charter's rights and freedoms above the status of posited rules.[123] The courts, she expresses, are committed to uphold the Charter rights.[124] "Seen in this light," she doubts whether "the type of utilitarian consideration" which counsel has ushered forth would satisfy her. Indeed, "[c]ertainly the guarantees of the *Charter* would be *illusory* if they could be ignored because it was *administratively convenient* to do so."[125] A focus upon the "considerable time and money" to be saved by existing posited procedures, "misses the point of the exercise under s. 1." The higher status attributed to section 7 rights "implicitly recognizes that a *balance of administrative convenience* does not override the need to adhere to these principles [in section 7]."[126] The justification must be "more compelling" than that.

(b) *The Judiciary's a Priori Duties*

Wilson seem to depart from a second rationalist boundary of Dickson's image of a constitution: namely, that law is objectively discoverable in a world independently from a judge's pre-understanding of that world. Now, Wilson too projects law as an objective entity. Yet, she entertains the very speculative issues which Dickson epitomizes as illegitimate. Traditionally, Canadian judges refrain from adjudicating upon executive decisions because of the open "moral and political considerations" in such a task, she acknowledges in *Operation Dismantle*.[127] In contrast, the constitutionality of the testing of cruise missles, quoting from Lord Radcliffe in a British case, inevitably "depends on an infinity of considerations, military and diplomatic, technical, psychological and moral, and of decisions, tentative or final, which are themselves past assessments of fact and part expectations and hopes."[128] The moral/political character of these considerations should not prevent a judge from reviewing them, according to Wilson. "However unsuited courts may be for the task, they are called upon all the time to decide questions of principle and policy," she notes.[129] This did not stop British, American, and Canadian judges from reviewing restrictive trade practices, the Sherman Act, or administrative tribunal decisions of such agencies as the Canadian Transport Commission or the CRTC respectively.

Wilson recognizes that the key issue in *Operation Dismantle* is not the efficacious "*ability* of judicial tribunals to make a decision on the questions presented."[130] Rather, the constitutional issue goes to a matter of *duty*: "whether the courts *should* or *must* rather than on whether they *can* deal with such matters."[131] That is, is it "*appropriate* or *obligatory* for the courts to decide the issue"?[132] The weightiness of the particular political consequences which a court is obligated to review should not detract from duty, she affirms. In her words, "the courts should not be too eager to relinquish their judicial review function simply because they are called upon to exercise it in relation to weighty matters of state."[133] "[I]t is *our obligation* under the *Charter* to do so," she reminds herself.[134] To evaluate a posited cabinet policy in terms of duty constitutes "a totally different question" from scrutinizing the empirical consequences or meritorious content of a cabinet policy, she believes.[135] The Charter, that is, raises *a priori* claims in an objective noumenal world in contrast to empirical consequentialist claims of a phenomenal world.

(c) *Wilson's Empiricist Constitution*

At the same time that she incorporates objectivist issues of obligation, Wilson differentiates the boundaries of her image from Dickson's "teleological" image. Dickson's purposive image of the Charter, she thinks, simply continues the "pith and substance" approach to traditional 'division of powers' analysis.[136] That approach distils the "constitutional value" represented in challenged legislation by distinguishing its primary legislative purpose from its merely incidental effects. That is, one "abstracts" the primary purpose from the broader spectrum of legislative effects. Only when the consequences directly reflect a primary statutory purpose do the effects take on analytic significance.[137] Wilson suggests that it is precisely the adoption of this purposive image of a constitution which explains the shallow, inadequate judicial decisions which have harmed civil liberties during the pre-Charter past.[138] Wilson believes that "the constitutional entrenchment of civil liberties in the *Canadian Charter of Rights and Freedoms* necessarily changes the analytic approach the courts must adopt in such cases."[139] The Charter is "first and foremost an effects-oriented document."[140] 'Whatever the purpose of a posited set of rules, do the rules impact upon an individual right?': that is, "the first stage of any *Charter* analysis," she claims.[141]

If Wilson pictures the Charter as "first and foremost" an effects-oriented document, how direct a nexus need there be between the statute and the negative impact of the statute upon duties/rights? First, she points out in *Big M Drug Mart* that the consequences need not be real or actual. They can be potential. In her words, "[i]n my view, so long as a statute has such an actual or *potential effect* on an entrenched right, it does not matter what the purpose behind the enactment was."[142] And again, "[o]nce the plaintiff can point to an actual *or potential* impingement on a protected right, it will not matter that the underlying legislative purpose is subject to conjecture."[143] Secondly, in *Operation Dismantle*, she widens her "effects" inquiry to include "an infinity of considerations," as noted above.[144] However unsuited judges are for the task, they have the authority and *the duty* to examine the effects of these complex considerations for constitutional rights. Yes, the consequences take the judiciary into the moral/political content of posited rules. Yes, judges have pursued such an enterprise before. No, judges should not shirk their responsibility to entertain such a policy-oriented, empirical inquiry. And yet, not all consequences offend constitutional guarantees, Wilson cautions in *Jones v. The Queen*.[145] "[T]rivial or insubstantial" effects should be excluded.

Having broadened the scope of legitimate socio-economic impact inquiry, Wilson then imposes a heavy burden upon government lawyers in their justification of restrictions upon Charter rights. In *Singh*, for example, she expresses "a particular disappointment" in "the limited scope of the factual material brought forward" by the state's counsel in support of the government's section 1 claim.[146] Wilson echoes the observations of a colleague to the effect that the state must offer sufficient empirical evidence to demonstrate a reasonable limit. Even if utilitarian considerations (such as costs and the volume of cases)[147] were considered relevant factors in justifying a limit to a Charter right (which, as we noted, she holds as irrelevant),[148] Wilson is dissatisfied with the scanty empirical evidence adduced to show the serious economic costs resulting from an award for *Singh*.[149] Similarly, in *Jones*, Wilson insists that government lawyers should offer more than a compelling social interest in education so as to save the School Act from constitutional attack.[150] Jones has refused to proceed through the regulatory machinery required of him to receive an exemption for the mandatory public school attendance of his children and approval of his academy as a private school. Government lawyers have failed to fulfil the section 1 onus of adducing evidence demonstrating that the regulatory machinery has impaired Jones's religious freedom as little as possible, given other alternatives. Further, the government lawyers have failed to demonstrate how the regulatory scheme in fact ensures that children would receive efficient schooling. Indeed, the government has offered not a single justification for the regulatory scheme.[151]

What is more, Wilson charges government lawyers with more than a heavy duty to proffer demonstrable empirical evidence justifying limits to a constitutional right. After a lengthy excursus into the theoretical nature of a right in *Macdonald*, she acknowledges a more general affirmative obligation on the state's part to make constitutional rights effective.[152] This positive duty contrasts with "a negative duty not to interfere with X's right to use his own language."[153] But from whence comes the positive duty? Certainly, the text of the Constitutional Acts, 1867 alone does not legitimate such a positive role on the part of the state. And the passive self-image of judges such as Laskin would ordinarily deter a judge from enforcing such a positive duty on legislators. Rather, Wilson finds two sources for the state's affirmative duty: first, Canadian constitutional history;[154] and second, her "initial premise ... that the essence of language is communication."[155] The latter social premise incorporates "the notion of understanding and being understood."[156] Thus, the textual right to use French in pleadings "recognizes and accommodates the litigant's right to understand and be understood."[157] This would work to ensure a "meaningful" or effective access to the courts and would join the text to "the needs" of the citizenry.[158]

But why does Wilson expect lawyers to examine the moral, psychological, military, and cultural consequences of legislation for real human beings? And why does she require lawyers to adduce demonstrable empirical evidence in their section 1 arguments? One answer lies in her judgment of *Société des Acadiens* v. *Association of Parents*[159] where the Société has claimed that the language rights of its group are infringed when one of the judges before whom the Société appears allegedly does not comprehend French adequately. Wilson aims to join the text called The Constitution Act with the social/cultural fabric of the Canadian community in her response to the challenge. More generally, a constitution for Wilson emanates from within the organic evolution of a society. Section 19(2) of the Charter provides, for example, that "Either English or French may be used by any person in, or in any pleading in or process issuing from, any court of New Brunswick." Wilson infers from the text that judges be able to understand the proceedings before them. But there lurk many issues behing this indeterminate conception of "understanding": "What level of understanding is required? Who decides whether the appropriate level is attained? Must the understanding be a direct understanding through the language itself or is understanding through the medium of translation adequate?"[160] These issues, in turn, hang upon a "broader and more difficult question": namely, "is the level of understanding required merely the level required for due process ... [o]r is the level to be determined in the context of the principle of equality of status of the two official languages in the court structure?"[161]

To respond to these issues, Wilson goes to her overall image of the text's language rights (especially section 16) and the Charter as a whole. She hypothesizes two conceptions of the guarantee: does section 16, for example, merely posit a "new constitutional standard" much like "a platonic assertion of good intention" without real legal consequence?[162] or, alternatively, does the text itself impose a "self-executing" obligation upon the government immediately to "root" equality of language rights "firmly in the Canadian reality"?[163] Wilson follows the first alternative. Section 16(1) of the text does not describe the present reality. Rather, it declares a goal.[164] That a gap persists between the goal and the cultural reality does not trigger constitutional relief. Rather, one must identify the stage of social/cultural growth or development at any particular time. That is, "where are we currently on the road to bilingualism and is the impugned conduct in keeping with that stage of development?"[165] So long as the governmental conduct coincides with the cultural norm of the appropriate historical stage, then government fulfils "the spirit of section 16." Wilson openly presumes that the judiciary's "understanding of what is significant and what is reasonable under present [political/cultural] conditions will evolve at a pace commensurate with social change."[166] Again, when considering the meaning and character of section 133's required use of French or English in Canadian courts, Wilson understands that section 133 "contained an *organic* principle of growth capable of responsing to changing social realities."[167] After all, the text's linguistic rights "grew out of our peculiar Canadian heritage and the evolution of our social and political history."[168] It would be strange, then, that lawyers would ahistorically arrest their interpretative enterprise with an *a priori* edict in 1982.

(d) *The Meaning of Charter Guarantees*

Wilson's "effects" image of the Charter, of course, presupposes that one knows the meaning of the Charter's rights. Her image concentrates upon the question 'knowing the meaning of a constitutional right, does a posited set of rules impact upon the right?' She herself acknowledges that the text of the Charter uses very open-ended, if not indeterminate, concepts such as the right to 'life,' the right to 'liberty,' and the right to 'security of the person,' all of which are "capable of a broad range of meaning."[169] The text leaves judges "with a conundrum" because section 7 reads "the principles of fundamental justice" instead of "natural justice" and "due process" which had been judicially construed and applied.[170] What do the terms of the Charter mean? How should one go about trying to discover their meaning? Do the text's concepts possess an inherent meaning? After all, she reminds the legal community in *Singh*, "it is incumbent upon the Court to give meaning to each of the elements, life, liberty and security of the person, which make up the 'right' contained in s. 7."[171]

Wilson responds to the latter questions in each of her early judgments. Dickson responds by going to the historical origins of a Charter concept. He studies its evolution with an eye to identifying its purpose. Wilson, in contrast, goes to normative political/moral theory presupposed in a concept. The source of theory is twofold. In *Singh* and *Big M Drug Mart* intuition grounds the theory. In *Operation Dismantle, Re. s. 94(2) Motor Vehicle Act B.S.B.C. 1979, Jones, Macdonald,* and *Retail Business Holidays,* Wilson increasingly appeals to the scholarly discourse of political and moral theory, much as lawyers and judges have appealed to precedent in earlier generations.

In *Singh*, for example, Wilson ultimately discovers "the meaning" of section 7 rights within her own intuition: "To return to the facts before the Court, it will be recalled that a Convention refugee is by definition a person who has a well-founded fear of persecution in the country from which he is fleeing. *In my view*, to deprive him of the avenues open to him under the Act to escape from that fear of persecution *must*, at the least, *impair* his right to life, liberty and security of the person in the narrow sense by counsel for the Minister."[172] Though one's return to one's homeland *may* not automatically cause a deprivation of the right to life or liberty, "I *cannot*, however, *accept*," she asserts, that such a return does not deprive one of one's security of the person.[173] Again, her meaning of the latter is an emotive or intuitive one. That is, her appeal is to a "it seems to me," or the term "*must*" mean, or "I cannot accept" that meaning. As she expresses it again, upon acknowledging that "unfortunately no clear meaning of the words emerges from the case law," "*It seems to me* that even if one adopts the narrow approach advocated by counsel for the Minister, 'security of the person' *must encompass* freedom from the threat of physical punishment or suffering as well as freedom from such punishment itself."[174] In *Singh*, Wilson is aided in the interpretative enterprise by the fact that all counsel agree, no doubt intuitively as well, that "at a minimum" "fundamental justice" in section 7 includes the notion of procedural fairness.[175]

Similarly, in *Big M Drug Mart* Wilson defines the freedom of conscience and religion by intuition. After expressing her "effects" approach to the Charter, she states that

Applying such reasoning to the case at bar, one can agree with Dickson J. at p. 337, that in enacting the *Lord's Day Act* "[t]he arm of the state requires all to remember the Lord's day of the Christians and to keep it holy," and that "[t]he protection of one religion and the concomitant non-protection of others imports disparate impact destructive of the religious freedom of the collectivity." *Accordingly*, the Act infringes upon the freedom of conscience and religion guaranteed in s. 2(a) of the *Charter*.[176]

Yes, Wilson exposes the *de facto* impact of the posited law. But she understands the impact in terms of a Charter right. And *that*, she leave undefined, perhaps inevitably so. Her "accordingly" expresses that the impact has offended her intuitive image of the freedom.

Wilson's posit of her own intuition serves as a convenient manner in which to resolve the moral/political issues which she recognizes as important. And this avenue has the support of one of the more renowned British philosophers of this century.[177] But intuition as the source of resolving ethical issues still seems to run counter to her insistence in *Operation Dismantle* that a judge should not substitute his/her opinion for that of the executive as to the merits or soundness of a policy.[178] For, if law is to remain objective, how can Wilson legitimately superimpose her opinions or intuitions upon the content of the higher, supreme law of a constitution? Her embrace of an intuitive source for law certainly resembles a positivism characteristic of the rationalist image of a constitution – only intuition replaces rules. Both entertain the objectivity of law. So, if Wilson really begins with a rationalist image of a constitution, her positing of her own intuitions may not render her image incoherent. Indeed, William Lederman, we shall see, shares and explains the need for our faith in the judge's ultimate posit of his/her intuition.[179] What may well render Wilson's image of a constitution incoherent is her earlier caution against a judge's substitution of her own intuition for the executive's and, more generally, Wilson's importation of empiricism into her otherwise rationalist image of a constitution. Of course, on this interpretation, Wilson like Dickson remains entrapped within the rationalist horizons from which she so deeply aspires to escape.

Now, Wilson does appeal to more than intuition in another series of judgments: *Operation Dismantle, Re B.C. Motor Vehicles Act, Jones, Macdonald,* and *Retail Business Holidays.* Here, she gives content to the Charter's concepts by seeking out ideal-directed political, moral, and legal theory as expounded by the professional theorists themselves. Wilson responds to the question 'could the facts as alleged violate section 7 of the *Charter?*' in *Operation Dismantle* by elaborating her own theory of rights grounded in her own intuitions. Her intuitions are aided this time, however, by appropriate quotations from leading liberal Anglo-American philosophers of this century: Mortimer J. Adler,[180] John Rawls,[181] Ronald Dworkin,[182] and Roscoe Pound.[183] No doubt, each of the four philosophers would shudder to think that their rights theories could be found in one sentence. And at least Dworkin would be astonished to see how one quotation could be used to legitimize the thesis which he has aspired to undermine.[184] The point is, though, that Wilson appeals to "theorists" to legitimate her intuitions. And she follows through with a theory about freedom.[185] Hers is the classic liberal theory of negative freedom: that is, that the state should not directly impinge upon or threaten the life or physical security of an assignable individual.[186] Because the cruise missile testing only concerns the relations between two sovereign states and because the testing does not directly harm "any member of the immediate political community," she thinks that the testing does not offend negative freedom. Accordingly, the testing of the cruise does not contravene section 7 of the Charter.

Similarly, in *Re B.C. Motor Vehicle Act*, Wilson recognizes "the conundrum" because the Charter's text asserts such an undefined concept as "the principles of fundamental justice." Again, intuition forms the grounding of her meaning. "We know what 'fundamental principles' are," she insists. "They are the basic, bedrock principles that underpin a system."[187] Not all principles of law are fundamental principles: "only those which are basic to our system of justice," she claims toward the end of her judgment.[188] As with Dickson, "it will be for the courts" to inform us as to those. Wilson uses legal theory to legitimize her intuitions.

She does so in two parts of the *B.C. Motor Vehicle Reference*. First, she thinks that the attachment of a mandatory imprisonment sanction to a statutory offence contravenes section 7 of the Charter because mandatory imprisonment has invariably been reserved in the past "for the more serious *mens rea* offences." She reviews the earliest beginnings of mandatory sentences and then goes to scholarly texts on the subject (Holdsworth's *A History of English Law*, Blackstone's *Commentaries*, Archbold's *Criminal Pleading, Evidence and Practice* [1938], Allan's *Legal Duties*, and Kenny's *Outlines of Criminal Law*).[189] In addition, a Privy Council (1931) and a Canadian Supreme Court judgment each help her to frame the theoretical principle that mandatory imprisonment *ought* to be reserved for the more serious *mens rea* offences. The 'theory' of criminal law suggests this to be a principle of fundamental justice. The text seems clear. Further explanation is unnecessary, aside from an 'I do not believe.'

This still does not resolve whether a mandatory imprisonment sentence offends fundamental justice if attached to *an absolute* liability offence. To respond to that question, Wilson again feels compelled to turn to the theory of punishment "for the answer." The theory of punishment, for her, is synonymous with the "main objectives of the penal system."[190] That is, the 'theory' to which she appeals concerns a descriptively oriented theory of posited sentencing rules as they exist, not an ideal directed theory. She uncovers "the theory" in a 1969 study on sentencing[191] and in a Federal Law Reform Commission study.[192] The key objectives of posited sentencing rules, in turn, aim to correlate a sentence with a posited offence: "[i]t is basic to any theory of punishment that the sentence imposed bear some relationship to the offence; it must be a 'fit' sentence proportionate to the seriousness of the offence."[193] A mandatory term of imprisonment for a statutory offence committed unknowingly, unwittingly, and after due diligence is "grossly excessive and inhumane." By violating the 'theory' of punishment it offends a principle of fundamental justice.

Later judgments during our five-year period under study showed Wilson to be more and more willing to discover the meaning of Charter rights in political/legal theory. In *Jones*, she appeals to John Stuart Mill's *On Liberty*[194] and to Dickson's paraphrase of Mill's principle of self-regarding conduct[195] for the meaning of "liberty" in section 7 of the Charter. In sorting out the content of language rights under section 133 of the Constitution Act, 1867, in *Macdonald*, Wilson surveys the theories of rights, liberties, powers, and duties in the writings of H.L.A. Hart (1954), W.N. Hohfeld (1923), Austin (1885), Julius Stone (1946), Hegel (1821), Salmond, and William Lerderman (1959).[196] And in *Retail Business Holidays* Wilson applies Ronald Dworkin's notions of "internal compromise," "integrity," "principle," and "checkerboard legislation" to reconstruct the objective of the Retail Business Holidays Act itself.[197]

5. THE RATIONALIST HOLD

Dickson and Wilson, alone among Canadian Supreme Court justices, have strenuously aspired to break from the rationalist strains embedded within their contemporary legal culture. Dickson imagines a constitution as a forward-looking set of ends or *telii* which emanate from the institutional history of legal doctrine. Wilson pictures a constitution through the eyes of an empiricist, an intuitionist, and a theorist combined. And yet, notwithstanding their efforts, both judges are entrapped within the boundaries of their inherited rationalist image of a constitution. Both adopt an instrumentalist picture of the text's claims from time to time. Both present an artificial barrier between their own subjectivist preferences and an objective law. And both ultimately fall back upon a policy, an intuition, or a theory as the 'bottom line' for the meaning of a right. In Chapter XI, I shall identify another strain of judgments within our history which shares the Dickson/Wilson desire to transcend our inherited rationalist boundaries. I shall show how these boundaries realistically entertain the sorts of issues which Dickson and Wilson so desperately wish to raise.

A restraining factor, though, lies in the fact that only Dickson and Wilson alone of Supreme Court justices consciously work out an alternative vision of law and the world. Estey, for example, pictures the Charter as positing a set of rules whose objective meaning inheres within the four corners of the text itself.[198] During the early months of the Charter's history, Gerald LaForest followed suit,[199] only to replace rules with posited policies in later months.[200] LeDain takes up the latter as the linchpin for his image of a constitution, we shall soon see.[201] The dominant image of a constitution, then, is a rationalist one which projects an apolitical, neutral, scientific role for lawyers and judges. This prism understands law as a set of rules and/or policies posited in an objective world whose meaning inheres in that world.

(a) *The Textualist Rationalism of Skapinker*

Law Society of Upper Canada v. *Skapinker* represents the Supreme Court's first opportunity to respond to the Charter.[202] The surface issue in *Skapinker* arises out of section 28(c) of Ontario's Law Society Act, which has required that all members of the bar be Canadian citizens. Skapinker, an American citizen at the time he commences proceedings,[203] claims that this posited requirement contravenes "the right to pursue the gaining of a livelihood in any province" as guaranteed in section 6(2)(b) of the Charter. Estey responds otherwise on behalf of a unanimous court. In a sense, Estey offers something for everyone in his judgment. Dickson and Wilson no doubt find Estey's response attractive because of the pre-eminence which Estey allots to the Charter at the start of his judgment. Lamer and Beetz, in contrast, probably find the rationalist-laden over-tones of the judgment attractive.[204] A close look at Estey's judgment shows that his elevated status for the Charter simply reflects how he pictures a constitution as a vertical, hierarchically posited set of rules, the Charter rules positing authority to legislative/judicial bodies to posit further rules. The meaning of all rules, Estey assumes, inheres within the text of the Charter itself.

(i) *The elevated status of a constitution* After restating lower court judgments, counsel's arguments, and the relevant textual sections in the posited law and the Charter, Estey begins by elevating the constitution over ordinary posited law. He characterizes the Charter as "not a statute or even a statute of the extraordinary nature of the *Canadian Bill of Rights*."[205] The latter is "of course, in form, the same as any other statute of Parliament ... It is however, not a part of the Constitution of the country."[206] The Charter is similar to the British North America Act, 1867 in status or legitimacy in that both serve as parent texts in the hierarchy of posited texts. Given that vertical hierarchy, judges are "here engaged in a new task" which has to recognize "the distinction between 'simple statutory interpretation' and 'a constitutional role'." As a constitutional text, the Charter embodies "the supreme law of Canada" which has "to guide and serve the Canadian community for a long time," much like a parent must, from conception, guide and serve a child for a long time.[207] The Charter offers "a new dimension, a new yardstick of reconciliation between the individual and the community and their respective rights ..."[208]

(ii) *A constitution as a text* What is the content of this constitution which has imbued judges with "a new task"? On the one hand Estey pictures it as "a living tree," as a "constituent or organic statute." This picture cautions him against a "narrow and technical interpretation" which "if not modulated by a sense of the unknowns of the future, can stunt the growth of the law and hence the community it serves."[209] On the other hand, he insists that the text of the Charter has created a "new dimension" – not a shift in cultural/political values or a consciousness that political institutions have proven inaccessible, or whatever. A constitution, for Estey's judges, begins and ends with a text.

When Estey returns to the text as the starting-point, he treats "the key issue in this appeal" as a matter of teasing out the objective meaning of one word in the text, "and." He offers "three arguably applicable readings" of section 6(2): first, one can interpret the word "and" following section 6(2)(a) conjunctively by adding the word "then"; secondly, one can interpret the word "and" disjunctively by deleting "and" from the text; or thirdly, one can read section 6(2)(a) and (b) "as though the conjunction 'and' were absent" but impute "a mobility aspect" to section 6(2)(a).[210] The latter interpretation separates, though not divorces, the two clauses from each other, he suggests. The key to the objective meaning of "and" is the heading, "Mobility Rights," inserted above section 6, according to Estey. Although Canadian, British, and American courts have not posited a clear guideline for the use of headings in the interpretation of statutes and although Estey can only speculate why the Charter framers include headings,[211] "[a]t the very minimum, the Court must take them into consideration when engaged in the process of discerning the meaning and application of the provisions of the Charter."[212] That is, Estey appeals to words within the text to interpret the word 'and' in the text. Further, "the extent of the influence of a heading in this process," in turn, hangs upon other textualist factors:

including (but the list is not intended to be all-embracing) the degree of difficulty by reason of ambiguity or obscurity in construing the section; the length and complexity of the provision; the apparent homogeneity of the provision appearing under the heading; the use of generic terminology in the heading; the presence or absence of a system of headings which appear to segregate the component elements of the *Charter*; and the relationship of the terminology employed in the heading to the substance of the headlined provision. Heterogeneous rights will be less likely shepherded by a heading than a homogeneous group of rights.[213]

The heading *must* be examined, he insists. Indeed, if one does not examine the heading "as part of the entire constitutional document," he speculates, a judge would be adopting "a technical rule of construction" even where the words have a "clear and unambiguous meaning."[214] Estey, then, presents as the sole hurdle the reconciliation of the words in the heading with the word "and" in section 6(2)(a).

Estey then goes to the heading "mobility rights." "[T]he expression 'Mobility Rights' *must mean* rights of the person to move about, within and outside the national boundaries," he insists.[215] The subject-matter of each of the subsections in the text itself, he thinks, supports his definitive assertion. In three paragraphs of unsurpassed rigour in the annals of rule rationalism, Estey works out the ramifications of the first two readings of "and" noted above in the light of both the terms "Mobility Rights" and "in any province."[216] *The text alone* makes it "reasonable to conclude" that *the text* has compelled him to adopt the third meaning of the word "and." That is, the text has directed him to read section 6(2)(a) and (b) "as though the conjunction 'and' were absent" and as though "a mobility aspect" were imputed. Accordingly, "the right to pursue the gaining of a livelihood" does not establish "a free standing right to work."

Ironically, Estey considers the "right to work" to be a narrow technical interpretation[217] because "a free standing right to work" apparently can only be discovered in isolation from the heading "Mobility Rights." By appealing to the words which the heading "must mean," Estey describes his textualist approach as consonant with a liberal interpretation. His conception of a "liberal" interpretation, then, obviously departs radically from Dickson's or Wilson's understanding of a "liberal" interpretation. Why Estey can consider his focus upon the objective meaning of the words in the text as a "liberal" interpretation hangs upon his deep image of a constitution as a text.

Estey could take other courses. He could gather the *telos* of section 6(2)(b) by tracing its historical origins and evolution in Western, or, at least, Anglo-American societies as Dickson does. He could study the works of Rawls, Dworkin, Aristotle, or others to appreciate the moral/political theory embedded within the particular right, as Wilson does. Or, he could consider the real or potential empirical effects which his preferred interpretation poses for real human beings in the gaining of their livelihood. Estey turns to none of these avenues because he cannot. And he cannot do so because, embedded within his understanding of a constitution, if not the world, there lies a deep deference to a posited, abstract text. That image delineates boundaries beyond which he cannot venture. The boundaries pre-censor how he interprets the text.

(iii) *A constitution as a posited text* If Estey pictures a constitution as a text, how can he reconcile that picture with the elevated "constitutional" status which he projects onto the text? Statutes, after all, are also texts. Estey has anxiously fretted about this question for, when he elaborates his general image of the Charter at the start of the *Skapinker* judgment, he makes a point of noting how the Charter has been posited. The text has taken "the form" of a British statute. But, once posited, the positing processes lose "their relevancy or shrink *to mere historical curiosity value* on the ultimate adoption of the instrument as the Constitution."[218] In other words, once posited, the text alone – not its historical or institutional genesis – embodies the complete constitution. The Charter differs little from the British North America Act in that respect, according to Estey. Both documents have been posited and the act of positing ends all inquiry into history, cultural norms, and the like. The positing of a parent text becomes indispensable in that, given that texts alone count, some text must authorize the positing of further rules in the hierarchy of rule-positing. Indeed, what make the Charter a supreme text is not the text itself, as Estey claims,[219] because a statutory text such as the Canadian Bill of Rights can posit and has posited its own supremacy without judicial acknowledgment. Rather, Estey's textualist *image* of a constitution comes first.[220] The image legitimizes the Charter as a parent text. The image delegitimizes the Canadian Bill of Rights as subservient to ordinary legislated rules. Finally, the image delineates the boundaries of what counts as both a "narrow" and a "liberal" interpretation.

(iv) *Estey's institutional self-image* Estey's image presents a "new task" for judges, a task which can be accomplished objectively, apolitically, scientifically. Estey makes this clear in the second sentence of his judgment: "*At the outset, let it be emphasized in the clearest possible language that* the issue before this Court in this appeal is not whether it is or is not in the interest of this community to require Canadian citizenship as a precondition to membership in the bar. Rather, *the only issue* is whether s. 28(c) of the *Law Society Act. supra*, is inconsistent with S. 6(2)(b) of the *Canadian Charter of Rights and Freedoms*."[221] That is, the only issue is one of textual coherence, in contrast to an issue of public policy. Estey feels compelled to emphasize the difference at the outset because, for him, a constitution is an abstract text which delineates abstract, concrete rules. And he poses the 'either/or,' 'text/policy' alternative as the only alternative because he is entrapped within a rationalist image of legal knowledge which entertains a subjective policyism as the only possible alternative to an objective text. If Estey were to admit that in the process of discovering objective rules one inevitably incorporates one's subjective views about the content of the posited rule, then the text can no longer be considered a legitimate source of law. Law would no longer remain objective. Rather, law would be subjective and, therefore, disqualified as legal knowledge.

Estey's insistence upon the objectivity of the posited text brings with it an ironic twist. The irony emanates not so much from the use of his self-described "liberal" approach to the text to produce a technical interpretation. Rather, one cannot help but find it ironic that when Estey discovers the meaning in the text he can do so with nothing but his emotive intuition. In *Skapinker*, he insists, "[t]he expression 'Mobility Rights' *must mean* ..."[222] What is the source of his meaning? Is it history? No. Is it political theory? No. Is it Estey's own unequivocal subjectivist intuition? Yes. And we have already seen that Estey is not alone in that regard.[223]

(b) *The Trappings of Policy/Values Rationalism*
Of course, Canadian jurists more frequently replace or supplement strict textual rules with social values as the key constituent of a constitution. Charter judgments during the Charter's first five years are no exception. Substituting or supplementing rules with values, Supreme Court justices still insist that constitutional law exists 'out there' in an objective world. Like rules, values are posited. Like rules, one can objectively assign weight to them, ascertain their immutable meaning, balance them against each other, and scientifically apply the values to diverse circumstances. Lamer, LaForest, LeDain, and McIntyre work out such a values-centred image of the Charter.[224]

In *Re B.C. Motor Vehicles Act*, for example, Lamer pictures federalism through a two-stages rationalistic prism. First, he claims that lawyers should distil or abstract "the constitutional value" embedded within the rules of a statute. Secondly, lawyers should then weigh that abstracted value against the "sphere of values" implanted within sections 91 and 92 of the British North America Act.[225] Lamer extends this "abstracted values" analytic technique to his Charter analysis. The Charter merely widens the range of values against which a lawyer can measure the statute's abstracted value: "[t]he truly novel features of the *Constitution Act, 1982* are that it has sanctioned the process of constitutional adjudication and has extended its scope so as to encompass *a broader range of values*."[226] The Charter has added individualistic values to the arsenal of governmental relationship values. This broader range of legitimate "relevant" values – not the text itself, or history, or the judiciary's institutional self-image – entrusted judges "with this new and onerous responsibility" of playing a more active role.[227] Unlike a posited rule, an abstracted value does not direct or "cause" one specific answer, partly because the value possesses an open-ended character, partly because values inevitably conflict with each other at an abstract level. Notwithstanding this apparent invitation to subjectivity, this group of Supreme Court judges retains a belief in an objective law. Objectivity remains, it is thought, if only jurists can learn to balance values scientifically in an *ad hoc* manner.[228] When the balancing process is "delicate," "inherently dynamic," and "unstable," as in labour relations, then the legislature should strike the balance of values.[229] Judges and the objectivity of law would thereby remain unscathed. Foreign authorities posit values 'out there' in an externalized world, just as they do rules.

The expansion of constitutional law to include values does not open the floodgates to the constitutionalization of judges' values. In *Re B.C. Motor Vehicles Act*, for example, Lamer expresses that "[t]he overriding and legitimate concern that courts ought not to question *the wisdom of enactments*, and the presumption that the legislator could not have intended same, have to some extent *distorted* the discussion surrounding the meaning of 'principles of fundamental justice'."[230] This "spectre of a judicial super-legislature" has led judges to restrict the meaning of section 7 narrowly to 'procedural fairness.' But Lamer is not haunted by this spectre. Why not? Because, "*[s]ince way back in time and even recently the courts have developed the common law beyond procedural safeguards without interfering with the 'merits or wisdom' of enactments*."[231] Courts "for a good many years" have considered the content of posited legislation. This is not "the novel feature of the *Constitution Act, 1982*." How can a judge consider the content of challenged statutes without evaluating their wisdom? By picturing a constitution through the lens of a balancing of policies. In *vires* issues judges have always distilled "the constitutional value," "the true meaning," or "an abstract" of the content of a posited enactment. But this process of abstracting values has precluded judges from considering "the appropriateness of policies underlying legislative enactments." Indeed, "the Constitution" (that is, the judge's self-image) 'compels' him not to do so. The task of a judge, in Lamer's eyes, is "to secure for persons 'the full benefit of the *Charter's protection'* ... *under s. 7 while avoiding adjudication of the merits of public policy.*"[232] This can be accomplished, Lamer thinks, by two methods: first, a purposive analysis; and second, the articulation of *objective and manageable standards.*[233]

Faith in objective and manageable standards as represented in abstracted values feeds Lamer's reluctance to give any but minimal weight to speeches in Parliament or to minutes and evidence of the special Joint Parliamentary Committee on the Constitution. Parliamentary speeches are "inherently unreliable" and of an "indeterminate nature." This indeterminacy, in turn, undermines Lamer's picture of an objective constitutional law. What, then, makes for objective standards? The fact that rules are posited. Lamer believes he can talk about values without evaluating the wisdom of legislative rules because he accepts a posited enactment as a 'given.' Only, instead of seeing rules in the enactment, he exposes the values lying behind the rules. If he did question or critique the Ends of those values, then he would be questioning their wisdom. But he does not believe that he does or can do so. He understands the purpose of a challenged statute in terms of the values presupposed in *that* enactment, not his own values. Lamer's unreserved deference to the 'givenness' of the posited enactment ensures the very objectivity of law which contemporary Canadian Supreme Court justices long to maintain.[234]

6. THE CLASH OF BOUNDARIES

The Charter experience adds something to constitutional imagery. The 'subject-matter' of Charter litigation – 'freedom of expression,' 'mobility rights,' 'language rights,' and the like – withers, upon close inspection, into a search for an appropriate image of a constitution. The text has stimulated lawyers and judges to reconsider their past boundaries of their images, to revise the boundaries, or to replace them. In this respect, the Charter experience reaffirms the collapse of traditional 'subject-matters' of constitutional law. What the experience adds is the realization that each judge and each lawyer project a network of particular boundaries which coincide with that person's individual image of a constitution. The boundaries delimit each person's response to surface issues triggered by a text. The objectivity and rationality of law – no matter how pivotal to a particular person's image – crumbles along with our pre-understanding of law as an encyclopaedic compendium of 'subject-matters.' Charter law collapses into Charter imagery. Four such images dominate the contemporary discourse of the Canadian Supreme Court. But within the boundaries of each image, legal knowledge seems so coherent, so ordered, so definitive, so objective.

Dickson elevates and separates the constitution from the rules posited in ordinary statutes and the Canadian Bill of Rights. In place of rules, the character of a constitution is constituted in *telii* or ends. Dickson understands the ends in the context of the genealogy of the text's concepts. Not content to leave the constitution in an *a priori* world, he connects a social boundary to a constitution in that one must understand the linkage of the ends with society. Against these boundaries, Dickson sees it as his mission – and that of other judges – to guard his image from attack by the executive and legislative arms of government.

Wilson, too, possesses identifiable boundaries of a constitutional image. She rejects the weak sense of rights which comes with utilitarian balancing. Her institutional role flows out of Kantian noumenal duties purged of empirical considerations of efficacy. Having immunized her institutional self from attack in the phenomenal world, Wilson urges that Dickson's boundary of a constitution be widened beyond the ends embedded in texts to include the empirical consequences of Charter rights. This widened boundary brings with it a heavier onus upon government lawyers to adduce social/economic data in justifying reasonable limits upon Charter rights. Rather than discovering an inherent meaning to Charter rights, as does Estey, Wilson expands the exegetical process to incorporate insights of professional philosophers.

Now, the above boundaries do not completely dominate the Dickson and Wilson prisms of a constitution. When Dickson begins to transpose the circumstances of the cases into his boundaries, he falls back into an instrumental rationality. He balances off social interests against each other, oblivious to the Ends and social history which he aspires to consider. Having loosened the chains of the contemporary and past legal culture, Dickson and Wilson freeze the world into an objectivist/subjectivist prism which pre-censors how they understand the world. Whereas Dickson sees himself as an objectivist scientist, Wilson ultimately grounds the meaning of the text in her own subjectivist intuitions. With our very identification of these conflicting boundaries of a constitutional image, law as an objective compendium of 'subject-matters' withdraws into the inward world which individual participants share with each other.

But that the boundaries of both Dickson's and Wilson's images of a constitution seriously clash with the boundaries of the others on the Supreme Court, there can be no doubt. At the one extreme, there lies Estey's textualist boundary which magnetically restrains his world of law to a text whose *a priori* meaning inheres in the text itself. At the other extreme, there lie the widened boundaries of LeDain and Lamer who aim to expose the social policies embedded in a text. Both sets of boundaries project the lawyer/judge as a scientist whose sole job it is to observe the objective world scientifically, impartially, and apolitically.

PART II:

THE RATIONALIST IMAGE OF A CONSTITUTION

PART I OF THIS ESSAY closely examined the actual discourse in the traditional 'subject-matters' of Canadian constitutional law. Constitutional discourse has predominantly assumed law to exist 'out there' in an objective world of horizontally posited 'subject-matters' under which officials vertically posited rules. The 'subject-matters' encompass a totality of social conduct. Secondary rules are ratiocinated from prior, given rules in the vertical hierarchy. Rational order flourishes. We have now discovered from what the discourse takes to be the 'leading' judgments and commentaries on the 'subject-matters,' though, that this 'subject-matter' approach to constitutional law presents only one picture of a constitution. More important, we have discovered that even the 'subject-matter' image of a constitution begins from *within* the consciousness of the spokespersons in the discourse. The search for an objective law invariably collapses into a spokesperson's self-examination as to what counts as 'a constitution' and what does not; what role the spokesperson should play within the image; what resource material counts as a legitimate source of law; and whether law is political.

Although the boundaries of the competing images of a constitution appear fragmentary in such subject-matters as the 'rule of law,' 'separation of powers,' 'section 96,' 'standing,' and 'evidence,' the judiciary clearly recognizes that the critical issue in law is not 'what are the vertically posited rules flowing under a particular subject-matter?'; rather, the first order question is 'what is my image of a constitution?' Fully coherent images of a constitution have flowered in such 'subject-matters' as 'constitutional amendment' and the 'Charter of Rights.' The most refined, and certainly dominant, image is permeated with rationalism. That rationalistic strain concentrates upon posited rules as the basic resource material in the context of the initial 'subject-matters,' supreme court responses to the Canadian Bill of Rights, and lower court reactions to the Charter of Rights. Values, sometimes described as policies, have more recently replaced rules as the major constituent of contemporary versions of rationalism. Dickson and Wilson, for example, have stridently aspired to break from the hold of rules only to find themselves entrapped in a 'values' version of the same dominant rationalist prism of law.

Part II of this essay carries the law of a constitution one step further. I aim here to identify the boundaries of various versions of a rationalist image of a constitution. In order to do so, we must understand why I have described the dominant image as 'rationalist.' For this project, I shall concentrate upon the analysis of the federal 'division of powers.' And I shall do so by widening the resource material of my study to include the leading scholarly commentaries of the law of Canadian federalism, beginning in the 1920s.

By widening the resource material of my study beyond judicial decisions, I do not intend to infer that scholarly essays or classroom texts have been politically controlling, intellectually influential, or even judicially observed. Nor do I wish to infer that legal scholarship has actually caused legal consciousness. Such inferences would be entertained only by one who understands the important issues of knowledge in terms of rational causality. Rather, legal scholarship should be understood much as I have shown how one should understand a judicial decision. Academic commentaries neither describe 'the law' nor analyse 'the law' nor prescribe what ought to be 'the law' because the law of a constitution does not live 'out there' in an objective reality. The scholarly essay, much as a judicial decision, expresses how the scholar's image of 'what is a constitution?' pre-censors the world. Like the judge, the scholar, too, often leaves the boundaries of his or her prism to prejudgment. I aim to make conscious what judge and scholar alike have hitherto left to prejudgments.

We have seen in Part 1 that the dominant prism through which contemporary Canadian judges have understood their world of law has had a rationalistic character. From horizontally posited 'subject-matters,' the lawyer/judge rationally uncovers a vertical hierarchy of posited rules or posited values. The lawyer/judge does so in a neutral, passive manner with a sustained faith in scientific rationality. So too, we shall see, a rationalism has permeated the dominant strains of Canadian constitutional thought since the 1920s. This rationalism did not originate with the judges or scholars themselves. Rather, their rationalist image of a constitution grew out of the deeper Enlightenment conception of rationality which lawyers have shared with some scientists, sociologists, economists, political scientists, and philosophers during this century.[1] Why all these disciplines have understood rationality in the terms they have is the subject of still another story.[2]

VIII

The Rule Rationalist Image of Federalism Law

Until the 1970s, a rule rationalist image of a constitution dominated Canadian legal discourse. We have experienced how the boundaries of this image solidify Laskin's responses to the *Patriation References*, 'standing,' 'extrinsic evidence,' 'section 96' interpretation, 'separation of powers,' the demise of the Canadian Bill of Rights, and the early reaction of lower court judges and some Supreme Court judges to the Canadian Charter of Rights and Freedoms. Interestingly, this same image permeates the scholarship of Canadian law professors. It is the scholars who clarify and refine the rule rationalist boundaries. Nowhere is their clarity better demonstrated than in their commentaries about the law of federalism.

These commentaries express how law is discoverable within a horizontal/vertical axis[1] 'out there,' independent of the commentator, judge, lawyer, or student. Posited rules divide human conduct along a horizontal axis of discrete, insulated 'subject-matters.' A legislated text – the British North America Act, 1867 to present renamed in 1982 as the Constitution Acts – posits the boundary lines between each 'subject-matter' and the next. Within each enclosed 'subject-matter,' legislators, judges, or bureaucrats posit a hierarchy of rules, doctrines, principles, and texts. The latter flow vertically, coherently, and rationally from the first premises within each 'subject-matter.' Meaning inheres in the rule. The lawyer's duty is to learn, describe, and apply the rules impartially, neutrally, scientifically, and passively. An arsenal of rational techniques aid the lawyer in this scientific enterprise. Together, the horizontal/vertical spectrum of 'subject-matters' and rules encompasses all existing and all future human conduct. In juridical terms, there exists "an exhaustiveness of legislative power" whereby "all powers executive and legislative, and all public property and revenues," are distributed between the two levels of government.[2] That is, the image leaves no human behaviour immune from the potential rational control of the posited rules within each 'subject-matter.' W.P.M. Kennedy, Albert Abel, Louis Philippe Pigeon, Jean Beetz, and others share this image of federalism law. It permeates their writings and their judgments. I call it a rule rationalist image.

1. OBJECTIVITY

William Lederman writes in his formative essay that the most important issue in law is "what is the nature of the reality about which man makes reasoned propositions?"[3] For the rationalist, reality is constituted in an objective, natural world external to the subjective feelings of a human being. The former offers a legitimate and valid source of legal knowledge; the latter an illegitimate and invalid source. This rigid separation of an objective from a subjective source of knowledge presents the first 'given' boundary in the various rationalist images of federalism law. From that boundary in the lawyer's consciousness, much else coherently flows.

First, the meaning of a rule inheres from within the words of the rule itself. This contrasts with another version of the rationalist image which suggests that one can glean the meaning of a rule from the social context within which the rule is framed or interpreted. As William P.M. Kennedy insists in an early commentary on Canadian federalism, the meaning of the British North America Act, 1867 must be expounded "*according to the terms set out in it*, finding the intention *from its words*, upholding it *precisely as framed*, ascertaining its *true meaning within itself* and clear of any qualifications which the Imperial Parliament has not expressed in it, *and apart from any questions of expediency or of political exigency.*"[4] His contemporary, Vincent MacDonald, describes interpretation as "an objective matter"[5] where a text serves as "its own and only interpreter."[6] Such abstruse words in sections 92 and 92 as "affecting" and "in relation to" possess definite, precise meanings with serious legal ramifications, according to MacDonald.[7] For Albert Abel – the eminent legal scientist – words are "self-defining," to be "taken as they stand and if, as they stand, they give no room for construction, that ends the matter."[8] Indeed, he claims that important constitutional crises could have been avoided if only lawyers had interpreted "of" to mean "of" instead of "in."[9]

Secondly, objectivism permeates the very manner in which a lawyer exercises choice in his or her analysis. For Abel[10] and Beetz[11] particularly, a lawyer should appeal to objective standards, external to the text and external to one's "frozen whims," "unconcious biases," and "policy preferences," to use Abel's terms. History, in Abel's view, obviously offers a needed external standard because history lends itself "to relatively objective examination and thus reduces the risk of unconcious biases and policy preferences which bedevil interpretation."[12] William Lederman, after distinguishing between the objective world of natural facts and the subjective world of personal values, insists that "objectively true or valid abstractions (ideas, concepts, universals) are possible for the human mind," in that concepts are an integral part of objective reality. The lawyer can check "the validity or truth of abstract propositions against objective reality by logical thought, experiment, observation, study and dialectical discussion."[13] The precise argumentative techniques are semantics,[14] analogical reasoning,[15] logic,[16] and accurate social/economic data.[17] Beetz characterizes a constitution discovered along these lines as immutable, permanent, overbearing, and abstract: "[l']immutabilité de l'interprétation constitutionnelle supposait enfin un certain rejet des notions purement relatives, des données quantitatives, de l'innommé, de la jurisprudence dite 'realiste' et purement descriptive, des considérations d'ordre surtout fonctionnel; elle supposait au contraire que l'on mette l'accent sur le qualitatif, l'approfondissement et la précision des concepts, la jurisprudence analytique."[18] Beetz informs us that to the extent that law emulates an objective rationality, law is legitimate.[19]

2. TEXTS

Imbued with a wish for an objective reality, rule rationalists project great deference to texts – particularly the texts of statutes and judgments. The primary text is the British North America Act, 1867. History, moral/political values, speculative moral/political philosophy, and social/economic interests, it is sometimes admitted, do enter the law-making process. But they do so only by accident, to the extent that the content of a text's rules incorporate values or the like. The lawyer or judge must not scrutinize the content of the rules in that the content contains subjectivist values. The latter are irrelevant and illegitimate sources of law. Kennedy strenuously complains that the primary text – the British North America Act, 1867 – is immunized from such national social issues as poverty, financial chaos, unemployment, and exploitation.[20] For him, the only way to overcome the gap between text and social crisis is to repeal the text *in toto* and to rewrite it "completely." Only then, could law remain objective and, at the same time, socially relevant.

Let us closely examine Pigeon's essays and judgments to understand how textualism permeates his image of a constitution. For Pigeon, the British North America Act, 1867 constitutes the exclusive source of a constitution. He elevates sections 91 and 92 to an entrenched position which neither level of government can amend.[21] In his first published essay, "Are the Provincial Legislatures Parliaments?" Pigeon concentrates entirely upon the precise words of the text.[22] By reading the word "Canada" in section 17 of the Act in its textual context of eleven other sections, Pigeon concludes that "Canada" connotes "the juristic federal unit" rather than merely a geographical entity.[23] The text posits each legislature "with sovereign authority" within its respective horizontal compartment. In another essay, "The Meaning of Provincial Autonomy," Pigeon challenges the pro-centralists by appealing to the actual words in sections 91 and 92.[24] Centralists pay "slight attention" to the "pregnant words" immediately following the POGG power, for example.[25] Further, Pigeon believes that the centralists erroneously offer a historical interpretation of the British North America Act, 1867 – erroneous because, quoting from *Brophy* v. *A.G. of Man.*,[26] "[t]he question is, not what may be supposed to have been intended, but what has been said."[27] That is, law emanates from the inherent words of a text, not the framers' intent. The 'givenness' of the text, he believes, constitutes "a fundamental rule of legal interpretation."[28]

Kennedy's and Pigeon's exclusive reliance upon a legislated text gives way to a more realistic assessment of the role of judicial texts in the writings of Vincent MacDonald. MacDonald writes in one essay, for example, that "[n]ot second in importance to the text of a constitution is the character, attitudes and personnel of its judicial expositor; for in a very real sense 'the constitution is what the judges say it is.' "[29] He goes one step further in another essay when he begins by saying that "[t]he starting point of this study is that the Canadian constitution is not to be found in the terms of the British North America Act, but in the terms of that act as interpreted by the courts in some hundreds of cases."[30] MacDonald condemns the Privy Council for having both "unconsciously translated into law their own views as to what is right or expedient"[31] and, at the same time, adopting a "literalistic" or "ultra-literalistic approach" to the British North America Act for over fifty years.[32] Along the latter lines, the legislated text serves as "the source of power"[33] or "the ultimate source and channel of governmental power."[34] Precisely because the text is so important, the Privy Council should have maintained a "constant effort to bring and keep the Constitution [that is, the BNA Act) up-to-date as the *source of power* adequate to present needs."[35] Instead, the Privy Council discovers federalism law "from its [the text's] own terms and scheme, rather than from authoritative guides to that intention known to every educated Canadian."[36]

Whether the text emanates from a court or a legislature, what legitimates the text as a source of law is that it has been posited according to a hierarchy of rules. The text posits horizontal and vertical rules; and the text, in turn, is posited. Although rules may well slowly evolve over time or may originate through an imperceptible historical genesis in political/moral values, it is not until some institution, itself posited by a higher ordered text, has formally posited the rule that the rule can be considered law. In addition to a value-laden genesis, the content of the rule might well direct the lawyer to inevitable value choices. But it is the official *positing* of the rule – not the moral character of the rule's content – which legitimates its content as law. Finally, jurists might well believe that rules describe social reality or, at least, that rules initially do so describe social reality when first posited (as Vincent MacDonald seems to express). But the *positing* of the rule, not the social reality presupposed in the initial enactment of the rule, again legitimates the rule as a source of law.

3. HORIZONTAL COMPARTMENTS

Now, this rule rationalist picture of reality imagines law as objective and as discoverable in pre-existing posited legislative/judicial texts. The objectivity and textualist boundaries of the rule rationalist image do not necessitate rules as the sole constituent of a constitution. For, one could read a poem, music sheet, play, or fragmented description of one's subconscious as if the latter were objective texts. What makes the difference between a rule and a play is that the picture of law projects that texts go on to delineate a horizontal line of compartments. The compartments, when considered as a whole, theoretically encompass all past, present, and future social conduct – or, so it is envisioned. Familiar compartments ring loud and clear: "peace, order and good government," "trade and commerce," "criminal law," "property and civil rights," and "matters of a local and private nature." The image treats each compartment as if it actually lived an autonomous life of its own. For, the 'subject-matter' or compartment is a 'given.' Within each compartment, the appropriate institution – legislature or court, federal or provincial – can posit rules vertically. The horizontal compartments, which join with the vertical rules, speak to the whole of social conduct: the categories in sections 91 and 92 of the British North America Act exhaust the whole field of law making.[37] Meaning inheres to the compartment. One rule causes the next in the vertical hierarchy – or so it seems. The image constructs a totality of human existence. The picture directs the lawyer/judge to the right answer. Jurists respond to surface issues as if the picture of a horizontal/vertical hierarchy of rules *causes* the answer.

Let us understand how one jurist, Pigeon, works out the boundary of a horizontal/vertical hierarchy.

A legislated text, the British North America Act, posits an "axiomatic" rule,[38] "the fundamental principle,"[39] a "general rule,"[40] a "basic principle,"[41] with "a special character."[42] How does Pigeon understand this axiomatic rule? First, the legislated text posits a boundary line marking out a space over which a social group or "minority" can dominate. Secondly, within each space, the minority is "mistress in her own house," possessing an autonomous "free movement within the area bounded by the limitations."[43] Thirdly, Pigeon compares this autonomous space with an individual's freedom:

[t]he true concept of autonomy is thus like the true concept of freedom. It implies limitations, but it also implies free movement within the area bounded by the limitations: one no longer enjoys freedom when free to move in one direction only. It should therefore be realized that autonomy means the right of being different, of acting differently. This is what freedom means for the individual; it is also what it must mean for provincial legislatures and governments. There is no longer any real autonomy for them to the extent that they are actually compelled, economically or otherwise, to act according to a specified pattern. Just as freedom means for the individual the right of choosing his own objective so long as it is not illegal, autonomy means for a province the privilege of defining its own policies.[44]

Fourth, the objective, textually imposed boundary line constitutes a "fundamental principle" because, without it, brute force posits the boundary line. The compartments within section 91 and 92 of the British North America Act, then, preserve civic peace among competing minorities.

Pigeon applies his compartmentalized picture of federalism law in judgment after judgment as a Supreme Court judge. In *Burns Foods Ltd.* v. *A.G. Man.*, for example, a contract has been signed outside the province of Manitoba.[45] That being the case, Pigeon finds that the contract falls beyond Manitoba's free space or jurisdiction. The strict, seemingly visible boundary line between the exclusive, total space of the national and of the provincial legislatures prevents the provinces from effectively controlling the "interprovincial trade" compartment. Similarly, the boundary line forecloses the national legislature from regulating the "local trade" compartment. Neither efficiency nor political goals can override the permanent and objective character of the compartments. The permanence and objective compartments allocate the control of production, purchase, and sale of commodities to the provincial compartment of "matters of a local and private nature" in section 92(16) of the BNA Act, Pigeon explains in *Re Agricultural Products Marketing Act*.[46] Similarly, the compartment of "administration of justice in the Province" in section 92(14) of the BNA Act excludes the federal parliament from creating courts other than for the purpose of administering federal, as opposed to provincial, laws.[47] And, when "a genuinely new problem [such as narcotics] which did not exist at the time of Confederation" arises, the federal residuary compartment of "peace, order and good government" casues the problem to be placed under the federal space unless the problem can be described as "merely local and private."[48]

4. THE VERTICAL RULES

This rule rationalist image of law projects a vertical hierarchy of rules in addition to a horizontal spectrum. Within each horizontal compartment, the assigned legislature can posit rules underneath each horizontal compartment. The vertical length of the rules grows through the autonomous ratiocination process of judges. Although the judges themselves may state the new rules, it seems as if one rule causes a secondary rule; the latter, in turn, causes exceptions to the general rule, and so on. The initial positing process of the rule itself – not its moral content – legitimates the rule as a part of the law of federalism.

When rules are first posited, it is generally assumed, they correspond with the objective natural world of "fact." Rules notionally categorize facts, Lederman explains again and again.[49] For Vincent MacDonald, because rules correspond with the social background of the judges, the legal scholar should concentrate upon the history, personnel, and mental attitudes of the Privy Council to appreciate the present rules.[50] But because the vertical ratiocination process itself is abstract, rational, and constructed by the mind, Kennedy, MacDonald, Beetz, and other rule rationalists quickly acknowledge that the vertical hierarchy of posited rules could well become divorced from social reality over time. "Federalism is legalism," Kennedy exclaims. "It is, at best, a second best."[51]

MacDonald describes how the vertical ratiocination process pushes even history and ideal-directed social values to the side.[52] The "rapid march of political, economic, social and ideological change" of the previous quarter-century has overtaken the basic text.[53] Social facts external to the text have "both [set] the judicial process in motion and provide the field for the operation of the results of that process."[54] When such a gap between vertically posited rules and social reality emerges, a constitutional amendment of the text serves as the only option to transcend the gap because of the inherent abstractness of the rules.

One jurist, Jean Beetz,[55] pushes the vertical hierarchy of pre-existing rules to the complete exhaustion of any gaps between the rules. On the one hand, Beetz admits that a judge should look beyond the form of the British North America Act to the text's "operation, at its effects and at the scale of its effects."[56] Provincial autonomy constitutes the reality (or "substance," to use his term) of the text. On the other hand, behind that "substance" there hovers an abstract notion or idea which Beetz calls "the Constitution." Permanent, overbearing, abstract, objective, "the Constitution" possesses an inherent imperativeness about it, independently of the jurist. Posited rules join the "substance" of a provincial autonomy with the idea of "the Constitution." "[T]he older the rule, the better it is," he claims, "for it has proved its justice and usefulness by its very duration."[57] If a posited rule were unfair or harmful, "man would have quickly found a way to get rid of it."[58] In contrast, a new rule is untried and unknown. Man mistrusts the unknown and is "partly afraid of it." Indeed, the notion of a rule itself implies "a certain duration": "[o]therwise it is an *ad hoc* rule. It is lacking in generality. It is lacking in certainty and therefore it is under suspicion of being arbitrary and illegitimate."[59] Thus, the lawyer must fall back upon pre-existing posited rules to join the form of a text with the substance of 'the Constitution.'

Beetz works out this general picture of pre-existing vertically posited rules within horizontal compartments in his *Dupond* judgment.[60] Dupond attacks the constitutionality of a Montreal by-law and ordinance. The by-law authorized the city's executive committee to, "by ordinance, take measures to prevent or suppress" the holding of assemblies, parades, or gatherings which endangered the safety, peace, or public order. The executive committee enacted an ordinance pursuant to the by-law. The ordinance prohibited "the holding of an assembly, parade or gathering anywhere and at any time on the public domain" for thiry days. Dupond claims that the by-law falls within the 'criminal law' compartment of section 91 of the British North America Act. As such, the boundary line demarcating 'criminal law' excludes the by-law from the province's "space" (jurisdiction).

Beetz responds to this possibility with the realization that posited rules constitute the whole of 'the Constitution.' The by-law and ordinance do not and must not allow for the creation of any uncertain, unknown, open-ended future rules. First, the by-law and ordinance prohibit the holding of *all* assemblies, parades, or gatherings, irrespective of religion, ideology, or political opinion. Secondly, a municipal officer has not been granted an uncontrolled discretion to enact new rules.[61] Thirdly, this pre-existing posited statutory rule contrasts with counsel's argument that the rule conflicts with the fundamental freedoms of speech, assembly, association, press, and religion. The latter are abstract, vague, metaphysical, and unknown concepts, antithetical to Beetz's preoccupation with known posited rules. In Beetz's own words,

I find it exceedingly difficult to deal with a submission couched in such general terms. What is it that distinguishes a right from a freedom and a fundamental freedom from a freedom which is not fundamental? Is there a correlation between freedom of speech and freedom of assembly on the one hand and, on the other, the right, if any, to hold a public meeting on the highway or in a park as opposed to a meeting open to the public on private land? How like or unlike each other are an assembly, a parade, a gathering, a demonstration, a procession? Modern parlance has fostered loose language upon lawyers. As was said by Sir Ivor Jennings, the English at least have no written constitution and so *they may divide their law logically.*[62]

Worse still, the right to hold public meetings on the public domain simply does not exist, "[b]eing unknown to English law." Being unknown, such a right "did not become part of the Canadian Constitution under the preamble of the *British North America Act, 1867*," according to Beetz.

5. THE JUDICIARY'S SELF-IMAGE

We have experienced that those jurists who understand reality through a rule rationalist prism project law as an objective autonomous system of rules. A posited text supplies the language for the necessary justificatory discourse. That discourse hypothesizes a horizontal scheme of self-contained compartments with a hierarchy of rules vertically posited under each compartment. Against this background, does a judge create rules? No. May a judge do so? No. Scholars/lawyers/judges observe the world: they do not create it. Their role is to apply pre-existing rules in an objective, impartial, passive, and neutral manner. Does some text, such as the British North America Act, posit such a neutral role? No. An *image* of a constitution which joins the above-described boundaries together encourages such a role. For Kennedy, for example, judges do not create rules because the inherent meaning emanating from the parent text is "to say the least of it, far from obscure."[63] Regretfully, he complains, the Privy Council had in fact created law in the process of having "regularly misquoted" and misunderstood the "exact words of the text.[64]

When the posited rules diverge from social reality, can a judge intervene to close the gap? Unequivocally no: '[i]t is not the function of the courts to change a statute so as to bring it into line with modern demands," Kennedy insists.[65] For MacDonald, a gap between rules and social reality calls for a textualist revolution rather than for an activist court. Albert Abel ignores the possibility of a gap, although his three-staged mechanism of analysis does contemplate inescapable choices.[66] In exercising choice, the judge must appeal neither to policies nor to "a *commedia del arte* constitution freely variable for each new occasion."[67] Such an activistic role would reconstitute judges into legislators instead of scientist/ adjudicators. Rather, choice should be exercised in terms of "some suitable standard" or on "a principled basis" external to the text itself.[68] Such an appeal to standards "above the rules and above the law," Beetz explains at length, legitimates the positing of a choice.[69] Pigeon, too, acknowledges the inevitability of choices in the application of rules to "borderline cases"[70] and in the interpretation of such indeterminate words as "substantial," "free," and the like.[71] But Pigeon rejects the "mathematical formulas" of scholars such as Abel,[72] for Pigeon's horizontal compartments allot a rule-making role for the legislature. Each legislature – not courts or the legal profession – possesses uncontrolled discretion to posit rules in the inevitable moral dilemmas which judges are otherwise required to face.[73] Pigeon thereby sustains the consistently passive self-image of a judge/lawyer within the rule rationalist prism of a constitution.

6. RATIONALITY

Given this scientific, impartial, politically neutral role for a jurist, what causes the ratiocination of one rule from another? Well, rationality itself. William Lederman synthesizes much of what I call 'rule' and 'policy rationalism' in order to express what he describes as an "orthodox" image of a constitution.[74] In working out his image he identifies five rationalist techniques which, he thinks, equip a lawyer to test the truthfulness of a rule as against objective reality. The techniques also aid a lawyer to discover the inherent true meaning of words in the rule.[75] Each technique speaks to a different element of rationality. First, semantics sharpens and systematically refines the inherent, objective meaning of a word.[76] Secondly, precedent aids this enterprise of discovery, in that the prior positing of a rule encompassing certain social conduct "in all probability foreclose[s] the question of the correct classification."[77] Precedent reduces uncertainty, making the parent text more meaningful.[78] Thirdly, one can clarify the "true meaning" of a rule's features by testing the application of the rule to diverse social facts.[79] Lederman describes this technique as analogical reasoning. Fourth, logic serves as a technique to develop the implications of a possible rule "through stages of decreasing abstraction in order to assess the detailed consequences of applying such propositions ..."[80] Lederman adds a fifth technique in rationality, more characteristic of policy than of rule-rationalism: namely, that a maximum quantity of social/economic data equips the lawyer/judge to ensure that a fact category of a rule actually corresponds with social reality.[81] These five constituents of rationality join to share an "hypothetico-deductive reasoning" method.[82] Lederman admits that this juridical rationality is not unlike the scientific method, for both use logical thought, experiment, observation, study, and dialectical discussion to uncover "objective reality."[83]

Of the extensive works concerning the law of Canadian federalism, the theses and argumentation of Albert Abel best bear witness to rationalist techniques.[84] The analytic technique which he prescribes for all demonstrates and advocates a methodical rationality which begins and ends with the fact category (the "class consciousness," as he calls it) of a given posited rule. The text of the British North America Act, 1867 possesses an inherently "comprehensive, intelligible and tidy" logic.[85] The text's posited rules constitute "a coherent universe."[86] The framers share a "harmonious and consistent" approach to Confederation.[87] Clear analysis flows from a three-staged "formula"[88] or "mechanism."[89] And the above-described techniques of rationality (semantics, precedent, analogy-making, and logic) inhere to the core of Abel's image of federalism law. Let us look more closely at his elegant three-staged formula for discovering Canadian federalism law.

First, the lawyer identifies the pith and substance or the "matter" of a challenged statute. Abel distinguishes the specific from the generic features of a statute. A lawyer concerns her/himself with the generic character of a statute because the "matter" of a statute is "an abstract of the statute's content," or "the true, full and *exact* summarisation" of "[w]hat's it all about?"[90] This first stage of his mechanism aims to identify the centre of gravity or generic character of a statute. At the second stage, a lawyer assigns content to the concept labels in sections 91 and 92.[91] Utilizing "the distinctive traditional materials and techniques of the law," the lawyer seeks out "an integrating principle" or "common trait"[92] of each class in sections 91 and 92. A section 91 or 92 class, for Abel, constructs a fact category, each being "distinct, occupying no common ground with any other."[93] Each class *exclusively* incorporates all social facts which potentially come within the fact category. And, each class acts as "[a member] of a coherent universe."[94] Any one class coexists with the next, forming "a compendium of governmental power allocated between the two levels without voids and without overlaps."[95]

In the third stage of Abel's "elegant mechanism" the lawyer asks whether a statute's matter (or centre of gravity) falls within one of the designated fact categories of sections 91 and 92.[96] Where one cannot find a fact category in sections 91 and 92 to encompass the feature of a statute, the residuary 'Peace, Order and Good Government' clause crystallizes. The critical stage in Abel's scientific enterprise has more often than not been omitted from constitutional analysis, Abel complains. Lawyers have mechanically labelled a statute "without any connecting demonstration" of how its features are contemplated by the fact category of a specific enumerated class in sections 91 or 92. The omission thereby collapses Abel's first and second stages of analysis.

Abel's zealous advocacy of rationality is not unlike that of Pigeon, Beetz, Kennedy, MacDonald, and Laskin the judge. Rationality joins the horizontal compartments with the vertical hierarchy. The 'correct' use of rationality leaves the lawyer/judge/scholar apolitical, passive, and impartial. What is more, conclusions "necessarily follow." Conclusions, if logically sound in terms of objective meaning, simply must be accepted. What is, ought to be. Rationality constitutes the *cause* of any particular rule, in terms of its genesis and its *telos* (or end). Because one ratiocinates a rule from which one must begin anew in the next "similar" circumstance, rationality effectively formulates the starting rules in each analytic exercise. Or, at least, so it seems.

IX

The Policy Rationalist Image of
Federalism Law

Not unlike our earlier subject-matters, so too what jurists take to be federalism law collapses into a search for an appropriate image of a constitution. Juxtaposed against rule rationalism, one can identify within the Canadian legal heritage the coherent boundaries of a competing image of a constitution. This image projects as law the exposed social policies or 'ought' values which lie behind the "wordship"[1] of posited rules. Influences by the American realist movement, a small group of Canadian legal scholars – John Willis,[2] Cecil Wright,[3] and Bora Laskin[4] – picture reality in terms of social facts rather than as posited rules. The lawyer/judge/scholar can discover social facts by techniques of an objective "rational assessment," to use Laskin's term.[5] A later generation of "process" realists encourages Noel Lyon to identify an 'ought' or ideal-directed character with the policies embedded within social reality.[6] Lyon renames them goal/values. He tries to demonstrate how a lawyer/judge/scholar can scientifically describe, analyse, and apply the goal/values with the same precision which Albert Abel pictures possible for rules. The Supreme Court's present chief justice, not unlike Lyon and the early Laskin, balances "the interests" or purposes of one Charter guarantee as against "the interests" of another, as if rights and law were scientifically and rationally quantifiable. Dickson calls his image of the constitution a "teleological" or "purposive" one.[7]

Now, Canadian scholars sometimes consider their policy/values image of federalism law as somehow different from the rule rationalist image. One jurist goes so far as to equate policy with natural law.[8] Others distinguish policy from rules in terms of the inevitable political character of judicial decision-making[9] or the realism of the 'law and society' movement.[10] 'Rules versus policy' serves as the ideological theme of law faculties and students for a generation at least.[11] I aim to explain how a policy image of a constitution shares two important continuities with a rule rationalist image. First, positivism inheres in the core of a policy image. For the early Laskin, for example, policies are posited by a legislature (and supplemented by a court); for Lederman, the judge is the source of the posited policies; for Lyon, the community; and for the 'law and society' commentators, a political elite and a political institution dressed as a court.[12] Secondly, the policy image shares with rule rationalism the technique of rationality. The policy image merely adds a broader resource material (social/economic facts and shared goals) and more diversified techniques of rationality (psychology, theory, and history).

1. TO PIERCE THE VEIL OF ABSTRACT RULES

One dominant motivating factor generates the policy rationalist image of federalism law: the need to pierce the veil of abstract rules in order to join law with a social reality beyond the rules. Bora Laskin as a young scholar sets the framework for this social realism in his early essays. The essays demonstrate a strident, open attack against those jurists who picture federalism law as a compendium of cold, rigid abstractions.[13] In his first published essay, for example, he describes how equity originates from "a maze of procedural technicality" only to lose its "elasticity" by the nineteenth century when precedents and stereotyped categories have overburdened equity.[14] Laskin joins abstract rules with the liberal individualism of John Stuart Mill. By exalting the individual "as an anarchic ideal" the Millian state arbitrates between the rights of competing acquisitive individuals.[15] As an arbiter, the state requires formal rules to oversee disputes. The legislature performs that function whereas judges nibble away at the rules in the form of distinctions and exceptions.[16]

Laskin's early ruthless realism reaches its apex in his classic 1947 essay "Peace, Order and Good Government' Re-examined." Laskin aims to show in that essay, among other things, that the Privy Council has created rigid, abstract distinctions without differences[17] as well as "[u]nnecessary, if not also innocuous, dicta."[18] These, in turn become "precious formulae" which the Privy Council mechanically applies to significant social legislation without any inquiry into the "social, factual considerations"[19] or the "matter" (or purpose) of the Canadian statute.[20] Duff and other Canadian judges then freeze the "artificial presuppositions" into magic formulae.[21]

Only Watson's *Local Prohibition dicta* break from this artificial, abstract rule rationalism by contemplating that local social/economic problems can juristically evolve into national federal problems.[22]

Laskin interprets Haldane's federalism judgments as the epitome of an unreal, formulaic image of a constitution. Laskin characterizes Haldane himself as "the generalizer *par excellence* ... with his often repeated formula."[23] Haldane pictures law "in terms of cold abstract logic, purporting to find its points of reference within the four corners of the *B.N.A.*."[24] Haldane's abstract picture constrains the potential impact of the 'POGG' clause to the point of imprisoning the "Canadian Constitution" in an emergency straight-jacket, oblivious to "practical," social/economic facts.[25] In *Toronto Electric Commissioners* v. *Snider*[26] Haldane proves himself to be "the arbiter *sans peur et sans reproche* ready to solve any problem by a prepared formula, invariable in its compounds, regardless of the matter to be solved."[27] In *Snider*, the federal Industrial Disputes Investigation Act, 1907 introduces a scheme for conciliation of labour disputes whereby the government can mandatorily postpone strikes or lockouts pending the termination of conciliation efforts. Serious work stoppages precede and follow the enactment of the Industrial Disputes Investigation Act. The social policy underlying the Act was the social need to restore public order in industrial relations throughout Canada, Laskin believes. But Haldane, he complains, has approached social and economic facts "with the *inflexible concepts* that are often the product of a *neat mind*, unwilling in the interests of some sort of *formal logic* to disarrange thought patterns that had been nicely fitted together."[28] Laskin finds *Snider* "almost shocking in its casualness" with "the now monotonous formulae of earlier cases" and with "[n]ot even a pretence at analysis ..."[29]

2. POLICY

If the realist lawyer aspires to pierce the veil of abstract rules, what lies behind the rules? Social reality. And how, exactly, can a lawyer find social reality? For Laskin the young scholar, the key is to identify "the matter" or social interests which pressed for the enactment of any indigenous Canadian statute. Once one has clarified "the matter" (or policy), the lawyer can then connect "the matter" of the statute to one of the enumerated heads in section 92 of the British North America Act, 1867 or to the introductory "Peace, Order and Good Government" clause in section 91, of which the latter's enumerated heads serve as mere examples.[30] By concentrating upon "the matter" of any challenged statute, Laskin can incorporate the "facts and circumstances which give rise to some social pressure for legislation"[31] into an analysis of the text of the British North America Act. He can thereby accurately describe his analytic method as an "interlocking one, in which the British North America Act and the challenged legislation react on one another and fix each other's meaning."[32] Further, Laskin's policy image of federalism law contemplates the law's entangled evolution with corresponding social forces. For, the "continual state of ferment ... [and] the constantly changing conditions of society"[33] render an inevitably temporary character to any judicial decision.[34] His concentration upon "the matter" of a statute – rather than superimposed foreign abstract rules – acknowledges that temporary character. The boundaries of the rule image of the Privy Council, in contrast, estops jurists from entertaining social/economic reality. Consequently, the rule image obstructs and impairs the natural evolution of Canadian society.

Whereas Bora Laskin focuses upon the social genesis of any Canadian enactment, Noel Lyon envisions social reality in terms of ideal-directed shared values. Statutes and judicial decisions constitute merely two of many sources – and not the most important sources – of those values.[35] Instead of being posited in statute form, a constitution emanates *from within a society* much as customary international law evolves from within the international community over time.[36] A sustained deference to a norm *constitutes* constitutional or customary international law. This constitutive process constrasts with an institution's conscious posit of a norm. As Lyon explains in his first essay: "[t]he term 'constitutive process' is not just a linguistic substitute for constitutional law.' The latter term conveys a reference to a *body of materials*. Policy-oriented analysis focuses inquiry on a *process*, and seeks to promote systematic and comprehensive inquiry about that process."[37] To the question 'what is the Canadian Constitution?' then, Lyon and a colleague respond with "[t]he constitution of a people is found in the attitudes and customs of its members and in the working practices of its institutions."[38] In the context of institutional *indicia* of acknowledged norms in Canada, Lyon and his co-editor, Atkey, identify "consistent patterns" supporting "shared value preferences directed toward common goals, however dimly perceived and unarticulated."[39] The competent lawyer should study "the actual patterns of behaviour" of a society's populace, not the formal abstract rules of its judicial elite. Indeed, "[t]o assert that there can be no such shared goals and values is to deny that we have a constitution at all," he writes in his formative essay.[40] By picturing a constitution in constitutive terms, Lyon and Atkey aim to redefine the lawyer's area of responsibility from the formal courtroom to "the larger framework" where s/he acts in a "non-legal capacity."[41]

3. THE DE FACTO ROLE OF JUDGES

The policy rationalists broaden the resource material and rationality techniques available to the competent lawyer. But what role do judges in fact play in the elaboration of federalism law? Beginning with the early writings of Bora Laskin, policy rationalists recognized that judges consciously shape federalism law according to their particular social/economic/political attitudes. The judiciary thereby indirectly controls governmental policies.[42] Let us examine the *de facto* role of the judiciary as pictured in the essays of Bora Laskin, Paul Weiler, Peter Russell, and two contemporary Quebec scholars, Robert Décary and Gil Rémillard.

Laskin acknowledges the contingent character of judicial decision-making at an early stage of his career: "[w]e may as well deny the existence of the court as to deny that judicial decisions are the products of social and economic and political considerations for which the words of the British North America Act are merely the vehicles of communication. The constitution is as open as the minds of those called upon to interpret it; it is as closed as their minds are closed."[43] Constitutional law students suffer from a "delusion" by even entertaining the notion "that constitutional adjudication is 'pure' law, divorced from social or economic or political (in the highest sense) views."[44] To the claim of one scholar that courts should "concentrate on what the law 'is' rather than what it should be," Laskin responds "[h]ow far can naivety go?"[45] In addition to being facetious he sometimes finds it "amusing (or, perhaps, sad)" to watch "the spectacle of judges with opposing views of the legislation charging each other with trespassing on policy, and each virtuously claiming to be concerned only with legal competence."[46]

Laskin again and again demonstrates how particular judicial decisions really reflect a judge's own social, economic, or political view rather than some abstract rule of law. He claims, for example, that beginning with his *Board of Commerce* judgment Duff has embarked upon his own course more out of a conscious policy choice than from "the dictate of *stare decisis*" or the "compulsion of Privy Council decisions."[47] Further, the bank taxation cases illustrate the impact of economic factors upon constitutional issues.[48] Social/economic factors influence and underlie the judicial treatment of provincial marketing and price-fixing schemes.[49] One can explain the "singular suppression" of the trade and commerce power, Laskin thinks, only in terms of the social and economic consequences which the marketing of natural products poses.[50] The *Sask. Farm Security Act Ref.* illustrates that "there is no inevitability in constitutional decision [-making]."[51] And each of the Supreme Court judges pegs his *Saumur* judgment squarely on social and religious issues.[52] We have already noted how Laskin concludes one essay by describing the text of the British North America Act as merely "the vehicles of communication" for social, economic, and political issues.[53] In concluding another essay he writes: "[m]y examination of the cases dealing with the Dominion's general power *does not indicate any inevitability* in the making of particular decisions; if anything, it indicates *conscious and deliberate choice of a policy* which required, for its advancement, *manipulations* which can only with difficulty be represented as ordinary judicial techniques."[54] And in another, he ends with "[i]ndeed, the judicial office *remains uniquely personal* amid all its institutional restraints."[55]

Notwithstanding his exposé of Haldane's personal political biases and the Canadian Supreme Court's parroting of those prejudices, Laskin retains an ingrained faith in the judiciary's ability to transcend personal bias in favour of objectively posited social interests or "the matter" embedded within indigenous Canadian statutes. Over the decades, other Canadian scholars share a faith in the existence of an objective social/ political reality beyond legal discourse. During the 1970s, for example, anglophone and francophone scholars reconciled themselves to the inevitably political character of federalism judgments. For Paul Weiler, for example, rules of law simply do not exist.[56] Over time, the "law-like" character of the text of the British North America Act, 1867 has slowly eroded. Why? In the first place, social change has eventually rendered "most of the original federal bargain outmoded." Secondly, because legislators have experiences difficulty in amending the written constitution, the draftspersons' original allocation of authority evolved "substantially" without a corresponding change in the constitution's form.[57] Through time, then, the original text has simply become irrelevant to "the real human and social issues." What remains of the constitution? Pure policy: constitutional challenges in the courtroom speak to "essentially political and economic conflict."[58]

Peter Russell, more than any other Canadian scholar, has worked out the full ramifications of the policy image of a constitution. Although he sometimes considers policy as a supplement to legal rules in his early writings,[59] by the 1970s Russell pictures a constitution solely in political terms. By 'political,' he means "the initiation of significant change in our customs, our laws, or institutions and the maintenance of some important features of the established order"[60] or, affirming David Easton's classic conception of "political," "the authoritative allocation of *values*."[61] In contrast to understanding the judiciary "as being essentially technical and non-political," Russell devotes his major study, *The Judiciary in Canada: The Third Branch of Government*, to the "firm conviction that judges exercise political power and that courts are part of the machinery of government."[62]

Russell complains that what I have called the rule rationalist image of a constitution has burdened jurists for more than a century. The image innocently excludes power as a legitimate factor in law-making. Rule rationalists have imagined that only legislators, not judges, make political judgments. Sections 91 and 92 of the British North American Act, 1867, it is supposed, distribute political power between the two sets of political entities: federal legislatures and provincial legislatures. In contrast, judges impartially adjudicate disputes by appealing to what they understand to be objective external rules. Because judges believe that they actually apply rules rationally, judges self-describe their role as neutral or apolitical vis-à-vis the presumed political actors. The 'constitution as rules,' according to Russell, "conditions him [the lawyer] to view social relations through the little slivers of life that are revealed in law reports."[63] Legalistic complacency with existing posited rules "completely blinds jurists from realising how seldom in fact the traditional legal remedies are relevant or available to the individual ..."[64] The rule blinders have "distracted us from the concerns which are most immediately related to the rights and liberty we might enjoy in the modern state."[65] This is particularly so when one studies the Canadian Supreme Court as a bilingual and bicultural institution.[66]

Why has a 'constitution as rules' blinded the legal community? Because, Russell emphasizes again and again, judicial decision-making inevitably revolves about political values rather than rules. Judges, lawyers, and scholars should finally recognize the *de facto* role of values. Once one appreciates the latter, one can "unmask value-judgments" hidden behind the "dispassionate legal reasoning," as Russell aimed to do in *The Supreme Court as a Bilingual and Bicultural Institution*.[67] The concentration upon formal posited rules has disguised "the hidden nature" of the judicial process.[68]

So, for example, the formal "filters" of a 'rules' image of a constitution condition "the more humanist and cosmopolitan English-speaking lawyers" to react spontaneously with "bored shrugs" to any claim that a common law *mentalité* has dominated the Supreme Court.[69] The image has diverted scholars from studying, first, the extrinsic political circumstances surrounding the rules and, second, the *de facto* political role of judges in their allocation of values.[70] We have noted that the critical issue for any "legal" scholar, according to Russell, is 'why has any particular issue arisen in a court?' And the resolution of *that* issue hangs upon "the delicate balancing of social priorities,"[71] as he demonstrates in his works again and again.

Anglophone scholars are not alone in their realistic exposé of the social policies and political values presupposed in federalism judgments. During the 1970s, Quebec scholars, too, pierce the contingent juristic doctrines only to find an openly federal bias embedded within them. Indeed, Robert Décary claims that the openly political values of the Canadian Supreme Court in the *Patriation Reference* have undermined the judiciary's credibility as an impartial, restrained arbitrator of federalism disputes.[72] The Majority of Seven, for example, held that "Par rapport *tout au moins* a la formule de modification, le processus en question ici ne vise pas la *modification d'une constitution complète*, mis plutôt *l'achèvement d'une constitution incomplète*. Il s'agit en *l'espèce* de la touche finale, d'ajouter *une pièce* a l'édifice constitutionnel ..."[73] This assertion proves feeble, according the Décary, because the Charter in fact has added "d'une *touche nouvelle*" rather than "de touche finale" to the Constitution. And the Court has admitted that the Charter "envisage la suppression d'un pouvoir législatif provincial." Décary notes how the argument of counsel for the group of eight provinces has considered "des déclarations de personnalités politiques importantes" as having the force of law.[74]

More important, Décary claims that the Supreme Court judges have in fact restated the issue of 'conventions' in a manner which harms Quebec's autonomy rule. According to the latter rule, Quebec is an autonomous province.[75] From that, one can deduce the further rule that Quebec possesses a veto power over any infringement of her legislative powers. But whereas the provinces have asked whether there exists a convention which requires provincial consent, the Supreme Court's Majority of Seven restates this very issue in terms of whether *unanimous* provincial consent is required: "le fond de la question est de déterminer si conventionnellement le consentment provincial est obligatoire or non si, en ce cas, il doit être unanime."[76] Décary describes how the Supreme Court, again and again in its judgment, has imposed "une échelle de valeur" as, for example, when it has expressed that "certaines conventions peuvent être plus importantes que certaines lois."[77] Finally, the Majority of Six has openly embraced a formal condemnation of governmental conduct when it has asserted that "le principe fédéral, dit-elle, est irréconciliable avec un état des affaires où l'action unilatérale des autorités fédérales peût entrainer la modification des pouvoirs législatifs provinciaux ... [C'est] le processus que porte atteinte au principe fédéral. C'est en tant que protection contre ce processus que le convention constitutionnelle est née."[78] The judiciary have usurped a political role and have thereby sacrificed their historic place as the guardian of the federal principle, a principle which, we have seen, Pigeon and Beetz hold deeply.

Gil Rémillard shares Décary's realistic assessment of the judiciary's role in an important essay, "Legality, Legitimacy and the Supreme Court."[79] He concedes that "the temptation is very much present in any judicial system to draw an arbitrary line between the theory of law and its practice in relation to the exercise of power."[80] Indeed, in his text *Le Fédéralisme Canadien*, Rémillard shows that "jusqu'à ces dernières années du moins, s'en est tenue à une interpretation strictement légaliste."[81] But the line between law and power is arbitrary or tautological. One should, instead, maintain "a strict link" between "the politico-socio-economic implication of the exercise of power and its theoretical scope."[82] In Rémillard's study of constitutional decisions, "le Comité judiciaire s'est montré à plusieurs reprises beaucoup plus politique que juridique."[83]

Rémillard argues that the Supreme Court of Canada has broken the arbitrary barrier between law and power in the *Patriation Reference*.[84] The key to Rémillard's image of a constitution lies in his distinction between legality and legitimacy. Because power is "natural" in the sense that one can find it among humans, animals, and plants, there flows from this natural fact of power an equally "instinctive corollary": namely, the abuse of power. "Man should thus consider power in an organised fashion on the basis of a more or less conscious social perception."[85] A constitution performs such a purpose in that a constitution subjects power to known legal rules.[86]

Rémillard believes that the Supreme Court judgment in the *Patriation Reference* has demonstrated how a constitution can actually become illegitimate, in that the state (or an institution of the state) exercises power legally under a constitution notwithstanding the fact that the electorate has not authorized the creation of the constitution. The Majority of Seven exclusively grounded the constitution in posited law. The Majority insisted upon formal legitimacy: "[a]ny exercise of the state's power must be subordinate to its respect of a higher rule."[87] At the same time, the Majority maintained that conventions, confined to political practice rather than law, do exist.[88] Conventions constitute "material legitimacy" in that they connect power to "the prevailing constitutional *values* or principles of the period" and "the wishes of the electorate."[89] The gulf between legality and legitimacy "calls into question the celebrated problem of the foundation of the state's authority."[90] Because the Supreme Court itself has reiterated that "the wishes of the electorate" constitute "the constitutional value" fundamental to responsible government and because the Canadian people "at no time" were consulted (nor had the Government in power requested a mandate from Canadians), the legitimacy of the *Patriation Reference* was "open to considerable criticism."[91]

Similarly, the subsequent *Québec Veto Reference* invited the Supreme Court to respond to "a strictly political question": namely whether a convention exists confirming Quebec's right to veto a constitutional amendment.[92] Again, only an appeal to the populace through a referendum could have "permanently" settled the issue of legitimacy, Rémillard claims.[93] Had the Quebecois disapproved of the Patriation Bill in such a referendum, patriation would be legal, though illegitimate, because legislators would exercise power without having been granted the legitimacy to exercise it. In the *Patriation Reference*, the Supreme Court considered the Patriation Bill legal, though immoral in political terms (that is, illegitimate). At the same time, the Court appealed to objectivist *indicia* for legitimacy such as the wishes of the electorate. The Court thereby left a vast gap between legality and legitimacy. In so doing the Court opened the door to unavoidable "important political conflicts."

4. THE OBJECTIVITY OF POLICY

Interestingly, at the same time that scholars have exposed the political character of judicial decisions about federalism, they maintain an objectivist image of law in that 'the law' of federalism lives 'out there' in an objective world independently of the jurist. At the same time that he criticizes the *Patriation Reference* Court for imposing value judgments which undermine the autonomy rule, Robert Décary resurrects the historic role of the Supreme Court as an impartial restrained arbitrator and guardian of a rule – the autonomy super-rule. Similarly, Gil Rémillard criticizes the Supreme Court's *Patriation Reference* and *Québec Veto Reference* for undermining the historic barrier between law and power. Rémillard prescribes that political issues be returned to the electorate in the form of a referendum, leaving an objective law to judges.

Indeed, the very legitimacy of judicial decisions hangs upon a longing for a clear separation of power from law, legitimacy from legality – as if there were and could be 'out there' an objective world which needs to be applied only for the asking. Even the devastating realism of Bora Laskin, Peter Russell, and Paul Weiler yearns for the judiciary's return to an objective legal order, politics being left to the legislature in a democratic society.

In place of the old natural rights talk, for example, Laskin advocates that jurists should impartially balance the costs and benefits of competing social interests.[94] Jurists should so so with a scientific eye for the future dominant social interests in the inevitable social evolution of society.[95] Ever ready to shed old abstract rules, the judge should "draw lines" between competing social interests, conscious of prior precedents and contemporary social facts.[96] Does Laskin contemplate that judges would actually replace politicians in this enterprise of closing the gap between legal abstractions and social reality? As both a scholar and a judge, his response is an unequivocal negative. Yes, judges and legislators complement each other in closing the gap.[97] But the legislature is far better equipped to do so.[98] Usually, judges can only "nibble away" at a rule whereas, in contrast, a legislature can frame a new rule to meet a new social situation without being compelled to align the new rule logically with pre-existing ones. In contrast to Albert Abel's deference to the text, Laskin supports the principle of legislative supremacy out of a concern for institutional efficacy. And this efficacy, he grounds in social realism.

What makes federalism law 'law,' then, is the objectivity, neutrality, and impartiality with which a jurist measures social interests. Haldane failed in that duty, Laskin believes, because Haldane had been biased in favour of the provinces from the start. Haldane's views "were not uninfluenced by his long apprenticeship, when at the Bar, as counsel for the provinces in at least ten cases …," Laskin declares.[99] The Privy Council overall has consciously and deliberately manipulated policies in a manner which "can only with difficulty be represented as ordinary judicial techniques."[100] By so openly exposing the Privy Council's bias and manipulative technique, Laskin inferentially appeals to the fundamental importance of the neutrality with which a judge should pursue his balancing role.

And all this, in turn, assumes that facts do exist 'out there,' separate from the judge and learned counsel. Social facts are facts. They are "the matter" of a statute – the very "matter" which forms the grounding of Laskin's whole analytic scheme. Laskin accepts the social facts which policies represent as 'givens.' They are his starting-point. The lawyer need only discover them. And this, s/he does by objective "rational assessment."[101] With the correct rational method which concentrates upon the facts, the reality, "the matter," we would finally grasp our just constitution. Laskin thereby replaces the abstract rules with social policies. But the pictured separation of an objective law from a subjective bias still inheres in the core of his method. And from that separation he cannot escape, as we have already seen in Part I of this essay.

Even Paul Weiler's piercing critique of the inevitably political content of federalism judgments presupposes that an objective federalism law is possible. Indeed, judges *must* escape from policy-making and this they could so only if judicial review of legislation were abolished, Weiler insists. This is what he means by "thinking about the unthinkable."[102] Weiler presents three legitimate functions for judges. First, granted the inherent objectivity of the meaning of words, judges can initially clarify a meaning in an effort to ascertain whether a posited enactment applies to one head of power over another.[103] An "appropriately restricted" judge should not seriously entertain vague doctrines such as "occupying the field," "pre-emption," or "implied conflicts." Secondly, a judge's primary duty is to adjudicate disputes by appealing to pre-existing posited rules and doctrines. That is, a judge/lawyer should limit one's examination to rules rather than to values.[104] Once a judge breaks from the rules to take "the intuitive leap," in Noel Lyons's words, the objectivity of the legal system is lost. Fiat remains.[105] Finally, a judge should proceed to hold a statute inoperative only "in an escapable contradiction of legal directives" between federal and provincial statutes.[106]

Weiler leaves it to the real political arena to resolve all political/ constitutional issues. Judges are simply not competent to discuss, consider, and posit values. In his words, "[t]he natural question to ask is whether our courts – especially the Supreme Court of Canada – are institutionally equipped to make the judgments required for *rational policy-making*."[107] In addition to being incompetent in policy matters, judges cannot possibly remain impartial when the federal government appoints the personnel of the courts and when the constitution does not guarantee the judiciary's independent status, the integrity of the appointment process, and the security of their tenure. The latter factors leave supreme court judges especially dependent upon the federal side in the inevitable political issues. As a consequence, Weiler places his faith in the legislature. Without the latter faith, his image of a constitution would leave a serious gap. Weiler plugs the gap. But he does so without questioning the objectivist underpinnings of his policy image of a constitution. Legislatures can more rationally resolve political issues than courts. And courts can rationally apply objective, apolitical norms in an impartial manner. Weiler adheres to the fact/value picture of reality.[108]

5. THE POSITIVISM OF POLICY

Now, the policy image of a constitution shares something more than objectivism with the rule rationalist image. Although some advocates of policy strikingly differentiate themselves from the sinister positivism of rules, a positivism too imbues their policy image. For, after all, some institution or person must posit the policies. For Laskin, the legislature ought to posit the policies in the form of "the matter" of a statute, although manipulative jurists such as Haldane oftentimes usurp the positing role. William Lederman, in contrast, contemplates that, ultimately, the judge himself or herself posits his or her own values. Unlike a scientist, Lederman reminds us, a jurist must distinguish good from evil, just from unjust.[109] This judgment takes the lawyer/judge/scholar beyond the reality of posited rules to value choices. Ultimately, one must choose or posit one value over another. Rationality merely clarifies one's choices. Lederman stresses that the most important moment arrives in the decision-making process when a judge posits *her* or *his* values. The judge's inevitable posit of a value explains why Lederman emphasizes the need for independent courts "of the first rank" in his earliest essays.[110] It explains why, for Lederman, "the essential order of society" would suddenly dissolve without "a complete and closed hierarchical system of propositions of authority."[111]

Although Noel Lyon aims to scientize what Lederman leaves to faith, Lyon, too, succumbs to the very positivism which entraps Lederman's ultimate value choices. In place of the judge, however, Lyon projects the community as the ultimate source of value allocation.[112] Noel Lyon's newly discovered techniques of rationality can only prolong the moment when a value choice must be posited. In "A Fresh Approach to Constitutional Law" Lyon acknowledges that his scientific model "contains no answers. It simply offers a descriptive framework for human activities that is comprehensive and subject to empirical reference."[113] He describes his image of a constitution (and of law) as an orderly sequential one, each stage of scientific investigation building upon the previous one. The rationality of his image leads eventually "to *the final creative task* with *some hope* that it will be performed *on as rational a basis* as the existing state of human knowledge will permit."[114] In their teaching text Lyon and

Atkey oftentimes remind the student that ongoing decision processes do not "in fact genuflect to neat organization charts."[115] Lyon and Atkey merely aspire to offer the "functional tools" to observe the processes. In "The Charter as a Mandate" Lyon again acknowledges that rationalism can only ensure "that judges themselves will be aware of all the choices they are in fact making and will seek the best available guidance on each of them before making *that intuitive leap* that usually ends the process of judicial decision."[116] Models speak to the need to clarify "starting points, destinations and guidance" in the reform of institutions, he claims in another essay. But the content of the models only points to "the direction of *the preferred* outcomes that *the stated* goals represent."[117] That is, models begin with posited goals.

Along similar lines, Lyon asserts in "Vague but Meaningful Generalities," that "[i]t is true that judgments *ultimately* must be made."[118] Jurists should use rationality, not ideology or doctrine, to clarify the Charter values. Ultimately, though, "[i]n fact, there are *no answers, just judgments* as to where lies the balance between total freedom and total control ..."[119] Indeed, linguistic analysis reveals the deception of "categorical truths." Lyon, in contrast, pictures that judges should infuse "a system of fundamental values ... into our law through a careful weighing, against the *relevant* circumstances, of the various claims to legal protexion ... and a *suitable* balance must be struck between those claims."[120] Rationality cannot determine the criterion of relevancy or the suitability of the balance or the legitimacy or fundamentality of the values. Only the simple, crude positing of a value in an ultimately "intuitive leap" can answer those questions. Lyon's image of a constitution cannot escape from the positivism of rationalism.

Canadian jurists finally acknowledge the undisguised positivistic character of the policy image of federalism law when law joins with power. The central issue for scholars such as Weiler, Russell, Décary, Rémillard, and Monaghan is 'what institution, class, profession or (presumably) sex possesses or ought to possess the authority to posit the ultimate value choices in a liberal-democratic state?'[121] Values inevitably lie at the core of law. Values speak to reality. That institution which allocates values, therefore, exercises effective power.[122] Formal rules, techniques of rationality, and objective policies merely camouflage the power to posit the policies/values.

Although values possess an ideal-directed character, they are grounded in social reality because judge and citizen alike believe in them deeply. As such, one can treat them as 'givens.' One can empirically verify them by reference to social behaviour, the latter existing as a natural fact. The natural fact of a shared acceptance de-legitimizes the value. That explains why Rémillard, for example, expresses such concern for the lack of conscious electoral choice for the Referendum Bill during the late 1970s. Rémillard measures the Bill's form against "the wishes of the electorate." The fact that the Supreme Court, rather than the electorate, posits the community's values triggers a cause for alarm. For Paul Weiler and Peter Russell, the elected officials should posit policies, although lawyers and judges have regretfully and wrongfully usurped that role. Indeed, the authoritative posit or allocation of one value over another renders a political character to judicial decision-making. Peter Russell himself defines "political" as the allocation of values. And, the final realization that judges in fact posit policies or values arouses these public-minded jurists to advocate judicial restraint, on the one hand, and a more realistic and systematic scrutiny of the content of the posited values, on the other. Not surprisingly, then, they advocate a broad spectrum of rational techniques to uncover the posited values.

6. EXPANDED TECHNIQUES OF RATIONALITY

The policy image of federalism law initially concentrates upon the admissibility and weight of 'extrinsic evidence.' Because Laskin's image begins with the social facts causing a statute's enactment, a lawyer/judge misdirects her/his analysis by limiting herself or himself to the four corners of a statute. To identify "the matter" of a statute, one must examine the social pressures leading to its enactment and this can be accomplished, Laskin believes, by expanding the lawyer's resource material to include the parliamentary discussion of a bill at its various legislative stages, the bill's legislative history, and the trend of social forces.[123] This expanded extrinsic evidence would offer "a rational basis" for constitutional determinations.[124] Without anchoring one's method in such empirical evidence, judgments would be arbitrary and, therefore, irrational.

Noel Lyon's concentration upon the community's values as opposed to "the matter" of legislation leads him to add formal documents, common law principles, unwritten conventions, practices, and moral/political attitudes to the arsenal of a policy lawyer.[125] As to common law principles alone, Lyon expands law's resource material far beyond the final appellate judgments to include

the decision of the lower court which is being appealed; the arguments of counsel for all parties at trial and on appeal; the pleadings and written argument filed by the parties at trial and on appeal; the procedural techniques used by the parties to delay or speed up the progress of the case; the negotiations transpiring between the parties prior to and during the commencement of the action; the nature of various third parties intervening in the case at trial and at the appellate level; and public comment through the mass media before, during, and after the case.[126]

Sometimes, judicial decision-makers mark their dominant value preferences in technical discussion. On other occasions, they consciously articulate their value preferences.[127] Lyon's own text demonstrates a wealth of material to which the lawyer should legitimately appeal in identifying the core of law. In addition to the traditional institutional sources of a court and a legislature, he considers "informal" institutions such as political parties, the mass media, political lobby groups, and protest groups.[128] The latter open up the scrutiny of sociology texts, Senate debates, House of Commons debates, media accounts, judicial decisions, and municipal by-laws.

To a broader resource material for the study of law, Noel Lyon adds social psychology. Until the early 1970s, according to Lyon, Canadian lawyers and scholars have groped for a subjective "hunch," intuition, or inarticulate major premise as the sole basis for the inevitable value choice.[129] Lawyers have been "only dimly aware" of their values. In his words, "legal scholars and lawyers who are expected to guide the judicial process know little or nothing beyond the observed biases and predispositions through which these unstated but central influences manifest themselves."[130] This occurs because the familial, institutional, and professional environments have "conditioned" or "programmed" values within one's subconscious.[131] He expresses his picture of lawyers and the impact of legal training in this way: "[t]he legal minds seems to prefer to operate intuitively. It is gradually programmed with a complex body of facts, principles, and attitudes, which it organizes according to patterns of training and experience so that it can be brought to bear on specific problems."[132] Lyon urges lawyers to scientize those intuitions.[133]

For Peter Russell, it seems, a more concentrated effort to utilize contemporary empirical techniques would "unmask" the value judgments hidden behind the formal "dispassionate" reasoning of rule lawyers.[134] Russell consistently attempts to support his advocacy of expanded rational techniques with extensive statistical research.[135] The critical issue for any legal scholar, he claims, is the empirical one: 'why has any particular issue arisen in a court?' To that end, he urges scholars to contemplate a broader set of issues:

Why was the statute drafted at this particular time? What were the social and economic interests that moulded and influenced the politicians who drafted that statute? Why do these cases come to court and what difference does it make that these cases as opposed to other issues come to court? How are those judicial decisions carried out and what kind of social and economic and political relations do they change? The key is for the scholar in the law school to at least be asking those questions, and not to live in a formal legal world where he is content with just looking at what is in the cases and the statutes.[136]

The empirical studies of Canadian law now constitute a 'school of thought.'[137]

Finally, policy rationalists add theory to their arsenal of rationality techniques. "Legal theory is important," Lyon expresses during the mid-1970s "because it shapes the questions we frame about the law and the way we respond to those questions in concrete cases."[138] Constitutional theory, he continues, is "especially important because it *determines the way we perceive* the functions and relationships of the various institutions of government and hence the quality of our system of representative government under law." Theory aids one in the enterprise of locating the content of a community's shared values. By identifying the underlying community values one can better understand the surface issues about which lawyers and other public officials debate.[139] And theory in the form of modelling offers policy-makers an opportunity to study an institution over a long time frame and "to effect fundamental changes in a highly stable system of institutions and processes where the key personnel, judges, usually remain in office for the rest of their working lives once they are appointed."[140]

Lyon's human rights essays[141] and "The Central Fallacy of Canadian Constitutional Law"[142] exemplify how one can use theory to expose the reality of shared values or judicial "intuitions" lying behind formal rules. He begins with the "unexamined assumption" of Canadian constitutional law: namely, that the Canadian legislatures enjoy a supremacy of the same character as the United Kingdom Parliament. This assumption he describes as being "deeply embedded in our legal thinking." That premise can be exposed only by going to legal theory in that, again, theory "shapes the questions we frame about the law."[143] When he examines the theoretical assumption or "mental act" of the Supreme Court judgments in the *Breathalyser Reference*,[144] for example, he finds that the "simplistic" English theory of legislative supremacy has dominated the reasons in the judgment. Indeed, Canadian constitutional law more generally has presupposed the English theory.[145]

Lyon aims to show in his essay "The Central Fallacy" how the continued acceptance of the English theory has left a vast gap between that theory on the one hand and actual Canadian value preferences on the other. Instead of concentrating exclusively upon both the texts of section 91 and 92 and the texts of judicial decisions interpreting sections 91 and 92, as had Albert Abel, Pigeon, and the rule rationalists, Noel Lyon urges an expansion of the lawyer's scope of inquiry to the entire British North America Act, 1867. Once the lawyer has accomplished that, s/he would be compelled to recognize that the BNA Act as a whole has vested judicial power exclusively in an independent judiciary "as a matter of law." Lyon builds upon his earlier argument, from 1972, where he has inferred a 'rule of law' value from section 99.[146] Section 99 has made it extremely difficult to remove judges; but there would be no point in securing judges from political interference, Lyon argues, if the executive or legislature could bypass judges whenever a government has found it expedient to do so.[147] The English theory of legislative supremacy has represented the latter possibility as valid, in that English theory has vested judicial power ultimately in the legislature. In contrast, because judicial independence exemplifies a shared value indigenous to Canada and because shared values are constitutive of a constitution, a simple legislative enactment cannot be used to alter the value of judicial independence. The latter constitutes a constitutional requirement. Accordingly, he reasons, only a formal constitutional amendment of the British North America Act, 1867 can legitimately change the requirement.[148]

7. RATIONAL ORDER

Positivism and rationalism permeate the juristic prisms of federalism law. We saw in the previous chapter that a very deep desire to picture a rational order fires the image of the constitution shared by Albert Abel, Beetz, Pigeon, and other rule rationalists. William Lederman, we have noted, seeks to synthesize rules and policies in an effort to prevent the dissolution of a rational universe. The policy rationalists too press themselves to repair the rational disorder allegedly wrought by the likes of Lord Haldane. By scientizing a lawyer's intuitions and a community's values, Noel Lyon seeks to order what is otherwise disordered. Once Peter Russell and Paul Weiler recognize the inevitable positivism of the rule and policy images of federalism law, they advocate the re-allocation of value choices from appointed judges to the majoritarian legislature. The real practice of judicial law-making contradicts the liberal-democratic theory of majoritarianism. Décary and Rémillard similarly long for a return to an "umpire" role for the judiciary. If the judiciary returned to an "umpire" role, the gap between legality and legitimacy would thereby collapse. In the process, of course, rule rationalism would be resurrected.

Canadian constitutional scholars, in the end, remain entrapped within the positivism and rationalism of our era. They picture law as possessing a genetic and logical beginning: namely, posited rules and policies. They imagine that, with sophisticated rational technique, rules/policies can actually *cause* legal answers. They differ only as to the institutional source of the posited rules/policies and the efficacy of considered rational techniques.

As a result of their image of a constitution, the constitutional law becomes an end-in-itself. Their image precludes any inquiry into the ends towards which a constitutional law might be evolving. History and prescriptive claims become asides, accidents. The image of a constitution – not a text, or a set of values, or even "the Constitution" – closes off any inquiry beyond the posited rules/policies themselves. Without a genetic beginning or a moral end, the law is deemed an end-in-itself, notwithstanding disclaimers to the contrary. Canadian jurists thereby elevate the means of rationality to the station of ends. And all out of a desperate need for rational order.

X

The Image of "Orthodox" Rationalism

The Canadian legal scholars we have studied in the past two chapters picture federalism law through two impressive images of a constitution. The one begins with a horizontal spectrum of 'subject-matters' below which legislators and judges vertically posit rules. Combined, the horizontal/vertical scheme regulates the whole of social conduct: past, present, and future. The second begins with social policies which legislators and judges in fact, though not in form, posit. Both images grant an extraordinary deference to the capacity of rationality to find, apply, elaborate, distinguish, and create the rules which encompass the whole of human conduct. Both prisms presuppose an inevitable posit of the rules or policies. What characterizes the two images in this shared rationalism and positivism, notwithstanding the apparent aspiration of Laskin and others to differentiate their piercing realism from the formalism of rule rationalism. Interestingly, this same shared rationalism and positivism characterizes a third image of federalism law. This image, which William R. Lederman describes as "orthodoxy," incorporates both posited rules with posited policies or values. We have already experienced in Chapter VII how Dickson responds to Charter challenges: first, by identifying the 'interests' or 'values' underlying a Charter right; secondly, by rationally balancing the competing 'interests' against the end(s) of the Charter.[1] Dickson's image of the Charter resembles orthodoxy's amalgam of rules and policies. To better appreciate the Dickson picture of the Charter as much as to complete the story of the law of Canadian federalism, let us examine closely how William Lederman works through "the dilemmas" of the "orthodox" image of a constitution.[2] In the process I aim to consolidate the general claim that scholars, as much as judges or lawyers, approach any 'subject-matter' of law with a pre-understanding or image of a constitution. The boundaries of this image pre-censor how one understands the 'subject-matter.' Lederman's writings finally clarify for us the boundaries of a 'balanced' or 'orthodox' image of a constitution which we have slowly been drawing from Canadian legal discourse in earlier chapters.

1. THE NATURE OF REALITY

The first clue to Lederman's image of a constitution lies within his early 1958 essay entitled "The Common Law System in Canada."[3] Lederman himself recognizes the essay as laying the groundwork for his later studies. Over twenty years later he notes that "... this essay does reveal and develop more fully than any other my continuing basic premises and beliefs concerning some of the principal issues of legal science and philosophy."[4] For Lederman, the critical issue for the lawyer is "what is the nature of the reality about which man makes reasoned propositions?"[5]

Jurists have offered two responses to that question, according to Lederman. First, the Blackstonian, who seems to resemble the character traits of "rule rationalists," claims that "certain basic self-evident legal principles are given which are potentially complete in their substantive scope."[6] The legal order is complete: what rules exist pre-exist. The Blackstonian accepts that, with the aid of Aristotelian logic, the lawyer can deduce detailed normative rules for *every* life-situation. Lederman likens the Blackstonian picture of legal results to a trigonometric table. Judges aim "to discern and apply all-sufficient pre-existing rules" in this "closed system."[7] The all-inclusive, self-sufficient legal order constitutes the whole of reality for the Blackstonian. Because what exists pre-existed, Lederman can accurately describe the legal method within this image as a "mechanical jurisprudence."[8] For the image leaves no room for creativity.

Lederman portrays that realists offer a second response to the general question of 'what is reality?' The Realists – or those whom I call "policy rationalists" – approach law much as scientists investigate physics and chemistry, Lederman believes. To understand the judicial process one must predict "*the largely irrational conduct* of judges in deciding what they have to decide."[9] Realists deny the existence of a closed, pre-existing system of rules which an Aristotelian rationality can discover. Realists believe, in Lederman's view, that one can and should study law in imitation of modern experimental natural science, using behaviourist psychology as a tool. Why? Because natural facts alone constitute reality. Only directly perceptible, concrete, physical things exist in nature. All else is external to nature and , therefore, unreal. Whereas physical, natural objects are facts, the human person's abstractions, creations, or limitations of nature are "completely subjective" and divorced from natural facts. Concepts and subjectivist feelings emanate from the world of value and constitute non-reality. Since the human mind creates rules of law as constructs, the rules are external to facts and they are, therefore, unreal.[10] With the aid of the behavioural sciences, the realists aimed to predict "the largely irrational conduct of judges."

Lederman rejects and, at the same time, tries to synthesize elements from both the Blackstonian and the realist response to the question of reality. By grounding his image of law in both rules and values, he believes his image is "an orthodox view." On the one hand he accepts the epistemological grounding of realism *in facts* and, on the other, he incorporates rules and other concepts into his image of 'what constitutes fact.' Yes, Lederman agrees with the Realists that facts constitute reality. Further, if something were not a fact, then it must be a subjective, arbitrary, unreal value. But, for Lederman, the 'is' world of fact does not stop with nature. Why not? Because common attribute, time and space, cause and effect relate physical objects to each other. These relationships among natural objects are "just as real and true" as the natural objects themselves, Lederman claims. What is crucial for him is that he understands ideas, abstractions, and universals to function so as to denote the common attributes of the relationships among natural objects. He groups the relationships together as concepts. Because Lederman considers these relationships as part of reality, Lederman can incorporate the concepts denoting those relationships as also part of 'fact,' of the 'is' world. Lederman thereby broadens the realists' world of fact to include relationships and their consequential representative concepts.

From this, Lederman reasons that concepts are "not mere figments existing in the mind only with no hold whatever on objective reality."[11] Concepts can be understood as true or false, valid or invalid. This is so because they denote or describe the relationships among natural objects. The concepts exist 'out there' to be discovered only for the asking. One can check the truth and validity of a conceptual proposition by connecting it to "the objective reality" of natural objects plus their relationships. Consequently, "logical thought, experiment, observation, study and dialectical discussion" serve as the means to test a proposition's truth and validity.[12]

2. RULES OF LAW AS REALITY

A rule of law constitutes a concept or abstraction. A rule of law joins or describes the relationships among natural facts. Lederman himself describes rules of law as "notional classes of facts or type-fact[s]."[13] By this he means that if one proves, first, that certain facts have actually occurred and, secondly, the facts fall within a "type-fact" or "fact category" of a rule, then the rule triggers a legal consequence. The rule imposes a duty upon some person or persons to adhere to a "specified type of conduct."[14] The "fact category" or "notional category of fact" prescribes certain features or criteria of facts. These features identify the real facts for legal purposes.[15] Lederman considers that the 'subject-matter' of a rule is a term used to refer to the two elements of a rule: all features within the fact category, and the prescribed rights and duties triggered by the fact category.[16] The judge's role is to examine the connection between a given notional fact category on the one hand and concrete natural facts on the other. The latter, he describes as "neutral,"[17] "non-verbal,"[18] or "non-legal facts."[19] This investigation of the relationship between a notional fact category and natural facts represents what Lederman means when he suggests that one can check the truth or validity of a rule of law (a conceptual proposition) against "the objective reality." Natural facts, again, constitute objective reality.[20] It makes sense, then, for Lederman to proceed to define rules of law as "precepts of human conduct employed as a means of social control in a politically mature community."[21] The rights and duties in the rule set out precepts or 'ought' claims of human conduct. The notional fact categories in the rules serve as the means to control social relationships, the latter being natural facts.

From this perspective one can appreciate Lederman's character of the parent text within his image of a constitution (and law). Sections 91 and 92 of the British North America Act, 1867 categorize notional categories of facts. When categorizing the distribution of legislative powers, "we approach the facts of life only through their legal aspects, that is, only to the extent that such facts have been incorporated in rules of law as the typical fact-situations contemplated by those rules."[22] That is, the lawyer understands social reality through the prisms of rules of law. Lederman believes that there are many such rules of law. Sections 91 and 92 offer a complete prism, "a *complete* system ... over *virtually the whole* range of actual and potential law-making."[23] Again, not unlike both the rule rationalist and Laskin's "social interests" images, sections 91 and 92 of the British North America Act, 1867 constitute "a *total* system" of distribution of rule-making.[24] The totality of present and future human conduct is encompassed within the scope of sections 91 and 92.

What sections 91 and 92 enumerate, then, are not classes of social relationships (that is, relationships among natural objects) but classes of laws or notional fact categories which, in turn, categorize social facts. That is why Lederman expresses that the framers could hace (more concisely and more clearly) phrased sections 91 and 92 of the British North America Act, 1867 by positing the power to enact *"laws coming within the classes of laws next hereinafter enumerated."*[25] Social facts (that is, the facts about the social relationships among natural persons) are legally neutral. Rules of law, in contrast, posit prescriptive criteria or features which identify certain neutral social facts as relevant to the features. Sections 91 and 92 categorize those rules of law.

3. RATIONALITY

Because sections 91 and 92 of the British North America Act, 1867 categorize rules of law which, in turn, identify relevant features for neutral social relationships and because the latter are "just as real and true" as the natural objects (such as human persons) themselves, Lederman concludes that one can test the truthfulness and validity of the rules against the objective reality (the social relationships). But how is one to do this? We have already seen in the previous chapter that Lederman accomplishes this with rationality or, in his words, with "logical thought, experiment, observation, study and dialectical discussion."[26]

Lederman's image of law (and reality), then, offers two functions for a lawyer/judge. First, s/he should ensure that concrete "real" social facts are connected to the features of the notional fact category in a rule. Secondly, s/he must join the subject-matter of the rule (the fact category plus the rights/duties) to the classification of rules in sections 91 and 92. Rationality aids the lawyer/judge in both enterprises. These two functions, in turn, require that the lawyer/judge discover "the true meaning" of the objects of investigation. One must discover the true meaning of the words in the fact category of a rule, in the rights/duties which the rule imposes, and in the enumerated general features of the classificatory rules in sections 91 and 92. Lederman understands that rationality can and will sort out "the true meaning" of the concepts.

We see in Chapter VIII that Lederman offers five analytical tools with which to discover the "true meaning" of rules and classificatory rules: semantics, precedent, analogical reasoning, logic, and the correspondence of the fact category of a rule and social reality.[27] Each tool speaks to a different element or technique of rationality. Lederman acknowledges the similarity of the five techniques, as a whole, to the scientific method.

He describes the latter in these terms: "Natural scientists must formulate their general working hypotheses about cause and effect, make logical deductions from them to define particular instances consistent therewith, and then devise verifying experiments or improve and refine their observations of reality to see whether particular instances can be made to happen, or do occur, as expected on the basis of the starting hypotheses."[28] Scientists create abstract concepts, as do jurists, from lower to higher levels. They constantly adjust their abstractions with the results of particular observations and experiments. On several occasions Lederman insists that legal reasoning shares the "hypothetico-deductive reasoning" method of natural science.[29] Juristic thinking particularly benefits from the experimental science method, "specifically from the tentative attitude of the natural scientist toward his premises and his scrupulous care to test and review their accuracy in relation to relevant real facts of experience."[30] Similarly, he writes, the jurist must carefully and constantly gather social facts to inquire whether the fact category of a rule represents an accurate reflection of the contemporary social reality.[31] In addition to the shared "hypothetico-deductive reasoning" method of law and science, both the scientist and the jurist faithfully revere an ordered universe. The "basic assumption" of science is not that "objective facts" exist, but that "fundamentally there is order in the universe, in other words that there is a realm of consistent inevitable cause and effect in nature."[32] Jurists, too, precensor the law with a "basic faith" in a natural order. That faith, we shall see, serves as the key to Lederman's image of a constitution. His metaphoric self-description of his image as "orthodox" acknowledges the importance of faith within his constitutional image.[33]

4. VALUES

The 'is' world of natural objects, social relationships and, concepts constitute reality for Lederman. But, ironically, Lederman comes to admit that neither the natural objects, nor social relationships, nor concepts ultimately serve as the determinant elements of a legal decision. For, in addition to the real world above, there exists an 'ought' or ideal-directed world. The jurist's choice of values in that 'ought' world ultimately determines any one judicial result. The jurist is compelled to *choose* values since "*logic alone is not in the end all-sufficient* for the purposes of *either* [scientific or juristic thought]."[34]

The jurist chooses one value over another at each stage of the scientific/juristic/rational method. First, the rights and duties attached to a notional fact category of a rule possess an 'ought' character.[35] A rule "prescribes particular results."[36] He characterizes law as normative or ideal-directed, not merely descriptive of social reality.[37] This characterization shows why, "using the word 'rights' in a very wide sense, all law is human rights law."[38] In the second place, one has to identify the dominant features of the notional fact category of a rule. The jurist does so by choosing from among competing values those features which s/he considers the most important. Thirdly, "unmentioned value premises" inescapably enter into the jurist's connection of the neutral, natural social facts to the notional rule.[39] So, in examining the "pith and substance" or 'subject-matter' (that is, the dominant features in the fact category plus the prescriptive duty/right) of any challenged statute, the jurist has to weigh the importance of the competing features. This weighing of competing features requires a judgment call. In the fourth place, this value- or feature-weighing process inevitably entraps every 'division of powers' and constitutional rights issue. The constitutional issue invariably becomes an issue of choice: "[i]s the statutory scheme at issue something that is better done province by province on the basis of provincial autonomy, or is it something better done uniformly over the whole country on a nation-wide basis?"[40] The particular values which one has to weigh are uniformity versus regional diversity, local versus central administration, and universalism versus minority claims.[41] Sometimes, one can find values overlapping,[42] complementary,[43] or even repugnant to each other. "Rationally," to use Lederman's term, one can weigh the values or features embedded within a challenged rule both towards the federal and the provincial direction.

Similarly, Lederman emphasizes on many occasions that bills of rights express inevitably conflicting values at a high level of generality.[44] Sometimes, one has to read into a human rights value a conflicting value from outside the bill. Although freedom of expression represents "a basic value of our society," for example, "considerations of decency, public order, and private reputation nevertheless provide values of equivalent generality which conflict and compete with freedom of expression, and which deserve to be given some effect in spite of and at the expense of freedom of expression."[45] On other occasions, the valies articulated within a human rights code conflict with each other. So, for example, equal protection of law can conflict with equal benefit of the law (where posited law grants beneficial differences between individuals and groups), both being guaranteed in section 15(1) of the Canadian Charter of Rights and Freedoms.[46] The Charter presents to judges and legislators the critical and inevitable need to find "acceptable comprises when societal values are in conflict" and to play "a vital part in elaborating and particularising general principles so that the people involved know in a meaningful way what is expected of them by the law and what they can expect from the law."[47]

In summary, semantics, precedent, analogical reasoning, logic, and the correspondence of a rule to social reality can take the lawyer/judge only so far. Logic can merely display the possible factors of equivalent logical value.[48] The scientific/juristic method of "hypothetico-deductive" reasoning does not and cannot assist in the ultimate choice of rule classification which one had to make.[49] The "final question of the jurist" is to choose one value from some "acceptable" system of values, Lederman continually repeats.[50] "But, for this final step, what system of values is to prevail with those who have the official duty of decision?"[51] Once again, "whence come the criteria of relative importance necessary for such a [value] decision?"[52]

Lederman offers several possible responses to that critical question. One response he gives is the extent of acceptance of the values.[53] "[C]ertain broadly accepted community values that judges will share" should figure, he writes as early as his 1958 theoretical essay.[54] He notes how both Pound and Jeremy Bentham support such a criterion of choosing values, Pound suggesting that a judge should compromise conflicting values so as to distribute social goods as widely as possible with the least friction and waste.[55] But, Canada being a pluralistic society, each social group seeks to promote its own selfish preferences. Further, in a "considerable" number of issues, one cannot find "coherent public attitudes at all, whether consensual or conflicting, on the preferences of valuation concerned."[56] Judges are ill-equipped to indulge in "continual mass psycho-analysis on the pleasure or pain producing propensities of actual or proposed rules of law."[57]

Accordingly, a judge ultimately favours that value which he believes to be the better or more worthy one. Although a judge chooses a value by verbally appealing to the reasonable or moral man, "the point is that often the only clue to these typical or objective values will be the judge's own personal standards of better or worse, right or wrong."[58] The judge is compelled ultimately to resort to his own values. This presents the reason why Lederman can characterize the critical moment in the judicial decision-making process as "the lonely moments of responsibility" or what others described as "the agony of decision". The most that one can expect of the judiciary's ultimate value choice is "straight thinking, industry, good faith, and a capacity to discount their own prejudices."[59]

5. THE POSITIVISM OF ORTHODOX RATIONALISM

Rationality permeates Lederman's image of a constitution "to the limit of human capacity."[60] We have now seen, however, that the jurist's enterprise does not entirely correspond with a scientist's endeavour to describe nature. The jurist is compelled to distinguish good from evil, just from unjust.[61] This necessitates, in turn, that one go beyond reality to an 'ought' world of value choices. Ultimately, the judge *posits* or imposes a value choice in his/her "lonely moment of responsibility." That is, the most important moment in the judge's decision-making process is imbued with a primitive positivism of values. Lederman is conscious of that paradox. The dialectical process of the "hypothetico-deductive" reasoning method can identify the values. Beyond that, the judge inevitably *imposes* the choice of value from an 'ought' world. The place of posited values within Lederman's image of a constitution helps to explain why Lederman believes so strongly in the need for "independent tribunals of the first rank."[62] Because constitutional issues inescapably trigger value choices and because the values inevitably favour one level of government over another, a legal system *requires* an independent court which can posit values between the rival governments. Otherwise, the judge's choice of value is "biased" in preference of the one over the other.

The role of posited values within his image of a constitution also helps to explain why Lederman emphasizes that jurists finally resolve difficult legal problems "by the dialectical and *authoritative* processes of court room or legislative chamber, rather than by experiment in the laboratory."[63] Indeed, any "advanced constitution *must designate official persons* and *invest them with authority* of the organised community *to speak the last word* for legal purposes."[64] In describing his image of a constitution as "orthodox," lying somewhere between the Blackstonians and the extreme realists, he admits that orthodoxy requires that one accept the judge's posit of values *on faith*: "[t]he essence of the orthodox view is that judges do proceed by reasonable means to decide what they have to decide, and that they are to be believed, *and indeed must be believed*, when they expound the principles or rules of law they respectively purport to use to decide their cases."[65] The citizenry simply *must* accept the judge's choice of a value. It must be the *judge's* choice − not some pressure group's or a legislature's. The judge's "last word" admittedly dampens down debate and articulates the choice of value. But it is crucial for Lederman to complete his image of a constitution by acknowledging the inevitable positivism in the jurist's non-scientific starting-points: "[t]he jurist *must* have certain starting assumptions about what human conduct ought to be, and he must develop the logical implications of his general propositions through stages of decreasing abstraction in order to assess the detailed consequences of applying such propositions ..."[66] Lederman's rationality begins with posited 'givens.' And it is the judge who posits the 'givens.' Unlike rule rationalism and Laskin's social interests image of a constitution, Lederman's posited 'givens' are consciously chosen values. These, in turn, emanate from an 'ought' world which finds no place in reality.

Why does Lederman acknowledge the supreme importance of there being an authoritative positing of values? Lederman constantly reminds himself that if the judge does not ultimately choose a value, chaos will result. "[D]isregard of the deciding judge's chosen rule," he writes, "leads to a sort of mysterious confusion, if not indeed to complete chaos."[67] Even the moderate sociological jurists, such as Pound and Cohen, placed "*faith* in the possibility of partially significant insights into the proper order and truth of human relations" in terms of ideal-directed claims.[68] If a judge does not have "the last word," Lederman reminds us, "*the essential order of society* based on law *will dissolve* in endless debate and procrastination, *or in civil war.*"[69] By deferring to the judge's authority (legitimacy) to posit value choices, Lederman can breathe a sigh of relief. His image of a constitution is complete: "we do get *a complete and closed hierarchical system* of propositions of authority," even though we do not know what guides a judge's decision.[70] Even at the point of positing a value, Lederman reflects, the jurist resembles a scientist. Both believe fundamentally that order exists in the universe.[71] One simply has to accept a judge's authority to impose values *on faith.* Unless one does so, rational disorder would follow. With that disorder, one's image of a constitution or, more correctly, Lederman's image of a constitution would collapse.

6. ORTHODOXY'S RATIONALISM

Like his contemporaries William Lederman remains entrapped in the rationalism of his age. On the one hand, he deeply believes in the core elements of what he calls the "hypothetico-deductive" methodology, because one can use techniques of rationality to clarify the meaning of rules and the alternatives of values from which the judge must inevitably choose.[72] To the objectivity of the analytic process, he adds "straight-thinking, industry, good faith, and a capacity to discount ... prejudices."[73] An independent court can "impartially" weigh the provincial and federal features of any challenged statute. In his words, "[t]he very purpose of the judge's secure and disinterested constitutional status is to free him from all other influences except those of *reason and conscience*."[74] Even after a judge has posited a value, "the legal process is better if judges and legislators are disposed to show constant concern for the gathering of relevant data in the realm of objective reality."[75] And all this is done through the tools of rationality: semantics, precedent, analogical reasoning, logic, and empiricism.

And yet, Lederman consciously criticizes this rationality. On its own, it excludes a consideration of the inevitable values in the decision-making process. "In effect, the inevitable value-judgment is made," he admits, "but its nature as a necessary choice between logically equal alternatives is unfortunately obscured for all concerned."[76] Rationality, then, plays an instrumental function in the identification, the application, and the logical/hypothetical ramifications of posited ends. But the ends are inevitably and crudely posited. That being so, William Lederman cannot escape from the positivism of his rationalist image of a constitution.

PART III:

AN IMAGE OF A CONSTITUTION
AND THE TEXT

CANADIAN LEGAL SCHOLARS, not unlike the judiciary, are entrapped in the scientism of our age. Trained in the formalist and objectivist virtues of posited rules, Kennedy, MacDonald, Abel, Pigeon, and Beetz express a coherent horizontal/vertical picture of rules as a 'given': all else their image projects as an illegitimate source of (legal) knowledge. Bora Laskin, as a young scholar, exposes the social interests lying behind posited rules. Noel Lyon advocates the scientific method as the way to identify community values more clearly. William Lederman's image of 'what counts' as law supplements rules with values. Peter Russell, Paul Weiler, and Robert Décary resignedly acknowledge the inevitable posit of subjectivist values in judicial decision-making. Determined to make the judiciary (and legal scholars) conscious of the political character of such values, they advocate that judges restrain their actions to rules. Thus, desirous of escaping from posited values, they succumb to posited rules as the only possible alternative. Both French and English scholars accept positivism and rationalism to the core. Their images differ as to what exactly is posited: for the one tradition, rules; for the second, values/policies; and for the third, rules supplemented with values/policies. Their images differ in their rationalistic techniques. But the three strains accept rules and/or values as a 'given' and presuppose that a rationalist technique can actually cause a purified objective law. If only one could refine the tools of rationality or replace the one posited constituent with another, judges and scholars, as scientists, could better discover the posited rules and/or values, adjust the latter into a cohesive whole, rationally cause subsidiary rules and/or values, more accurately predict their application in the phenomenal world, and more incisively explain the nature of law.

Against this background, we may now return to the legal discourse surrounding the traditional 'subject-matters' of what we have hitherto taken to be constitutional law. We know now that these 'subject-matters' coalesce, upon close study, into a deep question: namely, 'what is one's image of a constitution?' And we can better appreciate the power of the rationalist image of a constitution which permeates our 'subject-matter' in Part I of the essay. We have seen that Dickson and Wilson so wish to break from the restraining rationalist and positivist boundaries which encircle their understanding of (legal) reality. And yet, they too, uncontrollably, imperceptibly relapse into rationalist horizons not unlike generations of Canadian scholars before them. Lawyers are caught in a trap which projects posited rules and posited values/policies as the only possible constructs of legal knowledge. Rationalist technique has hitherto been our only hope of escape.

Part II of this essay has tried to understand 'why?' Instead of reading a judicial decision as a source of posited rules or policies, 'reasons for judgment' or a scholarly essay express one person's image of how one understands oneself and others. That understanding is delimited by inherited boundaries within which legitimate and valid (legal) knowledge is constituted. Beyond the boundaries, there dwells non-knowledge. It is illegitimate and invalid as a constituent of law. These boundaries, whose conjoining network I call an image, constrain one. They pre-censor how one understands the world. Canadian scholars are caught in a trap because the images which dominate their pre-understanding of the world leave only two alternatives available as to what is a constitution: either a constitution is made up of posited rules, or it is composed of posited values/policies. The one image clashes again and again with the other, the only escape apparently being a supplementation of the one with the other or a more rigorous scientistic methodology. Notwithstanding the intensity of their opposition, the dominant images share common boundaries: the positivism of the constituents and the rationalism of the method. Is there nothing left?

I now wish to return to our heritage and identify a distinctive and distinctively different image of a constitution. This image offers boundaries which, it seems, transcend – if not bypass – the rationalist trap which constrains our horizons. We see strains of this image in the teleologically oriented lower court judgments interpreting the Charter. Dickson's advocacy of an historically oriented, teleological image and Wilson's attempt to link the *a priori* concepts to an empirical context fill out the boundaries. But it is in the expression of Ivan Rand, jurist of the 1950s, that one uncovers the full contours of a teleological image.

Ivan Rand, judge and scholar, expresses an image of a constitution whose boundaries entertain issues of ideal-directed theory and social/cultural practice. That is, theory and practice are socially legitimate and epistemologically valid issues within the horizons of Rand's image of a constitution. In Chapter XIII, I shall suggest why the text of the Charter of Rights seems to trigger deep meta-issues of theory and a piercing scrutiny of social/cultural practice.[1] As to the former, for example, the text makes a surface claim to the effect that Charter rights are very special – indeed, so special that they are paramount over all institutional and social interests. In addition, the text suggests that Charter rights possess a universalist and permanent character. Jeremy Bentham most certainly would claim that the text suffers from the 'anarchical fallacies' of 'natural rights' thinking.[2] Further, like the duties derived from the various formulations of Kant's categorial imperative, the text's claims take on an 'ought' or ideal-directed character when transposed into the phenomenal or empirical world. That being so, the text's rights are not and cannot be descriptive of empirical reality. So to consider Charter rights would be illusionary, for, by their very nature, they are ideal-directed. As the text makes claims about action, so also it becomes crucial that the lawyer connect the 'ought' claims to social/cultural practice. And that requires a constitutional image which lets one ask questions of practice as well as of theory. The boundaries of Rand's image of constitution entertain both sets of inquiries.

The three rationalist images, in contrast, preclude the very sorts of surface issues which, one could argue, the Charter's text triggers. The rationalist images reflect a constitutional relativism which accepts the ends embedded in a society's posited laws and values as 'givens.' Similarly, the rationalist images constrict the lawyer to begin his/her analysis with the posited 'givens.' Being posited, it is illegitimate for the lawyer/scholar to question the ethical content or the social basis for the 'given' rules or values. The challenge for the contemporary lawyer is to picture a constitution which allows him/her to question the 'givens,' to connect the 'givens' to universalist human rights claims of theory, and to critique their reified character when divorced from social/cultural practice. Rand's image of a constitution begins to do just that.

XI

Rand's Teleological Image of a Constitution

Rand's judgments and essays depart from the rationalist image of a constitution. For the rationalist, the content of a constitution is posited. It is posited by the legislature, a judge, or 'the society.' The formal act of positing the rules, values, or policies pursuant to posited procedures legitimates the content of the rules or values. Rand's judgments do reflect strains of an historicism and of a rationalism. First, he uses a great wealth of historical evidence to support freedoms of discussion, religion, and the like.[1] Secondly, he invariably begins his analysis with a posited document (the British North America Act, 1867) and especially two sections thereof (ss. 91 and 92) as 'givens.'[2] Rand adds themes, though, which share the boundaries of Aristotle's image of a constitution as expressed in the *Constitution of Athens*[3] and the *Politics*.[4] In particular, the character of society —the social/cultural relationships of its peoples — constitutes the content of a constitution; its posited rules and values serve merely as *indicia* of that character. Rand gleans a character of Canadian society largely from institutional history and the history of ideas. Rand interestingly assumes that all members of Canadian (and British) society share similar political and social ideas over the centuries. From Canadian history Rand isolates whatever insights bear upon 'who is a citizen?' It is crucial to realize that, for Rand, a Citizenship Act does not posit 'who counts as a citizen.' Rather, one responds to that question by examining two further issues: first, what are the ends or *telii* of society? and secondly, who effectively shares in the power distribution of a society? These two sets of issues take Rand into the abstract noumenal world of theory and the social/cultural phenomenal world of practice. Rand examines the former in terms of the latter.

1. THE NOTION OF CITIZENSHIP

For Rand, a competent lawyer concentrates his/her attention and energies upon one critical inquiry: 'what are the necessary attributes and incidents of citizenship in Canada?' In responding to this issue, Rand develops a sense of which rights matter, how important they are, and how one should interpret them.

We have already seen in Chapter II what bearing 'citizenship' plays in Rand's 'rule of law' decision of *Roncarelli* v. *Duplessis*.[5] In that case Premier Duplessis has advised the liquor commissioner to revoke Roncarelli's liquor licence because Roncarelli furnishes bail fees for Jehovah's Witnesses. The government has arrested the Jehovah's Witnesses for distributing printed matter (*The Watch Tower* and *Awake*) allegedly contrary to local by-laws which require a licence for peddling any kind of wares. In a key paragraph to which I refer in Chapter II, Rand has this to say about Premier Duplessis's conduct:

To deny or revoke a permit because a citizen exercises an unchallengeable right totally irrelevant to the sale of liquor in a restaurant is equally beyond the scope of the discretion conferred. There was here not only revocation of the existing permit but a declaration of a future, definitive disqualification of the appellant to obtain one: it was to be "forever". This purports to divest his citizenship status of its incident of membership in the class of those of the public to whom such a privilege could be extended ... [W]hat could be more malicious than to punish this licensee for having done what he had an absolute right to do in a matter utterly irrelevant to the *Liquor Act*? Malice in the proper sense is simply acting for a reason and purpose knowingly foreign to the administration, to which was added here the element of intentional punishment by what was virtually vocation outlawry.[6]

This *dicta* raises at least five questions:
1 Why is the right *unchallengeable*?
2 Why is Roncarelli's *citizenship status* divested forever?
3 Why is the right *absolute*?
4 What is the right that is so absolute?
5 Why is citizenship status relevant at all?
We saw in Chapter II that historicist and rationalist images of a constitution constrain a lawyer from even considering these five questions. Although the historicist image projects a right as "unchallengeable" and "absolute" if one discovers the right embedded in institutional history, "citizenship status" is uneventful within a rationalist prism of

understanding law. Citizenship status matters only because an authoritative institution has posited a Citizenship Act. Posited rules may exclude a group of persons from being 'described' as citizens. Within the rationalist picture of a constitution, posited rights and posited values may be "challenged" in the form of a posited counter rule. Rights are "absolute" only to the extent that they are not so "challenged." An institution can amend or repeal any previously posited right. Accordingly, the moral content of a posited right possesses a relativistic character, varying in time and contingency. Certainly, "citizenship status" would not appear relevant within a rationalist prism in *Roncarelli* v. *Duplessis* in that the posited law has provided that the "Commission may cancel any permit at its discretion." Administrative discretion, not citizenship, constitutes the 'given' and that 'given' is rationally caused by a prior posited 'given': namely, the horizontal 'subject-matters' of section 92 of the British North America Act, 1867.

Only Rand's Aristotelian boundaries of a constitution can entertain the above five questions, because the core of Rand's image hangs upon 'who counts as a citizen?' Since Aristotle and arguably Rand ground citizenship in nature rather than in culture (or, more particularly, the posited rules or posited values of a culture), citizenship possesses a "natural" or "unchallengeable" character. That law is most "natural" or best where each and all persons within society share in the functions and benefits of political institutions.[7] Rand believes that his standard of equal sharing possesses a universal character.[8] Accordingly, the rights incidental to citizenship possess an "unchallengeable" and "absolute" character. Harm done to one's rights constitutes a harm *to one's person*.[9] There is a sense, then, that restriction of one's rights harms a person "forever." Legislative *fiat* cannot correct the harm because the harm contradicts nature, and nature universally applies to all, irrespective of convention or posited fiat.

Let us gain an understanding of Rand's image of a constitution as expressed in his own words in the paragraph quoted at length above.[10] When Rand states that Duplessis's denial or revocation of a liquor permit for a reason "totally irrelevant" to the purpose of a statute infringes an "unchallengeable," "absolute" right, Rand is expressing that constitutional rights emanate from a source other than posited rules or values. For, whatever the content of a posited rule or value, that rule or value cannot alter, repeal, or challenge an unchallengeable, absolute constitutional right. Rather than being grounded in posited rules, Rand's rights are those things which protect one's citizenship. Citizenship states one's membership in an association. To quote Rand from *Winner* v. *S.M.T.*

(Eastern) Ltd., "[c]itizenship is membership in a state; and in the citizen inhere those rights and duties, the correlatives of allegiance and protection, which are basic to that status."[11] Thus, the revocation of a right divests one of his or her "citizenship status." This harms a person "forever" because, if one is excluded from "citizenship status," one is not a natural person. As he puts it in *Switzman* v. *Ebling and A.-G. of Quebec*, "[l]iberty in this is little less *vital to man's mind and spirit* than breathing is to his physical existence. As such *an inherence in the individual* it is embodied in his status of *citizenship*."[12]

When he asserts in *Roncarelli* that the divestiture of citizenship is "forever," Rand expresses that neither the legislature nor the court can return his rights to Roncarelli. His rights exist outside the secular authority of a legislature or a court. This point is crucial for Rand's image of a constitution because it means that a formal legislative or judicial enactment simply cannot define 'who constitutes a citizen?' – at least, within Rand's image. Rand leaves himself with only one other possibility: namely, Aristotle's.[13] 'Who was a citizen?' hangs upon the character of a social whole in its historical context. The "complete citizen" is found only in the best constitution. Or, more correctly, the best constitution is that constitution where each and all are good persons ("the complete citizens").[14] One can be both a good person and a complete citizen because, by sharing in the functions and benefits of deliberative and judicial institutions, one is capable of ruling and being ruled.[15]

In summary, constitutional rights are "unchallengeable" and "absolute" for Rand because they inhere in citizenship status. "Complete" citizenship is entangled in the nature (or *telos*)[16] of a good person.

2. THE SOURCE OF A CONSTITUTION:
THE TELOS OF A GOOD PERSON

A *telos* is the consummated end toward which an organism grows. By identifying the ultimate end of an organism's activity, we can better understand the character – or social whole – of the organism. And so it is with constitutions.[17] One can find passages in Rand's judgments and essays where he connects a constitution with the *telos* of a human organism in a manner remarkably similiar to Aristotle's effort.

In *Switzman* v. *Ebling and A.-G. of Quebec* the landlord, Ebling, has cancelled Switzman's lease in reliance upon a provincial statute which makes it "illegal for any person, who possesses or occupies a house within the Province, to use it or allow any person to make use of it to propagate communism or bolshevism by any means whatsoever."[18] In invalidating Ebling's cancellation of the lease, Rand grounds his analysis in a "constitutional fact"; namely, "a capacity in men, acting freely and under self-restraints, to govern themselves" through "individual liberation from subjective as well as objective shackles."[19] This innate or *natural* capacity in persons to govern themselves applies to all persons. Consequently, the capacity of self-government possesses a universal character. In Rand's words, freedom of discussion emulates a universal character, "a unity of interest and significance extending equally to every part of the Dominion."[20] This same universal character renders Roncarelli's rights "unchallengeable" and "absolute."

But in *Switzman* Rand goes one step further by explicitly connecting that universal character to the *telos* of a human organism. In particular, Rand describes freedom of discussion as ultimately "the political expression of the *primary condition* of *social life, thought* and its communication by *language*."[21] In this one sentence Rand expresses the *telos* of a human organism in terms of a *social being* as opposed to an atomistic, self-sufficient individual. A social organism distinguishes itself from other organisms by thinking and talking. Similarly, in one of his later essays, Rand expresses that "an essential faculty of *complete man* ... appears to have been the utterance of ideas, opinions and propositions ..."[22] Elsewhere, he writes that "without the world of ideas, feelings, instincts and will with their communications, human beings would be of *another order in the animal kingdom*."[23] One grows into a complete person through the communication of ideas, opinions, and propositions. Communication with others makes one a *social* being. It also differentiates the human from other organisms. But one cannot reach one's end as a social being, Rand emphatically assures us, unless one experiences liberty in one's day-to-day life in that "[l]iberty in this is little less vital to man's mind and spirit *than breathing is to his physical existence*."[24] Precisely because liberty "[*inheres*] in the individual it is embodied in his status of citizenship," he suggests.[25] That is, liberty inheres in the natural person because liberty is entangled with the end of the human organism as a social being.

Rand again joins constitutional rights to the *telos* of a person in *Saumur* v. *City of Quebec*.[26] Saumur has argued as invalid a by-law which proscribes the distribution of "any book, pamphlet, booklet, circular or tract whatever without having previously obtained for so doing the written permission of the Chief of Police."[27] After citing several eighteenth- and nineteenth-century statutes which elevate prominence to religious freedom, Rand concludes that "[s]trictly speaking, civil rights arise from positive law; but freedom of speech, religion and the inviolability of the person are *original freedoms* which are at once the *necessary attributes* and modes of *self-expression of human beings* and the primary conditions of their community life within a legal order."[28] As he explains in one academic essay, the freedoms of expression serve as "essential attributes of man, his modes of self-expression."[29] Or, as he expresses in another essay, from the *telos* of a social personality "we derive the validity of self-respect and individual dignity."[30] That is, a constitution logically exists prior to posited law because a constitution states the necessary attributes for a person to flourish (*eudaimonia*).[31]

Rand connects a constitution with the *telos* of a person, again, in *Boucher* v. *R*.[32] The Duplessis Government has succeeded in having Boucher convicted of uttering a seditious libel contained in a four-page document entitled "Quebec's Burning Hate for God and Christ and Freedom Is the Shame of All Canada." Rand narrows the ancient elements of the crime of seditious libel so as to render the conviction invalid.[33] He restates 'the law.' His restatement takes account of the new "fundamental conceptions of government" which have evolved since the seventeenth century when Coke, as a reporter, had created the crime. Freedom of thought and discussion constitutes the new fundamental conception. After identifying the changes in the content of the crime brought on by the freedoms of thought and discussion, Rand feels compelled to join the constitutional freedoms of discussion with the *telos* of a human organism described above. "Freedom in thought and speech and disagreement in ideas and beliefs, on every conceivable subject, are of *the essence of our life*," he insisted.[34] But why so describe them as the essence of life? Does Rand understand a person's essence from some ideal-directed conception of a person? No. Rand discovers our essence from "daily experience": "[t]he clash of critical discussion on political, social and religious subjects has too deeply become *the stuff of daily experience* ..."[37] And in summarizing the thrust of the paragraph from which this sentence is drawn Rand repeats the connection between a constitution and the end of a flourishing life itself: "[s]imilarly in discontent, affection and hostility: as subjective incidents of controversy, they and the ideas which arouse them are *part of our living* which ultimately serve us in *stimulation*, in the clarification of *thought* and, as we believe, in the search for the *constitution* and *truth* of things generally."[36]

Rand links a constitution to the natural flourishing of a human organism in a positive sense. Why describe the freedoms of thought and discussion as *constitutional* rights? Because these and other incidents of citizenship are as vital to the *telos* of a human organism as is "breathing"

(*Switzman*); the "stuff of daily experience" (*Boucher*); the "necessary attributes ... of human beings" (*Saumur*); the "essential attributes of man" ("Some Aspects of Canadian Constitutionalism"); and the "essential faculty of complete man" ("Except by Due Process of Law"). But Rand adds something more about the incidents of citizenship. When a society's rulers attempt to modify, restrict, or repeal a good constitution grounded in the telos of a person, such rulers frustrate the *natural* growth of a person. That is, the posited laws obstruct the human organism from flourishing as a natural organism.

Rand makes this point in *Winner*.[37] Winner, an American citizen, operates a bus line between Boston and Halifax. Pursuant to a provincial statute he is granted a licence to operate the bus line, subject to the condition that he must prevent passengers from embarking and disembarking *within* the province of New Brunswick. In disregarding this condition, Winner is charged with a violation of the provincial enactment.

A close look at Rand's judgment, once again, shows him bent upon reconciling Winner's problem with the boundaries of Rand's Aristotelian image of a constitution. Rand initially suggests that Winner's right to use a highway is a precondition of the very existence of a state: "[h]ighways are a condition of the existence of an organized state: without them its life could not be carried on."[38] This empirical claim may or may not be supportable in an advanced industrial society. Having made the claim, though, Rand proceeds to connect Winner's constitutional right to use the highways with the *telos* of a human being. He does so in a negative fashion: "[t]o deny their use is to destroy the fundamental liberty of action of the individual, *to proscribe his participation in that life*." In addition, by denying Winner "liberty of action," the state prevents him from sharing in the benefits of civil society: "under such a ban, the *exercise of citizenship* would be at an end." To deny Winner the use of highways prevents him "from engaging in business at a post office or a customs house or a bank."[39] We shall soon see that "carrying on a business" constitutes an indispensable element of the *telos* of a person, in Rand's view. To impede the growth of business is unnatural because that obstruction forecloses the path along which human beings would otherwise naturally grow. Although Rand does not say so, it is only one small step to add Aristotle's important claim that such a constitution, being repressive of one's growth to her/his end, is perverse or unnatural.[40]

3. THE PERSON AS A SOCIAL BEING

If a person ever reaches his or her end, according to Rand, s/he will not remain a lonely, individualistic, atomistic being. Rather, s/he can reach his or her end only in association with others.

That Rand understands a person as a social being explains why he connects freedom of discussion to one's very social existence in the same contexts where he links the freedom to one's physical existence. So, for example, in the sentence preceding his claim in *Switzman* that "[l]iberty in this is little less vital to man's mind and spirit than breathing is to his physical existence," he reveals that freedom of expression is "the political expression of the primary condition of *social* life, thought and its communication by language."[41] Similarly, in *Saumur*, in the very sentence when he asserts that "freedom of speech, religion and the inviolability of the person are original freedoms which are at once the necessary attributes and modes of self-expression of human beings," Rand continues that the freedoms also serve as "the primary conditions of their [one's] community life within a legal order."[42] When he describes "freedom in thought and speech and disagreement in ideas and beliefs on every conceivable subject" as "the essence of our life" in *Boucher*, he envisions them as a part of "our compact of free society" and "*social* stability."[43] Finally, in *Winner*, Rand describes the free use of highways as "a condition of the existence of an organized state: *without them its life could not be carried on.*"[44] And, more directly, "[c]ivil life in this country consists of *inextricably intermingled activities* and *relations ...*" Between these passages in *Winner* one finds Rand explaining how the state's denial of a constitutional right proscribes participation in life itself.

The *telos* of a person lies in one's social relationships with others. It is not without reason, then, that Rand ties the flourishing of a human being with only certain kinds of social and political institutions. He explains in *Saumur* that if a government licensed the publication of pamphlets or books, the "basic condition" of the existence of a government would be "destroyed."[45] Why? Because "the Government, as licensor, becomes *disjoined from the citizenry*."[46] But why must the ruler be joined with the citizenry? Because, Rand informs us in *Switzman*, freedom of discussion constitutes "the primary condition of social life and of man's very existence."[47] That is, Rand continues, since man is a social being there exists "a capacity in men, acting freely and under self-restraints, to govern themselves." One can understand why Rand would conclude, without more, that "the endowment of parliamentary institutions is one and entire for the Dominion, that Legislatures and Parliament are permanent features of our constitutional structure."[48] Rand could attribute these permanent features to history or to some posited document (such as sections 17 and

35 of the British North America Act).[49] But he consciously avoids these options. Rather, democratic institutions are "one and entire" and "permanent features" of the end of a person: one's growth in association with others.

4. THE RELATIONSHIP BETWEEN A CONSTITUTION AND POSITED LAW: THE RULE OF LAW

Let us now return to the notion of the 'rule of law' in *Roncarelli v. Duplessis*.[50] We have seen that a constitution, for Rand, informs one as to 'who counts' as a citizen within a society. Posited rules do not define 'who counts.' The boundaries of Rand's image of a constitution prevent him from letting posited rules authoritatively define who qualifies as a citizen. Rand states as much in *Winner* when he suggests that a subject of a friendly foreign country "for practical purposes" "enjoys all the rights of the citizen."[51] Winner is an American citizen resident in the United States. Indeed, Rand would be hard pressed not to extend the scope of "citizenship" to landed immigrants, aliens, and all persons resident within the territory of Canada as well. As he expresses in one essay, whereas citizenship is grounded in *allegiance* in 1867 citizenship, by the early 1960s, is "necessarily embraced within the scope of the name Dominion as connoting the legislative creation of *an organized self-governing community*."[52] That is, 'who counts' as a citizen has evolved and been extended over time, notwithstanding the fact that the rules positing citizenship qualifications may have remained the same over the decades. Put another way, "the law of the land" as expressed in the Magna Carta and other ancient documents does "not seem to have meant law from time to time as it may be [posited]; it was the common law viewed as rooted in permanence ... as reason in the human establishment of England, as fixed precepts and principles of law by which the [s]overeign himself was bound; *natural law written in the constitution of man as part of nature*, and expressing itself in the unwritten law, *which not even the statutes of parliament could abridge, abrogate or supersede* without due process ..."[53] Rand pictures constitutional law as possessing a permanent, natural, paramount character in contrast to the temporal, constructed, weak sense of posited law.

No. Posited rules do not define 'who is a citizen?' Rather, Rand seeks out citizenship incidents in the evolution of the political theory of Canadian society. Rand transcribes the *telos* of a person into the juridical/political concept of citizenship. The *telos* of a human being, according to Rand, is to flourish. But to flourish, one needs liberty and the freedom to associate

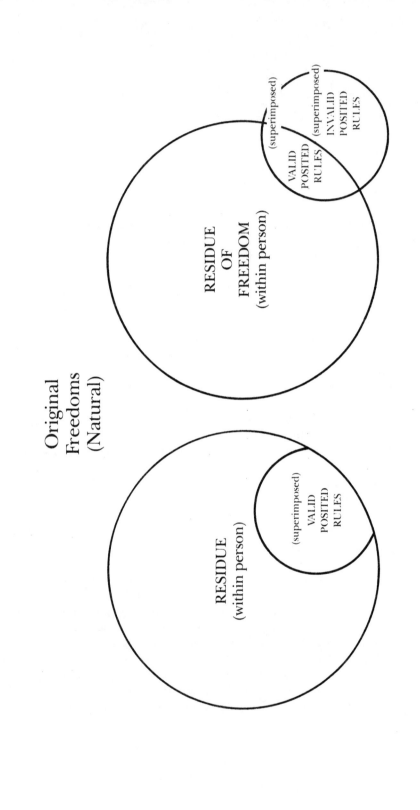

with others. One may well disagree with Rand's assessment of what constitutes the *telos* of a human being, as one might with Aristotle. But the crucial point for the constitutional lawyer is that Rand constructs a nexus between a constitution and 'who counts as a person.' By so doing he offers us horizons of a constitutional image which allow a lawyer to entertain questions which go to ideal-directed political theory, on the one hand, and the evolution of social/cultural practice, on the other. If posited rules do not declare 'who qualifies as a citizen?' and if the *telos* of a human being does do so, what exactly is the relationship between a constitution and posited law? One can best appreciate Rand's conception of the relationship by examining his metaphor of the circle in *Saumur*.[54]

Rand likens a constitution to the original circumference of a circle. Posited rules validly operate within that circle. But when the posited rules extend beyond the circumference, the rules are void. Rand's picture of the relationship between a constitution and posited law looks like the drawing on page 228. Rand describes the metaphor in this manner: "It is in the *circumscription* of these liberties by the creation of civil rights in persons who may be injured by their exercise, and by the sanctions of public law, that positive law operates. What we realize is the residue *inside* that periphery."[55] Or, to put the issue more clearly, the essence of a "civil right" is that positive law creates the right. This contrasts with "those freedoms that remain with the residue of unregulated conduct, fundamental, even 'natural' freedoms because they are not, so far, circumscribed by law."[56] Original freedoms compose the periphery. The periphery is unchallengeable, absolute, and universal. When posited rules conflict with the periphery, they are invalid.

In addition to the universal character of original freedoms, Rand adds that the circumference originates prior in time to posited law. That is why he describes the freedoms as "original freedoms." They exist prior to the existence of the state in point of time. The genesis of 'original freedoms' lies prior to posited law because the freedoms flow out of the natural *telos* of a person. In contrast, posited rules are a human construct. Given the contrast of a natural constitution with the cultural constructs of posited law, Rand can conclude that "[t]heir [that is, the original freedoms'] significant relation to our law in this, that under its principles to which there are only minor exceptions, there is no prior or antecedent restraint placed upon them: the penalties, civil or criminal, attach to *results* which *their exercise* may bring about, and apply as *consequential* incidents."[57] Thus, a constitution exists prior to posited rules and posited values. Priority lies, first, because of the character of constitutional rights, their character flowing from the *telos* of a person; and, secondly, because of the genesis of constitutional rights. Lawyers, even with the aid of rationality, simply cannot construct a constitution. Nor can posited law repeal a constitution. Posited law can validly punish one only if rules are posited out of respect for original constitutional rights. And when the posited rules contradict the incidents of citizenship entangled in the periphery of the circle, the posited rules are void. They are void because it is impossible for any secular institution to construct a thing which is conceptually and genetically prior to the original freedoms of the constitution.

Rand distinguishes constitutional law from posited law in at least two of his 'division of powers' judgments. Both concern the question whether the provincial and federal governments respectively can regulate trade and, if so, to what extent they may do so. On the one hand, section 91(2) of the British North America Act, 1867 provides that

(notwithstanding anything in this Act) the exclusive Legislative Authority of the Parliament of Canada extends to all Matters coming within the Classes of Subjects next hereinafter enumerated: that is to say,

2. The Regulation of Trade and Commerce.

On the other hand, section 92(13) of the BNA Act sets out that

92. In each Province the Legislature may exclusively make Laws in relation to Matters coming within the Classes of Subjects next hereinafter enumerated; that is to say,

13. Property and Civil Rights in the Province.

In *Ref. re Farm Products Marketing Act* Rand holds as invalid a provincial marketing scheme in that it has infringed the regulation of trade and commerce.[58] To respond to the surface issues presented by the British North America Act, 1867, Rand must understand the term "trade." He understands "trade" in terms of his overall image of 'what is a constitution?' He includes "trade" in the periphery of the circle, an original freedom bound up with the *telos* of a person in Canadian society. In this way, Rand immunizes trade from any restriction imposed by posited law: "[t]he production and exchange of goods as an economic activity does not take place by virtue of positive law or civil right; it is assumed as part of the *residual free activity* of men upon or around which law is imposed."[59] As an uninhibited and uninhibitable original freedom, "the true conception of trade (in contradistinction to the static nature of rights, civil or property [i.e. posited rights]) is that of a *dynamic*, the creation and flow of goods from production to consumption or utilization, as an *individualized* activity."[60] Rand understands trade as a "dynamic" or "flow" because, being a constituent element of the periphery of the circle, posited rules cannot legitimately and validly regulate the flourishing of trade. Trade is an "individualized" activity because it is caught up with the individual's end as a complete person, at least in Canadian society as Rand understands that society.

Of course, to be consistent, Rand should extend his analysus in *Re Farm Products Marketing Act* to immunize trade from federal regulation. But rule rationalism just weighs too heavily. Rand finds it necessary to frame his analysis within the 'given' of a posited text (the British North America Act, 1867). This text, in turn, supposedly sets out a complete set of rules. Because section 91(2) incorporates the word "trade" Rand finds it necessary to project that a federal parliament can regulate an original freedom in the periphery of the circle.

But we need not be too hasty in pointing to the contradiction in Rand's judgment. For, in *Murphy* v. *C.P.R. and Attorney General for Canada*, Rand faces a federal statute, the Canadian Wheat Board Act, which prohibits Murphy from "importing" grain from another province without a licence from the Wheat Board.[61] The CPR has refused to carry the grain in deference to the Wheat Board Act. Murphy contends that this federal statute contravenes section 121 of the British North America Act, 1867 which provides that "all Articles of the Growth, Produce or Manufacture of any one of the Provinces shall, from and after the union, be admitted free into each of the other Provinces." Once again, Rand describes trade as a "free current."[62] And "'[f]ree', in s. 121, means without impediment related to the traversing of a provincial boundary."[63] Rand insists in *Murphy* that trade still remains an indispensable element of the circle's original freedoms beyond the grasp of posited law: "what is preserved is a free flow of trade regulated in subsidiary features which are or have come to be looked upon as incidents of trade."[64] The Canadian Wheat Board Act, according to Rand, regulates the original freedom of trade in subsidiary features only. The Act merely "charges for services rendered in an administration of commodity distribution" and such charges would contrast with burdens imposed by Parliament for equalizing competition.[65] When one understands that the "true character" of the charge against Murphy constitutes merely "an incident in the administration of a comprehensive extra-provincial marketing scheme," Rand argues, the statute's "interference with the free current of trade across provincial lines disappears."[66] What the state – an artificially created abstraction – cannot do is substantially to regulate the original freedom of trade in the circle's periphery. As Rand understands it, the state (as represented in this case by the federal parliament) cannot posit laws which "in its essence and purpose" places "fetters upon or raises impediments to or otherwise restrict or limit the free flow of commerce across the Dominion as if provincial boundaries did not exist."[67] The "object" of section 121 of the British North America Act, then, "is to prohibit restraints on the movement of products."[68] Rand leaves the sanctity of his circle complete and untouched.

Thus, when one speaks of Rand as an adherent of the 'rule of law' one should not understand him as an advocate of the rule of posited law. Posited rules play a tertiary role in Rand's picture of the 'rule of law' and its relationship to his image of a constitution. Rather, he directs his focus to the question 'what is the end of a person?' The constituents of his response to that question compose the periphery of the circle. 'Who is a person' informs one as to 'which rights are constitutional rights, what is their meaning and when may the state restrict them?' One may seriously criticize Rand for his unsophisticated investigation of the *telos* of a person as embedded in Canadian socio-economic practice. One may question his assertions that the free flow of trade does in fact play an integral part in the *telos* of a person. But these two criticisms only go to show that Rand fails to transpose his image of a constitution to its logical completion with the rigour of social-economic analysis and the breadth of evidence which it requires. It is to the latter, then, that we must now turn.

5. THE RESOURCE MATERIAL OF A CONSTITUTION

But where does one look to find a society's response to the question 'what is the end of a person?' Like Aristotle, Rand urges us to investigate the socio-economic practice of a society and to do so within an historical context.

(a) *Socio-economic Practice*

A constitutional lawyer does not look for the *telos* of a person in posited rules of law, according to Rand. No, one looks to socio-economic practice. As his judgments in *Winner*, *Roncarelli*, *Re Farm Products Marketing Act*, and *Murphy* demonstrate, Rand interprets socio-economic life in Canada in terms of an interdependent, individualistic capitalism. His assessment of socio-economic reality shapes what rights lie in the periphery of the circle. His assessment also influences how he interprets their meaning.

Rand holds in *Winner*, for example, that interprovincial travel on highways constitutes "a condition of the existence of an organized state." Indeed, he believes that a citizen simply cannot participate in Canadian life without highways. Given this assessment of the purpose of life in a Canadian society, what elements of the constitution does Rand draw therefrom and why? Rand elicits two constituent elements from this assessment of the importance of interprovincial travel.

First, the social conception of persons in our society entitles us to a general constitutional right to work. In his words, "What this [the notion of citizenship] implies is that a province cannot, by depriving a Canadian of the means of working, force him to leave it: it cannot divest him of his right or capacity to remain and to engage in work there: that capacity inhering as a constituent element of his citizenship status is beyond nullification by provincial action."[69] The right to work encompasses, in turn, more than just the right to "work," he notes in his Royal Commission *Report*. 'The right to work' includes the right "to have work created to enable all to share in goods and services, for which, apart from inheritance or poverty, some form or badge of 'work' is held necessary."[70] That is, 'the right to work' encompasses the equal sharing of the products of society's work. If one becomes physically disabled, one still possesses a right to the community's products. Further, although the state may regulate a person's activities, the state (through the province) may not "divest him of his right" for that right is an indispensable attribute of citizenship. One's 'right to work' is thereby found in the periphery of the circle beyond the reach of posited law (including the posited law of the federal parliament, if one were consistent). 'The right to work' constitutes a significant attribute of citizenship.

Secondly, given Rand's appreciation of the economic *telos* of a person within Canadian society, there inheres in that *telos* the right of one to enter a province "except, conceivably, in temporary circumstances, for some local reason, as, for example, health."[71]

How can Rand discover what no other Canadian jurists had hitherto recognized: a constitutional right to work and to enter a province? The answer lies in the scope of legitimate constitutional inquiry for Rand. And that, in turn, hangs upon the boundaries of Rand's image of a constitution. For Rand, the proper role of a lawyer is to investigate the *telos* or end toward which one was growing. That *telos* emanates from social/cultural relationships rather than from some Platonic utopian enterprise, some Kantian *a priori* inquiry, or the lawyer's old "arid and unrealistic conceptualism" gleaned from the four corners of "the unaided text."[72]

Rand's competent lawyer must consider society's actual "[c]onditions and consequences."[73] Rand himself places the "engaging in business at a post office or a customs house or a bank" as a constituent element of the telos of a person in Canadian society.[74] To engage in business activity even in such secondary forums as a post office, customs house, or bank constitutes the *sine qua non* of social life for Rand. *From that social practice* he derives the incidents of citizenship in Canada. These incidents include the rights to work, to enter, and to travel.

Again, in *Roncarelli* Rand identifies an "unchallengeable," "absolute" citizenship right from his own investigation, however elementary, of socio-economic practice in Canada. What is the "unchallengeable," "absolute" right? The right to gain a livelihood *in the occupation of one's own choice* (through the sale of liquor in a restaurant in Roncarelli's case). But how does Rand find that right? He uncovers it in his own appreciation of the *telos* of a person in Canada. "The continuance of the permit over the years, as in this case," according to Rand, "not only recognizes its virtual necessity to a superior class restaurant but also its identification with the business carried on."[75] More important, "[a]s its exercise continues, the economic life of the holder [of a license] becomes progressively more deeply implicated with the privilege while at the same time his vocation becomes correspondingly dependent on it." As a consequence, to revoke Roncarelli's liquor licence constitutes "a punishment which inflicted on him, as it was intended to do, the destruction of his economic life as a restaurant keeper within the province."[76] Rand again makes it clear that such a right grows out of social/cultural practice in contemporary Canadian society when Rand precedes his final restatement of the 'rule of law' principle with the preface "in the presence of expanding administrative regulation of economic activities."[77]

Socio-economic practice in contemporary Canada embodies Rand's resource material. He may have inaccurately assessed the socio-economic practice (particularly, his *laissez-faire* description of economic practice in Canada). He may have inadequately investigated the socio-economic life in Canada in reaching his assessment. But the resource material from which he ascertains the *telos* of a person in Canada is clearly the socio-economic life about him. And that serves as a very different resource material from the institutional history of the historicist, or from the posited rules and posited values of the rationalist images of a constitution.

(b) *Historical Context*

Rand prefaces his 'rule of law' restatement with the condition "in the presence of expanding administrative regulation of economic activities."[78] He infers, of course, that in an earlier day when government had not regulated economic activities to the extent that it did in *Roncarelli's* time, Rand's conception of the *telos* of a person would have been very different. A government licence to carry on business would not be required. Even if it were, its revocation would not constitute a punishment in a primitive capitalist economy. Rand's preface, therefore, appeals to an important historical context from which he identifies the *telos* of a person and the constitutional rights incidental thereto.

Rand explains the importance of the historical context in *Boucher*. There, he examines the crime of seditious libel. He does so in the light of the historical evolution of the crime from its origins in the early seventeenth century. "But constitutional conceptions of a different order making rapid progress in the 19th century," he insists, "have necessitated a modification of the legal view of public criticism; and the administrators of what we call democratic government have come to be looked upon as servants, bound to carry out their duties accountably to the public."[79] Rand then informs us that history serves as the very essence of the common law. The latter, he envisions not in the rationalistic mould of a set of self-contained rules or values from which the lawyer deduces further rules and exceptions. Rather, he pictures the common law as a "flexible process of traditional reasoning upon significant *social and political matter*."[80] That social and political matter is synonymous with the term 'social/cultural practice' used in this essay. The critical boundary in Rand's image at this point is a historicist one. Rand insists that a constitution evolves and, as it does, a constitution gains a new and different *telos* or end of a person. In his words, a change in "social and political matter" induces changes in the "fundamental conceptions of government." The judge's proper duty is to replace the legal standards "deduced" from the former social and political matter with the "new jural conclusions."

XII

The Text and the Text's Questions

This essay claims that constitutional law, if it exists, exists only through an image of a constitution. The image pre-censors what lawyers/scholars/ judges take to be an objective world, separate and independent of the lawyer. This objectivist understanding of legal knowledge, I shall show in another essay, permeates the expression of such enlightenment rationalists as H.L.A. Hart and Ronald Dworkin as much as it does such natural law theorists as Aristotle and Aquinas. I have confined myself to Canadian legal discourse. To that end, I have demonstrated how our legal discourse is dominated by a rationalist pre-understanding of law as a horizontal/ vertical picture of 'subject-matters' whose content is posited in the form of rules and/or values/policies. In Parts I and II, though, we saw these 'subject-matters' break down into a sustained search for the appropriate boundaries of the dominant image in contemporary discourse. For, it is the image which gives legitimacy and truthfulness to one's response to a text. The boundaries, that is, demarcate law from non-law.

The second claim of this essay exposes several competing images of a constitution. Various versions of a rationalist image seem to dominate our discourse in every 'subject-matter' and most scholarly studies of our constitutional law. Both an historicist and a teleological image challenge the boundaries of the dominant image from time to time. Each image lies deeply rooted in past and present Canadian legal discourse.

But is there nothing left except imagery? Is there not one right image? Do not some images distort a true understanding of constitutional law? Is there not one image which is prescriptively better as a matter of ethical, political, or social theory? Once raised, trained, and educated within a rationalist prism of understanding, the temptation presses vibrantly to respond affirmatively. And yet, to succumb, without more, would undermine the general claim of this essay in addition to the judicial and scholarly expression studied in this essay. For, the enterprise would presuppose one objective truth called 'law' (renamed 'the right image') which judicial and scholarly expression suggests is just not there (here). That being so, one is further tempted to conclude that, though not ethically better, one particular image legitimates or permits the lawyer to raise certain issues which the other images foreclose. But that temptation too subtly shifts one into a comparative prescriptive analysis which hangs upon the prescriptive content of the very issues entertained (or foreclosed). Indeed, these might very well be the sorts of questions which a lawyer/judge/scholar ought not to raise as a matter of institutional role (self-image).

The issues entertained by an image, then, become crucial. If the issues are ethically, socially, or politically significant for lawyers to consider, then one image becomes instrumentally better to the extent that its boundaries entertain what the horizons of other images deny. If I can show how a particular text, such as the Canadian Charter of Rights and Freedoms, arguably triggers such a set of questions, then I can make the minimal claim that a practical lawyer should reconsider the boundaries of her/his own image of a constitution if s/he wishes to make sense of the text of the Charter or, more correctly, if s/he wishes to better understand the text. In this chapter, I shall identify such a set of issues and, in the final chapter, I shall reconsider the boundaries of an image of a constitution which entertains the latter questions.

Let me be more specific. I aim to make a case that the text of the Charter arguably triggers surface issues about the paramount, universal, and permanent character of the text's rights; the question of which social institution is to interpret the text; the role of critical reason in interpreting the text; and the indeterminate grounds upon which one may burden the text's rights. In contrast, we have observed in Part II of this essay how the rationalist images of a constitution preclude one from incorporating each of these particular dimensions, let alone their implications, from the horizons of legitimate legal enquiry. Instead of being paramount, later posited rules/values may override generally worded rights. Whereas the text arguably suggests that the text's rights are and ought to be universally shared by each and all, the rules and values of the rationalist image differentiate those classes of persons to whom the rules/values are to apply. As to the temporal dimension, the rationalist image contemplates that rights are *ad hoc* in that they may be repealed, amended, nullified, or impliedly altered by the simple posit of a different rule. Instead of a reinforced independent judiciary, the rationalist image projects that the legislature may create, modify, or repeal the very institution of a court. The boundaries sanction rational technique. Ultimately, instrumental technique, rather than critical reason, becomes the method of resolving disputes. Finally, the rationalist image suggests that determinate rules – not indeterminate notions of freedom and democracy – justify any socially legitimate and epistemologically valid criterion for burdening the text's rules.

Let us now make the case why the text of the Canadian Charter of Rights and Freedoms arguably triggers the above surface claims.

1. THE CHARACTER OF THE CHARTER'S RIGHTS

(a) *Paramountcy*
First, the text of the Charter arguably suggests that its rights are paramount over all other social and political considerations.

(i) *Guarantees* Section 1 states that the Charter '*guarantees*' the rights and freedoms set out in it. That is a strong verb. The Charter's rights and freedoms are intended to be guaranteed presumably in the sense that no official or institution acting on behalf of the state – whether that be Parliament, a provincial legislature, a court, or even a bank – can legally infringe the rights. In addition to being a strong verb, "guarantee" is an active verb. This strong active verb contrasts with section 25 of an earlier draft of the Charter Bill c-60 which provides that:

25. Nothing in this Charter shall be held to prevent such limitations on the exercise or enjoyment of any of the individual rights ... as are justifiable ...

Whereas section 25 of Bill c-60 makes the exceptions to the rights and freedoms paramount, the use of a strong, active verb in the final version of the text makes the rights and freedoms paramount.[1] Because this paramountcy is found in the first provision of the Charter and because section 1 expressly applies to all the rights and freedoms enumerated in the Charter, one can safely conclude that the paramountcy granted to the rights and freedoms is intended to set the general tone for the Constitution Act, 1982 as a whole.

The text of the Charter restates its "guaranteeing" effect in two other sections applicable to the whole Charter. Section 24 of the Charter authorizes any "appropriate and just" remedy where the rights or freedoms "as guaranteed by this Charter" have been infringed or denied.

Section 26 refers to "the guarantee in this Charter of certain rights and freedoms." Section 28 "guarantees" the text's rights as they apply to women. If something is "guaranteed," then that something must be very special.

(ii) *Subject only* The above guarantee is explicitly subject to only one exception. That one exception is found in the remaining words of section 1: "subject only to such reasonable limits prescribed by law as can be demonstrably justified in a free and democratic society."

But what are we to make of the word "only" in the phrase "subject only"? Presumably, it must mean something.[2] What meaning could "only" have? There are at least two possibilities: first, to strengthen the paramountcy granted to the rights and freedoms by the verb "guarantees"; and/or second, to ensure that officials would not add further exceptions to the rights and freedoms – other than the exception expressly set out in the remaining words of section 1. In either case, the addition of the adverb "only" fortifies the weighty paramountcy granted by the verb "guarantees" to the Charter's rights and freedoms.

(b) *Universality*

The rights guaranteed in sections 2, 3, 7–15, and 24 possess a sense of universality in that "everyone" "has" the rights (according to the wording of the Charter). If everyone – citizen and non-citizen, resident and non-resident – universally possesses the rights, then the rights cannot exist by virtue of any posited set of rules or values. Why not? Because a posited rule or value posits restrictive conditions to which the rule or value applies. Further, an ordinary posited rule or value posits a category of persons to whom the rule or value applies. Both the restrictive conditions and the category of persons of the posited rule/value share a relativistic or conditional character. This conditional scope of a posited right contrasts with the universal sharing by each and all as contemplated in the subjects "everyone" (s. 2, 7–12, 17), "every citizen" (s. 3, 6, 23), "every individual" (s. 15), "any member of the public in Canada" (s. 20), and "anyone" (s. 24). The adjective "fundamental" which describes the rights adds to the contrasting universalist character of Charter rights.[3] In this vein, posited rules or values cannot abridge the Charter rights without contradicting the universalist character of Charter rights. Nor may posited rules grant the rights to some persons and deny them to others.

(c) *Permanence*

Further, section 52 of the Constitution Act, 1982 seems to suggest a permanent character to the text's rights by expressly providing that "[t]he Constitution of Canada is the supreme law of Canada, and any law that is inconsistent with the provisions of the Constitution is, to the extent of the inconsistency, of no force or effect." Section 52(1) expressly defines "The Constitution of Canada" to include the Charter. Accordingly, any explicit or implicit attempt to ignore or override the paramount, universal, and permanent character of the text's universality and rights contradicts section 52(1).

Section 52(3) fortifies this permanent character in that an amendment to "the Constitution of Canada" "shall be made only" in accordance with the authority expressly provided in the Constitution Act, 1982. Section 38(1) makes the general procedure for such an amendment very difficult in that resolutions to the senate and house of commons must be accompanied by resolutions of the legislative assemblies of at least two-thirds of the provinces which have, in the aggregate, at least fifty percent of the population of all the provinces.

(d) *The Relationship of Section 33 to the Character of the Text's Rights*
Contrary to common opinion, it seems that section 33 of the Charter may reinforce the paramount, universal, and permanent character of the Charter's rights. Section 33 states that

33(1) Parliament or the legislature of a province may expressly declare in an Act of Parliament or of the legislature, as the case may be, that the Act or a provision thereof shall operate notwithstanding a provision included in section 2 or sections 7 to 15 of this Charter.

Section 33 confirms the suggested character of the text's rights for the following reasons.

First, because section 33 expressly refers to section 2 and section 7–15, and because sections 2 and 7–15 are subject to section 1 (by virtue of section 1), all legislative enactments –including any enactment which uses a section 33 clause – remain subject to section 1. That is, because a parliament or legislature may restrict section 2 and sections 7–15 rights only if such a restriction is a "reasonable limit prescribed by law as can be demonstrably justified in a free and democratic society" (by virtue of section 1), the legislative use of a section 33 *non obstante* clause must be read against section 1. This subjection of section 33 to section 1 is reinforced in that section 33 leaves section 24(1) untouched. And section 24 grants a wide-ranging authority to the judiciary to consider any remedy "appropriate and just in the circumstances" should a Charter right be "infringed *or denied*." The latter circumstance includes the express denial of a right by a legislature. And *that* is precisely the circumstance where a legislature expressly invokes a section 33 declaration. Furthermore, section 52(1) expressly provides that "The Constitution of Canada" is supreme. This includes sections 1 and 24(1). Accordingly, if sections 1 and 24(1) are ignored upon a section 33 declaration, section 52(1) is violated. And if parliament or the legislature proceeds upon a section 33 declaration as if sections 1 and 24(1) did not exist, parliament or the legislature conducts itself contrary to "[t]he Constitution of Canada."

Secondly, by explicitly referring only to section 2 and sections 7–15, section 33 confirms that neither Parliament nor a legislature may restrict democratic rights (sections 3 to 5), mobility rights (section 6), language rights (sections 16 to 22), minority language educational rights (section 23), aboriginal rights (section 25), rights existent prior to the Charter (section 26), multicultural rights (section 27), sexual equality (section 28), and denominational school rights (section 29). More correctly, the text would seem to suggest that neither a parliament nor a legislature may restrict such rights unless the restriction is a reasonable limit prescribed by law as can be demonstrably justified in a free and democratic society.

Thirdly, if a section 33 declaration overrides the section 1 guarantee and the section 24(1) judicial remedies clause, we would have an absurd consequence. The absurdity runs internal to the text: namely, the rights and freedoms existent prior to the Charter would be given a higher priority than the Charter's sections 2 and 7–15 rights. This ironic and absurd twist arises because section 33 consciously omits reference to section 26. And section 26 assures us that "the guarantee" or non-guarantee (if section 33 overrides sections 1 and 24(1)) "shall not be construed as denying the existence of any other rights or freedoms that exist in Canada." Those rights and freedoms, we have been reminded by the judges and politicians again and again, are not inconsequential.[4] This is particularly so for one who presupposes an historicist image of a constitution. But that the Charter should openly and expressly acknowledge that the character of rights prior to the Charter's enactment is of a weightier and deeper paramountcy and permanance than the Charter's own enumerated rights and freedoms is ironic in the least. Such an absurd consequence would leave one with the question: 'why enact the Charter of Rights in the first place?'

Finally, the Charter arguably confirms the paramountcy of the Charter's enumerated rights over a section 33 legislative declaration by section 33's use of the verb 'may.' The verb 'may' connotes a permission. But a permission is a privilege subject to the withholding or withdrawal of the permission by the grantor. The grantee of a permission does not possess a right or special claim to the privilege. Rather, the grantee is much like a beneficiary with this difference: the privilege or permission is granted upon the conditions precedent and conditions subsequent. The Constitution Acts, 1867–1987 generally, and the Charter in particular, enumerate the latter conditions. Accordingly, in the same way that Rand interprets "may" in the light of the purpose of the Liquor Act in *Roncarelli* v. *Duplessis*,[5] so too one should read a section 33 declaration in the light of the context and purpose of the Charter as a whole. And that purpose, it would seem, is to guarantee the paramount and permanent character of the enumerated rights. The text sets out ground rules or fundamental background conditions to the exercise of the state authority. Sections 1, 24(1), and 52(1) seem to reinforce the supremacy of those background conditions.

One can understand the importance of the permissive verb 'may' from a second perspective. Let us read 'may' consistently with the word 'law' in the Charter. The Charter's preamble states that the Charter is enacted because "Canada is founded upon principles that recognize ... the rule of law." Section 1 states that the rights may be "subject only" to reasonable limits "*prescribed by law*" as can be demonstrably justified in a free and democratic society. Section 15 posits that each individual is equal before and under *the law* and that each has the right to equal protection and equal benefit of the law. And section 52(1) states that the Constitution of Canada is *the supreme law* of Canada, and that *any law* that is inconsistent with that supreme law is of no force or effect.

But what is 'law'? We have seen in Part II that all versions of the rationalist image of a constitution equate law with the ultimate posit of rules or values. That is, the image pictures law as *fiat* although, as Lederman notes, sophisticated techniques may well hide that final picture. The text of the Charter contrasts with such a rationalist image in that its various provisions of the text incorporate an appeal to reason, not *fiat*, as the ultimate arbiter of controversies surrounding the text. Section 1 appeals to reason as the arbiter, for example, in that the text's enumerated rights may be infringed "subject only to such *reasonable* limits ... as can be demonstrably justified ..." Indeed, one might argue that many of the Charter's rights and freedoms constitute conditions necessary for the free flow of critical expression. Freedom of expression, mobility, due process, and formal equality would be unnecessary in a state which resolved disputes by an appeal to *fiat* over argument. That is, the text seems to make explicit the hitherto implicit ground rules for lawmaking by critical reason. And yet, the boundaries of a rationalist image of a constitution extend outwards to include fiat as a legitimate source of lawmaking.

Philosophers and judges alike understand critical expression as something more than just a 'freedom of expression,' 'freedom of mobility,' 'due process,' and the like.[6] Lon Fuller, John Rawls,[7] and the European Court of Human Rights in *Sunday Times* v. *U.K.*[8] suggest, for example, that law, to be law, must be certain, adequately accessible, and formulated with sufficient precision to enable the citizen to regulate his/her conduct. Certain accessible and precisely drafted rules would be unnecessary if one equated law with fiat. One can understand Rand's often quoted principle in *Roncarelli*, equally applicable to a section 33 declaration, in like vein: "there is no such thing as absolute and untrammelled 'discretion', that is that action can be taken on any ground or for any reason that can be suggested to the mind of the administrator."[9] "[N]o legislative Act can without express language, be taken to contemplate an unlimited arbitrary power exercisable for any purpose, however capricious or irrelevant, regardless of the nature or purpose of the statute," Rand emphasizes. The text of the Charter does not express that the state possesses "an unlimited arbitrary power exercisable for any purpose, however capricious or irrelevant." Quite the contrary.

2. WHO INTERPRETS?

If a section 33 declaration reinforces the paramount, permanent character of the Charter's rights, what is the purpose of section 33? At this point, I wish to distinguish the form and the forum of charter rights. Whatever their content, the text claims a paramount, universal, and permanent form to all Charter rights. That is what I mean by their character. The form of the rights still leaves untouched the question 'who interprets the text?' Is it the judiciary, the legislature, the executive, some university president, or some corporate official? That question goes to the forum or the institution which possesses the power to interpret the content to the rights and to enforce their paramountcy over posited law. And that issue has served as the dominant issue in Canadian constitutional history.

"Who interprets?' underlies the clash of the feudal and central courts during the late medieval period,[10] the legislature's challenge to the crown under the Stuarts,[11] the crown's deference to the legislature during the late seventeenth century,[12] and the legislature's making of cabinets during the nineteenth. No text claiming to be a "Constitutional Act," however clear its surface meaning, can undo the theme of 'who interprets' in the evolution of social/political practice in common law societies. But that theme does not end with Dicey's political supremacy of the legislature. We know now that the Canadian citizen does not directly participate in the legislative decisions which affect her/his life.[13] What is more, new institutions – multinational corporations, financial institutions, political parties, universities, television, the media, government bureaucracies, and the like – compete with legislators for influence. Indeed, the legislature rarely initiates legislative policy. And government agencies interpret/implement that policy once it takes its regulatory form. For almost thirty per cent of their history since 1914, Canadians have lived through alleged emergencies whereby legislatures delegated autocratic power to professional politician/bureaucrats with the effect that Canadians have been exiled, civil/political rights suspended, access to the courts denied, property confiscated, and a racial minority detained in camps.[14] Royal commissions document how, during "normal" conditions, legislatures have overseen a federal police which conducts illegal wiretaps, illegal mail openings, arson, infiltration of unions, and more.[15] Wealth and gender impact upon the citizen's effective participation in the body politic.[16] Judicially created rules subscribe to due process in financial relationships against social/economic circumstances which induce financial institutions to confiscate assets in a manner which contradicts every nerve of due process and equality of treatment.[17]

It is not surprising, against this background, that a charter which claims a paramount, permanent, and universal character to its content would speak to the theme of 'who interprets?' One can understand the text's response to this issue in two contexts.

On the one hand, the text immunizes the judiciary from executive or legislative intrusion into the judicial function (and what that entails, we have seen in Part I, hangs upon the judiciary's institutional self-image). Section 24 of the Charter authorizes the judiciary to grant "such remedy as the court considers appropriate and just in the circumstances." Section 52(1) immunizes section 24 from any ordinary posited enactment which impliedly or explicitly undermines the judiciary's authority to grant any remedy which a judge deems "appropriate and just in the circumstances." A judge "shall hold office during good behaviour" and can be removed only by Parliament alone (section 99(1)). Sections 101B and 101C, as provided in the Meech Lake Accord, speak to the political impartiality of the appointment process of supreme court judges vis-à-vis the provinces and federal governments. Section 101A constitutionalizes the Supreme Court of Canada in that, prior to 1987, the Supreme Court arguably existed only by virtue of an ordinary federal statute.[18] Section 41(g), as amended in the Meech Lake Accord, makes it highly improbable that the legislative or executive arms of government will successfully undermine the independence of the supreme court in that the senate, house of commons, and each legislative assembly must consent to any amendment concerning the Supreme Court. Finally, the structure of the text itself rigidly separates judicial functions from the legislative and executive arms of government. More particularly, the Constitution Act, 1867 separates those provisions relating to the judiciary from those concerning the legislature and executive.

On the other hand, section 33 grants a role to the legislature to set limits to (that is, to interpret) the text's rights when they seem to conflict with either freedom or democracy. Section 33 provides that the legislature must expressly state that it is addressing the issue of limits and the legislature must explicitly refer to that right in section 2 or 7–15 which it intends to restrict. But I have argued above that the use of section 33 must still accord with the conditions of section 1. After all, the rights are supposed to be paramount, permanent, universal, and thereby immune from repeal, whatever the institutional source of the repeal. A court, just as much as a legislature, bureaucrat, financier, or university president, can rule by fiat. The key to interpreting the text, I shall suggest below, is whether critical reason rather than posited fiat dominates the interpretative process. Presumably, a section 33 declaration will deter judges from critically scrutinizing a legislative enactment. But that is so not because the text's rights are posited, concrete, and *ad hoc* in character, but because a section 33 declaration sends a message that the legislature is taking over the interpretative function. On the basis of the study in Part 1 it is not difficult to picture a judge critically examining the content and circumstances of a section 33 declaration when the latter burdens the independence of the judiciary, disguisedly amends the text, seriously impacts upon "the structure of the constitution," or denies the very legitimacy of the text's rights for a period of time.

In like manner, one can understand the effect of section 2 of the Constitution Act, 1867 as amended in 1987 by the Meech Lake Accord. Section 2 provides as follows:

1. The *Constitution Act, 1867* is amended by adding thereto, immediately after section 1 thereof, the following section:

"2.(1) The Constitution of Canada *shall be interpreted* in a manner consistent with
(a) the recognition that the existence of French-speaking Canadians, centred in
Quebec but also present elsewhere in Canada, and English-speaking Canadians, concentrated outside Quebec but also present in Quebec, constitutes a
fundamental characteristic of Canada; and
(b) the recognition that Quebec constitutes within Canada a distinct society.
(2) The role of the Parliament of Canada and the provincial legislatures to
preserve the fundamental characteristic of Canada referred to in paragraph
(1)(a) is affirmed.
(3) The role of the legislature and Government of Quebec to preserve and
promote the distinct identity of Quebec referred to in paragraph (1)(b) is
affirmed.
(4) Nothing in this section derogates from the powers, rights or privileges of
Parliament or the Government of Canada, or of the legislatures or governments
of the provinces, including any powers, rights or privileges relating to
language."

First, note how the text of section 2 describes its own effect in terms of
"the role" of parliament and the legislatures (sections 2(2) and 2(3)), and
in terms of "interpretation": "The Constitution of Canada *shall be
interpreted in a manner* consistent with ..." To interpret a text, at least
according to long-standing constitutional doctrine, contrasts sharply with
rendering valid or repealing an enactment. The former goes to the
operation of an enactment; the latter to its legal "existence." Thus, it
would seem that section 2 of the Constitution Act can only authorize a
legislature to narrow the scope of a Charter right: section 2 cannot
override or render a Charter right null and void. Once again, the text
sustains the paramount, permanent, and universal character of the
Charter rights vis-à-vis ordinary posited enactments.

Secondly, if section 2 of the Constitution Act, 1867 as amended by
Meech Lake authorized the paramountcy of legislative enactments over
Charter rights, then section 2 would indirectly constitutionalize legislative
supremacy. But I have noted above how section 52 of the Constitution
Act, 1982 provides that "[t]he Constitution of Canada is the supreme law
of Canada." Although section 52(1) contemplates that "the Constitution"
might extend to conventionally acknowledged principles such as 'legislative supremacy,' the Charter is explicitly named as part of "the Constitution." Thus, the Constitution Act, 1982 entrenches constitutional
supremacy. To return to legislative supremacy as the principal content of
the Canadian constitution would require an explicit amendment to

section 52 of the Constitution Act, 1982. Although the Meech Lake Accord was enacted according to the proper amending procedure required of a section 52 amendment, the Accord specifically amends the Constitution Act, 1867, not section 52. Would the judiciary ever allow the amending procedure to be used in such an indirect manner?

Thirdly, even if the above arguments are fallacious, we are left with the question whether, in an effort "to preserve the fundamental characteristic of Canada [of the existence of French-speaking Canadians, centred in Quebec but also present elsewhere in Canada, and English-speaking Canadians, concentrated outside Quebec but also present in Quebec]" and "to preserve and promote the distinct identity of Quebec," a legislature may assume judicial functions as did the *Liyanage* legislature[19] or undermine the structure of the constitution as did the *Golak Nath*.[20] Could a legislature or executive award judicial office upon the payment of a fee? Could it appoint and dismiss judges at will? Could a legislature reverse the presumption of innocence or set the minimum sentence for all provincially created offences? Could a legislature indirectly chill, burden, restrict, or repeal the civil/political rights in sections 2–5 in an effort to preserve "a distinct society"? Could the legislature legalize a one-party state, for example? Or, for that matter, could a legislature deny certain civil/political rights to women to preserve the distinct society?

I intend these questions to be rhetorical because the suggested legislative enactments undermine the structure of a constitution of which the Charter's rights have a place. As India's Supreme Court once suggested,

The Constitution has given by its scheme a place of permanence to the fundamental freedoms ... The importance attached to the fundamental freedoms is so transcendental that a bill enacted by a unanimous vote of all the members of both the Houses is ineffective to derogate from its guaranteed exercise. It is not what the Parliament regards at a given moment as conducive to the public benefit, but what Part III declares protected, which determines the ambit of the freedom.[21]

And it is to the judiciary that one looks for the protection and enforcement of a constitution's scheme. By giving a place of paramountcy, universality, and permanence to the character of the text's rights, the text itself arguably suggests that the judiciary actively confront any legislative (or executive) enactment whose purpose or effect is to bypass, directly or indirectly, the text's rights out of any desire to preserve and promote "the fundamental characteristic of Canada" or "the district identity of

Quebec." The legislative use of section 33 of the Charter in conjunction with section 2 of the Constitution Act, 1867 as amended by the Meech Lake Accord, though most certainly triggering serious caution, initiates deep issues of 'what is a constitution?' rather than the abeyance of those issues. All public officials – legislators, judges, bureaucrats, university presidents, and bankers – must journey on to justify the legislative enactments in terms of freedom and democracy. For, Charter rights are subject only to reasonable limits *demonstrably justified in a free and democratic society*. That the limits are 'by posited law' does not end the discourse. Quite to the contrary. That discourse, we have seen again and again, takes us into one's image of 'what is a constitution?' And to that I shall turn in a minute.

3. THE ROLE OF CRITICAL REASON IN INTERPRETATION OF THE TEXT

The text, I now aim to suggest, triggers more than surface issues concerning the character of the text's rights and the institutional role of the judiciary in interpreting the rights. One can argue that the text arguably speaks to the process of interpreting the rights. Whereas the rationalist image of a constitution confines a lawyer to posited fiat as the ultimate interpretive source, the text seems to call upon the lawyer to resolve disputes in terms of critical reason. This dimension of the text is independent of the character of the rights and the set of issues surrounding 'who interprets?' The appeal to the Charter's rights constitutes special justifications for human conduct. An appeal to freedom of expression, for example, provides a justification for publishing seditious expression. An appeal to a Charter right constitutes a reason for serious censure against one who harms human conduct. The text seems to contemplate that lawyers appeal to reason, and a particular tradition of reason – critical reason – to interpret the text.

(a) *Rights as Reasons*

This characterization of a right coincides with how human rights theorists differentiate human rights from positive or civil rights. Richard Wasserstrom, for example, characterizes a right as providing "special kinds of grounds or reasons for making moral judgments of at least two kinds."[22] First, if a person has a right, s/he can properly cite that right as the *justification* for having acted in accordance with or in the exercise of that right. Secondly, to invade, interfere with, or deny another's rights constitutes, by itself, appropriate ground for serious censure and rebuke. H.L.A. Hart carries this connection between a right and the justificatory process one step further by suggesting that "a very important feature" of a moral right is that the right provides "a moral justification for limiting the freedom of another ..."[23] He argues that rights mark off an area of morality which involves concepts of justice, fairness, rights, and obligation. Rights speak to the ethics of right and wrong conduct rather than the ethics of the good life.

(b) *Reasons Which Do Not Count*

Arguably, the text suggests that a Charter right is not just any reason for social conduct. That is, it does not constitute just one reason to be balanced against others. Institutional efficacy (that is, for example, that the executive arm of government can more efficiently interpret and apply the text) and a political theory of majoritarianism also offer reasons for certain social conduct. But these reasons would not seem to count as compelling ones unless the legislature uses a section 33 declaration or unless one entertains a critical analysis of freedom and democracy (as triggered by section 1, I shall suggest below). In an important early essay on human rights Gregory Vlastos defines human rights as *prima facie* rights in that "the claims of any of them may be over-ruled in special circumstances."[24] But Vlastos stresses that not anything may count as an allowable exception: "[i]f *anything* may count as an allowable exception, then what does the right give us that we would otherwise lack?"[25] Only some reasons should count and he argues that those reasons should be the very considerations of justice which require us to uphold the special claim in the first place. And to suggest that efficacy or majoritarianism can outweigh constitutionalized human rights is to lower the latter to the plane of saying that "anything may count" as an allowable exception to the rights. The text would then become redundant as would the interpretive process triggered by the text.

(c) *The Appeal to Critical Reason*

But I might be wrong about this, and this very scepticism feeds critical reason as the engine of the interpretative enterprise. Critical reason contrasts sharply with the instrumental reason of the rationalist image uncovered in Parts I and II of this essay.

We saw in Parts I and II that lawyers/judges/scholars working within the rationalist boundaries of a constitution concentrate upon finding the most appropriate means to attain 'given,' non-debatable posited ends called rules and values. Reason within the rationalist image is understood as technique. The technique uncovers what is useful, appropriate, or 'best' in serving the posited ends. Precision, analytic rigour, impartiality, and objectivity characterize rational technique. Instrumental technique is the only form of reason, within the rationalist image, because the ends which reason serves are posited. Being posited, they are 'out of bounds.' To question their content takes the lawyer into the world of non-knowledge. In this way the boundaries of the rationalist image separate law from politics, objective technique from subjective values, 'hard' law from 'soft' law, 'practical' law from 'perspective' knowledge, 'is' from 'ought,' form from content. The boundaries of the rationalist image exclude any questioning of the content of the rules/values: such would be socially illegitimate and epistemologically untrue, or non-knowledge. Once the lawyer accepts the posited rules/values (ends) as 'givens,' s/he infers intermediate, secondary, and tertiary rules/values down a vertical hierarchy *ad infinitum*. An air of necessity imbues the lawyer's conclusions as if the lawyer can use rational technique to cause social conduct. Conclusions, that is, 'necessarily flow' as a part of an inexorable, inevitable, determinate rational order. Purified of the scrutiny of the empirical and theoretical content of the posited ends, the legal discourse takes on a life of its own. Ironically, the lawyer pictures her/himself as living in a 'practical' world of 'law' at the same time that the boundaries of the rationalist image immunize her/him from social/cultural practice, on the one hand, and theoretical questions of Right Conduct and the Good Life, on the other.

This pre-understanding of reason permeates every boundary of the rationalist image: the passive self-image of the judge/lawyer; the apolitical character of 'law'; the horizontal/vertical spectrum of rules/values; a resource material of rules and values; the rule's posit of 'who has standing?'; the external source of constitutional obligation; the separation and independence of judges from the political pressures beyond the boundaries; and the unquenchable drive for rational order. And all these boundaries exist 'out there,' extrinsic to the scholar as a scientist. To venture beyond these boundaries, the lawyer journeys into an unfamiliar, uncertain world of non-law, non-knowledge. The boundaries delineate the social legitimacy of the lawyer's enterprise. The boundaries inform one of the epistemological truthfulness of one's claims about (legal) knowledge.

This instrumental reason clashes with the critical reason entertained by the text of the Canadian Charter of Rights and Freedoms. The text colours its claims with a paramount, universal, and permanent character. The text tries to immunize from political pressure the judiciary's active scrutiny of the content of the posited ends. And, now, it seems to require lawyers to reflect critically upon the content of the posited ends. After all, the text's claims are justificatory statements about how one ought to act in social circumstances. The text states that the lawyer must assess those arguments against the content of posited rules/values in legal discourse. The text, then, triggers a critical reflection of the 'givenness' of the content of posited rules/values.

That critical reason takes the competent lawyer in two different directions.

First, precisely because the 'givenness' of the posited rules/values as supplemented by rational technique insulates the lawyer's interpretative enterprise from the social/cultural practice beyond the discourse sanctioned by the rationalist prisms of law, the critical reason of the text calls upon lawyers to expose that social/cultural practice lying behind the veil of discourse delimited by the image. Further, the competent lawyer/judge must examine whether the abstract *a priori* claims in the discourse descriptively coincide with the practice behind the curtain of the discourse. In the process, critical reason exposes the very rationalist boundaries which camouflage or pre-censor how the lawyer/judge/ scholar understands practice. To the extent that the lawyer accepts the claims in a text as a 'given' amidst social/cultural conditions of dependency and domination, for example, the boundaries of the rationalist images of a constitution blind the lawyer to unfreedom. Legal discourse within the rationalist images of law becomes ideological in the sense that it conceals or masks as 'unreal,' 'illegitimate,' 'impractical,' even 'utopian' the very social contradictions beyond the discourse.

So, for example, instead of understanding 'freedom of the press,' 'freedom of thought,' and 'freedom of conscience' as posited 'givens' from which the lawyer should rationally work out secondary rules/values with their exceptions along the encyclopaedic, enclosed horizontal/vertical spectrum of a rational order, the text urges the lawyer to join that very discourse to the power relationships within society. The lawyer may well come to understand how the boundaries of the rationalist image disguise the subtle unfreedom of the victims of the communications industry and the latter's posited 'givens.' In like vein, whereas the instrumental reason of the rationalist image of law pre-censors the lawyer to understand 'equality before and under the law' as the parroting of some *a priori* edict of some esteemed lawyer of another era or the inevitable conclusion in an encyclopaedic ratiocination process, the text of the Charter arguably offers 'equality rights' as hypotheses. The lawyer's duty is to test these hypotheses against the victims of the posited rules/values on the one hand and the power of the ideal-directed theory, on the other. In this manner, critical reason becomes the crucible in bridging the 'is' with the 'ought,' practice and theory, knowledge and non-knowledge. And all this rebounds off a text.

Critical reason takes the competent lawyer into a second direction, then. The text of the Charter offers the lawyer the opportunity to expose the social/cultural premises of the text's own hypotheses as well as the premises of the posited rules/values. The rationalist image of a constitution, we have seen, takes the social/cultural content of posited claims for granted. Whereas the lawyer unreflectively affirms the content of the posited rules/values within the rationalist prism, the text of the Charter destabilizes that affirmation. Whereas the boundaries of the rationalist image presuppose and aspire to enclose legal thought, critical reason aims to unleash the grip of such an enclosure. Whereas the boundaries of the rationalist image are determinate, the lawyer embued with critical reason continually reconsiders the ethical/political content of those boundaries. Critical reason, that is, exposes their rational indeterminacy and, by doing so, it sustains its own critical ethos.

4. THE INDETERMINACY OF THE TEXT

Once one appreciates the possibility that the text of the Charter may possess an indeterminate dimension, the rationalist image of a constitution once again forecloses another net of issues. Let me now suggest how one section of the text, its most important section, raises hypotheses about a just order rather than determinate assertions about a rational order.

The text of the Charter states, in section 1, that the text's rights may be burdened if the burden is a reasonable limit prescribed by law that is demonstrably justified. But by reference to what standard or argument is one to justify a limit to a Charter right demonstrably? Some argument is necessary, we have already seen. Must the argument be in terms of the purpose of a statute? Or is a judge given an open invitation to create the standard(s) of evaluation? The text's response to these two traditional suggestions is in the negative. Section 1 informs us that the argument in support of an impairment of a constitutional right must be evaluated in terms of a "*free and democratic society.*" These are the words of the text, not some judge's or mine. These words, then, become the most important words in the Charter. A restriction of a right must be demonstrably justified in terms of neither a free society nor a democratic society but of both a free and democratic society. But this form of argument, in turn, necessitates that the competent lawyer raise issues which the rationalist image of a constitution forecloses because they take one into a world hitherto repressed as illegitimate, a world characterized as non-knowledge.

(a) A Free Society

And what does this crucial term 'a free society' mean? As with the standard 'a democratic society' there is not one simple meaning; there are several. Accordingly, the outcome of any one constitutional challenge will depend upon the meaning lawyers adopt. If the scope is narrow, then it will be more difficult for a lawyer to justify demonstrably the connection between the impairment of a right and the necessity of the impairment for a free society. As a by-product, one's interpretation of 'a free society' will flavour the paramount, universal, permanent character of the rights as well as the role of judges, politicians, and university presidents in interpreting them.

Isaiah Berlin, for example, identifies two general traditions of freedom. The one, which he calls 'negative freedom,' suggests that a person is free "to the degree to which no man or body of men interferes with my activity."[26] Negative freedom asks "[w]hat is the area within which the subject – a person or group of persons – is or should be left to do or be what he is able to do or be, without interference by other persons?'[27] Positive freedom, in contrast, derives "from the wish or desire on the part of the individual to be his own master."[28] Positive freedom asks 'What, or who, is the source of control or interference that can determine someone to do, or be, this rather than that?'[29] Positive freedom contemplates a positive duty imposed upon the state to provide the socio-economic conditions for an individual to be his/her own master.

(i) *Mill's theory of negative freedom* John Stuart Mill elaborates the theory of negative freedom as well as anyone in his *On Liberty*.[30] Mill claims that he has discovered "one very simple principle," a practical principle, which delineates the boundary between legitimate societal harm to the individual and the individual's privacy. His principle, he thinks, governs society's relationship with the individual in all cases. He states the "the sole end for which mankind are warranted, individually or collectively, in interfering with the liberty of action" of any individual is self-defence or, to use his term, "self-protection." That is, society might rightfully exercise authority over an individual against the latter's will only for one reason: to prevent harm to others. Individuality ought to remain uncontrolled in all circumstances. As Mill asserts, "in the part which merely concerns himself, his independence is, of right, absolute. Over himself, over his own body and mind, the individual is sovereign."[31] The latter circumstances Mill describes as "self-regarding"; the former as "other-regarding."

What specific elements compose the "inner sphere of life," according to Mill? In the first place, the "inner sphere" comprises "the inward domain of consciousness" from which Mill derives liberty of conscience "in the most comprehensive sense," liberty of thought and feeling, and absolute freedom of opinion on all subjects. The freedom of expressing and publishing opinions, though "other-regarding," rests upon similar reasons and is "practically inseparable" from the inward liberty of thought. Secondly, the inner sphere of life requires liberty of tastes and pursuits unless such liberty harms others. Thirdly, there flows the freedom of association "for any purpose not involving harm to others." No society is "completely free" unless these three freedoms are "absolute and unqualified."[32]

In contrast, the outer sphere of life involves one's direct interventions with other persons. Mill's essay indicates two kinds of such interactions. First, there is activity "hurtful to others." Mill incorporates this category of "other-regarding" conduct into his initial statement of the principle. He curiously adds a second category, however.

On several occasions Mill states that one may harm the interests of another not only through one's acts but also through one's omissions. In his "Introduction," after setting out his principle, Mill states that there is a *prima facie* case to punish a person who fails to perform "many positive acts for the benefit of others, which he may rightfully be compelled to perform."[33] As examples, Mill offers such duties as the giving of evidence in court, the bearing of one's "fair share in the common defence, or in any other joint work necessary to the interest of the society of which he enjoys the protection," and the performance of "certain acts of benefience, such as saving a fellow creature's life, or interposing to protect the defenceless against ill-usage, things which *whenever it is obviously a man's duty to do* ..."[34] When Mill restates his principle of "self-regarding" conduct in Chapter IV he asserts that, although society is not founded upon a social contract, "every one who receives the protection of society owes a return for the benefit, and the fact of living in society renders it indispensable that each should be *bound to observe a certain line of conduct* towards the rest."[35] This "line of conduct" entails not only the maxim that one ought not to harm the interests of another but also that every person should bear "his share (to be fixed on some equitable principle) of the labours and sacrifices incurred for defending society or its members from injury and molestation." The latter involves an issue of "duty," we are told, and the duty is violated when "a distinct and assignable obligation to any other person or persons" is infringed.[36]

What examples does Mill provide of "self-regarding" conduct?[37] Muslims, he claims, express moral outrage towards Christians who eat pork simply because of the personal tastes and other self-regarding concerns of Christians. According to Mill, Southern Europeans believe married clergy to be irreligious, unchaste, indecent, gross, and disgusting. And, the Spanish state in Mill's day allegedly prohibits all forms of non-roman catholic public worship. Similarly, the puritans in New England and Great Britain have succeeded in pressuring their respective governments to enact statutes which preserve the sabbath as a day of rest for *all*, prohibit the sale of liquors except for medical purposes, and endeavour to repress all public as well as private amusements – including music, the theatre, and dance. These cases, Mill finds to be clear examples of "self-regarding" conduct. Despite the fact that a strong case can be made for prohibiting such personal "immoralities," according to Mill, such a prohibition has the consequence that society adopts the logic of the persecutors. We would be "admitting a principle of which we should resent as a gross injustice the application to ourselves."[38] The conduct in these examples, according to Mill, is individual, not social.

Mill admits that the boundary between "self-" and "other-regarding" conduct is not entirely clear-cut. "No person is an entirely isolated being," he recognizes.[39] It is "impossible for a person to do anything seriously or permanently hurtful to himself, without mischief reaching at least to his near connections, and often far beyond them," he continues. Having recognized the overlap between the two concepts, what then does Mill mean by "self-regarding" conduct?

(ii) *Berlin's theory of intentional constraints* Mill's principle of negative freedom is not so simple as he suggests, however. For, there are at least three theories of negative freedom. The first theory states that one is free to the extent that no other person or group *intentionally* harms one's self-regarding conduct. It is difficult to read Mill's principle as protecting only intentional harm. But Isaiah Berlin, who coins the distinction between negative and positive freedom, sometimes does so contemplate.

In the text of "Two Concepts of Liberty," Berlin writes that "[c]oercion implies the deliberate interference of other human beings."[40] And one's freedom is understood in terms of "how far [his possibilities of choice] are closed and opened by deliberate human 'acts'."[41] A person might find oneself "half-naked, illiterate, underfed and diseased" and yet her/his freedom would be "identical with that of professors, artists, and millionaires," according to Berlin. Unless and until the banker *deliberately* harms the self-regarding conduct of the farmer, the "half-naked, illiterate, underfed and diseased" person is free.

(iii) *The critical theory of unintentional economic constraints* C.B. Macpherson finds this situation unacceptable. Accordingly, he redefines negative freedom to mean unintentional as well as intentional impediments to one's freedom.[42] One can be unfree because of a lack of equal access to the means of life and the means of labour. A theory of negative freedom should incorporate issues concerning the unequal access to the means of life and labour inherent in capitalism, Macpherson argues.

(iv) *The critical theory of unintentional technological constraints* A fourth theory of negative freedom states that one should examine the unintentional impediments to one's private space in the social/cultural/technological context in addition to the economic context. This theory of negative freedom is embedded in the writings of the early critical theorists of the Frankfurt School.[43] For the early critical theorists a person is not "distinguished from and even antagonistic to the external exigencies" beyond "the private space" in which he remains "himself." Rather, a person is a social and socialized being whose autonomy must be perceived in a socialized context. This requires that we abandon "the view that character is to be explained in terms of the completely isolated individual."[44] As Horkheimer notes more than once,

The world which is given to the individual and which he must accept and take into account is, in its present and continuing form, a product of the activity of society as a whole. The objects we perceive in our surroundings – cities, villages, fields and woods – bear the mark of having been worked on by man. It is not only in clothing and appearance, in outward form and emotional make-up that men are the product of history. Even the way they see and hear is inseparable from the social life-process as it has evolved over the millennia.[45]

As a socialized being, power-relationships in a society at any given time colour one's character. One's "drives and passions, their characteristic dispositions and reaction-patterns," one's mind, one's ideas, one's basic concepts and judgments, one's "inmost life," one's preferences and desires: these are all "stamped by the power-relationships under which the social life-process unfolds at any time."[46] Against these power-relationships as a socialized being, man's essence is in a state of flux. The power-relationships vary through history and from society to society. So too, then, do the potentialities hidden behind those power-relationships. Accordingly, one should not engage in the depiction of some future world. That is utopian and, as such, mere fantasy. Rather, one should find oneself "in the grip of the present or the past and severed from the future."[47] It is the past and the here and now wherein one's potentialities are embedded.

The Mill/Berlin theory of negative freedom accepts the boundary demarcating one's space as a 'given,' as 'natural.'[48] Critical theory, in contrast, acknowledges that one is a socialized being. The "private space has been invaded and whittled down by technological reality. Mass production and mass distribution claim the *entire* individual, and industrial psychology has long since ceased to be confined to the factory ... The result is, not adjustment but *mimesis*: an immediate identification of the individual with *his* society and, through it, with the society as a whole."[49] Accordingly, the separation of the individual and society is "relativized."[50] Freedom of choice, though the precondition of other freedoms, is unreal behind the technological and social veil of appearances.[51] One's autonomy is surrendered in practice even though one may adhere to its importance in the abstract.[52] Thus, the inner sphere of life is really unfree in the sense of being dependent upon the ideas, decisions, and actions of other persons. The belief in that inner freedom is the very condition of unfreedom.[53] That belief in an inner freedom is an ideology.

Why is that so? By beginning with an atomistic individual, self-sufficient and separated from society, negative freedom must accommodate itself to the brute facts of technology and the social processes which bombard one's inner sphere of life daily. By accepting the sovereignty of the individual as a 'given,' one simply cannot grasp that one's freedom is determined from without. In truth, however, the individual is really powerless and the simplistic separation of one's being from society is rent by contradictions.[54] Thus, one's sense of personal independence and respect for dignity are "noble but abstract and naive"[55] because the individual's "dependence on the social conditions of real existence is forgotten."[56]

But once we remember that fact and once we realize that technology and society have made us unfree, we can regain control of the very autonomy which the early liberal writers originally sought. We shall recognize a new and sensitive human being beneath the veneer of an abstract, atomistic monad. One's relations with others will return to the grounding of the senses in place of that abstract criterion of property. The conditions necessary to fulfil those senses will be human needs. Freedom will be an immanent freedom in contrast to the abstract freedom which is necessarily imposed because it is abstract. Persons will be self-determinative and self-formative.

Ironically, it is precisely by acknowledging the socialized character of the person that the Critical Theorists hoped to restore the private dimension of the self which the bourgeois culture had once created.[57] By recognizing the socialized character of human beings, one could transcend the social constraints (the curtain of appearances) which repress the growth of one's potentialities. And behind that curtain there is a sensitive and "new" human being. The senses (seeing, hearing, smelling, touching, and tasting) become the "sources" of a new form of reason, a form which repels the instrumentalist reason of liberalism.[58] Marcuse urges that we return to the soul, "the traditional seat of everything that is truly human in man, tender, deep, immortal – the word which has become embarrassing, corny, false in established universe of discourse, has been desublimated ..."[59] The senses "discover and *can* discover by themselves, in their 'practice,' new (more gratifying) possibilities and capabilities."[60]

(v) *Positive freedom as self-direction* Negative freedom is only one side of the Charter's criteria for demonstrably justifiable infringements of the enumerated rights. The opposed concept is positive freedom. Positive freedom projects a positive duty upon the state to create conditions for one to be one's own master. It involves "freedom to" rather than "freedom from." As with negative freedom, so too positive freedom opens up into further competing theories of freedom.

First, sometimes positive freedom is understood in terms of the conditions necessary to foster a self-directing, self-determining human who is master of his/her own space.[61] If this conception of positive freedom were implemented, C.B. Macpherson tells us, "there would emerge not a pattern but a proliferation of many ways and styles of life which could not be prescribed and which would not necessarily conflict."[62]

(vi) *Freedom as the essential nature of a person* A second conception of positive freedom assumes that there is a true nature of a person lying behind the appearance of existence. A gap persists between the essence and appearance of a person, this theory claims. Our true essence should overtake the appearance of a person. When our essence coincides with existence, we shall finally be free.

(vii) *Positive freedom as participation* According to a third conception of positive freedom, a person is free to the extent that s/he participates "in the process by which [her/his] life is to be controlled."[63] Ronald Dworkin in one essay, for example, posits this theory of positive freedom as necessary for a citizen to take pride in a community: one can take pride in a community "in its present attractiveness – in the richness of its culture, the justice of its institutions, the imagination of its education – only if his life is one that in some way draws on and contributes to these public virtues."[64] More important, Dworkin suggests, "[s/h]e can identify himself with the future of the community, and accept present deprivation as sacrifice rather than tyranny, only if he has some power to help determine the shape of that future ..."[65] There appears to be a sense in which this community participation joins up with the first theory of positive freedom. If one cannot participate in determining the shape of a community's future, one is not master of oneself, nor self-directed, nor motivated by one's own conscious purposes. One will not have positive freedom in either the first or third senses.

(b) *A Choice of Freedom Theory*

The point, here, is not to argue why the text of the Charter supports one theory over another; rather, I have tried to identify radically different understandings of 'freedom,' the very 'freedom' upon which the text of the Charter lets everything hang. Although the priority of rights, their content, and the scrutiny of alleged infringements effectively hinge upon freedom, the text leaves our understanding of 'freedom' temporally tentative, and necessarily so. The text, then, encourages the competent lawyer to appreciate and to entertain the deep theoretical debates surrounding contemporary conceptions of freedom. But that inquiry, in turn, necessitates an image of a constitution which permits the lawyer/ judge even to consider such debates. The rationalist image enchains the lawyer's horizons so that such inquiries are illegitimate and invalid. What we seriously need is an image of a constitution which will foster an inquiry into freedom theory.[66]

(c) *A Democratic Society*

What more could possibly be said about democracy, a lawyer might retort, than that 'democracy is democracy'? 'You know, a society is obviously democratic or it is not,' the lawyer continues. When pushed, the lawyer of the past might add that democracy means 'majority rule.' 'The majority rules Canada and always has. Thus, if a burden upon a right is the sort of impairment for which one can find contemporary or past examples in Canadian legal discourse, then it is a limit demonstrably justified in a free and democratic society,' the argument goes. But under cross-examination, the lawyer with a rationalist image of a constitution can go no further. 'Democracy' is just one of those many unarticulated values, much like 'freedom.' It is a 'given' beyond which it is illegitimate for the lawyer/judge to venture.

The text of the Charter once again leaves another anchor concept indeterminate. Once again, many conflicting understandings of 'what is democracy' vie for our attention. And each offers very different consequences for constitutional analysis. In particular, the choice of the one conception over the other triggers different consequences for three important issues: first, 'which rights are the important ones?'; second, 'what is their context?'; and third, 'what level of scrutiny should a judge exercise in considering the content of any posited rule/value?'

(i) *The liberal theory of democracy* One theory of democracy, whose roots can be found in Hobbes, is a theory about political method. It states that the fair process by which decisions are made assures the justice of the outcome of that process. The process validates what goods ought to be produced, how much ought to be produced, what societal goals ought to be sought, and by what means. "Justice as Fairness," John Rawls once described his project.[67] So long as the institutional process is considered fair, so too the content of the outcome of that process in any particular circumstance will be just. That is, the fairness embedded in the procedure translates itself into the outcome.[68] These process theorists of democracy ask 'what property or properties of a procedure guarantee its fairness?' The process theory of democracy aims to justify at least three such background conditions as necessary properties for a fair political process.

First, *that there be formal political equality.*[69] The idea here is that every person counts for one vote and, as a corollary, that one person's vote is the equivalent of the next person's. The connection between formal political equality and fair institutional procedures underpins why liberals react against despotism, political privilege, and social status. Liberals correspondingly advocate that all persons – lord and tenant, labourer and owner, man and woman – be granted universal access to the political process. Similarly, liberals object to racial, religious, and other restrictions being placed upon candidates for political office. And their belief in political equality as a background condition for fair institutional procedures justifies their proscriptions against corruption or the gerrymandering of the political process.

Secondly, *that the political process will remain open over time only if the freedoms of expression, assembly, and religion are not infringed.* This background requirement ensures that all persons share in participating in the process, that minority groups will be heard, and that they will be able to compete with majorities in relative formal parity without fear or threat. Without the freedoms, the political process would not remain neutral among competing policies over time. Rather, the process would serve as a barrier for minorities wanting access to power.[70]

Thirdly, *that the majority will determine the outcome of the political process.*[71] Because procedural justice does not allow for an independent criterion of justice separate from and prior to the procedure by which public authority is constituted, a minority's view of the just outcome can neither override nor check the majority's. The rightness or wrongness, justice or injustice, of the individual outcome is irrelevant. In any case, because the political process operates against a background of formal political equality with equal liberties for all, the minority group one day may become the majority the next.

Against these three background conditions of fairness there are still further, differing varieties of democracy. Barry Holden tells us, for example, that whereas, traditionally, the individual has been given a negative role in passively choosing personal and policy options presented to him/her, modern process theories of democracy focus upon the plurality of elites or of interest groups.[72] In the elitist view, elites compete for positions of power. In order for democracy to exist, there must always remain a capacity for the electorate to remove an elite after having been offered a meaningful choice of elites during an election. The elitist theory emphasizes the importance of leadership (rather than programs), the elite's accountability, and the open mobility into the elite. In contrast, the pluralist theory of democracy focuses upon groups which influence government between elections. That is, it states that public policy crystallizes when groups pressure the decision-makers. The outcome of this process constitutes "the national interest" and "popular will." Laskin's image of a constitution, we have seen in Chapter IX, presupposes a pluralist theory of politics. The common feature of the traditional, elitist, and pluralist theories of democracy, whatever the niceties of their differences, is their focus upon *the processes* by which decisions are made. If that process is fair, then the outcome is a democratic one.

(ii) *The classical theory* The classical theory of democracy, most notably expounded by Aristotle and expressed by Rand, does not rest content with a fair political process.[73] Rather, it seeks an end which remains independent of and external to the process. It is just such a standard, rather than the process itself, which renders an outcome democratic. The external norm is variously described as "human dignity," "equal respect and concern," "human worth," the "development of the individual," or the equal sharing in deliberative and judicial office. Each norm in turn offers a different account for the content of the text's rights, the paramountcy of the rights, and the role of judges in interpreting the text. The common thread is that an open political process is justified not as an end in itself but as an effective means to ensure the growth of a human being. The more actively one participates in collective decisions, the more one gains in self-worth and the more one flourishes morally and intellectually, the classical theory claims.

(iii) *The implications for the text* Like 'freedom,' one's theory of 'democracy' raises corresponding implications for the interpretation of the text of the Charter.

What rights may be justifiably burdened in terms of democracy? If we take the process theory, those rights become indispensable if they ensure an open political process where the outcome will accurately reflect the majority's will. Accordingly, the freedoms of 'expression' (s. 1(b)), 'peaceful assembly' (s. 1(c)), and 'association' (s. 1(d)) become significant in ensuring the openness of the process and the policy/personnel choices of the elite. Freedoms of 'conscience' and 'religion' would be given a secondary role because of their distance from the fairness of the political process. The 'democratic rights' of the 'right to vote' (s. 3), the life of a legislature (s. 4), and the number of sittings of the legislature (s. 5) make for the possibility of a change in the governing elite. Formal 'equality rights' (s. 15) would be justified in terms of equal access to the political processes; French linguistic rights (s. 16–22) and aboriginal rights (s. 25 and s. 35) would protect two indigenous minorities which had been absent from the political elites over several centuries. To the extent that a posited rule/value burdens the fairness of the political process, then it cannot be demonstrably justified in terms of democracy. But to the extent that a legislative restriction against one of the above (or other enumerated rights) does not burden the conditions precedent for a fair political process, the restriction is demonstrably justified because the legislative will represents the majority's will.

In contrast, the classical theory of democracy suggests that the above inquiry is misdirected. The crucial issue for the classicist such as Rand is 'what are the conditions precedent for the flourishing of a person?' This requires that lawyers give substantive weight to the equality rights (s. 15), mobility rights (s. 6), equalization duties (s. 36), and the fundamental justice (s. 7) rights.

The two traditions of 'democracy' also favour the meaning which the rights should have. So, for example, the process theory of democracy would seem to require that one define 'freedom of expression' in terms of political expression and thereby exclude obscenity, libel, hate literature, and the like unless counsel could justify the content of the latter as political expressions. Freedoms of 'peaceful assembly' and of 'association' would protect political demonstrations, political interest groups, and political parties to the exclusion of economic and social organizations. The democratic rights would be understood to prevent the executive arm of government from eroding the Opposition's claim to rule. But the 'democratic rights' would not be extended to proscribe electoral laws which gerrymandered a constituency. Finally, the 'equality rights' would be understood to ensure the equal administration and equal application of the law. That is, formal equality before the political system would be the name of the game.

In contrast, the classical theory of democracy might not even entertain whether an obscene publication has a political content. Rather, it would encourage the lawyer to ask whether the repression of pornography is essential or demonstrably justifiable for the flourishing of human beings. The freedoms of 'peaceful assembly' and of 'association' would protect cultural, economic, religious, and social groups precisely because the individual grows in relationship with others as a social and socialized being. Freedoms of 'conscience,' 'belief,' and 'religion' would be given priority because of their nexus with the flourishing of an individual. The 'democratic rights' would be understood in terms of whether institutional arrangements (such as gerrymandering) demonstrated disrespect for the worth of a minority whose vote was thereby rendered ineffective. And 'equality rights' would be understood in a fashion which goes to the content of laws *per se* rather than equal access to the political system. Section 15 would be joined with the mobility rights (section 6), rights to life, liberty, and security of the person (section 7), and the equalization duties (section 36) in an effort to search for the social, economic, and cultural conditions for the full flourishing of persons as equals.

These competing democratic traditions, as with the traditions of freedom, raise contradictory ramifications for the role of judges in scrutinizing the alleged infringements of the text's rights. Whereas the process theory would require strict scrutiny of alleged infringements of sections 2, 3–5, 15, and a section 33 declaration, minimal scrutiny would be justifiable against alleged infringements of all other enumerated rights. In contrast, the classical theory of democracy would support strict scrutiny of alleged infringements of political and non-political expression, mobility rights, equality rights, and possibly fundamental justice rights. The courts would examine broad socio-economic factors, they would grant standing in a wider variety of cases, and they would scrutinize alleged infringements by large organizations which play an important role in the formation of human beings.

3. THE HYPOTHETICAL CHARACTER OF THE TEXT

The text of the Canadian Charter of Rights and Freedoms poses a critical problem. The text speaks to the character of its enumerated rights: their paramountcy, universality, and permanency. It arguably raises another set of issues which concentrate upon 'who interprets' the text. It arguably calls for the lawyer to appeal to critical reason, rather than instrumental reason, to interpret the text. And now, we see, it seems to take the lawyer into abstract moral/political theory. Upon closer consideration, we find that the arguably two most important words in the most important section of the text are not 'givens.' They are essentially contestable concepts. The choice of one theory of freedom or democracy will trigger one set of questions; the choice of another theory will trigger a second set. The text is rationally indeterminate.

Now, these very issues are excluded from the boundaries of the rationalist image of a constitution. The paramount, universal, and permanent character of the text's rights contrasts sharply with the character of a posited right within a rationalist image of a constitution. Whereas the rationalist image confines the creation, the duties, and the role of a court to the dictates of posited rules/values, the text, we have seen, calls upon judges/lawyers/public officials actively to interpret the text and to do so in the spirit of critical reason. Finally, whereas the rationalist image would constrict a lawyer to accept the posited meaning of "freedom" and "democracy" as a 'given,' freedom and democracy are indeterminate unknowns which beg the lawyer to journey beyond the inherited boundaries of the rationalist prism. Each tradition of 'freedom' and of 'democracy' possesses its own justificatory grounding. Each offers very different ramifications for the priority of rights, their content, and the role of judges/lawyers in interpreting the text. But the rule rationalist image of a constitution excludes an examination of all these questions, as do the policy and the orthodox images. Rationalism forecloses what the text of the Charter arguably begs the lawyer to inquire. That is why Ivan Rand's image of a constitution serves as a starting-point to re-examine the boundaries of our rationalist image of a constitution. Let me now begin the task.

XIII

An Image of a Constitution

The boundaries of an image of a constitution socially legitimate a lawyer's questions. Further, the boundaries differentiate true from untrue legal knowledge. If a lawyer asks one set of questions in order to advise her/his client or to argue a case, the boundaries foreclose other questions just as they repress the resolution of those questions. Legal discourse becomes complicated when opposing lawyers or different judges presuppose boundaries of opposing images of a constitution. But the very lawyering enterprise itself becomes misdirected, if not (ironically) irrational, when the lawyers/judges share one image of a constitution to interpret a text which arguably leads the lawyers/judges into one direction when the boundaries simply cannot entertain that direction without collapsing into themselves.

We have just experienced in Chapter XII how a case can be made that the Canadian Charter of Rights and Freedoms triggers one such set of issues and how the boundaries of the rationalist image of a constitution estop the lawyer from even addressing them as socially legitimate and epistemo-logically relevant inquiries. Whereas the rationalist image restricts the lawyer's resource material to posited rules and/or values possessing a transient, conditional, and *ad hoc* character, the text of the Charter arguably entertains a discourse about human rights with a paramount, universal, and permanent character. Whereas the rationalist image projects that the legislature alone ultimately interprets the text, the text arguably entertains that judges share that role with the legislature. Whereas the rationalist image restrains a lawyer's interpretive enterprise to an appeal to instrumental rationality, the text seems to raise issues which release critical reason as the source of legal knowledge. Finally, whereas the rationalist image directs a lawyer to interpret the words of a text as if they possessed a determinate content, the text of the Charter possesses an indeterminate content. Rather than ending discourse, as the rationalist image would have it do, the Charter opens up discourse around the deep, contradictory traditions embedded within each word.

The clash of images permeates contemporary legal discourse. By the end of Part I we identified the core of three such conflicting images: for the one, institutional history characterizes the image; for the second, rational technique supplements posited rules and/or values; and, for the third, the *telos* of society's social/cultural practice initiates another set of inquiries. Judges appeal to the boundaries of these images when they interpret any text for which lawyers claim constitutional import (it may well be that judges appeal to the boundaries when interpreting any text). They do so with respect to every important doctrine and 'subject-matter' of contemporary constitutional discourse: the 'rule of law,' the 'separation of powers,' the appointment of section 96 judges, standing, extrinsic evidence, constitutional amendment, the Canadian Bill of Rights, the Canadian Charter of Rights and Freedoms, and the division of federal/provincial authority. Each 'subject-matter,' we have experienced, collapses into a discourse about the boundaries of the competing images.

By the end of Part I we deciphered that one particular image of a constitution seems to dominate legal discourse. I called this image a rationalist image. We were able to see how sometimes posited rules, sometimes values, exclusively constitute the content of law within this image. Further, rational technique serves as the crucial method by which the lawyer 'uncovers' 'the law.' This analytic method presupposes that law 'lives' 'out there' in an objective world only to be discovered for the asking. Law 'lives' an autonomous life of its own along a horizontal/vertical axis.

By turning to Canadian scholarly discourse, we were better able to appreciate the precise boundaries of the rationalist image. Pigeon, Beetz, Kennedy, and Abel refine and clarify the boundaries of a rule rationalism. As a young scholar, Laskin reconsiders the boundaries of the latter by ruthlessly piercing the formality of posited rules. His image expands the lawyer's resource material and refines the rational technique to include the social interests embedded within any posited rules. Lyon demonstrates how one can scientize the discovery of the community's values by radically broadening the resource material of a lawyer and by adding social science methodology and political theory to technique. Lederman supplements posited rules with posited values, carrying rational technique to its limit at which point the lawyer must leap into the world of arbitrary values. Rémillard, Décary, Russell, and Weiler acknowledge the inevitable posit of values in legal discourse. That posit, which permeates their expression, renders judicial decision-making political. Reacting to the elitist and anti-majoritarian character of the judiciary's political choices of one value over the next, these lawyers/scholars implicitly urge the judiciary to return to the boundaries of rule rationalism in an effort to leave the political posit of values to the legislature. Like all jurists who prejudge the world through a rationalist prism, they are entrapped within boundaries which offer only two possibilities of what constitutes a constitution: if a constitution is not composed of posited rules, it must be made up of posited values. That very trap, we have just experienced in Chapter xii, forecloses the competent lawyer from entertaining a set of issues which the text of the Canadian Charter of Rights and Freedoms arguably poses.

That is why the first question in constitutional discourse is 'what is a constitution?'; not 'what is a just state?' Although more interesting and, in terms of who we are, far more important, lawyers cannot address the question 'what is a just state?' unless their images, their legal consciousness, their assumed prisms of pre-understanding the world allow them to ask issues of justice. More particularly, if lawyers are entrapped within the rationalist image of a constitution, the Canadian Charter will share the ignoble destiny of the Canadian Bill of Rights. What liberty or equality Canadians will experience in the future will be a mere historical accident, a mischievous aside. At least, that liberty or equality which we experience will dwell outside the scrutiny of critical reason. Only if we can break from the boundaries of the rationalist image, so firmly entrenched in the discourse of the courtroom and classroom: only then, will Canadian lawyers be able to pose the questions which a charter of paramount, permanent rights asks of them.

Now, we have experienced in Chapters vi, vii, and xi that there does lie embedded within the Canadian legal discourse one image of a constitution which entertains issues about the evolution of social/cultural practice on the one hand and the content of justice on the other. Rand contemplates issues which neither the historicist nor the rationalist image of a constitution can entertain. For Rand, a constitution is neither imposed by posited rules nor does it emanate from posited values. Echoing Aristotle, a constitution speaks to the conception of "citizenship" which finds itself in Canadian society at any point in time. "Citizenship" serves as Rand's juridical term for the *telos* or end of a person. Rand gleans that *telos* by studying the evolution of social/cultural practice. Rand finds embedded within that practice the end or *telos* of a citizen as a flourishing being. One flourishes as one socially interrelates with others. Because the consummated state (or *telos*) of a citizen is that of a social being, political institutions (such as legislatures, courts, the rule of law, or a federal structure) embody the natural outgrowth of a person. Rand finds the *telos* of a person by investigating or, more correctly, assuming socio-economic relationships in an historical context.

Rand's resolution of the first question is not a new one. His majestic effort lies in the line of a far older and, it will be argued elsewhere, far more enriching intellectual tradition whose roots go to Aristotle. The fundamental element common to both Aristotle and Rand is the indispensable nexus which joins a constitution with 'who counts as a person within any particular society' over time. Neither a legislature nor a court posits a conception of a person. Rather, 'who counts' emanates from the constitutive social components of a society. Rand does not investigate the Canadian social fabric with the rigour and insight which Aristotle demonstrates with respect to Sparta, Crete, Carthage, and Athens. Nor does Rand suggest that one constitution is prescriptively better than another, whereas Aristotle does do so. But both lawyers insist that one cannot talk about the content of a constitution without first asking 'who shares in the deliberative and judicial decision-making?' This study serves as their logical and genetic grounding for the content of a constitution.

Rand's image of a constitution raises two lines of inquiry for the contemporary competent lawyer. The first flows from the resource material of a constitution: the evolution of socio-economic practice within a society. The second orientates the lawyer toward the ideal-directed inquiry of 'who ought to be a citizen in Canadian society?' That these are the two very directions of inquiry which the text of the Charter may arguably beg, however, we saw in Chapter XII. Accordingly, let us work out the boundaries of both lines of inquiry.

1. A CONSTITUTION AS PRACTICE

The first line of constitutional inquiry concerns the relationship between the discourse and the social/cultural practices of a society, assuming the two differ. More recently, Foucault describes this as the relationship between knowledge and power. Assuming that there is a social/cultural practice separate from legal discourse (for example, practice certainly includes other discourses), the lawyer could identify social/cultural practice by investigating the very *indicia* which Aristotle uses in his studies of the constitutions of Sparta, Crete, Carthage, and Athens: namely, social practices, political practices, the distribution of wealth, economic obstacles to access to office, posited qualifications for judicial and deliberative office, the *de facto* relationship of one institution (say, the senior bureaucrats) to another (say, the house of commons), and the consequences as well as purposes of legislation. Aristotle aims to understand these *indicia* in terms of 'who are the *de facto* rulers and the *de facto* ruled?' Of course, Aristotle goes on to evaluate a constitution by assessing the extent to which one is a 'complete' or flourishing person. The flourishing person informs us of the end or *telos* of a person. That constitution is best where each citizen participates as a flourishing person. This essay, which understands a constitution in terms of imagery, contradicts Aristotle's teleological perspective because Aristotle suggests that there is one right *telos* toward which all persons are evolving and that this *telos* is a higher order of 'progress.'

What we can glean of benefit from Aristotle's image, though, is that power relationships replace history, posited rules, and posited values as the resource material of a constitution. A text, such as a Charter, does not offer institutional evidence of long-standing principles sanctioned by history. Nor does a constitution set out abstract rules from which a lawyer is expected to analogize secondary claims and exceptions. Nor is a constitution a compendium of values which the lawyer must balance against each other. Rather, a text, such as a statute, a judgment, or a self-named document called the Charter, states hypotheses about Goodness on the one hand and social/cultural practice on the other. A text does not start with 'givens.' Freedoms may or may not exist in practice. The lawyer's duty is to investigate whether, in fact, they do. So, "freedom[s] of the press, expression and thought" as "guaranteed" in section 2 of the Charter foment hypotheses begging inquiry into the relationship between the claim and the sophisticated means of thought control of an oligopolitistically controlled medium which projects a self-image of "objective," "impartial," "neutral" reporting of facts. Similarly, "equality in and before the law" is not understood in terms of some abstract mathematical model or the parroting of some esteemed lawyer from another society in another era. No. It is an hypothesis to be tested against the concentration of social, economic, or institutional power vis-à-vis groups and individuals within society. The real, concrete people behind the rationalist's abstract doctrines and values do not invariably share in the benefits or in the functions of deliberative and judicial offices. Equality in and before the law exists to the extent that they do share. The text of the Charter does not give meaning to "equality in and before the law." Nor can it, because of the indeterminate character of the content of the text. Only social/cultural practice can offer concrete insight into that content. Other texts – such as judgments – are merely *indicia* of that practice.

We cannot inform ourselves of the law of a constitution, however, by investigating social/cultural practice at some isolated point in time. For, constitutions evolve as do their purposes. And, further, one can best appreciate the end toward which a society is growing by identifying the genesis from which it began. Thus, history becomes a crucial component of the competent lawyer's enterprise.

Now, the *constitution as practice* presents a seemingly insurmountable paradox. Practice either departs from a charter's hypotheses or does not do so. Both events pose implications which the lawyer must avoid at all costs.

Now, let us assume that a lawyer interprets a text called a Constitution Act in a manner in which the text describes social/cultural practice. And, let us assume that practice actually departs from that description. Let us work out the ramifications for a constitutional text, if we continue to accept the Constitution Act as 'the constitution' and, alternatively, if we continue to assume social/cultural practice as 'the constitution.'

(a) *The Text as 'the Constitution'*

If we accept the *text as 'the constitution*,' then the text becomes a 'reality' in a society whose *practice* of rights really departs from the 'given.' This will have three consequences. First, the text will mask, conceal, or hide the lawyer from the very practice which contradicts the text's 'given.' By performing that function, we shall become blind to the social unfreedom which really exists in social/cultural practice. Secondly, because our reality will begin and end with the text, our denial of practice as a constituent of reality will serve to legitimize social unfreedom in practice. Consequently, the text of the Act and the interpretative discourse will function ideologically in that they will conceal, hide, distort, or mask the lawyer from the very social/cultural practice which opposes the descriptive claims in the Act and the discourse. Finally, the more seriously we take the text as describing practice, the more unrealistic our image of a constitution. We end up grounding our constitution in metaphysics rather than in the social/cultural experience, for we purge the latter from our prejudgments of reality.

(b) *Practice as 'the Constitution'*

Now, let us assume that social/cultural practice departs from the claims in a constitutional charter and that we accept practice as our 'given' reality. In this context, we shall naturally isolate the text as belonging to an ideal world. We shall picture the text and one's interpretation of the text as a utopian, "impractical" venture amidst the legal fraternity. The fraternity will likely defer to the text in order to explain or justify social/cultural practice, in that the legal fraternity, more than any other, prides itself in being in tune with 'practice' at the same time that it monopolizes interpretation of the text. The text takes on the role of Plato's forms, though the forms are understood through the prism of Socrates' adversaries: the sophists. The constitutional lawyer comes to accept practice as normal; indeed, as natural. Thus, the lawyer pictures the text as a perversion of the natural.

Thus the *constitution as practice* becomes an end in itself. Having discarded the text and the interpretation of the text as a utopian venture, the lawyer needs nothing else to complete his or her boundaries of reality. The *constitution as practice* is both self-sufficient and of intrinsic worth. In the process, the lawyer finds him/herself with no external claims to test, evaluate, or critique practice. And the universalist, permanent, and paramount claims in the text become an historical accident beyond the legitimate scrutiny of the lawyer.

2. THE CONSTITUTION AS INTERPRETATIVE DISCOURSE/PRACTICE

These two sets of ramifications, equally objectionable, flow from the possibility that practice actually departs from the text and the discourse interpreting the text. Let us now take a different tack. Let us assume that the interpretative discourse really does describe social/cultural practice. Once again, we are confronted with insurmountable hurdles. We shall not be able to entertain the possibility that there might be threshold claims outside the discourse/practice which are also necessary prerequisites of a just state. For, under our hypothesis, we shall exclude such justice issues from our boundaries of reality. Secondly, even if philosophers could identify such additional claims, the lawyer would have to discard them as utopian ventures divorced from the boundaries of his or her reality. The philosopher's responses would be rejected as impractical, irrelevant, and illegitimate. In either the first or second situations, the lawyer will have no realizable standard to assess whether the text is a Good one or a Bad one because reality is complete when our boundaries entertain the discourse/ practice. Constitutional discourse will begin and end within those boundaries.

Admittedly, the lawyer will proclaim the text as a Good one in that his/her prism of reality extends to the interpretative discourse and we have assumed, for argument's sake, that the discourse coincides with social/cultural practice. But is the text the best one? The just one? After all, we made a case in Chapter XII that the text of the Charter of Rights entertains ideal-directed claims about how we ought to conduct ourselves toward each other in addition to claims about social/cultural practice. And to what standard can we appeal if we wish to compare the Goodness of one society's constitutional experience with that of another? Indeed, can one make such prescriptive claims? And how can we entertain *that* question without knowing what we are entertaining? Justice and liberty, once again, become historical accidents. Because the lawyer's boundaries of *a constitution as practice/interpretative discourse* does not encompass issues of Goodness or Right Conduct, there is no ultimate set of standards to which the lawyer can appeal. Power becomes the clue to 'who wins?' And law becomes posited. Instrumental reason shall reign. The universalist, permanent, and paramount claims in the text become usurped into a well of constitutional relativism. And we must ask ourselves 'why have a "bottom line" text claiming paramountcy, universality, and permanence to begin with?' The text and the interpretative enterprises lose their reason to exist unless, of course, the discourse disguisedly functions to hide the lawyer and victim from social unfreedom.

A constitutional charter serves an objectionable role whether or not the interpretative discourse departs from social/cultural practice. If there is a way out of the paradox then we must return to the boundaries of our image of *a constitution as discourse/practice*. The latter assumed that the discourse either by itself or in conjunction with social/cultural practice was an end-in-itself. The text either coincided with practice or it did not. But the text/discourse was a 'given.' To escape from the trap, it would seem, we must treat the text as a set of hypotheses rather than as self-sufficient and complete 'givens.' On the one hand, the text may or may not coincide with social/cultural reality of power. On the other hand, the text may or may not make conclusive claims about justice and liberty. At last, we understand the role of a constitutional charter. The Charter hangs upon an 'if' clause. The text neither describes social/cultural practice as a fact nor makes conclusive claims about the ideal. Its character lies in the nature of hypotheses with which the lawyer may test the world of practice and world of theory. The text joins legal discourse to both worlds.

3. HYPOTHESES OF WHAT?

But the final question remains, 'an hypothesis of what?' To suggest that the Charter elaborates a series of hypotheses subjects one to the very constitutional relativism which enveloped the various rationalist images of a constitution examined in Part II. Something more is needed to escape from the relativistic hold. And 'that something' stems from the alleged character of the human rights which the Charter arguably entrenches: universality. The Charter hangs upon an 'if' clause. The text assumes that human rights exist universally among all human persons; that the interpretative enterprise should protect the paramountcy of the universal claims at all times; that lawyers should play a role in the interpretative project; and that they should do so by appealing to critical, rather than instrumental, reason. That 'if' clause or, more correctly, those 'if' clauses contradict the constitutional relativism which envelops the *constitution as practice*. The 'if' clauses assume that there might be one right answer about the *telos* or end of a person.

But the very existence of the 'if' clauses makes the Charter an hypothesis – nothing more nor less. And we have seen that treatment of the Charter as an hypothesis allows us to escape from the problems inherent in the *constitution as practice*. Thus, the Charter does not definitively inform us of the nature of a person. It offers hypotheses about the conditions precedent necessary to flourish as a Good person (community). As such, it does more than provide us with a set of standards with which to critique practice. It instructs us to ask further questions as to whether the hypotheses about the *telos* of a person are complete and sustainable.

At last, we can understand the law of a constitution as a unified whole and we can appreciate the role of a charter of rights within that whole. For a charter of rights raises the sorts of hypotheses which a society takes as important responses to the question 'what is the *telos* or end of a good person?' And *that* is the very enterprise which grounds Rand's image of a constitution. The law of a constitution depends upon 'who counts as a person?' within the social whole in its historical context. That question is answered, in turn, by an investigation of the extent to which each and all share in the benefits and the functions of citizenship. That constitution is best where each and all do so share.

Rand may well have erred in his assessment of the incidents of being a good person. And he may have been wrong in arguing that nature induces one to flourish as an end in itself. A charter of rights requires one to deliberate upon those very possibilities because its hypothetical nature as well as the meaning of its rights hangs upon their outcome. But only Rand's image of a constitution allows the lawyer to ask those questions. By self-reflecting about Rand's image of a constitution the lawyer can, at least, ask the right questions. S/he can discard the historicist and rationalist images as misdirected. And s/he shall come that much closer to resolving the very issues which a charter of rights begs. But Rand's image of a constitution, too, leaves us beset with issues.

To conclude that a constitutional charter is a set of hypotheses about theory and practice may envelop one in the same constitutional relativism which plagued a *constitution as interpretative discourse/practice* unless the hypotheses concern Goods with a paramount, universalist, and permanent character. First, can we reach the first principles of the Good without a jump to indemonstrable first principles – what Aristotle called "understanding" and Aquinas "divine reason"? Secondly, does not a constitutional image which projects a charter as a set of hypotheses of the Good assume that the content of the Good is really good rather than evil? Why should we assume that the Good's content is not just one more holocaust? And thirdly, does the lawyer's search for the Good presuppose that, external to Culture, there lives a universal, everlasting Nature? And, is not that dichotomy, itself, a cultural construct, albeit a deep one left over from the Greeks? And if so, does not the universal character of a constitutional charter collapse into a cultural relativism, the very relativism to which a *constitution as practice* succumbed? Is there nothing left? A constitutional charter as an hypothesis of the Good, then, is an hypothesis itself for everything hangs upon the content of the Good, if the Good is not a cultural construct.

4. CONCLUSION

The indeterminate character of the content of the Good underlines the never-ending role of theory in constitutional discourse. More than that, the indeterminacy of the Good reinforces the importance of practice for, without a consideration of social/cultural practice, theory takes on a reified, abstract life of its own with the risk that reified abstract thought becomes divorced from social/cultural practice. In the latter context, we have seen, an interpretative discourse can play a repressive function, cloaking and hiding the lawyer from the social unfreedom which his/her image of a constitution disguises. We are left, then, with the conclusion that if universalist, permanent, and paramount claims in a text are to serve some Good, then the lawyer must picture the text as unsynthesizable and unassimilable within any determinate, preconceived rational framework. Rather, a constitutional imagery rebounds off a text. And, if the character of the text's claims is to serve some end, the boundaries of the lawyer's image of a constitution must entertain a scrutiny of both theory and practice. The text's character calls upon practice to critique theory and theory to critique practice. Such an image of a constitution at least raises the possibility that a constitutional discourse will not become estranged from social/cultural practice on the one hand, and from becoming an instrument of constitutional and, therefore, ethical relativism, on the other. Only an image of a constitution whose boundaries entertain such continual critique can address the gap between the practice and theory of constitutional discourse. At last, lawyers will finally have found a role in alleviating the pain and suffering about them.

Notes

CHAPTER I

1 A.V. Dicey, *Introduction to the Study of the Law of the Constitution*, 10th ed. (Toronto: Macmillan 1959), at 23.
2 H.L.A. Hart, *The Concept of Law* (Oxford: Clarendon Press 1961), at 102.
3 See generally Immanuel Kant, *Grounding for the Metaphysics of Morals* (James W. Ellington, transl.,; Indianapolis, Cambridge: Hackett 1981).
4 Why I wish to do so is undoubtedly rooted in the writings of Max Horkheimer and Theodor Adorno. I have been particularly influenced in this context by Max Horkheimer and Theodor Adorno, *Dialectic of Enlightenment* (John Cumming, transl.; New York: Continuum 1972, 1944); Horkheimer, *Critical Theory: Selected Essays* (Matthew J. O'Connell et al. transl.; New York: Continuum 1982, 1968); Horkheimer, *Eclipse of Reason* (New York: Continuum 1974, 1947); Adorno, *Negative Dialectics* (E.B. Ashton transl.; New York: Continuum 1983, 1966); and Adorno, *Critique of Instrumental Reason* (Matthew J. O'Connell et al. transl.; New York: Seabury Press 1974).
5 Hans-Georg Gadamer, *Truth and Method* (New York: Crossroad 1985, 1975); *Reason in the Age of Science* (Frederick G. Lawrence, transl.; Cambridge: MIT Press 1981, 1976).
6 Jacques Derrida, *Of Grammatology* (Gayatri Chakravorty Spivak, transl.; Baltimore: Johns Hopkins University Press 1976, 1967).
7 Michel Foucault, *The Birth of the Prison* (Alan Sheridan, transl.; New York: Vintage 1979, 1975); *The History of Sexuality*, vol. 1: *An Introduction* (Robert Hurley, transl.; New York: Vintage Books 1980); and *The Use of Pleasure: The History of Sexuality*, vol. 2 (Robert Hurley, transl.; New York: Vintage 1986, 1984).

8 Paul Ricoeur, *The Conflict of Interpretations: Essays in Hermeneutics* (Don Ihde, transl.; Evanston: Northwestern University Press 1974); *History and Truth* (Charles A. Kelbley, transl.; Evanston: Northwestern University Press 1965).

9 The importance of this issue can be drawn from Georg Lukacs, *History and Class Consciousness* (R. Livingstone, transl.; Cambridge: MIT Press 1971, 1968); and Jean Baudrillard, *For a Critique of the Political Economy of the Sign* (Charles Levin, transl.; St Louis, Mo.: Telos Press 1981). Also see Jurgen Haberman, *The Theory of Communicative Action*, vol. 1: *Reason and the Rationalization of Society* (Thomas McCarthy, transl.; Boston: Beacon Press 1981).

One strain of contemporary feminist legal theory draws a connection between the dominant image (or "voice") and cultural practice. See, e.g., Carol Gilligan, *In a Different Voice* (Cambridge, Mass.: Harvard University Press 1982), and Williams, "Alchemical Notes: Reconstructing Ideals from Deconstructed Rights" (1987), 22 *Harv. C.R.-C.L. L. Rev.* 401.

I am also mindful of certain essays by Peter Gabel and Duncan Kennedy in the context of this issue. See esp. Gabel, "Reification in Legal Reasoning" (1980), 3 *Research in Law and Sociology* 25; "The Phenomenology of Rights-Consciousness and the Pact of the Withdrawn Selves" (1984), 62 *Texas L. Rev.* 1563; and Kennedy, "Toward a Historical Understanding of Legal Consciousness" (1980), 3 *Research in Law and Sociology* 3. Also see Balbus, "Commodity Form and Legal Form: An Essay on the 'Relative Autonomy' of Law" (1977), 11 *Law and Society Rev.* 571.

CHAPTER II

1 Aristotle tells us that it is "a positive danger," "a dangerous standard for action," for the Cretan council of elders to settle issues "at their own discretion" "by the mere will of men," rather than on the basis of written rules. Indeed, he goes so far as to suggest that that factor alone disqualifies the Cretan system from really being considered a constitution at all. Aristotle, *Politics* 1272a.

2 Chief Justice Coke insists that the king must live *under* the law as discovered by the "artificial reason" of lawyers. See, e.g., *Prohibitions del Roy* (1608), 12 *Co. Rep.* 63, 77 ER 1342 (KB).

3 For Dicey, "the universal rule or supremacy throughout the constitution of ordinary law" serves as one of the guiding first principles of the English Constitution. The Canadian Bill of Rights affirms that "men and institutions remain free only when freedom is founded upon respect for moral and spiritual values and the rule of law." The Charter of Rights "guarantees"

its rights "subject only" to limits "*prescribed by law*" in certain circumstances. And section 52(1) of the Charter guarantees the supremacy of this 'rule of law' requirement over any posited law which might suggest otherwise. A.V. Dicey, *Introduction to the Study of the Law of the Constitution*, 10th ed. (London: Macmillan 1965), at 34–5.

4 [1959] SCR 121.

5 [1985] 2 SCR 347.

6 See text infra chap. v, sect. 2. Also see, e.g., *Lavell v. A.-G. Can.*, [1974] SCR 1349, 11 RFL 333, 23 CRNS 197, 38 DLR (3d) 481; *R. v. Burnshine and Attorney General for Ontario (Intervenant)*, [1975] 1 SCR 693, [1974] 4 WWR 49, 25 CRNS 270, 15 CCC (2d) 505, 44 DLR (3d) 584. The Court's approach to the 'rule of law' in these two cases is discussed in Conklin, "The Utilitarian Theory of Equality before the Law" (1976), 8 *Ott. L. Rev.* 485. Also see Conklin and Ferguson, "The Burnshine Affair: Whatever Happened to Drybones and Equality before the Law" (1974), 22 *Chitty's L.J.* 303. Also see Tarnopolsky, "The Canadian Bill of Rights and the Supreme Court Decisions in Lavell and Burnshine: A Retreat from Drybones to Dicey?" (1974), 7 *Ott. L. Rev. 1*.

7 [1985] 1 SCR 721, at 749. Emphasis added.

8 Ibid., at 750. Emphasis added.

9 [1985] 1 SCR 613, at 645.

10 *Re Currie and Niagara Escarpment Comm.* (1984), 46 OR (2d) 484, 10 DLR (4th) 113 (HCJ).

11 Dicey, supra note 3, at 188. Dicey continues: "[i]n this sense the rule of law is contrasted with every system of government based on the exercise by persons in authority of wide, arbitrary, or discretionary powers of constraint."

12 Ibid., at 193.

13 Lon Fuller, *The Morality of Law* (New Haven and London: Yale University Press 1964), chap. 2.

14 John Rawls, *A Theory of Justice* (Cambridge, Mass.: Harvard University Press 1971), §38.

15 This is, first, that rules should be of a kind "which men can reasonably be expected to do and to avoid." Secondly, those who enact rules do so in good faith. Thirdly, impossibility of performance serves as a defence or, at least, a mitigating circumstance. See Rawls, ibid, at 236–7.

16 Ibid., at 238. This precept demands, according to Rawls, "that laws be known and expressly promulgated, that their meaning be clearly defined, that statutes be general both in statement and intent and not be used as a way of harming particular individuals who may be expressly named

(bills of attainder), that at least the more severe offenses be strictly construed, and that penal laws should not be retroactive to the disadvantage of those to whom they apply."

17 *Sunday Times* v. *U.K.* (1979), 2 EHRR 245 para. 46, 47, 49–53.

18 (1983), 41 OR (2d) 583, at 592; aff'd (1984) 45 OR (2d) 80; 2 OAC 388d (CA). Leave to appeal granted by SCC 3 April 1984; not reported at date of writing.

19 (1983), 41 OR (2d) 583, at 592.

20 [1985] 1 CTC 246, 57 NR 386.

21 Ibid., at 248.

22 Ibid.

23 Ibid.

24 Ibid., at 250.

25 Ibid., at 251.

26 The differences between procedural justice and substantive justice are set out in Conklin, "Clear Cases" (1981), 31 *U. Tor. L.J.* 231. Briefly, procedural justice looks to the fairness of the procedure by which a rule is made or administered whereas substantive justice looks to the justice of the content of the rule. The justice of the content of the rule would be understood in terms of corrective justice, distributive justice, or political justice. The latter concepts receive their first expression in Aristotle, *Nicomachean Ethics*, bk. v. For contemporary commentary in terms of law, see Weinrib, "Toward a Moral Theory of Negligence Law" (1983), 2 *Law & Philosophy* 37; Arnold, "Corrective Justice" (1980), 90 *Ethics* 180; John Finnis, *Natural Law and Natural Rights* (Oxford: Clarendon Press 1982), chap. 7; and Conklin and Morrison, "Public Issues in a Private Law World: The Case of the Appointment of a Receiver," forthcoming in (1988), 26 *Osgoode H.L.J.*

27 Thorson, "The International Commission of Jurists" (1957), 35 *Can. B. Rev.* 898, at 905–10.

28 See generally Kanyeihamba, "Constitutional Obligation in Developing Countries," and Aguda, "The Judiciary in a Developing Country" in M.L. Marasinghe and William E. Conklin, eds., *Essays on Third World Perspectives in Jurisprudence* (Singapore: Malayan Law Journal 1984).

29 [1959] SCR 121.

30 Ibid., at 142.

31 Ibid., at 141.

32 This very important issue forms the focus of Parts II and III. The traditional images of a constitution shared by Canadian jurists presuppose reason as instrumental rationality. See text infra chap. VIII–X. Rand expresses a very different conception of reason. See text infra chap. XI. See generally

Conklin, "The Legal Theory of Horkheimer and Adorno" (1985), 5 *Windsor Yearb. Access Justice* 230.

33 [1985] 1 SCR 721.

34 See Kanyeihamba, "Constitutional Obligation in Developing Countries" in M.L. Marasinghe and William E. Conklin, eds., *Essays on Third World Perspectives in Jurisprudence*, at 59–62; Reyntjens and Wolf-Phillips, "Revolution in the Legal System of Third World States," ibid., at 117–25; and Aguda, "The Judiciary in a Developing Country," ibid., at 144–8.

35 The Court cites the preamble of the Constitution Act, 1982 which provides "Whereas Canada is founded upon principles that recognize the supremacy of God and the *rule of law*" (Court's emphasis). The Court also claims "its implicit inclusion" in the preamble of the Constitution Act, 1867 by virtue of the words "with a Constitution similar in principle to that of the United Kingdom."

36 *Re Language Rights under S. 23 Manitoba Act, 1870 and S. 133 Constitution Act, 1867* (1985), 1 SCR 721, at 748i. Also see ibid., at 750f–h.

37 Ibid., at 750i.

38 Ibid., at 750j.

39 Ibid., at 751a. Emphasis added.

40 Ibid., at 766f; also see 752h.

41 Ibid., at 751d.

42 As quoted in ibid., at 752d. See generally text infra chap. IV.

43 Ibid., at 752h.

44 Ibid., at 758c, 765j.

45 Ibid., at 766a, 767c.

46 Ibid., at 766i.

47 Quoting approvingly (and with italics) from *Madzimbamuto* v. *Lardner-Burke*, [1969] 1 AC 645 (PC) at 740 in *Re Manitoba Language Rights* (1985) 1 SCR 721, at 761a.

48 Quoting approvingly from Albert Constantineau in *The De Facto Doctrine* (Toronto: Canada Law Bk 1910), at 5–6 in *Re Manitoba Language Rights* (1985) 1 SCR 721, at 755h–i.

49 Ibid.

50 Ibid., at 763i–j.

51 Ibid., at 758c. Emphasis added.

52 Ibid., at 758d–e. Emphasis added.

53 Ibid., at 760–6.

54 Ibid., at 763i–j.

55 Ibid., at 766a. Emphasis added.

56 Ibid., at 767a–b. Emphasis added.

57 Aristotle, *Politics*, bk. iv, c. 14.

58 Ibid., at 1298a.

59 Ibid., at 1299a.

60 Ibid., c. 16.

61 Charles Louis de Secondat Montesquieu (1689–1755), *L'Esprit des lois*, vol. 1, bk. 1, ch. 6, pp. 215–17 (1750), and reprinted in Morris R. Cohen and Felix S. Cohen, *Readings in Jurisprudence and Legal Philosophy* (Boston, Toronto: Little, Brown and Co. 1951), at 879. Montesquieu reasons that "[w]ere it joined with the legislature, the life and liberty of the subject would be exposed to arbitrary control; for the judge would be then the legislator. Were it joined to the executive power, the judge might behave with all the violence of the oppressor."

62 Thomas Jefferson, "Notes on the State of Virginia" [3rd Am. ed., 1801], at 174–5 and reprinted in Cohen and Cohen, ibid., at 880.

63 Noel Lyon opines that "In Canada, we have in the B.N.A. Act of 1867 a written basis for our formal institutions, their functions and power. From this document can be implied an intention that these institutions shall continue to exist and to apply the powers conferred on them in the performance of particular functions, thus providing legal authority for a principle of separation of powers." J. Noel Lyon and Ronald G. Atkey, eds., *Canadian Constitutional Law in a Modern Perspective* (Toronto: University of Toronto Press 1970), at 304. Lyon elaborated this argument in "Constitutional Validity of Sections 3 and 4 of the Public Order Regulations, 1970" (1972), 18 *McGill L.J.* 136 and "The Central Fallacy of Canadian Constitutional Law" (1976), 22 *McGill L.J.* 40. See generally text infra chap. ix.

   William Lederman claims that history, rather than the text, supports the separation of powers principle. Lederman, "Independence of Judiciary" (1956), 39 *Can. B. Rev.* 768 and 1138; reprinted in William Lederman, *Continuing Canadian Constitutional Dilemmas* (Toronto: Butterworth 1981), chap. 7.

64 Peter Hogg, author of the leading text *Constitutional Law of Canada*, emphatically states that "[t]here is no general 'separation of powers' in the Constitution Act, 1867. The Act does not separate the legislative, executive and judicial functions." Hogg insists that "each branch of government exercise only 'its own' function." 2nd ed. (Toronto: Carswell 1985), at 150–1. Hogg continues, "[a]s between the legislative and executive branches, any separation of powers would make little sense in a system of responsible government; and it is clearly established that the Act does not call for any such separation. As between the judicial and the two political branches, there is likewise no general separation of powers. Either the Parliament or the

Legislatures may by appropriate legislation confer non-judicial functions on the courts and (with one important exception, to be discussed) may confer judicial functions on bodies which are not courts." Hogg goes on to elaborate the exception: "the provincial Legislatures may not confer on a body other than a superior, district or county court judicial functions analogous to those performed by a superior, district or county court."

Judge Barry Strayer also asserts in his recent edition of *The Canadian Constitution and the Courts* that "[i]n considering the propriety or the legality of Canadian courts giving decisions on questions of constitutional validity, it is essential to keep in mind that they are not restricted by any concept of separation of powers." 2nd ed. (Toronto: Butterworths 1983), at 125. See discussion in text, infra, at notes 82 to 90.

One can find traces of the Hogg/Strayer opinion in the writings of Chief Justice Laskin and others. See the position of Laskin and others below in text between notes 89 and 102. Also see infra chap. VIII.

65 [1949] 4 DLR 199, [1949] WWR 586 (BCCA).

66 [1981] 2 FC 543, 130 DLR (3d) 433.

67 [1986] 2 SCR 56, at 75i–j.

68 [1985] 2 SCR 673, at 694–704.

69 [1949] 4 DLR 199.

70 Ibid., at 202. Emphasis added.

71 Ibid., at 206.

72 O'Halloran quoting from Coke C.J. O'Halloran's emphasis. [1949] 4 DLR 199, at 207.

73 [1949] 4 DLR 199, at 208. Emphasis added.

74 [1981] 2 FC 543, 130 DLR (3d) 433.

75 [1984] 1 FC 1010, 148 DLR (3d) 205, 48 NR 252 (App. Div.). Thurlow C.J. concentrates upon the meaning of "fixed and provided" in s. 100 (see esp. 1020–1024b), as does Heald (see esp. 1042e–1043b). Heald explicitly rejects Addy's historicist reliance upon convention, relying upon Laskin's majority judgment (the Majority of Seven) in the *Patriation Reference*, [1981] 1 SCR 753 (see text infra chap. IV). See esp. Heald at 1044d–1047f. Pratte, dissenting in the outcome, also shares a textualist image of a constitution: "I do not, therefore, find the solution of our problem in the history of the Constitution: That solution, in my opinion, must be found in the text of the *Constitution Act, 1867*" (1030e).

76 [1986] 2 SCR 56. For Dickson's image of a constitution as expressed in his Supreme Court judgment see generally text infra, at chap. VII, note 45. For the place of tradition within Dickson's image see, e.g., [1986], 2 SCR 56, at 69d, 70j, 72j.

77 See, e.g., [1985] 2 SCR 673, at 699j–702j. LeDain suggests that "[t]radition reinforced by public opinion, operating as an effective restraint upon executive or legislative action, is undoubtedly a very important objective condition tending to ensure the independence in fact of a tribunal." However, LeDain goes on to advise that s. 11(d) of the Charter "presupposes that it does not automatically exist by reason of tradition alone."

78 One should appreciate Dickson's view of history in the wider context of Dickson's teleological image of a constitution. See esp. infra chap. VII, note 45 and text between notes 35 and 52.

LeDain's emphasis upon history in *Beauregard* departs from his general 'policy balancing' image of a constitution which he has expressed in other Charter judgments. See generally text infra, chap. VII between notes 220 and 230. Also see chap. VII, note 200.

79 See text supra sect. 1(ii) and infra chap. XI.

80 Sections 99 and 100 provide as follows:

99 (1) Subject to subsection two of this section, the Judges of the Superior Courts shall hold office during good behaviour, but shall be removable by the Governor General on Address of the Senate and House of Commons.

(2) A Judge of a Superior Court, whether appointed before or after the coming into force of this section, shall cease to hold office upon attaining the age of seventy-five years, or upon the coming into force of this section if at that time he has already attained that age.

100 The Salaries, Allowances, and Pensions of the Judges of the Superior, District, and County Courts (except the Courts of Probate in Nova Scotia and New Brunswick), and of the Admiralty Courts in Cases where the Judges thereof are for the Time being paid by Salary, shall be fixed and provided by the Parliament of Canada.

101 The Parliament of Canada may, notwithstanding anything in this Act, from Time to Time provide for the Constitution, Maintenance, and Organization of a General Court of Appeal for Canada, and for the Establishment of any additional Courts for the better Administration of the Laws of Canada.

81 [1981] 2 FC 543, at 588c.

82 Ibid., at 588d, 588h; also see 590g–h.

83 Ibid., at 588i. Emphasis added.

84 Ibid.

85 Ibid.

86 H.L.A. Hart, *The Concept of Law* (Oxford: Clarendon Press 1961), at 79–88.

87 Supra note 64.

88 By this question I do not mean intellectual grounding (that is, 'how is the perspective justified?') but rather its anthropological grounding, although the two are undoubtedly connected. One's justificatory process no doubt adds to one's initial inward image of a constitution.

89 "Section 96 of the British North America Act" (1940), 18 *Can. B. Rev.* 517, at 523. Emphasis added. He cites *Ottawa Valley Power Co.* v. *Att. Gen. for Ontario*, [1936] 4 DLR 289, at 307, and *A.G. for Quebec* v. *Slanec and Grimstead*, [1933] 2 DLR 289, at 307 as authorities.

90 3rd ed. (Toronto: Carswell 1966), at 789; 3rd rev. ed. (1969), at 789; and 4th rev. ed. (1975), at 764.

91 Ibid.

92 Much of Chapter IX is devoted to showing why and how Laskin relies upon this 'given' boundary.

93 Ritchie C.J. in *Valin* v. *Langlois* (1879), 3 SCR 1, at 14 and quoted in Laskin, 3rd rev. ed., at 23: "the legislative power of the Local Assemblies is limited and confined to the subjects specifically assigned to them, while all other legislative powers, including what is specially assigned to the Dominion Parliament is conferred on that Parliament ..."

94 *Liquidators of the Maritime Bank* v. *Receiver-General of N.B.*, [1892] AC 437, at 442 as quoted in Laskin, 3rd rev. ed., at 23. Emphasis added.

95 Quoting from *A.-G. Ont.* v. *A.-G. Can.*, [1912] AC 571, 3 DLR 509 at 513 in Laskin, 3rd rev. ed., at 70.

96 (1887), 12 AC 575 (Privy Council), at 588; in Laskin, 3rd rev. ed., at 70.

97 Laskin, 3rd rev. ed., at 789. Emphasis added.

98 Ibid.

99 Section 4 of the Statute of Westminster, 1931 22 Geo. V, c. 4 provides that 'No Act of Parliament of the United Kingdom passed after the commencement of this Act shall extend, or be deemed to extend, to a Dominion as part of the law of that Dominion, unless it is expressly declared in that Act that that Dominion has requested, and consented to, the enactment thereof."

100 Laskin, 3rd rev. ed., at 789; 4th ed., at 764. Laskin does seem to suggest, however, that one can imply the existence and independence of the courts from the British North America Act. He continues the above quoted assertion with "[i]mplicit in the Act is, of course, a guaranteed jurisdiction to rule on the validity of legislation." Laskin seems to derive this implied power from the particular fact that a superior court may entertain constitutional objections to the proceedings of an inferior court even though the latter has limited the time within which one could make such objections. He then continues that "[t]he *British North America Act*, moreover, as-

sumes but without explicitly so declaring, that provincial superior Courts have a constitutional existence. Since their existence is expressive of function, there has been from time to time reference in the case law to inherent jurisdiction." Laskin, 3rd rev. ed., at 789. However one assesses Laskin's logical connections between his particular example regarding appellate appeal and his general claim about "a guaranteed jurisdiction" and "a constitutional existence" for courts, he deduces his claim from a posited set of rules in contrast to Rand's notion of citizenship or the O'Halloran/Addy reliance upon history.

101 He mentions limitations such as constitutional amendment, British legislation which expressly or "by necessary intendment" extends to Canada, legislation with extraterritorial effect, the reservation of bills, the disallowance of legislation, succession to the throne, and the office of governor-general. See Laskin, "Note on Limitations on Legislative Power" in Laskin, 3rd rev. ed., at 70–1.

Laskin continues with other possible limitations to the legislative power such as the office of.lieutenant-governor, indirect taxation by the federal parliament for provincial purposes, inter-delegation as between parliament and provincial legislatures, the want of treaty implementing power, "the explicit guarantees" of section 93, later provisions regarding denominational schools (e.g., regarding Newfoundland), the use of French and English as protected by section 133, and Abbott's "implicit limitation against federal interference with freedom of debate and discussion in addition to the express limitation against provincial interference in that respect." (See Laskin, 3rd rev. ed., at 73–4.) But it is significant that Laskin does not list the 'independence of the courts' as an exception to his general principle of the exhaustive totality of legislative power. He merely mentions "the protected tenure of Judges under section 99, subject, however, to compulsory retirement at age 75" (Laskin, 3rd rev. ed., at 74). Furthermore, the limitations which Laskin does note flow from the silence or "gaps" on the subjects in the posited set of rules in the British North America Act, 1867 itself. The appropriate legislative institution can later fill in the gaps.

102 [1981] 1 SCR 714.

103 That is, "[o]ur Constitution does not separate the legislative, executive, and judicial functions and insist that each branch of government exercise only it own function. Thus it is clear that the Legislature of Ontario may confer non-judicial functions on the courts of Ontario and, subject to S. 96 of the B.N.A. Act, 1867 which lies at the heart of the present appeal, confer judicial functions on a body which is not a court." Ibid., at 728.

104 Ibid.

105 Ibid., at 734–6.
106 Ibid., at 748.
107 Hogg, supra note 64, at 161.
108 [1981] 1 SCR 714, at 735.
109 Ibid., at 750. Emphasis added.
110 [1938] 1 DLR 593.
111 "It is difficult to avoid the conclusion that whatever be the definition given to Court of Justice, or judicial power, the sections in question do purport to clothe the Board with the functions of a Court, and to vest in it judicial powers ... Their Lordships have found it unnecessary to discuss in detail how far some of the powers alleged to be judicial are in fact merely administrative." Ibid., at 595–6 (DLR).
112 [1938] SCR 398; [1938] 2 DLR 497 (SCC).
113 Ibid., at 512 (DLR). Emphasis added.
114 [1949] AC 134; [1948] 4 DLR 673.
115 Ibid., at 680 (DLR). Emphasis added.
116 Ibid.
117 Ibid., at 682.
118 For Laskin's full image of a constitution as a young scholar see text, infra, chap. IX.
119 Laskin, "Municipal Tax Assessment and Section 96 of the British North America Act: The Olympia Bowling Alleys Case" (1955), 33 Can. B. Rev. 993, at 996.
120 Ibid., at 999.
121 I consider Laskin's teaching materials (supra note 100) as representative of "Laskin the teacher." His image of a constitution embedded in his teaching materials departs in some respects from his image in his writings. The latter image is elaborated in text infra chap. IX.
122 Laskin, "Municipal Tax Assessment and Section 96 ...," at 1017.
123 [1981] 2 SCR 220, 127 DLR (3d) 1, 38 NR 541.
124 Ibid., at 237 SCR.
125 Ibid., at 238 SCR.
126 Ibid., at 237 SCR.
127 [1981] 2 SCR 413, 127 DLR (3d) 513.
128 Ibid., at 427 SCR.
129 In L'Atelier 7 Inc. v. Babin et al. (1983), 148 DLR (3d) 609, at 624, and overruled in [1983] 2 SCR 364 the Quebec Court of Appeal invalidates a provincially appointed board with authority very similar to that in Residential Tenancies. The "mark of a judicial power," according to Malouf J.A., is "the existence of a dispute between parties." In addition, "a court is called

upon to enforce a series of recogni[s]ed rules in an equitable and impartial manner." A court resolves a dispute about the litigants' rights rather than the general social welfare. Whereas the Court of Appeal holds that the Quebec Régie performs a judicial function, the Supreme Court of Canada observes that the Régie does not proceed "in the manner of a court." In any case, Chouinard finds historical evidence which demonstrates that a provincially appointed tribunal has had jurisdiction over lessor/lessee matters between 1821 and 1965.

130 *Re B.C. Family Relations Act*, [1982] 1 SCR 62.
131 Ibid., at 93.
132 Ibid., at 107.
133 Ibid.
134 Hogg, supra note 64, at 151.
135 *McEvoy v. A.-G. of N.B. and A.-G. Can.*, [1983] 1 SCR 704, at 718–19; (1983), 148 DLR (3d) 25, at 37: "It has long been the rule that s. 96, although in terms an appointing power, must be addressed *in functional terms* lest its application be eroded. What then, is the relation between the proposed new statutory Court and s. 96? This is *the key constitutional issue* in the present case ..." Emphasis added.

CHAPTER III

1 [1976] 2 SCR 265; (1975), 5 NR 43; 55 DLR (3d) 632.
2 Ibid., at 268.
3 Ibid., at 271.
4 Ibid., at 268.
5 [1938] SCR 100.
6 [1953] 2 SCR 299.
7 [1957] SCR 285.
8 [1981] 2 SCR 575; 130 DLR (3d) 588.
9 An abortion was authorized when the mother's life or health was endangered.
10 See supra chap. II, sect 2(b) and sect. 3(c).
11 Ibid., at 578–9 (SCR).
12 Ibid., at 587.
13 Ibid., at 578.
14 *Ref. re Amendment of the Constitution of Canada (Nos. 1, 2 and 3)*, [1981] 1 SCR 753, at 852, 125 DLR (3d) 1, 1 CPR 59.
15 [1975] 1 SCR 138, 43 DLR (3d) 1.
16 [1981] 2 SCR 575, at 593, quoting from *Thorson v. A.G. Can.*, [1975] 1 SCR 138, at 162–3; 43 DLR (3d) 1. Emphasis added.

17 [1986] 2 SCR 607.

18 Ibid., at 631a.

19 See text supra note 2.

20 [1986] 2 SCR 607, at 633b.

21 See text supra note 3.

22 [1986] 2 SCR 607, at 632.

23 See text supra note 4.

24 [1986] 2 SCR 607, at 633f–g.

25 *A.G. Ont.* v. *A.G. Can.* (Validity of References Case), [1912] AC 571, 3 DLR 509 (JCPC).

26 Ibid., at 582 (AC).

27 Ibid.

28 Ibid., at 252, 584. The Privy Council continued, "or of public confidence in it, or with the free access to an unbiased [sic] tribunal of appeal to which litigants in the provincial [c]ourts are of right entitled."

29 Ibid.

30 Ibid., at 583.

31 Ibid.

32 Ibid., at 582.

33 Ibid., at 588.

34 Ibid., at 589.

35 Ibid.

36 Ibid., at 583.

37 Ibid., at 584.

38 Ibid.

39 In holding the London Resolutions inadmissible, for example, the Privy Council once explained that "[t]he Courts were left largely with their tools of *logic* and *precedent*, with contemporary or past legislative comparisons, with such *rules* of construction as they chose to apply, with *dictionaries* and other *works of reference* and, above all, with *their own particular philosophies* of federalism in general and Canadian federalism in particular." *A.-G. Ont.* v. *Winner*, [1954] AC 541, as cited in Laskin, infra note 43, at 154. Emphasis added. Although "their own particular philosophies of federalism in general and Canadian federalism in particular" are "above all" important, they "would be more telling the more there was adherence to a principle of strict construction."

Similarly, the leading early essay on the subject of evidence in constitutional proceedings explains that "in the overwhelming majority of them [that is, BNA Act cases], the *ratio decidendi* depended on reasoning entirely divorced from external sources or references." Kennedy, "The British

North America Act: Past and Future" (1937), 15 *Can. B. Rev.* 393, at 394.
Quoted with approval in *Cairns Construction Ltd.* v. *Government of Saskat-chewan* (1958), 16 DLR (2d) 465, 27 WWR 297. For Kennedy's image of a
constitution see generally text infra chap. VIII.

Vincent C. MacDonald advocates the same approach two years later.
"Constitutional Interpretation and Extrinsic Evidence" (1939), 17 *Can.
B. Rev.* 77, esp. at 81. For MacDonald's image of a constitution see generally
text infra chap. VIII.

The Canadian courts adopt the same conclusion, at least until recently.
For early decisions see, e.g., *Gosselin* v. *The King* (1903), 33 SCR 255. Cf.
St. Catherines Milling & Lumber Co. v. *The Queen* (1886), 13 SCR 577, at 606–7
where Strong J., dissenting, holds that courts must have recourse to
external aids derived from the surrounding circumstances and the history
of the subject-matter. Without such assistance, "the task of interpretation
would degenerate into mere speculation and guess work."

In 1958, the Saskatchewan Court of Appeal expresses a rule rationalist
image in *Cairns Construction Ltd.* v. *Government of Saskatchewan* with the
effect of excluding the evidence of economists which has gone to the issue
of whether a particular tax is direct or indirect.

The definition of a tax is "now one of law" set down in a pre-established
rule independent of an economist's opinion, or for that matter, a judge's.
(1958), 16 DLR (2d) 465, 27 WWR 297. The Court adopts the conclusions of
Kennedy and MacDonald in supra notes 34 and 35.

In *Home Oil Distributors Ltd.* v. *A.G.B.C.*, Davis of the Supreme Court of
Canada goes so far as to suggest that "[i]t would be a dangerous course"
to admit extraneous material such as a royal commission report because,
quoting affirmatively from an 1852 text, the court "must endeavour to
attain for ourselves the *true* meaning of the language employed – in the
Article and Liturgy." [1940] SCR 444, at 452; [1940] 2 DLR 609 quoting
from *The Case of the Rev. G.C. Gorham against the Bishop of Exeter* per
Langdale (1852, PC) in Edmund F. Moore, *Special Report* (1952), at 462.

And in *Ref. re Validity of Wartime Leasehold Regulations* the Supreme Court
per Rinfret asserts that a reference is not "a proper case" to admit evidence
concerning the facts underlying an alleged emergency even though the
"facts" of an emergency authorize the use of the POGG power over otherwise valid provincial authority. [1950] SCR 124, [1950] 2 DLR 1.

40 [1976] 2 SCR 373, 68 DLR (3d) 452, 9 NR 541.
41 Ibid., at 467–8 (DLR).
42 Ibid., at 468.
43 *Canadian Constitutional Law*, 3rd rev. ed. (Toronto: Carswell 1969), at 152.

44 *Maher* v. *Town of Portland* [1874] PC in Laskin, ibid., at 153.

45 See quotation of *Winner* Court supra note 39.

46 *St. Catherines Milling & Lumber Co.* v. *The Queen* (1886), 13 SCR 577 in Laskin, supra note 43, at 155.

47 Laskin, ibid., at 186.

48 Ibid., at 188. Since Laskin's sentence is difficult to follow, I quote it in whole: "Apart from this, there is a problem of constitutional construction in Canada which, although related to, stands above the use of extrinsic materials in connection with impugned statutes; and that is whether the scope or content of the various heads of legislative power is broad or ample enough to make reliance on anything more than precedent and logic worth while in assessing the validity of legislation."

49 [1981] 1 SCR 714, 37 NR 158.

50 See text supra chap. II, sect. 3.

51 Ibid., at 721. Quoting from J.D. Whyte and W.R. Lederman, *Canadian Constitutional Law*, 2nd ed. (Toronto: Butterworths 1977), at 229. Emphasis added.

52 Ibid., at 723.

53 Parts II and III attempt to show why this enterprise would be irrational.

54 (1984) 53 NR 268, 8 DLR (4th) 1 (SCC).

55 Ibid., at 18 (DLR).

56 Ibid., at 19.

57 Ibid., at 19, quoting Dickson in *Re Residential Tenancies Act, 1979*, [1981] 1 SCR 714 at 721. For discussion of latter see supra, chap. II, sect. 3(a).

58 Ibid., at 19–20. Emphasis added.

59 [1930] AC 124.

60 (1984), 8 DLR (4th) 1 at 20.

61 Ibid.

62 See text infra chap. IV.

CHAPTER IV

1 *Ref. re Legislative Authority of Parliament of Canada*, [1980] 1 SCR 54; (1980), 102 DLR (3d) 1, 30 NR 271.

2 *Ref. re Amendment of the Constitution of Canada (Nos. 1, 2 and 3)*, [1981] 1 SCR 753, 125 DLR (3d) 1, 1 CPR 59.

3 *Re A.G. Que and A.G. Can.* (1983), 45 NR 317, 140 DLR (3d) 385.

4 Hereinafter cited as the Minority of Two.

5 Hereinafter cited as the Minority of Three.

6 A former clerk to Laskin suggests that the Majority of Seven "bears the

distinctive style and flare of Chief Justice Laskin." The Martland/Ritchie dissent possesses "the precise and logical flow of Mr. Justice Martland's writing." The Majority of Six "reflects the style and structure as well as the constitutional expertise of Mr. Justice Beetz." The dissenting judgment of Laskin, Estey, and McIntyre "once again has the ring of Chief Justice Laskin." See MacKay, "Judicial Process in the Supreme Court of Canada: The Patriation Reference and Its Implications for the *Charter of Rights*" (1983), 21 *Osgoode H.L.J.* 55, at 62, 63.

7 *Re A.G. Que and A.G. Can. (Que. Veto Ref.)*, [1982] 2 SCR 793; (1983), 45 NR 317, 140 DLR (3d) 385 (SCC).

8 Lederman, "The Supreme Court of Canada and Basic Constitutional Amendment" in Peter Russell, Robert Décary, William Lederman, Noel Lyon, and Dan Soberman, *The Court and the Constitution: Comments on the Supreme Court Reference on Constitutional Amendment* (Kingston: Institute of Intergovernmental Relations 1982), at 46–7 and discussed further in Lederman, "Canadian Constitutional Amending Procedures: 1867–1982" (1984), 32 *Amer. J. Compar. L.* 339, at 349.

I have paraphrased Lederman's first question. He adds another: "what kind of federal constitution is it [the constitution]?" This issue, I intend to show in Part II, cannot be raised or answered until one addresses the first question of constitutional law: what is one's image of a constitution?

For Lederman's image of a constitution, see generally text, *infra*, chap. x.

9 "Constitutional Theory and the Martland-Ritchie Dissent" in Peter Russell et al., *The Court and the Constitution*, at 57.

Also see Lyon's earlier essay which set out his claim more generally: "The Central Fallacy of Canadian Constitutional Law" (1976), 22 *McGill L.J.* 40.

For Lyon's image of a constitution, see generally text, *infra*, chap. IX.

10 "Law and Convention: A Peep behind the Patriation Case" in E.W. MacKay, ed., *The Canadian Charter of Rights: Law Practice Revolutionized* (Halifax: Dalhousie Law School 1982), at 30.

11 See generally text, *infra*, chap. VIII, sect. 2.

12 Indeed, it may well be that fact which explains what Peter Hogg describes as the "formal peculiarity" of the decision. The usual format would be for the four judges who signed the majority judgments on both issues to write a single opinion, with each of the remaining four judges agreeing or dissenting thereto. Instead, there are four opinions, two on each issue. See Hogg, "Comment" (1982), 60 *Can. B. Rev.* 307, at 313.

13 Lyon, "Constitutional Theory and the Martland-Ritchie Dissent," *supra* note 9, at 59.

14 *Ref. re Legislative Authority of Canada* [1980] 1 SCR 54, at 65–6, (1980) 102 DLR (3d) 1, 30 NR 271.

15 Ibid., at 67.

16 Ibid., at 77. Emphasis added.

17 Ibid.

18 *Ref. re Amendment of the Constitution of Canada (Nos. 1, 2 and 3)*, [1981] 1 SCR 753, 125 DLR (3d) 1, 1 CPR 59.

19 Actually, these are the third and second questions respectively in the actual framing of the reference questions. All judgments deal with them in reverse order, however.

20 [1981] 1 SCR 753, at 774–5; (1982) 125 DLR (3d) 1.

21 Ibid., at 783 (Majority of Seven). References will be to the Majority of Seven – that is, are conventions a matter of law? – unless otherwise stated.

22 Ibid., at 803.

23 Ibid., at 849 (Minority of Three).

24 Ibid., at 784.

25 Ibid., at 781.

26 Ibid., at 783.

27 Ibid., at 788.

28 Ibid., at 801.

29 Ibid., at 859 (Minority of Three).

30 Ibid., at 801.

31 Ibid., at 858 (Minority of Three). Emphasis added.

32 Ibid.

33 Ibid., at 852 (Minority of Three). Emphasis added.

34 Ibid., at 853–4 (Minority of Three).

35 Ibid., at 854 (Minority of Three).

36 Ibid., at 855 (Minority of Three), quoting from Dicey still.

37 Ibid., at 854.

38 See generally text, infra, chap. VIII.

39 Ibid., at 856 (Minority of Three).

40 Ibid., at 775. Emphasis added.

41 Ibid., at 783.

42 Ibid., at 788.

43 Ibid., at 849.

44 Ibid., at 856.

45 Ibid., at 873.

46 Ibid., at 858.

47 Ibid., at 803.

48 Ibid., at 804. Emphasis added.

49 Ibid., at 808.
50 Ibid., at 853.
51 Ibid., at 873.
52 Ibid.
53 Ibid., at 842.
54 Ibid., at 826.
55 Ibid., at 830.
56 Ibid., at 831. Emphasis added.
57 Ibid., at 841.
58 Ibid., at 844–5.
59 Ibid., at 880.
60 Ibid.
61 Ibid., at 874.
62 Ibid., at 880.
63 Ibid., at 878.
64 Ibid., at 883.
65 Ibid., at 880–1.
66 Ibid., at 821.
67 Ibid.
68 Ibid., at 836.
69 Ibid., at 840.
70 Ibid., at 841.
71 Ibid.
72 Ibid., at 848.
73 Ibid., at 877. Emphasis added.
74 See text supra note 56.
75 Ibid. Emphasis added.
76 Ibid., at 883.
77 Ibid., at 884.
78 Ibid., at 881.
79 Ibid., at 880–1.
80 Ibid., at 883.
81 *Re A.G. Que and A.G. Can. (Que. Veto Ref.)*, [1982] 2 SCR 793; (1983), 45 NR 317, 140 DLR (3d) 385.
82 Ibid., at 816g. Emphasis added.
83 Ibid., quoting W. Ivor Jennings, *The Law and the Constitution*, 5th ed. (London: University of London Press 1959), at 816b–e, and affirmed in the *Patriation Reference* [1981] 1 SCR 753, at 888. Emphasis added.
84 Ibid., at 815h. Emphasis added.
85 Ibid., at 816c–d.

86 Ibid., at 803a.
87 Ibid., at 816i.
88 Ibid., at 803a.

CHAPTER V

1 RSC 1970, Appendix III, as am. SC 1970–71–72, c. 38, s. 29.
2 *R.* v. *Drybones*, [1970] SCR 282.
3 After reviewing the restrictive interpretation of s. 1(b) of the Canadian Bill of Rights over the years, Dickson resignedly acknowledges in *Queen* v. *Beauregard* [1986] 2 SCR 56, at 90d that "I believe the day has passed when it might have been appropriate to re-evaluate those concerns and to reassess the direction this Court has taken in interpreting that document." Similarly, Dickson gives minimal effect to the Bill in *PSAC* v. *Canada* [1987] 1 SCR 424, at 451f–j when he leaves it open as to whether s. 1(b) of the Bill might not even require "some rational explanation for the legislative focus ..."

   Only Beetz and Wilson seem to give the Bill sufficiently wide scope and effect as to render legislation inoperative. See, e.g., *Queen* v. *Beauregard* [1986] 2 SCR 56, at 100–21 per Beetz and *PSAC* v. *Canada* [1987] 1 SCR 424, at 458d–e per Wilson.
4 See, e.g., Government of Canada, *The Constitutional Amendment Bill: Text and Explanatory Notes* (Ottawa: Information Canada 1978), at 4; idem, *The Constitutional Amendment Bill, 1978: Explanatory Document* (Ottawa: Information Canada 1978), at 8–12; idem, *A Time for Action: Highlights of the Federal Government's Proposals for the Renewal of the Canadian Federation* (Ottawa: Information Canada 1978), at 2, 9.

   Also see, e.g., idem, *Proposal for a Constitutional Charter of Human Rights* (Ottawa: Queen's Printer 1968); idem, *The Constitution and the People of Canada* (Ottawa: Queen's Printer 1969), at 16, 18; Special Joint Committee of Senate and House of Commons on Constitution of Canada, *Final Report*, 4th sess., 28th Parl. (Ottawa: Information Canada 1972), at 18–19.
5 See, e.g., Hogg, "A Comparison of the Canadian Charter of Rights and Freedoms with the Canadian Bill of Rights" in Walter S. Tarnopolsky and Gerald A. Beaudoin, eds., *The Canadian Charter of Rights and Freedoms: Commentary* (Toronto: Carswell 1982).
6 See, e.g., Tarnopolsky, "The Canadian Bill of Rights and the Supreme Court Decisions in Lavell and Burnshine: A Retreat from Drybones to Dicey?" (1974), 7 *Ott. L. Rev.* 1.
7 See, e.g., Conklin and Ferguson, "The Burnshine Affair: Whatever

Happened to Drybones and Equality before the Law?" (1974), 22 *Chitty's L.J.* 303; Hogg, "Comment" (1974), 52 *Can. B. Rev.* 264.

8 Supra note 1, s. 2. Emphasis added.

9 Ibid., s. 5(2).

10 Ibid. Emphasis added.

11 [1970] SCR 282, 9 DLR (3d) 473.

12 In *R.* v. *Reale*, e.g., the Ontario Court of Appeal reconsiders the common law right of an accused to be present at his own trial because of the Bill's enactment, (1973), 13 CCC (2d) 345 (Ont. CA), *aff'd* by Sup. Ct. Can. in [1975] 2 SCR 624; (1974), 5 NR 169 (7 to 2 with Grandpré and Judson dissenting).

13 [1972] SCR 889, 18 CR (NS) 281, 7 CCC (2d) 181, 26 DLR (3d) 603.

14 [1972] SCR 926, 18 CR (NS) 308, 7 CCC (2d) 417, 28 DLR (3d) 1.

15 *Singh et al.* v. *M.E.I.* [1985] 1 SCR 177, at 228.

16 *R.* v. *Miller and Cockriell* [1977] 2 SCR 680, [1976] 5 WWR 711, 38 CR (NS) 139, 31 CCC (2d) 177, 70 DLR (3d) 324.

17 [1970] SCR 282, 9 DLR (3d) 473.

18 Ibid., at 305–6 SCR, 491 DLR. Emphasis added.

19 Ibid., at 306.

20 Ibid.

21 Of course, it is not. For more important constituents of the principle of legislative supremacy, see generally Conklin, "Pickin and Its Applicability to Canada" (1975), 25 *U. Tor. L.J.* 193.

22 [1974] SCR 1349, at 1390.

23 [1975] 1 SCR 693; (1974), 44 DLR (3d) 584.

24 [1976] 1 SCR 171; (1975), 52 DLR (3d) 548.

25 [1970] SCR 282, 9 DLR (3d) 473.

26 Ibid., at 299 SCR, 477 DLR. Emphasis added.

27 See text infra note 53.

28 [1974] SCR 1349, 11 RFL 333, 23 CR (NS) 197, 38 DLR (3d) 481.

29 [1977] 2 SCR 680, [1976] 5 WWR 711, 38 CR (NS) 139, 31 CCC (2d) 177, 70 DLR (3d) 324; *aff'g* [1975] 6 WWR 1, 33 CR (NS) 129, 24 CCC (2d) 401, 63 DLR (3d) 193 (BCCA).

30 "To suggest that the provisions of the *Bill of Rights* have the effect of making the whole *Indian Act* inoperative as discriminatory is to assert that the Bill *has rendered Parliament powerless* to exercise the authority entrusted to it under the constitution of enacting legislation which treats Indians living on Reserves differently from other Canadians in relation to their property and civil rights." [1974] SCR 1349, at 1359. Emphasis added.

Ritchie goes on to return approvingly to the *Drybones dicta* of Pigeon that

If one of the effects of the *Canadian Bill of Rights* is to render inoperative all legal provisions whereby Indians as such are not dealt with in the same way as the general public, the conclusion is inescapable that Parliament ... has also made any future use of federal legislative authority over them [i.e., Indians] subject to the requirement of expressly declaring every time "that the law shall operate notwithstanding the *Canadian Bill of Rights*." *I find it very difficult to believe ... one would have expected this important change to be made explicitly not surreptitiously so to speak.*
Ibid., at 1361–2, quoting Pigeon in [1970] SCR 282, at 304. Emphasis added. Ritchie then uses this dictum to rebut the contention that judges should employ the Canadian Bill of Rights to override special legislation. Ibid., at 1361.

31 One can trace this notion back to Ritchie's judgment in *Robertson and Rosetanni v. The Queen*, [1963] SCR 651, at 654ff., to Pigeon's dissenting opinion in *R. v. Drybones*, [1970] SCR 282, at 305, and to Ritchie's judgment in *Curr v. The Queen*, [1972] SCR 889. The "frozen meaning" doctrine is approved and applied in *A.G. Canada v. Lavell*, [1974] SCR 1349, per Ritchie, and in *The Queen v. Burnshire*, [1975] 1 SCR 693, per Martland as well as in *R. v. Miller and Cockriell*, [1977] 2 SCR 680, per Ritchie.

For some problems with the 'frozen meaning' doctrine see generally Conklin and Ferguson, "The Burnshine Affair: Whatever Happened to Drybones and Equality before the Law?" supra note 7, at 305–7.

32 [1977] 2 SCR 680, [1976] 5 WWR 711.

33 Ibid., at 704 SCR, 715 WWR.

34 Ibid., at 704 SCR, 716 WWR. Of course, the prime minister who introduced the Canadian Bill of Rights into Parliament stated that he did so precisely because Canadian courts and common law rights had failed to protect the individual. He expressly mentioned the internment and deportation of Japanese Canadians by Order-in-Council during and after the Second World War. See Hansard (1960), vol. 6, at 5942 and vol. 7, at 7544 (Diefenbaker). Furthermore, the preamble to the Bill clearly infers that Parliament believed the common law had inadequately protected the rights and freedoms: "And being desirous of *enshrining* these principles and the human rights and fundamental freedoms derived from them, in a Bill of Rights *which shall ... ensure the protection* of these rights and freedoms in Canada." Emphasis added. Finally, if the Bill did not purport to create some new rights why did Parliament find it necessary to "recognise" their existence as well as to "declare" existence?

35 [1977] 2 SCR 680, at 705–6; [1976] 5 WWR 711, at 717.

36 [1980] 2 SCR 370, 54 CCC (2d) 129, 114 DLR (3d) 393.

37 Infra note 42.
38 See note 36, at 393 SCR, 148 CCC, 412 DLR.
39 Ibid., at 394 SCR, 148 CCC, 413 DLR.
40 [1975] 1 SCR 693, at 705. Emphasis added.
41 Ibid., at 707. Emphasis added.
42 [1972] SCR 889.
43 [1975] 1 SCR 693.
44 [1972] SCR 889, at 899. Emphasis added.
45 Ibid., at 902. Emphasis added.
46 [1975] 1 SCR 693, at 714. Emphasis added.
47 *Morgentaler v. The Queen* [1976] 1 SCR 616.
48 Ibid., at 635. Emphasis added.
49 Ibid., at 636.
50 [1976] 1 SCR 170.
51 Ibid., at 184.
52 Some of the common law's dominant jurists – Bracton, Coke, Blackstone, Austin, and Dicey – share this apolitical image of the court. See generally Conklin, "The Utilitarian Theory of Equality before the Law" (1976), 8 *Ott. L. Rev.* 485, at fn. 10–16.
53 [1974] SCR 1349.
54 Ibid., at 1366.
55 Ibid. Emphasis added. Beetz notes in *R. v. Beauregard* [1986] 2 SCR 56, at 107 that Ritchie applied a broader test in later cases. Of five equality cases after *Burnshire*, only one alludes to Dicey's 'formal equality' doctrine. Ibid., at 106.
56 [1975] 1 SCR 693.
57 Ibid., at 705.
58 Ibid. Emphasis added.
59 Pigeon similarly imputed the adjective 'existing.' See supra notes 16–18.
60 [1974] SCR 1349.
61 For an explanation of the doctrine see generally in William E. Conklin, *In Defence of Fundamental Rights* (Alphen aan den Rijn/Germantown, Md.: Sijthoff & Noordhof 1979), at 103–22, esp. fn. 130. For Commonwealth experiences see Conklin, "The Role of Third World Courts during Alleged Emergencies" in M.L.A. Marasinghe and William E. Conklin, eds., *Essays on Third World Perspectives in Jurisprudence* (Singapore: Malayan Law Journal 1984).
62 For a recent example, see, e.g., *Queen v. Beauregard* [1986] 2 SCR 56, at 110i–111b per Beetz. For American and Canadian examples see the

references in Conklin, "The Utilitarian Theory of Equality before the Law," supra note 52, at fn. 66–74.

63 The majority of the Supreme Court has maintained this minimal rationalization process after the Bill's demise. See, e.g., *PSAC* v. *Canada* [1987] 1 SCR 424, at 451i. In *The Queen* v. *Beauregard* [1986] 2 SCR 56, at 90a–b, Dickson insists that the "short history of 'equality before the law' under s. 1(b) of the *Canadian Bill of Rights* demonstrates that a majority of the Court was never prepared to review impugned legislation according to an exacting standard which would demand of Parliament the most carefully tailored, finely crafted legislation." After asserting, without argument, that he can see "no objection" to the legislative role, Dickson maintains at 91a–c that "[o]nce it is accepted that the general substance of the law is consistent with the valid federal objective ... and that it is not discriminatory to draw some line ... I do not think the jurisprudence I have summarized above allows the courts to be overly critical in reviewing the precise line drawn ..."

64 [1975] 1 SCR 693.

65 Ibid., at 698 quoting Judson J. in *Turcotte* v. *The Queen* [1970] SCR 843 and restated "to seek to reform and benefit persons within that younger age group" at 707.

66 Ibid., at 707.

67 Ibid., quoting Laskin in *Curr* v. *The Queen*, [1972] SCR 889, at 899.

68 [1979] 1 SCR 183.

69 Ibid., at 192.

70 Ibid., at 192, 193.

71 Since the demise of the Canadian Bill of Rights in the late 1970s, our judges understand "validity" of the legislative purpose in terms of a justifiable social policy. This widens the sorts of considerations which may be used to justify "validity." See, e.g., *The Queen* v. *Beauregard* [1986] 2 SCR 56, at 90h–j per Dickson and *PSAC* v. *Canada* [1986] 2 SCR 56, at 90h–j per Dickson, and *PSAC* v. *Canada* [1987] 1 SCR 56, at 451i per Dickson. Of course, the shift in understanding "validity" from the rules of s. 91–92 to the social policies embedded in a statute coincides with the policy rationalist image of a constitution identified infra chap. IX.

72 [1970] SCR 282.

73 Ibid., at 306.

74 [1974] SCR 1349.

75 Ibid., at 1358. "[W]herever any question arises as to the effect of any of the provisions of the Bill, it is to be resolved within the framework of the *B.N.A. Act*. It follows, in my view, that the effect of the *Bill of Rights* on the

Indian Act can only be considered in light of the provisions of s. 91(24) of the *B.N.A. Act.*"

76 [1975] 1 SCR 693, at 707–8.

77 [1976] 1 SCR 170.

78 Ibid., at 205. Beetz proceeds to interpret *Lavell* in terms of the "validity" of Parliament's objective vis-à-vis the higher ordered rule in section 91 (24) of the British North America Act, 1867. The "Constitution" is the British North America Act. The rules in the British North America Act (s. 91(24)) "solely" authorize Parliament to bestow upon a federal minister, rather than a provincial surrogate court, the power to appoint an administrator to the estate of a deceased Indian. If the Canadian Bill of Rights – or, for that matter, the principles embedded in our history which, according to the court, the Bill restates – modifies that authority in any manner, "such a consequence would be tantamount to an amendment of *The British North America Act, 1867.*" Ibid., at 210. The logic is sound, but only if one accepts the boundary of a hierarchy of posited rules.

79 He suggests that the Bill itself has been enacted in order "to 'reflect the respect of Parliament for its constitution,'" [1976] 1 SCR 170, at 191. Since the British North America Acts constitutes the whole of 'the Constitution,' Ritchie explains, "I cannot believe that the special Indian status so clearly recognized in the *British North America Act* is to be whittled away without express legislation being passed by the Parliament of Canada to that effect." Ibid., at 191–2. Ritchie "could not believe it" because his straightforward image of a constitution does not allow him to do so. But his logical deduction from that image makes the very enactment of the Bill redundant.

80 (1979) 1 SCR 183, at 190. Section 91(2A) has "imposed on Parliament" the responsibility of discharging a scheme of unemployment insurance. The federal objective in the legislative rule at issue is valid because the British North America Act authorizes it. Accordingly, because the objective is valid, "[a]ny inequality between the sexes in this area *is not created by legislation but by nature.*" Emphasis added.

81 [1980] 2 SCR 370. In this case, section 91(7) has authorized the National Defence Act which, in turn, has created the rule allegedly conflicting with the Bill. Given the premise that the British North America Act rules constitute the whole of the Constitution (along with the boundaries of a passive self-image and apolitical law), "this is obviously legislation enacted for the purpose of achieving a valid federal objective." Also see text infra chap. VIII.

82 (1980) 2 SCR 370, at 393.

83 Ibid., at 393–4. Emphasis added.

CHAPTER VI

1 [1981] 1 SCR 753.
2 (1982), 1 CRR 298, at 304; 37 OR (2d) 189, at 199; 136 DLR (3d) 69, at 75.
3 Ibid., at 305, 199 OR, 76 DLR. Emphasis added.
4 Ibid., at 306, 200–1 OR, 77 DLR. Emphasis added.
5 R. v. Gallant (1983), 2 CRR 144, at 150.
6 See, e.g., R. v. Homier (1983), 2 CRR 215, at 220 per Hay (Ont. Prov. Ct.); R. v. Mills (1983), 2 CRR 300, at 310 per Baker (Ont. Prov. Ct.); R. v. Currie (1984), 5 CRR 339, at 344–5 per MacDonald (NSCA); Rolbin v. The Queen (1983), 2 CRR 166, at 171 per Boilard (Que. Sup. Ct.); R. v. Altseimer (1983), 2 CRR 119, at 124; 38 OR (2d) 783, at 788 per Zuber (CA).
7 (1983), 41 OR (2d) 225, at 244; 145 DLR (3d) 638, at 658 (CA). Emphasis added.
8 (1983), 38 OR (2d) 783, at 788; 2 CRR 119, at 124.
9 Ibid. Emphasis added.
10 See, e.g., Rolbin v. The Queen (1982), s CRR 166, at 170 per Boilard (Que. Sup. Ct.); P.P.G. Industries Can. Ltd. v. A.-G. of Canada (1983), 4 CRR 193, at 202; 42 BCLR 334, at 345; 146 DLR (3d) 261, at 274 per Seaton (dissenting) (BCCA); Re T.L.W. (1984), 5 CRR 241, at 245–6 per Nevins (Ont. Prov. Ct.); R. v. W.; R. v. L. (1983), 1 CCC (3d) 268, at 272 per Vogelsang (Ont. Prov. Ct.); R. v. Carter (1984), 18 MVR 9, at 13 per Brooke (Ont. CA); R. v. Santa (1984), 6 CRR 244, at 251 per King (Sask. Prov. Ct.). An Ontario County Court "fully considered the very serious message" of Zuber in Re U.S.A. and Copses (1983), 4 CRR 3, at 14–15. Also see Zuber (dissenting) in R. v. Duguay, Murphy and Sevigny (1986), 17 CRR 203, at 219–20 (Ont. CA).
11 (1982), 2 CRR 156.
12 Ibid., at 164. Emphasis added.
13 Ref. Re Public Service Employee Relations Act, Labour Relations Act and Police Officers Collective Bargaining Act, [1985] 2 WWR 289, at 301, 35 Alta. L.R. (2d) 124, at 136.
14 (1983), 8 CCC (3d) 33, at 35; 3 DLR (4th) 361 (Man. CA).
15 Ibid., at 363. Emphasis added.
16 Reynolds v. A.G. B.C. (1984), 52 BCLR 394, at 399–400.
17 R. v. Therens, [1985] 1 SCR 613, at 645. Emphasis added.
18 Re Ont. Film and Video Appreciation Soc., and Ont. Bd. of Censors (1983), 41 OR (2d) 583, at 592 (Div. Ct.).
19 [1985] 1 CTC 246, 57 NR 386 (FCA).

20 See, e.g., *Ref. Res. 12(1) of Juvenile Delinquents Act* (1982), 29 RFL (2d) 1, at 9 per Smith (Ont. HC): "[I]n my view, sovereignty of Parliament has been dealt a mild blow. The courts and Parliament are no longer the repositories of constitutional law rights. The *Charter* will prevail subject only to the non-obstante provisions in s. 33 of the *Charter*."

21 [1984] 3 WWR 481, 10 DLR (4th) 198 (BCCA).

22 Ibid., at 490, 207 DLR.

23 Ibid., at 491, 208 DLR.

24 Ibid., at 491–2, 208 DLR. Emphasis added in previous quotations.

25 Ibid., at 495, 211 DLR.

26 (1983), 41 OR (2d) 113.

27 Ibid., at 130. Emphasis added.

28 *R.* v. *Coombs* (1987), 22 CRR 374, at 383.

29 See text supra chap. v.

30 (1982), 38 OR (2d) 705, at 717; 2 CRR 131, at 143; 141 DLR (3d) 412, at 425 (HC). The Court then uses an objectivist test to describe the rule's purpose: it is a purpose "which members of a free and democratic society such as Canada would accept and embrace." See text infra sect. 1(d).

31 *Germain* v. *The Queen* (1985), 10 CRR 232, at 241–2 (Alta. QB). Emphasis added.

32 *Service Employees Internat. Union Local 204* v. *Broadway Manor Nursing Home et al.* (1985), 10 CRR 37, at 114 (Ont. Div. Ct.).

33 *R.* v. *Duguay, Murphy and Sevigny* (1986), 17 CRR 203, at 219.

34 The word "disgusting" is one such word. Both the tests for criminal conduct and the test for "law" in s. 1 of the Charter require "objective" criteria. See, e.g., *R.* v. *Glassman and Bogyo* (1987), 24 CCC 242, at 254–5 per Harris (Ont. Prov. Ct.).

35 And an "association," he thinks, can be equated with neither the purpose of an association nor the means (such as picketing) by which the association achieves its purpose. [1984] 3 WWR 481, 10 DLR (4th) 198 (BCCA).

36 (1986), 17 CRR 334, at 342 (BC Youth Ct.).

37 Ibid., at 343.

38 (1986), 17 CRR 117, at 125 (BC Prov. Ct.).

39 (1983), 4 CRR 193, 42 BCLR 334, 146 DLR (3d) 261 (BCCA).

40 Ibid. at 201, 344 BCLR, 273 DLR.

41 *R.* v. *Altseimer* (1983), 2 CRR 119, at 124; (1982), 38 OR (2d) 783, at 788 (Ont. CA), as discussed in text supra at notes 7–8.

42 (1984), 4 CRR 88.

43 Ibid., at 92.

44 *R.* v. *Linklater* (1983) 4 CRR 179. Emphasis added. Dictionaries aid in the

discovery of the plain meaning of Charter rights. See, e.g., *Re Application for Order under s. 466(1) of the Code* (1987), 22 CRR 282, at 288–9.

45 *Joplin* v. *Chief Constable of the City of Vancouver et al.* (1983), 4 CRR 208, at 212.

46 See text supra subsection 1(c).

47 *Re Edmonton Journal and A.-G. for Alta. et al.* (1983), 4 CRR 296.

48 Ibid., at 302. Emphasis added.

49 (1985), 10 CRR 37.

50 Ibid., at 54.

51 Ibid. Emphasis added.

52 Ibid., at 55. Emphasis added.

53 Ibid., at 56.

54 Finch of the British Columbia Supreme Court has this in mind when he suggests that "liberty must derive its meaning from an examination of every case where s. 7 is called in aid. Only in finding case by case the conduct which lies within or without its protection, will the great concept of liberty take on practical meaning." *R.* v. *Robson* (1984), 11 CRR 206, at 211. Along the same lines, McDonald follows such a process of citation to support the immutable definition of 'liberty' and 'security of the person' in *R.* v. *Neale,* (1986), 17 CRR 282, at 290–9 (Alta. QB). In *R.* v. *Leclerc* (1983), 1 CCC (3d) 422, at 427 (Que. SC), Savoie takes judicial notice of "the fact" that Canada is a free and democratic society. That "fact" provides the framework to justify a reversal of the onus of proof.

55 (1983), 41 OR (2d) 113, at 124. Emphasis added. Similarly, in *R.* v. *S.B.* (1983), 1 CCC (3d) 73, at 81–2 (BCSC), Bouck explains that subjectivist explanations for the Charter's meaning have not been well received in history and are not particularly convincing. One can steer away from the subjectivist trap, he thinks by studying how other societies have limited rights.

56 In *Southam,* supra n. 49, the Court reviews the practice at issue in the United States, Australia, New Zealand, and the United Kingdom. In *National Citizens' Coalition* v. *A.G. Can.,* [1984] 5 WWR 436, 11 DLR (4th) 481, the Alberta Queen's Bench makes particular reference to the experience in the United States. In *Canadian Newspapers Co.* v. *A.G. Can.* (1985), 49 OR (2d) 557, 44 CR (3d) 97, the Ontario Court of Appeal studies, legislation in four Australian states, the United Kingdom, New Zealand, and the United States. In reading the first 16 volumes of the CRR one is hard-pressed to find a judge who has varied from the Big Four. One recent judgment serves as an exception. See *Black* v. *Law Society of Alta.* (1986), 20 CRR 117, per Kerans (Alta. CA).

57 (1983), 4 CRR 193, at 207; 42 BCLR 334, at 351; 146 DLR (3d) 261, at 279. Emphasis added.

58 (1983), 38 OR (2d) 705, at 715; 2 CRR 131, at 141; 141 DLR (3d) 412, at 423 per Evans (HC). Emphasis added. Auxier applies this objectivist test in *Shewchuk* v. *Ricard* (1986), 17 CRR 117, at 125.

59 (1983), 3 CCC (3d) 147 (Man. QB) where Scollin has to ascertain the meaning of "would bring the administration of justice into disrepute" in s. 24(2) of the Charter.

60 *Re Retail Dept. Store Union and Gov't of Sask.* (1985), 10 CRR 1, at 13, for example.

61 (1984), 5 CRR 1 (BCCA).

62 Ibid., at 10. Emphasis added.

63 See, e.g., *R.* v. *Leemhuis* (1985), 11 CRR 337, at 343–4 (BC Co. Ct.).

64 *Que. Assn. of Protestant School Bds.* v. *A.G. Que. (No. 2)* (1983), 140 DLR (3d) 33, at 77 (Que. SC).

65 Ibid., at 90.

66 See text supra sect. 1(b).

67 *R.* v. *Robinson* (1984), 5 CRR 25, at 28 per Boland (Ont. HC).

68 *Service Employees' International Union, Local 204* v. *Broadway Manor Nursing Home et al.* (1985), 10 CRR 37, at 65 (Ont. Div. Ct.). Emphasis added.

69 Galligan insists that judges should presume that the politicians "have not acted capriciously, selfishly, arbitrarily or with ulterior motives." Politicians act with "honestly held opinions of what is for the common good." Indeed, he states, "I can think of no reason why legislators cannot be considered to have acted rationally when they enact legislation." Ibid., at 66.

70 As one judge in *Broadway Manor* puts it, "[t]he Court is not concerned with the question of whether the political judgment was right or wrong regarding which one of the many available solutions or measures was the most appropriate. The electorate will be the judge." Ibid., at 117–18 per Smith. In *R.* v. *Morgentaler* (1986), 17 CRR 223, at 249, the Ontario Court of Appeal reiterates that "it is not the role of the courts to pass on the policy or wisdom of legislation. That is a matter for Parliament and the Legislatures of the provinces." One such "policy" matter concerns a woman's right to terminate her pregnancy, at what stage and subject to what safeguards. Also see *Qually* v. *Qually* (1987), 5 RFL (3d) 365, at 370, where Dickson (Sask. CA) cautions against the expansion of the Charter's rights beyond their objective meaning: "[t]he words of Parliament [*sic* the Charter] must be given their ordinary meaning, not some fanciful and imaginative scope that would encourage resourceful counsel and sympathetic judges to make up whatever deficiency they perceive in the existing list of protected

rights. Security of the person means no more than a right to physical security."

71 *R. v. McKinlay Transport Ltd. et al.* (1987), 22 CRR 219, at 229.

72 *Re Latham and Sol. Gen. of Can. et al.* (1985), 10 CRR 120, at 131.

73 (1985), 12 CRR 45, at 57.

74 Ibid., at 59.

75 Martin expresses the balancing process in this manner: "The criminal justice system in free and democratic societies involves a constant quest to find and maintain a proper balance between the competing interests of effective law enforcement and the right of the individual to be free from unwarranted intrusion by the State and to be secure from abuse of power; a balance which is difficult to achieve and difficult to maintain." *R. v. Noble* (1984), 48 OR (2d) 643, at 661; 14 DLR (4th) 216, at 234. Also see *R. v. Rao* (1984), 46 OR (2d) 80, at 106–7; 9 DLR (4th) 542, at 567–9; *Re Southam Inc. and the Queen (No. 1)* (1983), 41 OR (2d) 113, at 130; *Re New Garden Restaurant and Tavern Ltd. et al. & Min. Nat. Revenue* (1984), 43 OR (2d) 417 (H. Ct.); *Thomson Newspapers Ltd. v. Dir. of Investigation and Research* (1986), 21 CRR 1 (Ont. HC), at 15–16 per Holland.

76 (1984), 43 OR (2d) 596, at 598.

77 Ibid.

78 (1983), 8 CCC (3d) 153, at 166; *aff'd* (1984), 10 CCC (3d) 573 (BCCA). Also see *Re Cromier and B.C. Teachers Fed'n* (1987), 24 CRR 271, at 286–91 per Lambert (BCAA) where, after setting out a universalist, non-positivist theory of the Charter (at 284–5), Lambert insists that freedom of expression triggers a balancing of social interests.

79 *R. v. Kresanoski* (1985), 58 AR 377 (QB). Also see *Re Cromier and B.C. Teachers Federation* (1987), 24 CRR 271, at 286–91 per Lambert (BCCA).

80 *Re R. and Beason* (1984), 43 OR (2d) 65; 7 CRR 65 (CA).

81 Ibid., at 79 OR, 79 CRR 65. Also see *Christie v. The Queen* (1986), 20 CRR 358, at 360 per MacDonald (PEISC).

82 *Re State of Wisconsin and Armstrong* (1973), 10 CCC (2d) 271, at 297–8; 32 DLR (3d) 265, at 291–2. Quoted at length and affirmed in *Re U.S.A. and Green* (1983) 42 OR (2d) 325, at 330–2 per Van Camp (HC). Also see *Re Howard and Presiding Officer of Inmate Disciplinary Court of Stony Mountain Institution* (1986), 17 CRR 5, 34 (FCA), where MacGuigan suggests that there is a "sliding standard" of "fundamental justice" varying with the "particular degree of liberty at stake and the particular procedural safeguard in question." This scale "may involve the balancing of competing interests."

83 *R. v. Bryant* (1985), 11 CRR 219, at 225 per Blair.

84 (1984), 11 CRR 302, at 306 (Ont. HC). The Court of Appeal in *Rauca* similarly

prefaces its balancing exercise with "[in] approaching the question *objectively*, it is recognized that the listed rights and freedoms are never absolute and that there are always qualifications and limitations to allow for the protection of other competing interests in a democratic society." (1983), 41 OR (2d) 225, at 241; 145 DLR (3d) 638, at 655. Emphasis added.

85 *Ford* c. *P.G. Du Québec*, [1985] CS 147, at 159 per Boudreault.

86 [1984] 5 WWR 436, at 453, 11 DLR (4th) 481, at 496 per Medhurst.

87 The concept seems to have first taken hold in *A.-G. N.S. et al. v. MacIntyre*, [1982] 1 SCR 175, at 186–7 per Dickson and followed in *Re Southam Inc. and The Queen*, (1984), 48 OR (2d) 678, at 696 (HC); *Re Southam Inc. and The Queen (No. 1)* (1983), 41 OR (2d) 113, at 121 per MacKinnon (CA); and *Can. Newspapers Co. v. A.G. Can.* (1985), 49 OR (2d) 557, at 576 per Howland (CA).

88 *R. v. Oakes* [1986] 1 SCR 103. See generally text, chap. VII infra, between notes 92 and 100.

89 (1986) 22 CRR 66, at 83 (BCCA), quoting from *Oakes*, supra. Also see *Badger v. A.-G. Man.* (1986), 21 CRR 277 (Man. QB) at 284 where Scollin holds section 31(d) of the Elections Act, R.S. Man. 1980 unconstitutional in that it disqualifies persons from voting in provincial elections, contrary to section 3 of the Charter. The blanket disqualification of every prisoner even disqualifies persons imprisoned for an inadvertent commission of an absolute liability offence. Thus, there is a lack of a rational connection between the absolute disqualification and the unexpressed purpose "of preserving the currency of the franchise and both symbolically and practically stigmatizing those who deliberately breach their duty to society" (at 283). The critical point for our purposes is that the lower courts, with one exception (see infra note 91), do not explain why any given legislative objective is of "pressing and substantial importance." Nor can they, without going beyond the given posited objective or their own subjective political preferences. Such an inquiry taking them into unfamiliar terrain, lower court judges accept the posited ends as a 'given.' They then scientifically refine the means legislated to accomplish the given end. Also see *Ref. Re Yukon Election Residency Requirements* (1987), 22 CRR 193, at 196–7 (Yukon CA), per Nemetz, and *Shewchuk v. Ricard* (1987), 24 CRR 45, at 64 per Macfarlane (BCCA).

90 Also see *Re Fraser and A.-G. N.S.* (1987), 24 CRR 193, where Grant (NSSC, TD), at 210–12, grounds the "sufficient importance" and "pressing and substantial" importance of the objective of legislation restricting political activities of a public servant in "I am satisfied" and "I consider." Neither argument nor evidence is offered as to *why* the restrictive legislation is so

"pressing and substantial." Grant then assesses the rational connection of the means to the given objective by ushering forth the similar existent restrictions of political freedoms in other provinces (see 213–19), Great Britain (221–2), the United States (222), and the Kernaghan Report (223–5). What is ought to be.

91 *Black* v. *Law Soc. Alta.* (1986) 20 CRR 117 (Alta. CA), per Kerans esp. at 143–8.

92 As Marshall expresses it in *R.* v. *Fatt* (1987), 24 CRR 259, at 269 (NWTSC), "[t]his case then raises quite serious questions as well in regard to court policy, the policy of this court, and the question of the degree of recognition to be given to cultural pluralism, in the context of aboriginal communities in the Arctic ... Values and conceptions ultimately beget custom, and finally law ..." Similarly, in *Baxter* v. *Baxter* (1984), 36 RFL (2d) 186, at 189, Pennell (Ont. HC) explains that all family law derives from the "public policy" which fixes the status of the marriage transaction as a civil contract. Given that policy, all else flows including the scope of "freedom of conscience and religion."

93 See, e.g., *Collins* v. *R.* (1982), 31 CR (3d) 283 (Ont. Co. Ct.); *Black* v. *Law Soc. of Alta.* (1984), 22 *Alta. L.R.* (2d) 214, 13 DLR (4th) 436 (QB); *Re Ont. Film and Video Appreciation Soc., and Ont. Bd. of Censors* (1983), 41 OR (2d) 583, 147 DLR (3d) 58 (Div. Ct.); *aff'd* (1984), 45 OR (2d) 80, 5 DLR (4th) 766 (CA); *R.* v. *Pohoretsky*; *R.* v. *Ramage*; *R.* v. *L.A.R.* [1985] 3 WWR 289; 32 *Man. R.* (2d) 291 (CA).

94 As to Charter values, Tarnopolsky expresses the distinction in this way: "it is not for the courts to express their opinion concerning the justification for this constitutional entrenchment of a policy of pluralistic cultural preservation and enhancement [in s. 27]. Nor should the courts avoid giving it any significance. It is merely *our duty* to try to define how the Charter 'shall be interpreted' in light of this provision." *R.* v. *Videoflicks* (1985), 48 OR (2d) 395, at 426; 5 OAC 1 (CA). Emphasis added.

95 The Ontario Court of Appeal, e.g., unanimously expresses this point in *R.* v. *Morgentaler, Smoling and Scott*: "It is important to reiterate once again that it is not the role of the courts to pass on the policy or wisdom of legislation. That is a matter for Parliament and the Legislatures of the provinces. Whether a woman should have a right to terminate her pregnancy and at what stage and subject to what safeguards are policy considerations." (1986), 52 OR (2d) 353, at 379.

96 Ibid., at 385.

97 Dickson first expresses this point in *Hunter* v. *Southam*: "While the courts are guardians of the Constitution and of individual's rights under it, it is

the legislature's responsibility to enact legislation that embodies appropriate safeguards to comply with the Constitution's requirements. It should not fall to the courts to fill in the details that will render legislative lacunae constitutional." [1984] 2 SCR 145, at 169; 14 CCC (3d) 97, at 115. In *R.* v. *Noble*, for example, counsel urge the court to read into the Narcotic Control Act and Food and Drug Act a sub-rule which would restrict their authorization of writs of assistance to circumstances where it is not feasible to obtain a warrant. The Ontario Court of Appeal, following Dickson's lead, finds that "[s]uch a rewriting of the provisions of s. 10(1)(a) would involve altering the entire basis and structure of the present provisions which, in my view, would constitute as profound a change in the existing legislation as that which was proposed in Hunter ..." (1984), 48 OR (2d) 643, at 666; 14 DLR (4th) 216, at 238–9 per Martin. On the other hand, judges sometimes realistically acknowledge a new rule-creating role which, they think, the Charter has thrust upon them. "The novelty [of the Charter]," the Black Court recognizes, "arises because, in its very generality, the Canadian [limitations] clause does not just offer rules for interpretation; rather it invites the courts to make the rules." *Black* v. *Law Soc. Alta.* (1986), 20 CRR 117, at 141 (CA). With an apparent absence of guidelines, judges either retrench "with concern" or recognized, as does the Black Court, that the Charter "requires a judge to be more than a lawyer."

98 *Re Southam Inc. and The Queen (No. 1)* (1983), 41 OR (2d) 113, at 129; 146 DLR (3d) 408, at 424 per MacKinnon. Emphasis added. Or, as the Court of Appeal expresses in *Rauca*, "[i]n approaching the question [of s. 1] *objectively*, it is recognized that the listed rights and freedoms are never absolute and that there are always qualifications and limitations to allow for the protection of other competing interests in a democratic society." That is, the values or interests inhere in the words and in the society at large. They exist separate from and independent of the judge. *Re Federal Republic of Germany and Rauca* (1983), 41 OR (2d) 225, at 241; 145 DLR (3d) 638, at 655. Emphasis added.

99 In *R.* v. *Konechny*, for example, the court has to determine the meaning of the words "arbitrarily imprisoned" as guaranteed in section 9's "right not to be arbitrarily detained and imprisoned." [1984] 2 WWR 481, 25 MVR 132. Lambert, dissenting holds that a posited rule imposing an imprisonment sentence is arbitrary if the sentence is required without regard to the circumstances and "without a *reasoned* application of the legal principles of sentencing." Ibid., at 492, at 128 MVR. Again, section 9 means that "each case must be individually considered and a process of reasoning applied to that individual case." The sentence must be "*rationally* imposed" on the

particular individual. Ibid., at 493, 149 MVR. Emphasis added. Similarly, Macfarlane for the majority insists that section 52 of the Constitution Act, 1982 "does not mean that judges have been authorized to substitute their opinion for that of the legislature which under our democratic system is empowered to enunciate public policy." Macfarlane believes he could respect his self-image and, at the same time, strike down the legislative policy if the latter were "without rational basis" or without a "rational reason." Ibid., at 503. Macdonald adds that "[t]he perception of intelligent, reasonable members of the public provides a helpful test." Ibid., at 496, 152 MVR.

100 *Belliveau* v. *The Queen* (1985), 12 CRR 1, at 5–6. Emphasis added.

101 *Que. Assn. of Protestant School Bds.* v. *A.G. Que. (No. 2)* (1982), 140 DLR (3d) 33, at 77 (Que. Sup. Ct.).

102 See, e.g., *R.* v. *Bryant* (1984), 48 OR (2d) 732, at 754f–g per Houlden (Ont. CA); *Re Klein and Law Society of Upper Canada* (1985), 50 OR (2d) 118, at 128f per Henry (Div. Ct.); *Re Global Communications and A.-G. Can.* (1983), 42 OR (2d) 13, at 20e per Linden (H. Ct.); *aff'd*, refer to (1984), 44 OR (2d) 609, at 625g per Thorson (CA); *Re U.S.A. and Smith* (1984), 44 OR (2d) 705, at 722a and 727f–g per Houlden (CA).

103 *Re Southam Inc. and The Queen* (1983), 41 OR (2d) 113, at 130; 146 DLR (3d) 408, at 425 (CA). Emphasis added.

104 *Que. Assn. of Protestant School Bds.* v. *A.G. Que. (No. 2)* (1982), 140 DLR (3d) 33, at 66 (Que. Sup. Ct.).

105 See *R.* v. *X.* (1984), 43 OR (2d) 685, at 689g per Linden (H. Ct.).

106 *R.* v. *Slaney* (1986), 18 CRR 332, at 338 (Nfld. CA) per Mahoney.

107 See, e.g., *Re Mitchell and The Queen* (1983), 42 OR (2d) 481, at 505g per Linden (H. Ct.).

108 *Black* v. *Law Soc. of Alta.* (1984), 33 Alta. L.R. (2d) 214, at 247; 13 DLR (4th) 436, at 467 (QB).

109 *Collins* v. *R.* (1982), 31 CR (3d) 283, at 285 (Ont. Co. Ct.).

110 See supra note 91.

111 *Que. Assn. of Protestant School Bds.* v. *A.G. Que. (No. 2)* (1982), 140 DLR (3d) 33 (Que. Sup. Ct.). For *Oakes*, see note 88.

112 Ibid., at 77. Emphasis added.

113 See, e.g., *Black* v. *Law Soc. of Alta.* (1984), 33 Alta. L.R. (2d) 214, at 247; 13 DLR (4th) 436, at 467 (QB).

114 See, e.g., *Re Ont. Film and Video Appreciation Soc. and Ont. Bd. of Censors* (1984), 45 OR (2d) 80 (CA), *aff'g* (1983), 41 OR (2d) 583, at 590 (Div. Ct.).

115 *Res. 94(2) of Motor Vehicle Act (B.C.)*, (1984), 5 CRR 148, at 151, *aff'd* [1985] 2 SCR 486.

116 *R.* v. *Big M Drug Mart* (1984), 5 CRR 281, at 301, *aff'd* [1985] 3 SCR 295. Emphasis added.

117 *R.* v. *Vermette* (1983), 3 CRR 12, at 21 per Greenberg.

118 *R.* v. *Lace* (1983), 3 CRR 48, at 51. Emphasis added. His authority is Laskin's *dicta* in *Hogan* v. *The Queen*, [1975] 2 SCR 574, at 597, that "[t]he Canadian Bill of Rights is a halfway house between a purely common-law regime and a constitutional one. It may aptly be described as a quasi-constitutional instrument." If Laskin did not describe the Bill as constitutional instrument, he certainly did not "specifically" point out that it was "merely statutory." Quite to the contrary. It was a "quasi-constitutional instrument" and Laskin gave the text that status.

   Rogers of the Nova Scotia Supreme Court cites the same *Hogan dicta* for distinguishing between the two instruments. See *R. Lindsay* (1983), 4 CRR 35, at 38–9. He also cites *dicta* from Laskin in *Curr* v. *The Queen*, [1972] SCR 889, at 899, which, to the contrary, has actually contemplated that the Bill can be used to deny effect to a substantive legislative measure if "compelling reasons" are advanced.

119 *R.* v. *McKenzie* (1983), 4 CRR 262, at 263 per Stevenson.

120 *R.* v. *Ahearn* (1984), 5 CRR 355, at 359 per Campbell (PEISC).

121 *R.* v. *Carroll* (1985), 10 CRR 202, at 213 (PEISC). Also see *R.* v. *Smith* (1985), 11 CRR 283, at 285 (BC Co. Ct.); *MacBain* v. *Cdn. Human Rights Comm'n* (1985), 11 CRR 319, at 328–9 (FCTD); *Yue* v. *U.S.A.* (1985), 12 CRR 63, at 69 (Ont. HC); *R* v. *Schwartz* (1985), 12 CRR 107, at 115 (Man. CA); *Re Budge and Workers' Compensation Bd* (1985), 12 CRR 375, at 378 (Alta. QB).

122 See, e.g., *R.* v. *Minardi* (1983), 2 CRR 193, at 199 and 201 per Graburn (Ont. Co. Ct.), where a wider scope is granted to the right against unreasonable search and seizure. Also see *R.* v. *Ahearn* (1984), 5 CRR 355, at 359 per Campbell (PEISC, where the elevation of the right to instruct counsel "from its former quasi-constitutional status" widens the meaning of the word "detention."

123 See, e.g., *R.* v. *Minardi* (1983), 2 CRR 193, at 200–1 per Graburn (Ont. Co. Ct.); *R.* v. *Big M Drug Mart* (1984), 5 CRR 281, at 298–9 (Alta. Prov. Ct.).

124 See, e.g., *R.* v. *Minardi* (1983), 2 CRR 193, at 201 per Graburn (Ont. Co. Ct.).

125 [1930] AC 124, at 136.

126 *R.* v. *Cohen* (1984), 5 CRR 181, at 199, quoting from Walter Tarnopolsky and G. Beaudoin, eds., *Canadian Charter of Rights and Freedoms: A Commentary* (Toronto: Carswell 1982).

127 *Johnson and Amalgamated Transit Union, Local 113* v. *The Queen* (1985), 13 CRR 331, at 335 per Steele. Also see *R.* v. *Ahearn* (1983), 3 CCC (3d) 454, at 457–8 and 459 per Campbell (PEISC).

128 *R.* v. *Oquataq* (1985), 13 CRR 370, at 383 per Marshall.

129 See *Service Employees' International Union, Local 204* v. *Broadway Manor Nursing Home et al.* (1985), 10 CRR 37, at 109 per Smith (Ont. Div. Ct.).

130 Also see *R.* v. *Manninen* (1984), 43 OR (2d) 731, at 741–2 (CA).

131 *Ref. re Constitutional Validity of s. 12 Juvenile Delinquents Act* (1983), 2 CRR 84, at 91 (Ont. HC).

132 In the words of Smith in *Service Employees' International Union, Local 204* v. *Broadway Manor Nursing et al.* (1985), 10 CRR 37, at 109 (Ont. Div. Ct.), "[t]he courts however have been entrusted with the awesome responsibility and power of enforcing and applying it [the Charter], a power which they never solicited and will only exercise as part of their solemn duty of interpreting the law."

133 *R.* v. *Manninen* (1984), 43 OR (2d) 731, at 739. Also see *R.* v. *Menzies* (1987), 24 CRR 92, at 103–4 per Misener (Ont. Dist. Ct.).

134 *R.* v. *Manninen* (1984), 43 DLR (2d) 731, quoting approvingly from Laskin in *Brownridge* v. *The Queen*, [1972] SCR 926, at 952–3.

135 *Hoogbruin and Raffa* v. *A.G. of B.C. et al.* (1986), 20 CRR 1 (BCCA), at 6.

136 *Robinson* v. *Saunders et al.* (1984), 46 OR (2d) 51, at 58b per Clements.

137 *Re Service Employees' Int'l Union* v. *Broadway Manor Nursing Home et al.* (1984), 44 OR (2d) 392, at 417c–e per Galligan (Div. Ct.). Emphasis added.

138 *Re Southam Inc. and the Queen (No. 1)* (1983), 41 OR (2d) 113, at 123f (CA).

139 See William E. Conklin, *In Defence of Fundamental Rights* (Alphen aan den Rijn/Germantown, Md.: Sijthoff & Noordhoff, 1979), chap. 1.

140 (1983), 41 OR (2d) 187 (CA).

141 Ibid., at 203.

142 Ibid., at 210. Emphasis added.

143 Ibid., at 214.

144 (1984), 47 OR (2d) 353.

145 Ibid., at 405–6. Emphasis added.

146 *Re Ont. Film and Video Appreciation Soc. and Ont. Bd. of Censors* (1983), 41 OR (2d) 583, at 589 (Div. Ct.); *Re Southam Inc. and The Queen (No. 1)* (1983), 41 OR (2d) 113, at 123 (Ont. CA); and *Southam Inc.* v. *Hunter et al.* (1983), 147 DLR (3d) 420, at 426 (Alta. CA). Cited in *Morgentaler*, supra note 144, at 406–7

147 (1984), 47 OR (2d) 353, at 408. Emphasis added. Similarly, in *Balderstone et al. and the Queen* (1983) 2 CCC (3d) 37, at 46–7, Scollin (Man. QB) claims that the "wealth of legal tradition" sustains "the real worth of the guarantees themselves." Legal tradition restrained the judiciary from translating the Charter into "rule by a judicial oligarchy." Under the weight of the past, Scollin simply cannot borrow "fundamental substantive, as well as proce-

dural, change" under the blanket of "fundamental justice" in s. 7. Ibid., at 47.

148 *R. v. Morgentaler, Smoling and Scott* (1986), 52 OR (2d) 353, at 377: "Some rights have their basis in common law or statute law. Some are so deeply rooted in our traditions and way of life as to be fundamental and could be classified as part of life, liberty and security of the person. The right to choose one's partner in marriage, and the decision whether or not to have children, would fall in this category, as would the right to physical control of one's person, such as the right to clothe oneself, take medical advice and decide whether or not to act on this advice. ... Even such fundamental rights are *not absolute.* They *may be controlled by the common law or by statute.* They must accommodate the rights of others." Emphasis added.

149 *R. v. Cohn* (1985), 48 OR (2d) 65 (CA).

150 Ibid., at 87–91.

151 Ibid., at 82e.

152 Ibid., at 91c. Emphasis added.

153 *R. v. Bryant* (1984), 48 OR (2d) 732 (CA). For the policy rationalism presupposed in the judgment, see text supra between notes 75 and 85.

154 *R. v. Bryant* (1984), 48 OR (2d) 732, at 747. Emphasis added.

155 *Re R. and Morrison* (1983), 47 OR (2d) 185, at 207.

156 *R v. Therens* (1984), 5 CRR 157, at 173. For a discussion of the Supreme Court's image of the Charter in the context of this case see infra chap. VII.

157 [1930] AC 124, at 136. Emphasis added.

158 *Re Southam Inc. and The Queen (No. 1)* (1983), 41 OR (2d) 113, at 123b.

159 See, generally, Conklin, supra note 139, chap. 1–3.

160 (1983), 41 OR (2d) 43, at 52e–f. Emphasis added.

161 *R. v. MacIntyre et al.* (1983), 69 CCC (2d) 162, at 166. Emphasis added.

162 *Black v. Law Soc. Alta.* (1986), 20 CRR 117 (Alta. CA), at 141.

163 Ibid., at 143–8.

164 Ibid., at 159–60.

165 *Re Service Employees' Int'l Union v. Broadway Manor Nursing Home et al.* (1984), 44 OR (2d) 392.

166 Ibid., at 461d.

167 Ibid., at 462c–d. Similarly, in *Re Retail, Wholesale & Dept. Store Union and Govt. of Sask.* (1986), 19 DLR (4th) 609 (Sask. CA), Bayda holds that freedom of association means more than the freedom to join an association: "*[T]o be* in association means *to act* in association, for, it is metaphysically impossible for a human being to exist in a state of inanimateness, or in a state of no movement, or as it were, in a state of mere beingness. For a

human being, to be is to act. Thomas Aquinas, in his *Summa Contra Gentiles* (111, 69) brands with error 'those who deprive natural things of their own actions.' Etienne Gibson, in his work *Being and some Philosophers* (Medieval Studies of Tor. Inc.), at 184, ... continued 'because the very nature of being is here at stake. Not: to be, then to act, but: *to be is to act*' [judge's emphasis]." Ibid., at 615. Emphasis added.

168 *Re Service Employees Int'l Union* v. *Broadway Nursing Home et al.* (1983), 44 OR (2d) 392. Ibid., at 464c. Emphasis added.

169 Ibid., at 464g.

170 *R.* v. *Red Hot Video* (1985), 15 CRR 206.

171 Ibid., at 229. Emphasis added.

172 Ibid. Emphasis added.

173 (1985), 19 DLR (4th) 609.

174 Ibid., at 615.

CHAPTER VII

1 *A.-G. Qué.* v. *Québec Protestant School Bds. et al.*, [1984] 2 SCR 66. In other unanimous judgments the Court simply adopts the reasons which one of the justices renders that day on a similar case. See, e.g., *Trask* v. *The Queen*, [1985] 1 SCR 655 and *Rahn* v. *The Queen*, [1985] SCR 659 which adopt the reasons in *R.* v. *Therens*, [1985] 1 SCR 613, although four separate judgments are rendered in the latter.

2 Pursuant to section 72 of Quebec's French Language Charter, instruction is to be given in French in all grades unless (a) one's father or mother has received his or her elementary education in English, in Quebec; (b) one's father or mother has been domiciled in Quebec on 26 August 1977 and he or she has received his or her elementary instruction in English outside Quebec; one is lawfully receiving one's education in English in his or her last year of school in Quebec before 26 August 1977; or one's young brothers and sisters have been receiving their education in English in their last year of school in Quebec before 26 August 1977.

3 Ibid., at 79a–c.

4 Ibid., at 79d. Emphasis added.

5 See, e.g., supra chap. VI, sect. 4.

6 *A.-G. (Qué.)* v. *Québec Protestant School Bds. et al.* [1984] 2 SCR 66, at 79f. Emphasis added.

7 Ibid., at 79f. One should also note how the Court continually referred to the Charter as "the Constitution," thereby elevating the status of the text.

8 Ibid., at 79h.

9 Ibid., at 81g.
10 Ibid., at 82b.
11 Ibid., at 84a.
12 Ibid., at 84f.
13 Ibid., at 84d.
14 Ibid., at 79f.
15 Ibid., at 85g. Emphasis added.
16 F.E. Peters, *Greek Philosophical Terms: A Historical Lexicon* (New York: New York University Press 1967), at 191.
17 *A.-G. (Qué.)* v. *Québec Protestant Separate School Bds. et al.*, [1984] 2 SCR 66, at 79a.
18 [1984] 2 SCR 145, 155c–d.
19 *Edwards* v. *A.-G. for Can.*, [1930] AC 124, at 136 as quoted in ibid., at 156a.
20 [1980] AC 319, at 328 as quoted in ibid., at 156d.
21 Ibid., at 156e. Emphasis added.
22 *R.* v. *Big M Drug Mart*, [1985] 1 SCR 295, at 344g. Emphasis added.
23 *R.* v. *Big M Drug Mart*, [1985] 1 SCR 295. Dickson begins by summarizing how the provincial appellate judge has distinguished the Charter from the Canadian Bill of Rights in terms of the "enhanced status" of the former and the mere declaratory language of the latter. Dickson concentrates upon the former factor. Judges have restrictively interpreted the Canadian Bill of Rights, according to Dickson, because judges have simply not projected a "distinctive nature and status to that document." Ibid., at 308b–g, 342h. Also see *Société des Acadiens* v. *Assoc. of Parents*, [1986] 1 SCR 549 at 567c; Dickson, "The Role of the Supreme Court of Canada" in (1984, October), 3 *Advocates Soc. J.* 3.
24 *R.* v. *Big M Drug Mart*, [1985] 1 SCR 295, at 342i.
25 Ibid., at 342j–343n. Also see *R.* v. *Oakes*, [1986] 1 SCR 103, at 124h. In any case, "the day has passed when it might have been appropriate to re-evaluate those concerns and to reassess the direction this Court has taken in interpreting that document" (i.e., the Canadian Bill of Rights). *Beauregard* v. *Canada*, [1986] 2 SCR 56, at 90d.
26 *Hunter* v. *Southam*, [1984] 2 SCR 145, at 155f.
27 *R.* v. *Big M Drug Mart*, [1985] 1 SCR 295, at 344g.
28 *R.* v. *Big M Drug Mart*, [1985] 1 SCR 295, at 313f, 349d–f. *Ref. re. Compulsory Arbitration*, [1987] 1 SCR 313, at 360i–361b.
29 Ibid., at 313f–g.
30 See text supra chap. III, sect. 3(a).
31 *Hunter* v. *Southam, Inc.*, [1984] 2 SCR 145, at 155f, 169a.
32 Ibid., at 169a–b.
33 *Operation Dismantle* v. *The Queen*, [1985] 1 SCR 441, at 447j, 455g–h.

34 *R.* v. *Big M Drug Mart Ltd.* [1985] 1 SCR 295, at 314a–b.

35 *R.* v. *Beauregard,* [1986] 2 SCR 56, at 73f. Dickson's emphasis.

36 See, e.g., *Hunter* v. *Southam,* [1984] 2 SCR 145, at 156g, 157c; *R.* v. *Big M Drug Mart,* [1985] 1 SCR 295, at 344d.

37 *Hunter* v. *Southam,* [1984] 2 SCR 145, at 155d–f. Emphasis added.

38 *R.* v. *Big M Drug Mart,* [1985] 1 SCR 295, at 343i. His emphasis.

39 [1930] AC 124, at 136. Emphasis added.

40 *Hunter* v. *Southam* [1984] 2 SCR 145, at 155j.

41 Joseph Owens, *A History of Ancient Western Philosophy* (Eaglewood Cliffs, NJ: Prentice-Hall 1959), at 311–12.

42 "What each thing is when its growth is completed we call the nature of that thing, whether it be a man or a horse or a family." *Politics* 1252b9.

43 "In the sphere of man's life (as in all life generally), birth has a first beginning [that is, the union of parents] but the ends attained from such a beginning is only a step to some further end." *Ethics* I.7, 1097b 2–21.

44 See generally *Politics* bk. I–III, *The Constitution of Athens* and *Ethics* v, x. 1179b–1181b624.

45 *R.* v. *Beauregard,* [1986] 2 SCR 56, at 81e.

46 *Big M Drug Mart* [1985] 2 SCR 145, at 344e. Emphasis added. Also see *Société des Acadiens* v. *Assoc. of Parents,* [1986] 1 SCR 549, at 560c.

47 See generally Plato's dialogues, *Euthyphro* and *Phaedo.* Of course, Plato's equation of a *telos* with the Forms is the subject of varying interpretations. See generally Cherniss, "The Philosophical Economy of the Theory of Ideas"; Wedberg, "The Theory of Ideas," and Cross and Woozley, "Knowledge, Belief and the Forms" in Gregory Vlastos, *Plato I (A Collection of Critical Essays): Metaphysical Epistemology* (Garden City, NY: Anchor Books 1971).

48 See, e.g., *Hunter* v. *Southam,* [1985] 2 SCR 145, at 155d–f.

49 *Société des Acadiens* v. *Assoc. of Parents,* [1986] 1 SCR 549, at 565h.

50 Ibid., at 567c.

51 This sense of a *telos* is the subject of Conklin, "The Legal Theory of Horkheimer and Adorno" (1985), 5 *Windsor Yearb. Access Justice* 230. Also see Kaplan, "Can Rational Instrumentalism Do All That?: Reply to Professor Conklin," ibid., at 381.

52 [1984] 2 SCR 145, at 155f.

53 Ibid., at 155d; 158e–g.

54 Ibid., at 155c: "It is clear that the meaning of 'unreasonable' cannot be determined by recourse to a dictionary, nor for that matter, by reference to the rules of statutory construction."

55 Ibid., at 155d–f, 160a.

56 Ibid., at 157e–159j, 167f–h.

57 Ibid., at 157e–159j.

58 Ibid., at 167f.

59 [1985] 1 SCR 295, at 344j–346a. Also see, e.g., Rand in *Boucher* v. *The King* [1951] SCR 265.

60 Ibid., at 313f–g, 349d.

61 Ibid., at 342j–343g.

62 Ibid., at 344e–i.

63 Ibid., at 317i–319f.

64 Ibid., at 319f–331a.

65 Ibid., at 334i, 344f.

66 Ibid., at 344i.

67 Ibid., at 346i.

68 [1986] 1 SCR 549.

69 Ibid., at 560a.

70 Ibid., at 564d–e.

71 Ibid., at 564e. Emphasis added.

72 [1986] 2 SCR 56.

73 See esp. ibid., at 69–76.

74 *R.* v. *Big M Drug Mart*, [1985] 1 SCR 295, at 331h.

75 *Hunter* v. *Southam*, [1984] 2 SCR 145, at 157a.

76 *R.* v. *Big M Drug Mart*, supra note 74, at 332a.

77 [1986] 1 SCR 103, at 119j–120b.

78 [1986] 1 SCR 549, at 568c.

79 Ibid., at 566g.

80 *Edwards Books and Art Ltd. et al.* v. *Queen*, [1986] 2 SCR 713, at 758h–759i.

81 See, e.g., *Hunter* v. *Southam*, [1985] 2 SCR 145, at 155g.

82 See text supra, chap. 3, sect. 3(a)(i).

83 *R.* v. *Big M Drug Mart* [1985] 1 SCR 295, at 353i.

84 *Operation Dismantle* v. *The Queen*, [1985] 1 SCR 441, at 447j, 455f–g.

85 Ibid., at 447j–448a, 455g–h.

86 *Hunter* v. *Southam*, [1984] 2 SCR 145, at 169a.

87 *Queen* v. *Beauregard*, [1986] 2 SCR 56, at 77b. Dickson stresses that "[o]n the insitutional plane, judicial independence means the preservation of the separateness and integrity of the judicial branch and a guarantee of its freedom from unwarranted intrusions by, or even intertwining with, the legislative and executive branches." Ibid., at 77c–d.

88 *Hunter* v. *Southam*, [1984] 2 SCR 145, at 157d, 159g–160a, 161j–162d, 169j–170a. Also see *R.* v. *Big M Drug Mart Ltd.*, [1985] 1 SCR 295, at 344d; *Re Fraser*, [1985] 2 SCR 455; *R.* v. *Oakes*, [1986] 1 SCR 103, at 139c; *Edwards*

Books & Art Ltd. v. *Queen*, [1986] 2 SCR 713, at 769h–783e. The latter concerns Dickson's use of "interest balancing" in s. 1 of the Charter.

89 See text supra chap. VI, sect. 2.

90 See *Hunter* v. *Southam*, [1984] 2 SCR 145, at 160–70.

91 *Re Fraser and Public Service Staff Relations Bd.*, [1985] 2 SCR 455, at 458. Dickson states that this is not a Charter case as counsel apparently did not argue a provision of the Charter. However, he certainly argued an infringement of freedom of expression.

92 Ibid., at 470–2.

93 *R.* v. *Big M Drug Mart*, [1985] 1 SCR 295, at 352e. Utilitarian balancing also permeates his treatment of s. 1 in a recent series of labour legislation judgments. *Public Service Alliance of Canada & A.G. Man.* v. *R.*, [1987] 1 SCR 424, at 439–51; *RWDSU* v. *Sask.*, [1987] 1 SCR 460, at 476d–483e; *Ref. re. Compulsory Arbitration*, [1987] 1 SCR 313, at 373g–386d. Also see his assessment of "the importance" of the legislative objectives in *Edwards Books & Art Ltd.* v. *Queen*, [1986] 2 SCR 713, at 769h–783e.

94 *R.* v. *Oakes*, [1986] 1 SCR 103, at 138j–139. However, in *Public Service Alliance of Canada & A.G. Man.* v. *R.*, [1987] 1 SCR 424, at 439j–440g, Dickson asserts that an objective is of "sufficient importance" if there is "a serious problem" when an act is passed. In this case it was inflation. Dickson refers to double digit inflation, a higher inflation rate in Canada than in the United States, and failed restraint policies of the late 1970s. He seems to give great weight to the judiciary's perception of the Anti-Inflation Act a decade earlier. Because inflation is a "pressing and substantial concern" in the early 1970s, this constitutes Dickson's labelling of it as an important objective for overriding freedom of associating in 1987.

95 For these issues see generally text infra chap. XI.

96 *Edwards Books & Art Ltd.* v. *The Queen*, [1986] 2 SCR 713, at 770. In *Public Service Alliance of Canada & A.G. Man.* v. *R.*, [1987] 1 SCR 424, Dickson cautions against assessing "the effectiveness or wisdom of various government strategies for solving pressing economic problems" (at 442a). A study of the relative importance of the causes of inflation is out (at 442b). And "a high degree of deference" ought to be reserved for the Government's posited means (at 442d). Dickson accepts the Government's rationale for the means used as a 'given.' See esp. 444f–445b.

97 *Hunter* v. *Southam*, [1984] 2 SCR 145, at 166i.

98 [1985] 1 SCR 494.

99 Ibid., at 508h. Emphasis added.

100 See esp., *Operation Dismantle* v. *The Queen*, [1985] 1 SCR 441, at 450–2.

101 Ibid., at 451f–g.

102 Ibid., at 452c.

103 Ibid., at 453b.

104 Ibid., at 453c.

105 Ibid., at 453h, 454a.

106 Ibid., at 454f–g.

107 Ibid., at 454i. Emphasis added.

108 Ibid., at 455b–c.

109 Ibid., at 456a. Emphasis added.

110 *Singh et al.* v. *M.E.I.*, [1985] 1 SCR 177, at 209g–h.

111 Ibid., at 205b–g, 206h.

See also the summary of the David B. Goodman Lectures delivered by Wilson at the University of Toronto Law School as reported by Peter Calamai in *National*, December 1985, at 3.

112 *Singh et al.* v. *M.E.I.*, [1985] 1 SCR 177, at 218f; *R.* v. *Big M Drug Mart Ltd.* [1985] 1 SCR 295, at 361d–f. Also see above-reported lectures.

113 *Singh et al.* v. *M.E.I.*, [1985] 1 SCR 178, at 218d: "It seems to me that it is important to bear in mind that the rights and freedoms set out in the *Charter* are fundamental to the political structure of Canada and are guaranteed by the *Charter* as part of the supreme law of our nation."

114 *R.* v. *Big M Drug Mart Ltd.*, [1985] 1 SCR 295; *Operation Dismantle* v. *The Queen*, [1985] 1 SCR 441; *Re Constitutional Questions Act and s. 94(2) of the Motor Vehicle Act, R.S.B.C. 1979*, [1985] 2 SCR 486; *Macdonald* v. *City of Montreal*, [1986] 1 SCR 460; *Société des Acadiens.* v. *Assoc. of Parents*, [1986] 1 SCR 549. *Public Service Alliance of Canada & A.G. Man.* v. *R.*, [1987] 1 SCR 424; *RWDSU* v. *Sask.*, [1987] 1 SCR 460; *R.* v. *Smith*, [1987] 1 SCR 1045; *Canada* v. *Schmidt*, [1987] 1 SCR 499; *United States* v. *Allard*, [1987] 1 SCR 564; *R.* v. *Rahey*, [1987] 1 SCR 588.

115 *Govt. of Sask et al.* v. *Retail, Wholesale and Dept. Store Union, Local 544, 496, 635 and 955*, [1987] 1 SCR 460, at 487a. Wilson's emphasis. Wilson continues that the prevention of economic harm to a particular sector is not *per se* of weighty enough importance to override a constitutional right. Rather, economic regulation which offends as fundamental freedom must be done in response to "a serious threat to the well-being of the body politic or a substantial segment of it" (at 487f).

116 [1985] 1 SCR 177.

117 Counsel also argues that the procedures violate s. 2(e) of the Canadian Bill of Rights. Wilson decides on the Charter claim whereas Beetz decides on the Canadian Bill of Rights issue. For the latter see text supra chap. v, note 9.

118 See *Singh et al.* v. *M.E.I.*, [1985] 1 SCR 177, at 209b–g.

119 For a description and discussion of the latter see generally William E. Conklin, *In Defence of Fundamental Rights* (Alphen aan den Rijn/Germantown, Md.: Sijthoff & Noordhoff 1979), at 132–46. However, for a series of utilitarian arguments for a strong sense of rights, see Scanlon, "Rights, Goals and Fairness" in Jeremy Waldron, ed., *Theories of Rights* (Oxford: Oxford University Press 1984), chap. VI.

120 *Operation Dismantle* v. *The Queen*, [1985] 1 SCR 441, at 488i–490a.

121 See, e.g., *Singh et al* v. *M.E.I.*, [1985] 1 SCR 177, at 217b. Similarly, in *R.* v. *Therens*, the police have not informed the accused of his right to retain and instruct counsel without delay and have thereupon taken his breath for analysis. Estey believes that "[h]ere the police authority has flagrantly violated a *Charter* right without any statutory authority for so doing." [1985] 1 SCR 613, at 621i. To admit the evidence "would *clearly* 'bring the administration of justice into disrepute'." Ibid., at 622d. He continues, however, that he is "strongly of the view" that he should *not* explain what "the administration of justice into disrepute" means: "I am strongly of the view that it would be most improvident for this Court to expatiate, in these early days of life with the *Charter*, upon the meaning of the expression 'administration of justice' and particularly its outer limits." In this case, he thinks, the facts *clearly* fall within the meaning of the concept, whatever the concept means. What it means is what Estey intuitively feels it means. One cannot discover that intuition inherent in the words of the posited text, Estey's own disclaimer to the contrary.

122 Ibid., at 218b.

123 Supra note 113.

124 *Singh et al.* v. *M.E.I.*, [1985] 1 SCR 178, at 218c. "I think that in determining whether a particular limitation is a reasonable limit ... it is important to remember that the courts are conducting this inquiry *in light of a commitment* to uphold the rights and freedoms set out in the other sections of the *Charter*." Emphasis added.

125 Ibid., at 218j. Emphasis added.

126 Ibid., at 219b. Emphasis added.

127 *Operation Dismantle* v. *The Queen*, [1985] 1 SCR 441, at 465h.

128 *Chandler* v. *D.P.P.* [1962] 3 All ER 142, at 151 (HL) as quoted by Wilson in italics in *Operation Dismantle*, ibid., at 465d–e.

129 Ibid., at 465i–466a.

130 Ibid., at 466i. Her italics.

131 Ibid., at 467a. Her italics.

132 Ibid., at 467b. Emphasis added.

133 Ibid., at 471f–g.

134 Ibid., at 472i and 474a. Emphasis added.

135 Ibid., at 472d

136 *R. v. Big M Drug Mart*, [1985] 1 SCR 295, at 357a–d, 360g–h.

137 Ibid., at 358a.

138 See Conklin, *In Defence of Fundamental Rights*, supra note 119, at 29–41, 168–71, 223–6 where this is discussed.

139 *R. v. Big M Drug Mart*, [1985] 1 SCR 295, at 359e. Emphasis added.

140 Ibid., at 360a.

141 Ibid., at 360a, 360i–361a.

142 Ibid., at 361d. Emphasis added.

143 Ibid., at 361e. Emphasis added.

144 *Operation Dismantle v. The Queen*, [1985] 1 SCR 441, at 465d–f; quoting and approving dicta from Lord Radcliffe in *Chandler v. D.P.P.*, [1962] 3 All ER 142, at 151 (HC). See supra note 128.

145 *Jones v. The Queen*, [1986] 2 SCR 284, at 313j–314.

146 *Singh et al. v. M.E.I.*, [1985] 1 SCR 177, at 217e.

147 Ibid., at 217i–j, quoting from Estey in *Law Soc. of Upper Can. v. Skapinker*, [1984] 1 SCR 357, at 384.

148 See text supra sect. 4a.

149 *Singh et al. v. M.E.I.*, [1985] 2 SCR 177, at 220e.

150 *Jones v. The Queen*, [1986] 2 SCR 284, at 315e.

151 Ibid., at 322i–j. Similarly, in *Public Service Alliance and A.-G. Man. v. R.*, [1987] 1 SCR 424, at 457i–458a, the Government limited the freedom of public services employees to bargain collectively and to strike in order to persuade the general public to enter voluntarily into employment agreements of wage increases of 6 per cent and 5 per cent for each of the next two years respectively. But the Government offered no evidence that this had actually induced voluntary compliance in the private sector. Thus, public sector employees are arbitrarily and inequitably differentiated from private sector employees.

   Similarly, in *Gov't of Sask. et al. v. Retail, Wholesale & Dept. Store Union, Locals 544, 496, 635 & 955*, [1987] 1 SCR 460, at 490a–f, Wilson complains that Government lawyers have failed to adduce weighty evidence establishing economic harm to dairy workers and the public brought on by a lockout or strike of milk processing facilities. Indeed, the only evidence consists of affidavits sworn by union representatives and some "inherently unreliable" newspaper clippings.

152 *Macdonald v. City of Montreal*, [1986] 1 SCR 460, at 538a.

153 Ibid., at 541c.

154 Ibid., at 537d–539a.

155 Ibid., at 543h.

156 Ibid., at 543h–j.

157 Ibid., at 543j–544a.

158 Ibid., at 537.

159 [1986] 1 SCR 549.

160 Ibid., at 609i–j. The theme of negative freedom provides a core element in the evolution of liberal thought. See generally John Stuart Mill, *On Liberty* (Mary Warnock, ed.; Glasgow: Wm. Collins and Sons 1962), at 130; T.H. Green, *The Principles of Political Obligation* (J.R. Rodman, ed.; New York: Crofts 1964), who criticizes the conception of negative freedom; Isaiah Berlin, "Introduction" and "Two Concepts of Liberty" in *Four Essays on Liberty* (London: Oxford University Press 1969).

The notion is discussed in Conklin, *In Defence of Fundamental Rights*, supra note 119, chap. 4 and 6; MacCallum Jr., "Negative and Positive Freedom" in Peter Laslett, W.G. Runciman, and Quentin Skinner, eds., *Philosophy, Politics & Society*, 4th series (New York: Barnes and Noble 1972); Siedentop, "Two Liberal Traditions" in Alan Ryan, ed., *The Idea of Freedom* (Oxford: Oxford University Press 1979); Taylor, "What's Wrong with Negative Liberty," ibid.; Dworkin, "What Liberalism Isn't" in (1983), 29 *New York Rev. of Books* 47.

161 *Société des Acadiens* v. *Association of Parents* [1986] 1 SCR 549, at 610a.

162 Ibid., at 615f.

163 Ibid., at 617g.

164 Ibid., at 619b.

165 Ibid., at 619f.

166 Ibid., at 620c.

167 Ibid., at 625a. Emphasis added.

168 Ibid., at 638j–639.

169 *Singh et al.* v. *M.E.I.*, [1985] 2 SCR 177, at 205b.

170 *Re s. 94(2) of Motor Vehicle Act, R.S.B.C. 1979*, [1985] 2 SCR 486, at 530d–i.

171 *Singh et al.* v. *M.E.I.* [1985 1 SCR 177, at 205i.

172 Ibid., at 205i–206b. Emphasis added to "In my view," and "must."

173 Ibid., at 206g. Emphasis added.

174 Ibid., at 207h. Emphasis added.

175 Ibid., at 212j.

176 *R.* v. *Big M Drug Mart*, [1985] 1 SCR 295, at 361a–b. Emphasis added.

177 G.E. Moore. See *Principia Ethica* (1903), c. 1, 5–21 and reprinted in A.I. Melden, ed., *Ethical Theories*, 2nd ed. rev. (Englewood Cliffs, NJ: Prentice-Hall 1967), at 515–25.

178 *Operation Dismantle* v. *The Queen*, [1985] 1 SCR 441, at 472a–b.

179 See generally text infra chap. x.
180 *Operation Dismantle*, supra note 178, at 488g: *Six Great Ideas* (New York: Macmillan 1981), at 144.
181 *Operation Dismantle*, at 489d: *A Theory of Justice* (Cambridge, Mass.: Harvard University Press 1971), at 213.
182 Ibid., at 489i: *Taking Rights Seriously* (London: Duckworth 1977), at 267.
183 Ibid., at 489j: *Jurisprudence*, vol. 4 (St Paul, Minn.: West Publishing 1959), at 56.
184 Wilson uses Dworkin's quotation along with the others to support a "weak" sense of rights. As to how Dworkin tried to undermine Wilson's thesis see generally Conklin, *In Defence of Fundamental Rights*, supra note 119, at 230–43. Wilson's conception of rights hardly departs from the weak sense adopted by her predecessors. See Conklin, ibid., at 241–3.
There is also little doubt that Rawls would be concerned that his sentence was taken out of context. See Conklin, ibid., chap. 5.
185 *Operation Dismantle v. The Queen*, [1985] 1 SCR 441, at 490a–h.
186 Ibid., at 490a, 490i–j. See generally supra note 160. Also see Conklin, *In Defence of Fundamental Rights*, chap. 4.
187 *Re s. 94(2) of Motor Vehicle Act, R.S.B.C. 1979*, [1985] 2 SCR 486, at 530f.
188 Ibid., at 531f.
189 Ibid., at 526b–528c.
190 Ibid., at 532e–534a.
191 Nigel Walker, *Sentencing in a Rational Society* (London: Allen Lane 1969) and discussed in *Re s. 94(2) of Motor Vehicle Act*, ibid., at 532e–i.
192 *Working Paper II – Imprisonment and Release* (Studies on Imprisonment, 1976), at 10, in *Re s. 94(2)*, ibid., at 532j.
193 *Re s. 94(2) of Motor Vehicle Act, R.S.B.C. 1979*, [1985] 2 SCR 486, at 533g.
194 *Jones v. The Queen*, [1986] 2 SCR 284, ay 318j.
195 Ibid., at 310j–311a.
196 *Macdonald v. City of Montreal*, [1986] 1 SCR 460, at 515–24.
197 *Edwards Books & Art Ltd. v. Queen*, [1986] 2 SCR 713, at 809c–810a.
198 See esp., *Law Soc. of Upper Canada v. Skapinker*, [1984] 1 SCR 357.
199 For examples of LaForest's strict textual rationalism see *Krug v. The Queen* [1985] 2 SCR 255; *Spencer v. The Queen* [1985] 2 SCR 278.
200 See, e.g., *Jones v. The Queen*, [1986] 2 SCR 284, esp. at 304–7.
201 See, e.g., LeDain in *R. v. Therens*, [1985] 1 SCR 613, who consciously rejects a textualist approach to the constitution at 633c by adopting Wilberforce's *dicta* in *Min. Hom. Affairs v. Fisher*, [1980] AC 319, at 328 and supporting the Saskatchewan Court of Appeal reasons in *Therens* (1983), 5 CCC (3d) 409, at 423–4. LeDain distinguishes his image of the Charter from his image of

the Canadian Bill of Rights at 637f–g, 639d–h, and incorporates posited values to supplement posited rules at 651i–654c.

202 *Law Soc. of Upper Canada* v. *Skapinker*, [1984] 1 SCR 357, at 365d.

203 Skapinker subsequently became a Canadian citizen in the course of his proceedings and was admitted to the bar. An intervenor, Richardson, for all practical purposes replaced Skapinker, although Skapinker still appeared before the Supreme Court to argue his case.

204 Beetz's image of the Charter coincides with his image of the constitution generally. See text infra chap. VIII.

McIntyre also signs the Estey judgment in *Skapinker*. Although his *Dubois* judgment reflects a textual rationalism, some of his judgments in the 1970s reflect a desire to break from rule rationalism entirely. See e.g., *R.* v. *Miller and Cockriell* (1975), 63 DLR (3d) 193 (BCCA), McIntyre dissenting, at 256–7. His more recent labour relations judgments reflect the contours of a policy rationalism. See generally *Ref. re. Compulsory Arbitration*, [1987] 1 SCR 313 per McIntyre, at 414b–420b and *Govt. of Sask.* v. *Retail, Wholesale & Dept. Store Union, Locals 544, 496, 635 & 955*, [1987] 1 SCR 460 per McIntyre, at 484i–j.

205 See esp., *Law Soc. of Upper Canada* v. *Skapinker*, [1984] 1 SCR 357, at 365d.

206 Ibid., at 366a.

207 Ibid., at 366g.

208 Ibid., at 366i. Note, however, that if the Charter does not posit a specific right – e.g. to bargain collectively or to strike – then the claimed right is excluded from constitutional protection. See *Ref. re. Compulsory Arbitration*, [1987] 1 SCR 313 per LeDain, at 391f–j.

209 Ibid., at 366h.

210 Ibid., at 369a–j. Also see how Estey understands various courts as presenting the central issue in s. 29 of the Charter as a question of the meaning of "by" and "or under" in *Re: An Act to Amend the Education Act*, [1987] 1 SCR 1148, at 1208a–1209e. Section 29 provides that "[n]othing in this Charter abrogates or derogates from any rights or privileges guaranteed by or under the Constitution ..." Estey finds it unnecessary to work over the meaning of "by" and "under" because of the adverb, "guaranteed."

211 *Law Soc. of Upper Canada* v. *Skapinker*, [1984] 1 SCR 357, at 376d–h.

212 Ibid., at 376h.

213 Ibid., at 376j–377a.

214 Ibid., at 377g.

215 Ibid., at 377i. Emphasis added.

216 Ibid., at 369a–j.

217 Ibid., at 377g. Cf Laskin, "Mobility Rights under the Charter" (1982), 4
    Sup. Ct. L. Rev. 89.

218 *Law Soc. of Upper Canada* v. *Skapinker*, [1984] 1 SCR 357, at 365f. Emphasis
    added.

219 Estey claims that the rules within the text itself (in the form of s. 52 and the
    complex amendment rules) elevate the status of the text. See *Law Soc. of
    Upper Canada* v. *Skapinker*, [1984] 1 SCR 357, at 366f. There seems to be an
    internal circularity in this reasoning: the Charter is supreme; the Charter
    posits the rules; and the rules of the Charter (section 52 and the amending
    rules) posit the Charter to an elevated status. Of course, this circularity
    "makes sense" within an image of a constitution which sets texts as the
    delimiting source of law and which posits the texts as positing a vertical
    hierarchy of rules. See generally text infra, chap. VIII.

220 Closely follow how Estey's whole argument in *Skapinker*, ibid., at 368j–385
    presupposes that a constitution's boundaries begin and end with a text
    posited at the top of the hierarchy of texts.

221 Ibid., at 359j–360a. Emphasis added.

222 Ibid., at 377i. Emphasis added.

223 See discussion supra concerning Wilson's intuitionism. Similarly, in *R.* v.
    Therens, the police have not informed the accused of his right to retain
    and instruct counsel without delay and have thereupon taken his breath for
    analysis. Estey believes that "[h]ere the police authority has flagrantly
    violated a Charter right without any statutory authority for so doing."
    [1985] 1 SCR 613, at 621i. To admit the evidence "would *clearly* 'bring the
    administration of justice into disrepute'." Ibid., at 622d. He continues,
    however, that he is "strongly of the view" that he should *not* explain what
    "the administration of justice into disrepute" means: "I am strongly of
    the view that it would be most improvident for this Court to expatiate, in
    these early days of life with the *Charter*, upon the meaning of the expres-
    sion 'administration of justice' and particularly its outer limits." Ibid., at
    662e. In this case, he thinks, the facts *clearly* fall within the meaning of
    the concept, whatever the concept means. What it means is what Estey
    intuitively feels it means. One cannot discover that intuition inherent in
    the words of the posited text, Estey's own disclaimer to the contrary.

224 For Beetz's image of a constitution see generally text infra chap. VIII. More
    recently, Beetz has expressed a 'balancing of social interests' image of a
    constitution. See, e.g., *Manitoba (A.G.)* v. *Metropolitan Stores Ltd.*, [1987] 1
    SCR 110, at 129g–150e, where Beetz weighs the efficacious and "public"
    interests in granting injunctive relief before constitutional invalidity has
    been finally decided on the merits.

225 *Re s. 94(2) of Motor Vehicle Act, R.S.B.C. 1979*, [1985] 2 SCR 486, at 496a–d.
226 Ibid., at 496e. Emphasis added.
227 Ibid., at 497j.
228 In *Mills* v. *The Queen*, [1986] 1 SCR 863, at 925a–d, Lamer identifies four
    values underlying the guarantee of a trial within a reasonable time. In
    Jones v. *The Queen*, [1986] 2 SCR 284, at 307c, LaForest understands the
    guarantee of "liberty" in section 7 also as a matter of "balancing." "Some
    pragmatism is involved in balancing between fairness and efficiency," he
    admonishes, when one is abstracting the policy of a challenged statute.
    Ibid., at 304e. More generally, he writes later in *Jones*, the Charter protects
    rights "only within the limits of reason" (ibid., at 305i), "reason" being
    understood in policy balancing terms. Also see LaForest in *R.* v. *Rahey*,
    [1987] 1 SCR 588, at 642c–648b where he balances off the interests un-
    derlying a right to trial within a reasonable time (s. 11(b)). Also see LeDain
    in *R.* v. *Therens*, [1985] 1 SCR 613 and McIntyre in *R.* v. *Rahey*, [1987] 1
    SCR 588, at 608h–j.
229 *Ref. re. Compulsory Arbitration*, [1987] 1 SCR 313, per McIntyre at 414b–420c.
230 *Re s. 94(2) of Motor Vehicle Act, R.S.B.C. 1979*, [1985] 2 SCR 486, at 498g–h.
    Emphasis added. Also see *R.* v. *Rahey*, [1987] 1 SCR 588, at 609a where
    Lamer supports "an objective standard" for s. 11(b).
231 Ibid., at 499b. Emphasis added.
232 Ibid., at 499d–e. Emphasis added.
233 Similarly, in *Mills* v. *The Queen*, [1986] 1 SCR 863, Lamer explains that the
    growing impairment of an accused's liberty is "easily and objectively
    ascertainable." Ibid., at 925e. "[T]he only realistic means" to protect one's
    security is by "an objective standard." Ibid., at 925i. The alternative, he
    adjudges, is subjectivity: every individual can satisfy harm to her/his security
    by demonstrating subjective anxiety, stress, or stigmatization as a result of a
    criminal charge. This subjective test would be "well nigh impossible" to
    prove. Accordingly, Lamer insists upon creating what he deems to be an
    objective test for the reasonableness of a trial delay. Ibid., at 931i–j.
        Similarly, in *R.* v. *Collins*, [1987] 1 SCR 265, at 282f–283b Lamer projects
    a rational objectivity into s. 24(2) of the Charter. Section 24(2) authorizes
    the exclusion of evidence if its admission "would bring the administration
    of justice into disrepute." The latter hangs upon how "the reasonable man,
    dispassionate and fully apprised of the circumstances of the case" would
    view the admission. Of course, this reasonable person "is usually the
    average person in the community, but only when that community's current
    mood is reasonable." Also see McIntyre, ibid., at 292b–e.
234 In one of the last judgments in our five-year period, McIntyre expounds a

more sophisticated explanation of the objectivist character of Charter values. The language, structure and history of the text, constitutional tradition, and the history, traditions, and underlying philosophies of Canadian societies combine to grant determinate meaning to the Charter's rights. *Ref re Compulsory Arbitration*, [1987] 1 SCR 313, at 394i. These factors make posited, pre-Charter rules relevant to the McIntyre interpretative process. However, McIntyre ultimately rejects history and tradition as an acceptable grounding for the meaning of 'freedom of association' at 406b.

PART II

1 See generally Conklin, "The Legal Theory of Horkheimer and Adorno" (1985), 5 *Windsor Yearb. Access Justice* 230.
2 See, e.g., Hans-Georg Gadamer, *Truth and Method* (New York: Crossroad 1985, 1975); Jurgen Habermas, *The Theory of Communicative Action*, vol. 1: *Reason and the Rationalization of Society* (Boston: Beacon Press 1981); Richard Bernstein, *Beyond Objectivism and Relativism: Science, Hermeneutics and Praxis* (Philadelphia: University of Pennsylvania Press 1983); Susan J. Herman, *Hermeneutics and the Sociology of Knowledge* (Cambridge: Polity Press 1986); Richard Rorty, *Philosophy and the Mirror of Nature* (Princeton: Princeton University Press 1979).

CHAPTER VIII

1 In Part I, the generic term "rules" is used to cover both horizontal compartments and vertically posited rules, tests, principles, and doctrines. I borrow the 'vertical' and 'horizontal' concept from Kennedy, "Toward an Historical Understanding of Legal Consciousness" (1980), 3 *Research in Law & Sociology* 3.
2 The principle of the exhaustiveness of legislative power appears to have gone unquestioned by Canadian courts and legislators since it was initially laid down in the Privy Council decision of *Dow v. Black* (1875), LR 6 PC 272; 44 LJPC 52. See also *Valin v. Langlois* (1879), 5 App. Cas. 115; 49 LJPC 37; *Russell v. Reg.* (1882), 7 App. Cas. 829; 51 LJPC 77; *Lambe's Case* (1887), 12 App. Cas. 575; 56 LJPC 87; *Liquidators of the Maritime Bank* v. *Receiver-General of N.B.* [1892] AC 437; *In Re Prohibitory Liquor Laws* (1895), 24 SCR 170; and *Brophy's Case* (1895), AC 202; 64 LJPC 70. Note, for example, the recent decision of *Dupond v. City of Montreal* (1978), 19 NR 478 (SCC). Authors of texts on Canadian constitutional law have accepted the courts' premise in their traditional descriptively oriented examination of

the law. William H.P. Clement states in *The Law of the Canadian Constitution*, 3rd ed. (Toronto: Carswell 1916), at 453, for example, that "the whole field of self-government in Canada is covered in the distribution of legislative power effected by the British North America Act. Whatever belongs to self-government in Canada belongs either to the Dominion or to the provinces within the limits of the Act. Whatever is not thereby given to the provincial legislatures rests with the parliament of Canada." A.H.F. Lefroy in his *Canada's Federal System* (Toronto: Carswell 1913) asserts: "There is, then, no possible kind of legislation relating to the internal affairs of Canada, which cannot be enacted either by the Dominion parliament or by the provincial legislatures. If the subject-matter of an Act is not within the jurisdiction of the provincial legislatures, acting either severally or in concert with each other, it is within the jurisdiction of the Dominion parliament ..." (at 96–7). In his earlier *Legislative Power in Canada* (Toronto: Toronto Law Book & Publishing Co. 1897–8), at 244, Lefroy emphasizes that the exclusive authority of the legislature is "as plenary and ample within the limits prescribed by section 92 as the Imperial Parliament, in the plenitude of its power, possessed and could bestow." Its authority is "absolute" (270ff.). The 1939 Senate Report on the BNA Act reaffirms this proposition (Senate of Canada, *Report Relating to the Enactment of the British North America Act, 1867* (1939), at 14ff.). Finally, the most influential text on constitutional law in English-speaking Canada acknowledges that although sections 91 and 92 are not entirely exhaustive, the qualifications to the exhaustiveness principle merely flow from other "fundamental" provisions of the BNA Act (such as sections 133 or 91(1)) rather than from customary constitutional law. B. Laskin, *Canadian Constitutional Law*, rev. 3rd ed. (Toronto: Carswell 1969), at 92–3.

3 Lederman, "The Common Law System in Canada" [hereinafter cited as "The Common Law System"] in Edward McWhinney, ed., *Canadian Jurisprudence: The Civil Law and Common Law in Canada* (Toronto: Carswell 1958) and reprinted in W.R. Lederman, *Continuing Canadian Constitutional Dilemmas* (Toronto: Butterworths 1981), at 17. Twenty years later Lederman notes that "... this essay does reveal and develop more fully than any other my continuing basic premises and beliefs concerning some of the principle issues of legal science and philosophy" (ibid., at 42–3).

4 Kennedy, "The British North America Act: Past and Future" (1937) 15 *Can. B. Rev.* 393, at 393. Emphasis added.

5 MacDonald, "Judicial Interpretation of the Canadian Constitution" (1935–6), 1 *U. Tor. L.J.* 260, at 272; "Constitutional Interpretation and Extrinsic Evidence" (1939), 17 *Can. B. Rev.* 77, at 79.

6 MacDonald, "Constitutional Interpretation and Extrinsic Evidence," at 79.

7 MacDonald, "The Canadian Constitution Seventy Years After" (1937), 15 *Can. B. Rev.* 401, at 423. MacDonald claims, e.g., that a "basic misreading of these vital sections dominated judicial interpretation" for three decades. See MacDonald, "The Constitution in a Changing World" (1948), 26 *Can. B. Rev.* 21, at 30.

8 Abel, "The Neglected Logic of 91 and 92" [hereinafter cited as "The Neglected Logic"] (1969), 19 *U. Tor. L.J.* 487, at 503.

9 Abel, "What Peace, Order and Good Government?" (1968–9), 7–8 *Western Ont. L. Rev.* 1, at 1

10 Abel, "The Neglected Logic," at 503–4.

11 Beetz, "Les Attitudes changeantes du Québec à l'endroit de la Constitution de 1867" [hereinafter cited as "Les Attitudes changeantes"] in P.A. Crepeau and C.B. MacPherson, *The Future of Canadian Federalism* 113 (Toronto: University of Toronto Press 1965), at 115.

12 Abel, "The Neglected Logic," at 504.

13 Lederman, "The Common Law System," supra note 3, at 17.

14 See Lederman, "The Common Law System," at 18; "Classification of Laws and the British North America Act" [hereinafter cited as "Classification of Laws"] in J.A. Corry, F.C. Cronkite, and E.F. Whitmore, eds., *Legal Essays in Honour of Arthur Moxon* (Toronto: University of Toronto Press 1953), and reprinted in Lederman, *Continuing Canadian Constitutional Dilemmas*, supra note 3, chap. 12, at 242. Lederman, "Unity and Diversity in Canadian Federalism: Ideals and Methods of Moderation" (1975), 53 *Can. B. Rev.* 597 and reprinted in Lederman, *Continuing Canadian Constitutional Dilemmas*, chap. 15, at 301.

15 Lederman, "Classification of Laws," at 237; "The Common Law System," at 36.

16 Lederman, "The Common Law System," at 24.

17 Ibid., at 34.

18 Beetz, "Les Attitudes changeantes," supra note 11, at 120.

19 Beetz, "Reflections on Continuity and Change in Law Reform" (1972), 22 *Univ. Tor. L.J.* 129, at 131.

20 Kennedy, "The British North America Act: Past and Future," supra note 4, at 398; and "The Interpretation of the British North America Act" (1942–4), 8 *Camb. L.J.* 146, at 152.

21 *Re Agricultural Products Marketing Act*, [1978] 2 SCR 1198.

22 (1943), 21 *Can. B. Rev* 826.

23 Ibid., at 828–9.

24 (1951), 29 *Can. B. Rev.* 1126.

25 Ibid., at 1128.

26 [1895] AC 202, at 216.

27 Pigeon, "The Meaning of Provincial Autonomy" (1951), 29 *Can. B. Rev.* 1126, at fn. 6

28 Ibid., at 1128. Also see how much weight Pigeon gives to the new text, the Canadian Charter, in "L'Effectivité des décisions de justice en droit public interne [constitutionnel]" (1985), 26 *Les Cahiers de Droit* 995.

29 MacDonald, "The Canadian Constitution Seventy Years After," supra note 7, at 427.

30 MacDonald, "Judicial Interpretation of the Canadian Constitution," supra note 5, at 260.

31 MacDonald, "The Constitution in a Changing World," supra note 7, at 22.

32 Ibid., at 23, 32.

33 Ibid., at 24.

34 Ibid., at 22.

35 Ibid., at 24. Emphasis added.

36 Ibid., at 23.

37 See generally Kennedy, "The Interpretation of the British North America Act," supra note 20, at 146, 148, 150–1.

38 Pigeon, "Brief" to the Joint Committee on Human Rights and Fundamental Freedoms (1948), 26 *Can. B. Rev.* 706, at 714.

39 Pigeon, 'The Meaning of Provincial Autonomy,' supra note 27, at 1135.

40 *R. v. Thomas Fuller Construction* [1980] 1 SCR 695.

41 *Re Agricultural Products Marketing Act* [1978] 2 SCR 1198.

42 Pigeon, "Are the Provincial Legislatures Parliaments?" (1943), 21 *Can. B. Rev.* 826, at 827

43 Pigeon, "The Meaning of Provincial Autonomy," at 1132–3.

44 Ibid.

45 [1975] 1 SCR 494.

46 [1978] 2 SCR 1198, at 1297.

47 *R. v. Thomas Fuller Construction* [1980] 1 SCR 695, at 713.

48 *R. v. Hauser* [1979] 1 SCR 984, at 1000.

49 He describes rules of law as "notional classes of facts or type-facts." See Lederman, "Classification of Laws," supra note 14. Also see Lederman, "The Common Law System," supra note 3, at 17; "The Balanced Interpretation of the Federal Distribution of Legislative Powers in Canada" in P.A. Crepeau and C.B. MacPherson, eds., *The Future of Canadian Federalism,* supra note 11, and reprinted in Lederman, *Continuing Canadian Constitutional Dilemmas,* supra note 3, chap. 14, at 268.

50 See MacDonald, "The Constitution in a Changing World," supra note 7, at 23.

51 Kennedy, "The British North America Act: Past and Future," supra note 4, at 400.

52 MacDonald, "Judicial Interpretation of the Canadian Constitution," supra note 5, at 268; "Constitutional Interpretation and Extrinsic Evidence," supra note 5, at 83.

53 MacDonald, "The Constitution in a Changing World," at 22.

54 Ibid., at 24. Also see MacDonald, "The Canadian Constitution Seventy Years After," supra note 7, at 412.

55 Formerly of the Faculty of Law, University of Montreal (1953–70), and currently a Supreme Court judge (since 1974).

56 The judge's duty is to examine "the reality of the matter or of the matters with which in effect they deal." See *Re Anti-Inflation Act* [1976] 2 SCR 373, at 452. Also see Beetz, "Les Attitudes changeantes," supra note 11, at 117.

57 Beetz, "Reflections on Continuity and Change in Law Reform," supra note 19, at 130.

58 Ibid., at 130, fn. 2.

59 Ibid., at 132.

60 *A.-G. Can.* v. *Dupond*; *Dupond* v. *A.-G. Can.* [1978] 2 SCR 770.

61 To the contrary. Authority has been vested in the executive committee of the city. The latter can exercise its authority only after the directors of the police department and of the city's law department have expressed "that an exceptional situation warrants preventive measures." Their report must render reasons, the reasons must be justified in terms of the by-law's standard, and the prohibition must be temporary. Thus, the by-law and ordinance posit a clear, known, certain rule.

62 Quoting from Jennings, "The Right of Assembly in England" (1931–2), 9 *N.Y.U. Law Q. Rev.* 217 in *A.-G. Can.* v. *Dupond*; *Dupond* v. *A.-G. Can.* [1978] 2 SCR 770, at 796, 798. Emphasis added.

63 Kennedy, "The Interpretation of the British North America Act," supra note 20, at 153.

64 Ibid., at 156, 153.

65 Kennedy, "The British North America Act: Past and Future," supra note 4, at 398.
    In his essay "The State and the Law" Kennedy suggests that "[w]e must not confuse it [law] with some preconceived moral or ethical system." W.P.M. Kennedy, *Some Aspects of the Theories and Workings of Constitutional Law* (New York: Macmillan 1924), at 15. He continues that "[l]aw has necessarily neither any moral significance nor absolutist claim ... by 'law' we

must mean only those regulations which enable the state to carry out its peculiar functions."

66 Abel, "The Neglected Logic of 91 and 92," supra note 8, at 488, 491, 497, 510, 512.

67 Ibid., at 520, fn. 108; Also see Abel, "The Anti-Inflation Judgment: Right Answer to the Wrong Question?" (1976), 26 *U. Tor. L.J.* 409, at 444.

68 Abel, "The Neglected Logic," at 503–4.

69 Beetz describes this neutral reasoning process in "Les Attitudes changeantes":

> En réalité, cette méthode d'interpretation, bien loin d'élaborer des règles *neutres, objectives, désintéressées* qui permettraient uniquement de trouver la signification d'un texte et l'intention de son auteur, dicte à l'inteprète des maximes d'ordre public qui mettent on oeuvre des critères fondementaux auxquels l'on veut accorder la priorité même à l'encontre, dans certains cas, de la volonté expresse du législateur.

> Supra note 11, at 115. Emphasis added. Beetz juxtaposes this neutral appeal to external standards with an appeal to force in *A.-G. Can.* v. *Dupond*; *Dupond* v. *A.-G. Can.* [1978] 2 SCR 770, at 797.

70 Pigeon, "French Canada's Attitude to the Canadian Constitution" in E. McWhinney, ed., *Canadian Jurisprudence: The Civil Law and Common Law in Canada*, supra note 3, at 33.

71 Pigeon, "The Meaning of Provincial Autonomy," supra note 27, at 1131.

72 Ibid., at 1131.

73 See ibid., at 1133, 1135; also see Pigeon in McWhinney, supra note 70, at 33.

74 See generally Lederman, "The Common Law System," supra note 3.

75 See esp. ibid., at 17.

76 Ibid., at 18.

77 Lederman, "Classification of Laws," supra note 14, at 242.

78 See generally Lederman, "Unity and Diversity in Canadian Federalism," supra note 14, at 301.

79 Lederman, "Classification of Laws," at 237.

80 Lederman, "The Common Law System," at 22. He distinguishes this from a logic which deduces rules from "assumed first principles." He believes that the stated "consequences" form of logic has actually "prevailed" in the common law and chancery courts. See ibid., at 34–5.

81 See ibid., at 34.

82 Ibid., at 21–3.

83 Ibid., at 17. He describes the scientific method in these terms:

> Natural scientists must formulate their general working hypotheses about cause and effect, make logical deductions from them to define particular

instances consistent therewith, and then devise verifying experiments or improve and refine their observations of reality to see whether particular instances can be made to happen, or do occur, as expected on the basis of the starting hypotheses (at 20).

Scientists create abstract concepts, as do jurists, from lower to higher levels. They constantly adjust their abstractions with the results of particular observations and experiments. Juristic thinking has particularly benefited from the experimental science method: "specifically from the tentative attitude of the natural scientist toward his premises and his scrupulous care to test and review their accuracy in relation to relevant real facts of experience" (ibid., at 22). Similarly, the jurist must carefully and constantly gather social facts to inquire whether the fact category of a rule bears an accurate reflection with the contemporary social reality (ibid., at 34–5). Also see Lederman, "Classification of Laws," supra note 14, at 232.

84 Abel received his LLM and SJD from Harvard Law School in 1937 and 1943 respectively. His teaching assignments covered several law schools: Washington University (St Louis) (1937–9), West Virginia (1940–55), Harvard (1950–1, as a visiting professor) as well as summer terms at Iowa, George Washington, and Ohio State. In 1955 he joined the Law Faculty at the University of Toronto, where he remained until his death.

85 Abel, "The Neglected Logic," supra note 8, at 512.

86 Ibid., at 499, 500.

87 Ibid., at 504.

88 Ibid., at 520.

89 Ibid., at 521.

90 Ibid., at 490. Emphasis added.

91 Ibid., at 497. See generally Abel, "What Peace, Order and Good Government?" supra note 9.

92 Ibid., at 503.

93 Ibid., at 508.

94 Ibid., at 499. He describes a section 91 or 92 class in one of his last essays in this manner:

Court-created or text-created, a class of subjects by its nature is a class, meaning that it has members and so of necessity is an aggregate. Court-created or text-created, no class of subjects can be so self-contained that its implementation can avoid 'touching on,' that is incidentally affecting, activities whose regulation in the main belongs under some other class of subjects.

Abel, "The Anti-Inflation Judgment," supra note 67, at 429.

95 Abel, "The Neglected Logic," supra note 8, at 499.

96 As Albert Abel puts it, "The matter so particularized is the key, the 'classes of subjects' so generalised the lock, to the portal of constitutionality. They must fit together. The Act says that the 'matter' must be one 'coming within' an appropriate 'class of subject' for exclusive competence to be attributed to parliament or to a legislative assembly." Ibid., at 507.

CHAPTER IX

1 Wright, "An Extra-Legal Approach to Law" (1932), 10 *Can. B. Rev.* 1, at 6.
2 "Statute Interpretation in a Nutshell" (1938), 16 *Can. B. Rev.* 1; "Three Approaches to Administrative Law: The Judicial, the Conceptual, and the Functional" (1935–6), 1 *U. Tor. L.J.* 53; "The McRuer Report: Lawyers' Values and Civil Servants' Values" (1968), 18 *U. Tor. L.J.* 351.
3 See supra note 1.
4 See Laskin, "The Protection of Interests by Statute and the Problem of 'Contracting Out'" [hereinafter cited as "The Protection of Interests"] (1938), 16 *Can. B. Rev.* 669; "'Peace, Order and Good Government' Re-Examined" (1947) 25 *Can. B. Rev.* 1054; "Tests for the Validity of Legislation: What's the 'Matter'?" (1955–6), 11 *U. of Tor. L.J.* 114; "The Supreme Court of Canada: A Final Court of and for Canadians" (1951) 29 *Can. B. Rev.* 1038.
5 *Harrison* v. *Carswell* [1976] 2 SCR 200, at 208.
6 See generally text supra chap. VIII, sect. 56.
7 See esp. text supra chap. VIII, sect. 2.
8 Mark MacGuigan, for example, rejects a "positivistic" image of a constitution which projects as "ideologically neutral, embodying no lofty statements of ideals and parading no value judgments" (in "The Privy Council and the Supreme Court: A Jurisprudential Analysis" (1966) 4 *Alta. L. Rev.* 419, at 419). He also rejects a "sociological" image which concentrates upon "native" judicial bodies alive to indigenous social conditions. MacGuigan describes his image as "essentially a natural-law one" (ibid., at 421). MacGuigan considers his image a non-positivist natural law one because "[t]he ultimate decision had to be a value judgment, or, if you prefer, a policy decision" (ibid., at 425). If judges cannot reach their decisions rationally, then the only possible alternative, he imagines, is a "values" approach. If only courts considered "the historically documented intention of the Fathers" and a 'Brandeis Brief' revelation of contemporary exigencies, their "natural law" or values method would be more appealing. Ironically, MacGuigan condemns the textualism of the Privy Council as "positivistic" without realizing what Lederman has: namely, that judges equally posit the values which MacGuigan erroneously labels "natural law" (425–6).

9 See generally, Russell, "The Political Purposes of the Canadian Charter of Rights and Freedoms" (1983), 61 *Can. B. Rev.* 30; idem, "Bold Statescraft, Questionable Jurisprudence" in Keith Banting and Richard Simeon, eds., *And No One Cheered: Federalism, Democracy and the Constitution Act* (Toronto: Methuen 1983), at 210; idem, "Judicial Power in Canada's Political Culture" in M.L. Friedland, ed., *Courts and Trials: A Multidisciplinary Approach* (Toronto: University of Toronto Press 1975), at 75; idem, "The Political Role of the Supreme Court of Canada in Its First Century" (1975), 53 *Can. B. Rev.* 576, at 576; idem, "The Jurisdiction of the Supreme Court of Canada: Present Policies and a Programme for Reform" (1968), 6 *Osgoode H.L.J.* 1, at 5; idem, "A Democratic Approach to Civil Liberties" (1969), 19 *U. Tor. L.J.* 109, at 128–9.

Also see Robert Décary, "Le Pouvoir judiciare face au jeu politique" in Peter Russell, Robert Décary, William Lederman, Noel Lyon, and D. Soberman, *The Court and the Constitution: Comments on the Supreme Court Reference on Constitutional Amendment* (Kingston: Institute of Intergovernmental Relations, Queen's University 1982), Gil Rémillard, "Legality, Legitimacy and the Supreme Court" in Keith Banting and Richard Simeon, eds., *And No One Cheered* (Toronto: Methuen 1983), at 189.

This political orientation appears to have seen its first full discussion in Paul Weiler, *In the Last Resort: A Critical Study of the Supreme Court of Canada* (Toronto: Carswell/Methuen 1974). Also see Monahan, "At Doctrine's Twilight: The Structure of Canadian Federalism" (1984), 34 *U. Tor. L.J.* 47, esp. at 90–9 where Monahan penetratingly elaborates an image of a constitution very similar to Weiler's.

This essayist also tries to differentiate a political image of a constitution from rule rationalism in Conklin, "Clear Cases" (1981), 31 *U. Tor. L.J.* 231; and "A Practical Legal Education" (1982), 7 *Dalhousie L.J.* 122, although I also attempt to transcend a 'policy' image of law without realizing the positivist character of the prescribed approach.

10 See generally Russell, "Overcoming Legal Formalism: The Treatment of the Constitution, the Courts and Judicial Behaviour in Canadian Political Science" (1986), 1 *Can. J. Law and Society* 5.

11 See, e.g., Consultative Group on Research and Education in Law, *Law and Learning* (Ottawa: Social Sciences & Humanities Research Council 1983), esp. chap. 2, 4, 10. Also see Veitch, "The Vocation of Our Era for Legal Education" (1979), 44 *Sask. L. Rev.* 19, at 31ff. Campbell, "Toward an Improved Legal Education: Is There Anyone Out There?" (1978), 44 *Sask. L. Rev.* 81, esp. at 89–96; and Conklin, "A Practical Legal Education," supra note 9.

12 See generally the essays discussed in Russell, supra note 9; and see *Law and Learning*, supra note 11.

13 See esp. Laskin, "The Protection of Interests" and "'Peace, Order and Good Government' Re-Examined," supra note 4. Also see idem, "Book Review" (1967), 10 *Can. Pub. Admin.* 514, at 517 in reviewing G.P. Browne, *The Judicial Committee and the British North America Act* (Toronto: University of Toronto Press 1967). Laskin described the rule rationalist image as "sterile" (at 514) and "a stupidity" (at 516). Also see his support for the policy realism of J. Noel Lyon and Ronald G. Atkey, *Canadian Constitutional Law in a Modern Perspective* [hereinafter cited as *Canadian Constitutional Law*] (Toronto: University of Toronto Press 1970) in (1971), 10 *U. Western Ont. L. Rev.* 195.

14 Laskin, "The Protection of Interests," at 670–1.

15 Ibid., at 669–73.

16 Ibid., at 671.

17 Laskin, "'Peace, Order and Good Government' Re-examined," at 1061.

18 Ibid., at 1056.

19 Ibid., at 1080.

20 Ibid., at 1067.

21 Ibid., at 1068–9.

22 In *Local Prohibition Case, A.-G. Ont.* v. *A.-G. Can.* [1896] AC 348, at 361, Watson states:

> Their Lordships do not doubt that some matters, in their origin local and provincial, might attain such dimensions as to affect the body politic of the Dominion, and to justify the Canadian Parliament in passing laws for their regulation or abolition in the interest of the Dominion. But great caution must be observed in distinguishing between that which is local and provincial, and therefore within the jurisdiction of the provincial legislatures, and that which has ceased to be merely local or provincial, and has become matter of national concern, in such sense as to bring it within the jurisdiction of the Parliament of Canada.

Watson's *dictum*, Laskin believes, makes "allowance for a social and economic development of Canada" ("'Peace, Order and Good Government' Re-examined" at 1068) by requiring the legal community to go directly to Canadian statutes, freed of the Privy Council's artificial abstractions. Canadian statutes are the critical source of social/economic reality because, following Holmes, a legislature – as opposed to a court – best reflects the myriad contending social forces at any one time. See, e.g., "The Protection of Interests," supra note 4, at 669 and 673. Laskin gains much from Holmes (see, e.g., ibid., at 671) who, in turn, was heavily influenced by Darwin. See Conklin, "The Political Theory of Mr. Justice Holmes" (1978), 26 *Chitty's L.J.* 200.

23 Laskin, "Tests for the Validity of Legislation," supra note 4, 116.
24 Laskin, "'Peace, Order and Good Government' Re-examined," at 1059–60.
25 Ibid., at 1076.
26 [1925] AC 396.
27 Laskin, "'Peace, Order and Good Government' Re-examined," at 1077.
28 Ibid. Emphasis added.
29 Ibid., at 1080.
30 Laskin, "'Peace, Order and Good Government' Re-examined," at 1057.
31 Ibid., at 1069.
32 Laskin, "The Protection of Interests," at 669.
34 Laskin, "The Supreme Court of Canada," supra note 4, at 1071.
35 Even a judicially elaborated text in the form of Reasons for Judgment does not constitute the source of law as represented by Vincent MacDonald, Bora Laskin, and other realists. Indeed, "traditional analyses" of Canadian constitutional law have erroneously assumed for too long that appellate courts actually render the only significant public law decisions. See generally Lyon and Atkey, *Canadian Constitutional Law*, supra note 13, at 128. To imagine that a constitution's source lies in a text's formal rules reflects "the heavy hand of positivism" and positivism's "inhibiting attitudes." Lyon, "A Fresh Approach to Constitutional Law: Use of a Policy-Science Model" [hereinafter cited as "A Fresh Approach"] (1967), 45 *Can. B. Rev.* 554, at 554.
36 Noel Lyon's writings demonstrate the deep influence of Harold D. Lasswell and M.S. McDougal upon Lyon while he was a student at the Yale Law School during the 1950s. Several of his more recent essays acknowledge the influence of Lasswell and McDougal upon his own image of a constitution. In "The Teleological Mandate of the Fundamental Freedoms Guarantee; What to Do with Vague but Meaningful Generalities" [hereinafter cited as "The Teleological Mandate"] (1982), 4 *Sup. Ct. L. Rev.* 57 at fn. 7, Lyon notes that Lasswell and McDougal's "Criteria for a Theory about Law" (1971), 44 *So. Calif. L. Rev.* 362, has provided the tools for Lyon and Atkey's "attempt to re-shape Canadian constitutional analysis around a policy-science framework" in Lyon and Atkey, *Canadian Constitutional Law*. The appeal of models to Lyon is influenced by Harold Lasswell, *The Future of Political Science* (New York: Atherton Prd. 1963). See Lyon, "Modelling as an Approach to Judicial Reform" in (1981), 1 *Windsor Yearb. Access Justice* 281 at fn. 3. It is not a coincidence that a former colleague and associate of Lasswell and McDougal, Oscar Schacter, best elaborates and publicizes this element of public international law. See Schacter, "The Evolving Law of International Development" (1976), 15 *Colum. Int'l Dev't* 1; "Towards a Theory of International Obligation" (1968), 8 *Va. J. Int'l L.* 300 and reprinted in S.M.

Schwebel, ed., *The Effectiveness of International Decisions* (Leyden: Sijthoff 1971).

37 Lyon, "A Fresh Approach," supra note 35, at 559. Emphasis Lyon's.

38 J. Noel Lyon and Ronald G. Atkey, *Canadian Constitutional Law*, at 70.

39 Shared goal/values constitute the exclusive content of a constitution. By utilizing a broad range of historical and contemporary institutional materials, for example, Lyon and Atkey identify and clarify the content of fundamental shared judicial values: judicial restraint, judicial ingenuity, separation of powers, and the rule of law. They focus upon processes whereby such protected values crystallized as political activities, "development and protection of the public mind," security and well-being, recognition of the individual person, economic activities, conscience and religious activities, creative activities, and the bonds of human affection. Language rights, they believe, synthesize both historically enshrined and contemporary values within the Canadian body politic. Finally, Lyon and Atkey do not examine Canadian federalism in terms of "the logic" of the text, as has Albert Abel, or the social/political interest groups causing the enactment of Canadian statutes as has Laskin, or the notional categories of rules as has Lederman. Rather, the 'modern perspective' image of a constitution identifies the value preferences shared by both federal and provincial governments over time in their judicial and non-judicial, formal and informal processes of decision-making. Lyon and Atkey demonstrate how parties have deferred to such shared value preferences as competence in relation to political processes, safety, health and general well-being, autonomy of decision-making, wealth, respect for persons, an enlightened public mind, creative expression, and the family and other human associations.

40 Lyon, "A Fresh Approach," at 561.

41 Lyon and Ronald Atkey, *Canadian Constitutional Law*, at vi.

42 Laskin, "Tests for the Validity of Legislation," supra note 4, at 127. Also see the writings of Weiler and Russell cited supra note 9.

43 Laskin, "Tests for the Validity of Legislation," at 127.

44 Ibid., at 117.

45 Laskin, "Book Review" (1967), 10 *Can. Pub. Admin.* 514, at 517 in reviewing G.P. Browne, *The Judicial Committee and the British North America Act.* See supra note 13.

46 Laskin, "Tests for the Validity of Legislation," at 119.

47 Laskin, "'Peace, Order and Good Government' Re-examined," supra note 4, at 1056.

48 Laskin, "Tests for the Validity of Legislation," at 119.

49 Ibid., at 118.

50 Ibid., at 120–1.

51 Ibid., at 121.

52 Ibid., at 123.

53 Supra note 32.

54 Laskin, "'Peace, Order and Good Government' Re-examined," at 1086. Emphasis added.

55 Bora Laskin, *The Institutional Character of the Judge* (Jerusalem: Magnes Press, Hebrew University 1972), at 24. Emphasis added.

56 Weiler implicitly longs to return to the old days when judges actually appealed to objective legal standards. See, e.g., Weiler, "Two Models of Judicial Decision-Making" (1968), 46 *Can. B. Rev.* 406.

57 See Weiler, "The Supreme Court of Canada and Canadian Federalism" (1973), 11 *Osgoode H.L.J.* 225, at 236.

58 See ibid., at 226.

59 See generally Russell, *The Supreme Court of Canada as a Bilingual and Bicultural Institution*, vol. 1 (Ottawa: Information Canada 1969), at 176–7.

60 See Russell, "Judicial Power," supra note 9, at 75.

61 See Russell, "The Political Role," supra note 9, at 576. Emphasis added.

62 (Toronto: McGraw-Hill 1987), at 3. Also see Russell, "The Jurisdiction," supra note 9, at 5.

63 See Russell, "A Democratic Approach to Civil Liberties," supra note 9, at 128–9.

64 Ibid., at 129.

65 Ibid., at 131.

66 See generally Russell, *The Supreme Court of Canada*, supra note 59, at 176–7.

67 Ibid.

68 Russell, "Judicial Power," at 75.

69 Russell, "The Political Role," at 579.

70 Ibid., at 576.

71 Russell, "A Democratic Approach to Civil Liberties," at 123.

72 "Le Pouvoir judicaire face au jeu politique," supra note 9. For an earlier exposition of the political bias of the federally appointed judiciary see generally, e.g., Royal Commission of Inquiry on Constitutional Problems, Report, vol. 2 (Quebec: Province de Québec 1956).

73 Ibid., at 29. Décary's emphasis.

74 Ibid., at 29.

75 Louis-Philippe Pigeon explains and appeals to this "axiomatic rule," "fundamental principle," "general rule," "basic principle," "special character" of provincial autonomy in his several academic essays and many

federalism decisions. See generally, e.g., Pigeon, *Brief* to the Joint Committee on Human Rights and Fundamental Rights (1948), 26 *Can. B. Rev.* 706, at 714; "The Meaning of Provincial Autonomy" (1951), 29 *Can. B. Rev.* 1126; *R. v. Thomas Fuller Construction*, [1980] 1 SCR 695; *Re Agricultural Products Marketing Act*, [1978] 2 SCR 1198; and "Are the Provincial Legislatures Parliaments?" (1943), 21 *Can. B. Rev.* 826. The axiomatic rule states that provincial parliaments (and federal parliaments) are "mistresses in their own house." Pigeon grounds the rule in four sources: Sankey's "interprovincial compact" or "original contract" image of Confederation; the constitutional requirement that only the British Parliament can amend sections 91 and 92 of the BNA Act, 1867; Sankey's "mistress in her own house" *dicta* in the *Persons Case* [1930] AC 124; and French Canada's attitude of the treaty character of the Canadian constitution.

76 As quoted in Décary "Le Pouvoir Judiciare Face au Jeu Politique," supra note 9, at 37

77 Ibid., at 31.

78 As quoted in ibid., at 39.

79 Supra note 9.

80 Ibid., at 189.

81 *Le Fédéralisme Canadien* (Montreal: Québec/Amérique 1983), at 258. See esp. 227–57.

82 Rémillard, "Legality, Legitimacy and the Supreme Court," supra note 9, at 189.

83 Rémillard, *Le Fédéralisme Canadien*, at 258, See esp. 218–26.

84 For a discussion of the case see generally text supra chap. IV.

85 Rémillard, "Legality, Legitimacy and the Supreme Court" at 190.

86 Ibid., at 191.

87 Ibid., at 192.

88 Ibid., at 193.

89 Ibid., at 194. Emphasis added.

90 Ibid., at 193.

91 Ibid., at 200.

92 Ibid. See generally text supra chap. IV between notes 78 and 86.

93 Ibid., at 200–1.

94 Laskin, "The Protection of Interests," supra note 4, at 670. The old "natural rights" talk, Laskin complains, serves "no good purpose to discuss at too great length."

95 It is not difficult to see the influence of Holmes, Brandeis, Frankfurter, and other utilitarians upon the young Laskin. See generally William E. Conklin, *In Defence of Fundamental Rights* (Alphen aan den Rijn/Germantown, Md.:

Sijthoff & Noordhoff 1979), at 236–41. Also see Conklin, "The Political
Theory of Mr. Justice Holmes," supra note 22.

96 Thirty-five years after Laskin has advanced his balancing role for judges, he
still maintains that a judge should balance the competing social interests
at issue in any one case. See *Harrison v. Carswell* [1976] 2 SCR 200, at 208.

97 Laskin, "The Protection of Interests," at 695.

98 Ibid., at 671.

99 Laskin, "'Peace, Order and Good Government' Re-examined," supra note
4, at 1055.

100 Ibid., at 1086.

101 See *Harrison v. Carswell*, [1976] 2 SCR 200, at 208.

102 See Weiler, "Of Judges and Scholars: Reflections in a Centennial Year"
(1975) 53 *Can. B. Rev.* 563, at 574.

103 See Weiler, "The Supreme Court of Canada and Canadian Federalism,"
supra note 57, at 244.

104 See esp. Weiler, "Two Models of Judicial Decision-Making," supra note 56.

105 See, e.g., Weiler, "The Supreme Court ...," at 231–2.

106 Ibid., at 244. Weiler consistently uses the term "inoperative" rather than
"invalid." All statutes, then, are constitutionally valid. Only rarely is a
statute ever inoperative.

107 See Weiler, "The Supreme Court ...," at 238. Emphasis added.

108 For Peter Russell's views on this issue, see, e.g., "A Democratic Approach to
Civil Liberties," supra note 9. Also see Peter Russell, *The Judiciary in
Canada* (Toronto: McGraw-Hill 1987), at 16–17.

109 See Lederman, "The Common Law System in Canada" in Edward
McWhinney, ed., *Canadian Jurisprudence: The Civil Law and Common Law in
Canada* (Toronto: Carswell 1958) and reprinted in W.R. Lederman, *Continuing Canadian Constitutional Dilemmas* (Toronto: Butterworths 1981) 11,
at 22.

110 Lederman, "Classification of Laws and the British North America Act" in
J.A. Corry, F.C. Cronkite, and E.F. Whitmore, eds., *Legal Essays in Honour of
Arthur Moxon* (Toronto: University of Toronto Press 1953) and reprinted in
Lederman, *Continuing Canadian Constitutional Dilemmas*, chap. 12, at 229.
Also see Lederman, "The Independence of the Judiciary" (1956), 34 *Can.
B. Rev.* 769, 1139 and reprinted in Lederman, ibid., chap. 7.

111 Lederman, "The Common Law System in Canada," at 41.

112 Indeed, he dreads a judiciary who, like the Privy Council, would "once
again inadvertently subvert the will of the people, this time expressed as
higher law rather than mere statute, *to their own judgment* ..." (Lyon, "Vague
but Meaningful Generalities," supra note 36, at 242; emphasis added).

Indeed, Lyon rejects as "a very bad idea" any suggestion that Charter judges should evaluate the wisdom of legislation. Why? "[B]ecause it suggests that they are to decide cases according to something other than law," Lyon responds. See Lyon, "The Charter as a Mandate for New Ways of Thinking about Law" (1984), 9 *Queen's L.J.* 241, at 242. And the community's values, not judge's value choices, constituted the law.

113 Supra note 37, 557–8.
114 Ibid., at 558. Emphasis added.
115 See, e.g., Lyon and Atkey, *Canadian Constitutional Law*, supra note 13, at 634.
116 Supra note 112, at 242. Emphasis added.
117 Lyon, "Modelling as an Approach to Judicial Reform," supra note 36, at 283–4. Emphasis added.
118 "The Teleological Mandate," supra note 36, at 58. Emphasis added.
119 Ibid., at 65. Emphasis added.
120 Ibid., at 72. Emphasis added.
121 See generally the essays cited supra note 9.
122 By 'power,' Peter Russell means "the initiation of significant changes in our customs, our laws, or institutions and the maintenance of some important features of the established order." See "Judicial Power," supra note 9, at 75. He affirms David Easton's classic conception of power as "the authoritative allocation of values." See Russell, "The Political Role of the Supreme Court in Its First Century," supra note 9, at 576. Emphasis added.
123 See Laskin, "The Protection of Interests," supra note 4, at 699.
124 Laskin, "'Peace, Order and Good Government' Re-examined," supra note 4, at 1060.
125 Lyon and Atkey, *Canadian Constitutional Law*, supra note 13, at 75.
126 Ibid., at 129.
127 Ibid., at 118.
128 Ibid., at 255–78. "Informal" institutions play "a substantial role in constitutional decisions and policy" (at 255).
129 Lyon, "A Fresh Approach," supra note 35, at 556–7.
130 Ibid., at 557.
131 See Lyon and Atkey, *Canadian Constitutional Law*, at 50, and Lyon, "A Fresh Approach," at 557.
132 Lyon, "A Fresh Approach," at 557.
133 See Lyon and Atkey, *Canadian Constitutional Law*, at 71.
134 See, e.g., Russell, "A Democratic Approach to Civil Liberties," supra note 9, at 128–9.
135 See, e.g., Russell, *The Supreme Court as a Bilingual and Bicultural Institution*,

supra note 59; "The Political Role of the Supreme Court of Canada," supra note 9; and "The Jurisdiction of the Supreme Court of Canada," supra note 9. One cannot help but be impressed with the detailed empirical data which Russell marshals in his political analysis of *The Judiciary in Canada: The Third Branch of Government*, supra note 108.

136 See, e.g., Russell, "The Prognosis for Research in Law Schools" in National Conference on Law and Learning, *Proceedings*, 1 and 2 Dec. 1983, at 128. Also see his essays cited supra note 9, esp. "A Democratic Approach ..."

137 See the research summarized in Russell, "Overcoming Legal Formalism," supra note 10. Also see essays in *Windsor Yearb. Access Justice*, vols. 1–6.

138 Lyon, "The Central Fallacy of Canadian Constitutional Law" (1976), 22 *McGill L.J.* 40, at 40.

139 See, e.g., Lyon, "Constitutional Theory and the Martland/Ritchie Dissent" in Peter Russell, Robert Décary, William Lederman, Noel Lyon, and D. Soberman, *The Court and the Constitution: Comments on the Supreme Court Reference on Constitutional Amendment* (Kingston: Institute of Intergovernmental Relations, Queen's University 1982) where Lyon argues that the majority and minority opinions in the *Patriation Reference* reflect "fundamentally different conceptions of the law of the Canadian Constitution" (at 57). Reprinted in (1981) 7 *Queen's L.J.*, at 135.

140 Lyon, "Modelling," supra note 36, at 282.

141 In his "Central Fallacy" essay, for example, Lyon demonstrates how the English theory of legislative supremacy has again coloured the Canadian legal community's picture of an "implied bill of rights" and the Canadian Bill of Rights (supra note 138, 50–1). Although the latter, again, represents shared fundamental rights values within the Canadian political processes, the retained English theory has had a negative impact upon the values. Similarly, on a more constructive bent, Lyon urges lawyers to move outward from the text of the Charter of Rights "in search of a general context of meaning that is shaped by *the political tradition* the Charter is meant to reflect." See "The Charter as a Mandate ..." supra note 112, at 242. Emphasis added. Political theory offers the contemporary lawyer "a good general perspective." The political theory to which one should appeal can be found in the writings of Corry and Hodgetts, Robert Dahl, Daniel Bell, *Brown* v. *Board of Education*, John Stuart Mill, Devlin, Chaim Perelman, Ronald Dworkin, and others.

142 Lyon, "The Central Fallacy," supra note 138.

143 Ibid., at 40.

144 *Ref re. Proclamation of Section 16 of the Criminal Law Amendment Act., 1968–69*, [1970] SCR 777; (1970), 10 DLR (3d) 669.

145 See Lyon, "The Central Fallacy," at 40–1. Also see Lyon, "Constitutional Theory and the Martland/Ritchie Dissent," supra note 139, at 59, 63.
146 Lyon, "Constitutional Validity of Sections 3 and 4 of the Public Order Regulations, 1970" (1972), 18 *McGill L.J.* 136.
147 Ibid., at 143.
148 Lyon, "The Central Fallacy," at 47.

CHAPTER X

1 See esp. text, supra chap. VII, sect. 3.
2 Lederman himself was particularly conscious of the "dilemmas" emanating from his image. What the fundamental dilemma was we shall see below. He called his major book *Continuing Canadian Constitutional Dilemmas.*
3 [hereinafter cited as "The Common Law System"] Edward McWhinney, ed., *Canadian Jurisprudence: The Civil Law and Common Law in Canada* (Toronto: Carswell 1958) and reprinted in W.R. Lederman, *Continuing Canadian Constitution Dilemmas* (Toronto: Butterworths 1981), chap. 2.
4 Lederman, "The Common Law System," at 42–3.
5 Ibid., at 17.
6 Ibid., at 14–15. At 12, Lederman describes the Blackstonian vision as "a substantively complete and closed system of justice – a detailed natural law system – that was progressively discovered by the judges as its various pre-existing parts were needed."
7 Ibid., at 15.
8 Ibid., at 17.
9 Ibid., at 15. Emphasis added.
10 See esp. ibid., at 17–18, 20–21.
11 Ibid., at 17.
12 Ibid.
13 Lederman, "Classification of Laws and the British North America Act" [hereinafter cited as "Classification of Laws"] in *Continuing Canadian Constitutional Dilemmas,* supra note 3, chap. 12, at 230.
14 Lederman, "The Common Law System," at 25.
15 Lederman, "Classification of Laws," at 230.
16 Ibid., at 239.
17 Ibid., at 230, 233, 237.
18 Ibid., at 232.
19 Ibid., at 230.
20 See text supra between notes 4 and 6.
21 Lederman, "Classification of Laws," at 230.

22 Lederman, "The Balanced Interpretation of the Federal Distribution of Legislative Powers in Canada" [hereinafter cited as "The Balanced Interpretation"] in P.A. Crepeau and C.B. MacPherson, eds., *The Future of Canadian Federalism* (Toronto: University of Toronto Press 1965) and reprinted in Lederman, *Continuing Canadian Constitutional Dilemmas*, supra note 3, chap. 14 at 268.

23 "Unity and Diversity in Canadian Federalism: Ideals and Methods of Moderation" (1975), 53 *Can. B. Rev.* 597, reprinted in Lederman, *Continuing Canadian Constitutional Dilemmas*, chap. 15 at 285. Emphasis added.

24 Ibid., at 290. Emphasis added.

25 Lederman, "Classification of Laws," at 239. Emphasis his own.

26 Lederman, "The Common Law System," at 17.

27 See generally text supra chap. VIII, sect. 6.

28 Lederman, "The Common Law System," at 20.

29 Ibid., at 20, 23.

30 Ibid., at 22.

31 Ibid., at 34–5. Also see Lederman, "Classification of Laws," at 232.

32 Lederman, "The Common Law System," at 20.

33 See text infra sect. 4. I am indebted to Dev Bains, a former student of mine, for showing me the importance of faith within Lederman's image of a constitution.

34 Lederman, "The Common Law System," at 19–20. Emphasis Lederman's.

35 Lederman, "Classification of Laws," at 234.

36 Ibid., at 232.

37 Lederman, "The Balanced Interpretation," supra note 22, at 268.

38 Lederman, "The Canadian Constitution and the Protection of Human Rights" in R.St.J. MacDonald and J.P. Humphrey, eds., *The Practice of Freedom* (Toronto: Butterworths 1979) and reprinted in Lederman, *Continuing Canadian Constitutional Dilemmas*, supra note 3, chap. 24, at 403.

39 Lederman, "The Common Law System," at 40.

40 Lederman, "The Balanced Interpretation," at 276.

41 Lederman, "Classification of Laws," at 241.

42 Ibid., at 245.

43 Lederman, "Unity and Diversity in Canadian Federalism," supra note 23, at 300.

44 See, e.g., Lederman, "The Canadian Constitution and the Protection of Human Rights," supra note 38, at 405; "Securing Human Rights in a Renewed Confederation" in Richard Simeon, ed., *Must Canada Fail?* (Montreal and London: McGill-Queen's University Press 1977) and reprinted in Lederman, *Continuing Canadian Constitutional Dilemmas*,

supra note 3, chap. 26, at 421ff. "The Power of the Judges and the New Canadian Charter of Rights and Freedoms" [1982] *U.B.C.L. Rev.* 1, at 2, 4.

45 Lederman, "The Canadian Constitution and the Protection of Human Rights," at 408.
46 Lederman, "The Power of the Judges ...," at 4.
47 Ibid., at 7.
48 Lederman, "Classification of Laws," at 238.
49 Ibid., at 241.
50 Lederman, "The Common Law System," at 22.
51 Ibid., at 38.
52 Lederman, "Classification of Laws," at 241.
53 Ibid., at 241.
54 Lederman, "The Common Law System," at 38.
55 Ibid., at 38–9.
56 Ibid., at 38.
57 Ibid., at 39.
58 Ibid., at 40.
59 Lederman, "Classification of Laws," at 241.
60 See esp. Lederman, "The Common Law System," at 16.
61 See esp. ibid., at 22.
62 Lederman, "Classification of Laws," at 229. Also see Lederman, "The Independence of the Judiciary" (1956), 34 *Can. B. Rev.* 769, 1139 and reprinted in Lederman, *Continuing Canadian Constitutional Dilemmas*, supra note 3, chap. 7.
63 Ibid. Emphasis added.
64 Lederman, "The Common Law System," at 41. Emphasis added.
65 Ibid., at 16. Emphasis added. In a similar vein Lederman points out at 34 that Roscoe Pound and Morris R. Cohen, advocates of the orthodox picture of reality, "do have faith in the possibility of partially significant insights into the proper order and truth of human relations, and are convinced of the need to strive for such insights for legal purposes in terms of generalized normative propositions."
66 Lederman, "The Common Law System," at 21–2.
67 Ibid. at 30.
68 Ibid., at 34. Emphasis added.
69 Ibid., at 41. Emphasis added.
70 Ibid. Emphasis added.
71 Lederman, "The Balanced Interpretation," at 276.
72 Lederman, "Classification of Laws," at 242.

73 Ibid., at 241.
74 Lederman, "The Common Law System," at 42. Emphasis added.
75 Ibid., at 24.
76 Lederman, "Classification of Laws," at 246.

PART III

1 These issues can also be gleaned from the text infra chap. v–vii.
2 Bentham, "Anarchical Fallacies" (1843) in A.E. Melden, ed., *Human Rights* (Belmont, Calif.: Wadsworth 1970), at 28.

CHAPTER XI

1 The historicist element of his judgments is discussed in William E. Conklin, *In Defence of Fundamental Rights* (Alphen aan den Rijn/Germantown, Md.: Sijthoff & Noordhoff 1979), at 37–41.
2 The rationalist element of his judgments is discussed in Conklin, ibid., at 39–40.
3 Kurt von Kritz and Ernst Kapp, transl.; (New York: Haffner Press 1950, 1974)
4 See esp. bks. i–iii.
5 [1959] SCR 121. See text supra chap. ii, sect. 1.
6 Ibid., at 141. See text supra chap. ii following note 26.
7 See esp. Royal Commission Inquiry into Labour Disputes, *Report* ("The Rand Report"), at 7–11. Cf. Aristotle, *Politics* 1274b 32 to 1275b 21.
8 See Rand, "Law in a Plural Society in a Crisis Age" in E. McWhinney, ed., *Canadian Jurisprudence: The Civil Law and Common Law in Canada* (Toronto: Carswell 1958), at xv. Cf. Aristotle, *Politics* 1278a40 to 1279a24; Johnson, "Who Is Aristotle's Citizen?" (1984), 29 *Phronesis* 73.
9 The connection of rights to the person or personality is a constant theme in Rand's essays and his judgments. For the former see Rand, "Some Aspects of Canadian Constitutionalism" (1960) 38 *Can. B. Rev.* 135, at 155; "Except by Due Process of Law" (1961), 2 *Osgoode H.L.J.* 171, at 178; and "The Role of an Independent Judiciary in Preserving Freedom" (1951) 9 *U. Tor. L.J.* 1, at 2–4.
10 Supra note 6.
11 [1951] SCR 887, at 918.
12 [1957] SCR 285, at 306. Emphasis added.
13 See text, supra note 1. See esp. Aristotle, *Politics* 1274b–1280a. Also, see generally Aristotle, *Constitution of Athens* (New York: Haffner Press 1950).

14 See *Politics* 1279a–b; *Nichomachean Ethics* 1161a–b.

15 See *Politics* 1276b, 33–9.

16 *Telos* is defined as "completion, end, purpose" in F.E. Peters, *Greek Philosophical Terms* (New York: New York University Press 1967), at 191.

17 See *Ethics* I.7, 1097b22 to 1098a8.

18 [1957] SCR 285, at 288.

19 Ibid., at 306.

20 Ibid.

21 Ibid. Emphasis added.

22 Rand, "Except by Due Process of Law," supra note 9, at 178. Emphasis added.

23 Rand, "Some Aspects of Canadian Constitutionalism," supra note 9, at 155. Emphasis added.

24 *Switzman v. Ebling*, [1957] SCR 285, at 306–7. Emphasis added.

25 Ibid., at 306–7. Emphasis added.

26 [1953] 2 SCR 299.

27 Ibid., at 325.

28 Ibid., at 329. Emphasis added.

29 Rand, "Some Aspects ...," at 155

30 Rand, "The Role of an Independent Judiciary ...," supra note 9, at 2.

31 Aristotle concludes that the *telos* of the human organism is to pursue *eudaimonia* or to flourish. This, he defines as "the energy and practice of goodness, to a degree of perfection, and in a mode which is absolute and not relative" (*Politics* 1332a). Throughout most of the *Ethics*, Aristotle describes *eudaimonia* as a state of character which makes one good and which causes one to perform one's function well.

32 [1951] SCR 265.

33 For a discussion of the elements of the crime and their political presuppositions see generally Conklin, "The Origins of the Law of Sedition" (1973), 15 *Crim. L.Q.* 277.

34 [1951] SCR 265, at 288. Emphasis added.

35 Ibid. Emphasis added.

36 Ibid. Emphasis added.

37 *Winner v. S.M.T. (Eastern) Ltd.*, [1951] SCR 887.

38 Ibid., at 920. Emphasis added.

39 Ibid.

40 *Politics* 1279a.

41 [1957] SCR 285, at 306. Emphasis added.

42 [1953] 2 SCR 299, at 329. Emphasis added.

43 [1951] SCR 265, at 288. Emphasis added.

44 [1951] SCR 887, at 920. Emphasis added.

45 [1953] 2 SCR 299, at 330. Emphasis added.

46 Ibid. Emphasis added.

47 [1957] SCR 285, at 306. Although he only refers to men in his judgments and academic essays, I presume that he also intends to include women. One cannot make this assumption of Aristotle, of course. See, e.g., Susan Moller Okin, *Women in Western Political Thought* (Princeton: Princeton University Press 1979), chap. 4.

48 Ibid., at 307.

49 S. 7 provides as follows: "There shall be One Parliament for Canada, consisting of the Queen, an Upper House styled the Senate, and the House of Commons." For such an argument see Conklin, *In Defence of Fundamental Rights*, supra note 2, at 27–9.

50 [1959] SCR 121. See text supra chap. II, sect. 1.

51 [1951] SCR 887, at 920.

52 Rand, "Some Aspects ...," supra note 9, at 155. Emphasis added.

53 Rand, "Except by Due Process of Law," supra note 9, at 177. Emphasis added.

54 [1953] 2 SCR 299.

55 Ibid., at 329. Emphasis added.

56 Rand, "Some Aspects ..." at 154.

57 [1953] 2 SCR 299, at 329. Emphasis added.

58 [1957] SCR 198.

59 Ibid., at 211. Emphasis added.

60 Ibid. Emphasis added.

61 [1958] SCR 626.

62 Ibid., at 638.

63 Ibid., at 638.

64 Ibid., at 642.

65 Ibid., at 639.

66 Ibid., at 638.

67 Ibid., at 642.

68 Ibid.

69 [1951] SCR 887, at 919.

70 *Report* supra note 7, at 8.

71 *Winner* v. *S.M.T. (Eastern) Ltd.*, [1951] SCR 887, at 919.

72 See Rand, "Some Aspects ...," supra note 9, at 151.

73 Ibid., at 152. See generally Lederman, "Mr. Justice Rand and Canada's Federal Constitution" (1979–80), 18 *U. Western Ont. L. Rev.* 31 and reprinted in William R. Lederman, *Continuing Canadian Constitutional Dilemmas* (Toronto: Butterworths 1981), chap. 23 at 389.

74 *Winner* v. *S.M.T. (Eastern) Ltd.*, [1951] SCR 887, at 920.

75 [1959] SCR 121, at 139–40

76 Ibid., at 141.

77 The restatement reads as follows:

That, in the presence of expanding administrative regulation of economic activities, such a step and its consequences are to be suffered by the victim without recourse or remedy, that an administration according to law is to be superseded by action dictated by and according to the arbitrary likes, dislikes and irrelevant purposes of public officers acting beyond their duty, would signalise the beginning of disintegration of the rule of law as a fundamental postulate of our constitutional structure.

78 Ibid.

79 [1951] SCR 265, at 286.

80 Ibid. Emphasis added.

CHAPTER XII

1 Bill c-60: Constitutional Amendment Act, 3d sess., 30th Parl., 26–27 Eliz. II, 1977–8. For an analysis of the limitations clause in the Bill see generally William E. Conklin, "Appendix" to *In Defence of Fundamental Rights* (Alphen aan den Rijn/Germantown, Md.: Sijthoff & Noordhoff, 1979).

2 A general interpretation principle is that every word in a legislative text is presumed to mean something. See generally E.A. Driedger, *Construction of Statutes*, 2nd ed. (Toronto: Butterworths 1983), at 89–92, 128–30; S.G.G. Edgar, *Craies on Statute Law*, 7th ed. (London: Sweet & Maxwell 1971), at 159–60; G. Granville Sharp and Brian Galpin, *Maxwell on the Interpretation of Statutes*, 10th ed. (London: Sweet & Maxwell 1953), at 1–2.

3 For the import of a text's description of its rights as *fundamental* or *human* see generally Conklin, *In Defence of Fundamental Rights*, supra note 1, esp. "Introduction." Senate approval need not be required if, within 180 days after adoption of a resolution by the House, the House again adopts the resolution (s. 47(1)).

4 However, when introducing the Bill, the prime minister of the day reminded the House of Commons of the exile of Canadians ordered after the Second World War "by a simple expedient of a declaration that there was a continuing emergency." See Hansard (1960) vol. 6, at 5942. Diefenbaker believed that the Bill would have "a tremendous effect, because there are in existence statutes which have the effect of denying those rights ..." See generally Hansard (1960) vol. 7, at 7544.

5 [1959] SCR 121. See text supra chap. 2, sect. 1(b).

6 One can glean what I mean by critical expression in Conklin, "The Legal Theory of Horkheimer and Adorno" (1985), 5 *Windsor Yearb. Access Justice* 230. Also see text infra sect. 3c.

7 See generally text supra chap. II, sect. 1, where these authors are discussed in this context.

8 (1979), 28 EHRR 245.

9 [1959] SCR 121, at 140.

10 See generally A.K.R. Kiralfy, *Potter's Historical Introduction to English Law and Its Institutions*, 4th ed. (London: Sweet & Maxwell 1958); Theodore Plucknett, *A Concise History of the Common Law*, 5th ed. (London, Butterworths 1956); J.E.A. Jolliffe, *The Constitutional History of Medieval England, from the English Settlement to 1485*, 4th ed. (New York: Norton, 1967), chap. 4.2, 5.2; G.R. Elton, *The Tudor Constitution: Documents and Commentary* (Cambridge: Cambridge University Press 1972), chap. 6–8; Carl Stephenson and Frederich George Marcham, *Sources of English Constitutional History*, vol. 1 (New York and London: Harper & Row 1972); H.G. Hanbury, *English Courts of Law* (London, New York, Toronto: Oxford 1967), chap. 1–4; Radcliffe and Cross, *The English Legal System*, 5th ed. (London: Butterworths 1971), chap. 1–6; F.W. Maitland, *The Constitutional History of England*, ed. H.A.L. Fiser (Cambridge: Cambridge University Press 1968), at 105–41.

11 See esp. J.P. Kenyon, *The Stuart Constitution 1603–1688* (Cambridge: Cambridge University Press 1969); Stephenson and Marcham, *Sources ...*, at sect VII; vol. 2 at sect. 1x and x; David Lindsay Keir, *The Constitutional History of Modern Britain since 1485*, 8th ed. (New York: Norton, 1966), chap. IV and V; J.W. Allen, *English Political Thought 1603–1644* (London: Archon Books 1967).

12 See E.N. Williams, *The Eighteenth Century Constitution: Documents and Commentary* (Cambridge: Cambridge University Press 1970), chap. 1; Keir, *The Constitutional History ...*, chap. 5; Stephenson and Marcham, *Sources ...*, sect. 10 and 11; G.P. Gooch, *English Democratic Ideas in the 17th Century*, 2nd ed. (New York: Harper & Row 1959); J.H. Plumb, *The Growth of Political Stability in England 1675–1725* (London: Peregrine 1967); George Burton Adams and H. Morse Stephens, *Select Documents of English Constitutional History* (New York: Macmillan 1929), at 339–475.

13 This point is discussed and documented in Conklin, *In Defence of Fundamental Rights*, supra note 1, at 78–9.

14 See generally Marx, "The Emergency Power and Civil Liberties in Canada" (1970), 16 *McGill L.J.* 39; "The 'Apprehended Insurrection' of October 1970 and the Judicial Function" (1972) 7 *U.B.C.L. Rev.* 55; Phillips,

"Canada's Internal Security" (1946), 12 *Can. J. Economics & Political Sc.* 18; Dennis Smith, *Bleeding Hearts ... Bleeding Country: Canada and the Quebec Crisis* (Edmonton: Hurtig 1971).

15 See, e.g., Commission of Inquiry re Certain Activities of RCMP, *First Report: Security and Information* (Ottawa: Information Canada 1979), esp at 1–8; *Second Report: Freedom and Security under the Law* (1981), esp. at 49–53, 103–4, 112–8, 149–50, 161–2, 201–3, 210–13, 221–2, 341–59; *Third Report: Activities and the Question of Governmental Knowledge* (1981), esp at 94, 111–15, 127–32, 181, 189–206, 221–9, 231–3, 271–6.

16 Does this really need documentation?

17 This is documented and explained in Conklin and Morrison, "Public Issues in a Public Law World: The Case of the Appointment of a Receiver" (1988), 26 *Osgoode H.L.J.* Also see Conklin, "Victims of Commercial Law" (1985), 8 *Can. Community L.J.* 67.

18 However, see Joseph Eliot Magnet, *Constitutional Law of Canada: Cases, Notes and Materials*, 1st ed. (Toronto: Carswell 1982), at 39.

19 [1967] 1 AC 259; [1966] All ER 650 (PC). For an interesting commentary of this case in the context of Canadian texts see generally Lyon, "Constitutional Validity of Sections 3 and 4 of the Public Order Regulations, 1970" (1922), 18 *McGill L.J.* 136, at 141–4. It is also discussed in the context of Third World constitutions in Conklin, "The Role of Third World Courts during Alleged Emergencies" in M.L.A. Marasinghe and William E. Conklin, eds., *Essays on Third World Perspectives in Jurisprudence* (Singapore: Malayan Law Journal 1984), at 92–5.

20 *Golak Nath* v. *State of Punjab* AIR 1967 SC 1943.

21 *Golak Nath* v. *State of Punjab* AIR 1967 SC 1943, at 1657 para. 22.

22 Wasserstrom, "Rights, Human Rights and Racial Discrimination" (1964), 61 *J. Phil* 20. and reprinted in *Human Rights*, ed. A.E. Melden (Belmont, Calif.: Wadsworth 1970), at 82. For an interesting series of essays written in response to Wasserstrom's argument see generally Pocklington, "Against Inflating Human Rights" (1982), 2 *Windsor Yearb. Access Justice* 77; McDonald, "The Roots of the Concept of Human Rights: A Response to Professor Pocklington," ibid., at 295; La Selva, "Moral Rights, Ideal Rights and Human Rights," ibid., at 312; Ajzenstat, "Liberalism, Compromise and Moral Absolutes," ibid., at 320; and Pocklington, "Morals, Politics, and the Inflation of Human Rights," ibid., at 331.

23 Hart, "Are There Any Natural Rights?" 64 *Phil. Rev.* 175 (April 1955) and reprinted in A.E. Melden, *Human Rights*, at 64.

24 Vlastos, "Justice and Equality" in R.B. Brandt, ed., *Social Justice* (Englewood Cliffs: Prentice-Hall 1962) and reprinted in Melden, *Human Rights*, 76, at 82.

25 Ibid., at 83 in Melden. Emphasis his own.

26 Isaiah Berlin, *Four Essays on Liberty* (London: Oxford University Press 1969), at 122.

27 Ibid., at 121–2.

28 Ibid., at 131.

29 Ibid., at 122.

30 Mill did not originate the theory. One can trace it back to Hobbes, if not earlier. See *Leviathan*, ed. Michael Oakeshott (New York: Collier 1962), chap. 21. For juridical expressions of this theory see, e.g., Pigeon's understanding of the axiomatic rule of provincial autonomy and its connection to freedom. Supra chapter viii text between notes 37 and 49.

31 John Stuart Mill, *On Liberty*, ed. Mary Warnock (Glasgow: Wm. Collins 1962), at 135.

32 See ibid., at 138.

33 Ibid., at 136.

34 Ibid. Emphasis added.

35 Ibid., at 205. Emphasis added.

36 Ibid., at 212.

37 See generally ibid., at 215–25.

38 Ibid., at 218.

39 Ibid., at 210–11.

40 Berlin, *Four Essays on Liberty*, supra note 26, at 122. LeDain expresses this theory juridically in the context of the independence of the courts in *Valente* v. *Queen*, [1985] 2 SCR 673, at 686c–g.

41 Ibid., at 130, fn. 1.

42 C.B. MacPherson, *Democratic Theory* (Oxford: Oxford University Press 1973), chap. 5.

43 See generally Conklin, "The Legal Theory of Horkheimer and Adorno" (1985), 5 *Windsor Yearb. Access Justice* 230, and Kaplan, "Can Rational Instrumentalism Do All That?: Reply to Professor Conklin," ibid., at 381.

44 See generally Max Horkheimer and Theodor W. Adorno, *Dialectic of Enlightenment* (John Cummings, transl.; New York: Continuum 1944, 1972), esp. xv, 30–2, 54–6, 83–6, 90–3, 120–1, 124–6, 154–6, 172, 198–9, 209–11, 241–2.

45 Max Horkheimer, "Traditional and Critical Theory" in *Critical Theory: Selected Essays* (Matthew J. O'Connell et al., transl.; New York: Herder and Herder 1972), at 200.

46 "Authority and the Family," ibid., at 69.

47 Herbert Marcuse, "Philosophy and Critical Theory" in *Negations: Essays in Critical Theory* (Boston: Beacon Press 1968), at 155.

48 See generally Theodor W. Adorno, *Negative Dialectics* (New York: Continuum 1983), pt. III, chap. 1.

49 Herbert Marcuse, *One Dimensional Man* (Boston: Beacon Press 1964), at 10. His emphasis.

50 Horkheimer, "Traditional and Critical Theory," supra note 45, at 207.

51 Herbert Marcuse, "Freedom and the Historical Imperative" in *Studies in Critical Philosophy* (London: NLB 1972), at 223.

52 Marcuse, "A Study on Authority: Introduction," ibid., at 51.

53 Ibid., at 52.

54 Horkheimer, *Critical Theory*, supra note 45, at 77–9.

55 "Authority and the Family," in *Critical Theory*, at 92. Berlin, *Four Essays on Liberty*, supra note 26, at 133ff.

56 Ibid., at 78; John Stuart Mill, *On Liberty*, supra note 31, at 135–6.

57 Herbert Marcuse, *Counter Revolution and Revolt* (Boston: Beacon Press 1972), at 48. A further problem is that an investigation of the true nature of a human being is rooted in a positivistic epistemology. Thus, the enterprise of grounding freedom in the essential nature of human beings is subject to the same criticisms which have been made of positivism. See generally Susan J. Hekman, *Hermeneutics and the Sociology of Knowledge* (Cambridge: Polity Press 1986), chap. 1. More generally, although the search for a "true essence" is reflective of the logocentric premise of Western thought, post-structuralists have critiqued the cultural underpinnings of that premise. See, e.g., Jacques Derrida, *Of Grammatology* (Gayatri Chakravorty Spivak, transl.; Baltimore, Md.: Johns Hopkins University Press 1974, 1976).

58 Ibid., at 63–4.

59 Herbert Marcuse, *An Essay on Liberation* (Boston: Beacon Press 1969), at 36.

60 Marcuse, *Counter Revolution*, at 71.

The return to the soul in man "presupposes a type of man with a different sensitivity as well as consciousness: men who would speak a different language, have different gestures, follow different impulses; men who have developed an instinctual barrier against cruelty, brutality, ugliness ... the social division of labor ... would be shaped by men and women who have the good conscience of being human, tender, sensuous, who are no longer ashamed of themselves ... The imagination of such men and women would fashion their reason and tend to make the process of production a process of creation." Marcuse, *An Essay on Liberation*, at 21.

61 Berlin, *Four Essays on Liberty*, supra note 26, at 131.

The *'positive' sense* of the word 'liberty' *derives from the wish on the part of the individual to be his own master.* I wish *my life and decisions to depend on myself* not *on external forces of whatever kind.* I wish *to be the instrument of my own, not of other men's, acts of will.* I wish to be a subject, not an object; to be moved by reasons, by conscious purposes, which are my own, not by causes which affect me, as it were, from outside. I *wish to be somebody, not nobody;* a doer – deciding, not being decided for, self-directed and not acted upon by external nature or by other men as if I were a thing, or an animal, or a slave incapable of playing a human role, that is, of conceiving goals and policies of my own and realizing them. This is at least part of what I mean when I say that I am *rational,* and that it is my reason that distinguishes me as a human being from the rest of the world. I wish, above all, to be conscious of myself as a thinking, willing, active being, bearing responsibility for my choices and able to explain them by references to my own ideas and purposes. I feel free to the degree that I believe this to be true, and enslaved to the degree that I am made to realize that it is not.

Emphasis added. See generally Charles Taylor, "What's Wrong with Negative Freedom" in Alan Ryan, ed., *The Idea of Freedom* (Oxford: Oxford University Press 1979).

62 MacPherson, *Democratic Theory,* supra note 42, at 111–12.

63 Berlin, *Four Essays on Liberty,* supra note 26, at 131. This theory is reflected in some language rights cases. See, e.g., *Société des Acadiens* v. *Assoc. of Parents* [1986] 1 SCR 549, at 562d–j per Dickson; *Macdonald* v. *City of Montreal,* [1986] 1 SCR 460, at 541c per Wilson.

64 Dworkin, "Why Liberals Should Believe in Equality" (1983), 30 *N.Y. Rev. Books* 32 (3 Feb. 1983), at 34.

65 Ibid.

66 Which rights are most important? Negative freedom suggests that the right to life as guaranteed in section 7 is the most precious. If the state can take away one's life, whether intentionally or unintentionally, there is nothing else to remain to protect against coercion (except the soul). Freedoms of conscience, thought, belief, and opinion as guaranteed in sections 2(a) and 2(b) would be next in importance because they are linked so closely to the inner sphere of life assumed in the three theories of negative freedom. The 'fundamental justice' and 'due process' requirements of sections 7 to 13 ensure that the state will not harm one's negative freedom without following procedural fairness.

The unintentional interference theories of negative freedom would add the equality rights and equalization duties in sections 15 and 36 respectively.

In contrast, positive freedom theories would give priority to the equality rights, mobility rights, freedoms of expression, peaceful assembly and association, language and educational rights, and the equalization duties. The participation theory of positive freedom would obviously focus upon the democratic rights and freedoms of expression, political assembly and political association.

And how do the competing freedom theories influence the meaning of the rights? Negative freedom would define its priority rights enumerated above as widely as possible. As Berlin asserted, "[t]he wide the area of non-interference the wider my freedom." The intentional interference theory of negative freedom would confine the meaning of the Charter rights to a civil/political context. The unintentional theories of negative freedom would expand the meaning of the rights to the socio-economic and technological contexts. This expanded meaning would also be shared by the self-direction theory of positive freedom. The participation theory of positive freedom would extend the 'democratic rights' to social and economic organizations which control, influence, or decide the choices in a person's life. That is, the state action doctrine in section 32 would be widely interpreted. Indeed, the state would have the duty to dismantle large-scale, anonymous organizations, including its own, in an effort to create conditions whereby persons would be able to participate effectively in autonomous decision-making.

Finally, the competing theories of freedom offer competing levels of scrutiny of alleged infringements of rights. Negative freedom would call for strict scrutiny of alleged infringements of sections 7 to 13, and 2(a), 2(b), including instances of a section 33 declaration involving such rights. All other rights would involve minimum scrutiny. The unintentional interference theories of negative freedom would widen the spectrum of demonstrably justified interferences with any enumerated right. Positive freedom would likewise have the same effect. But it would suggest strict scrutiny of alleged infringements of sections 15, 6, 36, 28, language rights, minority language education rights, aboriginal rights, and the freedoms of religion and association. Even the use of a section 33 declaration would not lessen the rigour of strict scrutiny of such rights.

67 John Rawls, *A Theory of Justice* (Cambridge, Mass.: Harvard University Press 1971), chap. 1.

68 See also Brian Barry, *Political Argument* (London: Routledge & Kegan Paul, 1965), chap. 4, 6; Robert A. Dahl, *A Preface to Democratic Theory* (Chicago: University of Chicago Press 1963); and "Procedural Justice" in Laslett and Fishkin, eds., *Philosophy, Politics and Society*, 5th series (Oxford: Basil Blackwell 1979). See generally *Politics* bk. III and IV. Also see text supra chap. XIII.

69 See generally J.S. Mill, *Considerations on Representative Government* (New York: Bobbs-Merrill 1958); Harriet Taylor Mill, "Enfranchisement of Women" in J.S. Mill and H. Taylor Mill, *Essays on Sex Equality* (Alice S. Rossi, ed.; Chicago & London: University of Chicago Press 1970); and James Mill, *Essays on Government* (New York: Liberal Arts Press, 1955). The Warren Court associated itself with this background condition. See, e.g., *Reynolds* v. *Sims*, 377 U.S. 533, 84 S. Ct. 1362, 12 L. Ed 2d 500; *Kramer* v. *Union Free School Dist. No. 15*, 395 U.S. 621, 89 S. Ct. 1886, 23 L. Ed. 2d 583 (1969); *Shapiro* v. *Thompson* 394 U.S. 618, 89 S. Ct. 1322, 22 L. Ed. 2d 600 (1969).

70 This particular conception of the place of freedom of expression in the political process can be found most prominently in the writings and judgments of Holmes J. See, e.g., *Gitlow* v. *New York* 268 U.S. 652, 45 S. Ct. 625, 69 L. Ed. 1138 (1925). It would appear that the reason why Holmes did not hold restrictions upon the teaching of the German language as an infringement of free speech was that political speech and the political process had not been infringed. See, e.g., *Meyer* v. *Nebraska*, 26 U.S. 390, 43 S. Ct. 625, 67 L. Ed. 1042 (1923); *Bartels* v. *State of Iowa*, 262 U.S. 400, 43 S. Ct. 628 (1923); *Holmes-Laski Letters: 1916–1935* ed. M.D. Howe (Cambridge, Mass.: Harvard University Press 1953), at 202–3 dated 23 July 1925 and at 75 dated 31 March 1917.

71 See John Locke, *Treatise of Government* (New York: Appleton-Century-Crofts 1937), chap. 7, 8, 11–13, 19.

72 Barry Holden, *The Nature of Democracy* (New York: Barnes & Noble 1974), at 68–72, 155–62.

Subject Index

Name Index

Abel, Albert, 7, 174–5, 182, 183–4, 216, 267
Addy, J., 124
Aquinas, T., 132, 236, 275
Aristotle, 29, 140, 219, 236, 262, 268–70, 275, 278 n1
Auxier, J., 107

Bayda, J., 132
Beetz, Jean, 7, 174–5, 180–1, 184, 216, 267
Bentham, Jeremy, 217
Berlin, Isaiah, 253, 255–6, 353 n61
Blair, J., 127
Bracton, 5
Bryant, J., 127
Burke, Edmund, 6

Cardozo, J., 126
Coke, Edward, 5

Dea, J., 109
Décary, Robert, 192, 194, 216, 267
Derrida, Jacques, vi, 14
Deschenes, Jules, 111, 119, 120
de Tocqueville, A., 132
Dicey, A.V., 11, 71–2, 80–1, 84

Dickson, Brian, 8, 36–8, 42–3, 60, 137–45, 144–8, 204
Dworkin, Ronald, 236, 259

Essen, J., 105–7
Estey, W., 42–3, 160–4
Evans, J., 106

Foucault, Michel, 14, 269
Fuller, Lou, 23

Gadamer, Hans, vi, 14
Galligan, J., 109, 112
Gilson, Etienne, 132

Hall, J., 103–4
Hart, H.L.A., 11, 236, 249
Hobbes, Thomas, 260
Hogg, Peter, 46, 282 n64
Holden, Barry, 261–2
Holland, J., 128
Horkheimer, Max, 256–8
Hugesson, J., 105

Jefferson, T., 29
Jennings, I., 81

Index of Cases Reviewed